Daniel Hellinger
Webster University

Dennis R. Judd
University of Missouri–St. Louis

The Democratic Facade

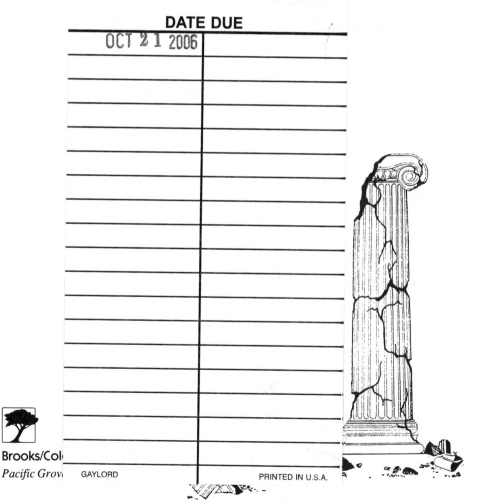

Brooks/Cole

Pacific Grove

With thanks and love to my wife, Joann,
for many years of support and encouragement
—Daniel Hellinger

To John Berg
—Dennis Judd

Consulting Editor: Roger R. Davidson
Sponsoring Editor: Cynthia C. Stormer
Editorial Assistant: Cathleen S. Collins
Production Service Manager: Joan Marsh
Production Service: Matrix Productions
Manuscript Editor: Vicki Nelson
Permissions Editor: Marie DuBois
Interior Design: Paul Quin, InfoTech
Cover Design: Sharon Kinghan
Cover Illustration: Sharon Kinghan
Typesetting: Jabula Publishing
Cover Printing: Malloy Lithographing, Inc.
Printing and Binding: Malloy Lithographing, Inc.

Brooks/Cole Publishing Company
A Division of Wadsworth, Inc.

Printed in the United States of America
10 9 8 7 6 5 4 3 2 1

Library of Congress Cataloging-in-Publication Data

Hellinger, Daniel
    The democratic facade / Daniel Hellinger, Dennis R. Judd.
      p.   cm.
    Includes bibliographical references and index.
    ISBN: 0-534-15228-7
      1. Political participation—United States. 2. Political socialization—United States.
3. Political planning—United States. 4. Legitimacy of governments—United States.
5. Elite (Social sciences)—United States. 6. United States—Politics and government.
I. Judd, Dennis R. II. Title.
JK1764.H45   1991
320.973—dc20

                            90-23199
                                CIP

Preface

The real ground of the difference between oligarchy and democracy is poverty and riches. It is inevitable that any constitution should be an oligarchy if the rulers under it are rulers by virtue of riches....

Aristotle *

We have written this book around a provocative thesis describing American politics as a facade structured to evoke symbols of democratic participation but also designed to ensure that control by elites is not endangered by the mobilization of populist majorities. This book is grounded firmly in the literature of the political science profession, and unlike most of the critical books on the market, it is not based on a neo-Marxist theme nor does it stress the inequalities and power relationships inherent in the capitalist system. There are several excellent books that tie the problems of American democracy to capitalism. Our focus is somewhat different. We describe how elites have structured and manipulated the "rules of the game" and the institutions of American politics to protect wealth and privilege.

As we indicate in chapter 1, elites have changed over the 200 years of American history, and the political strategies appropriate or available to elites in one period have been replaced by strategies in another. By providing a richly textured account of America's political history, we seek to avoid any interpretation that the composition of elites is static, or that elites remain in power by conspiring to do so. In every political system, elites will try to manipulate political institutions and processes to their advantage. No doubt they often do this by working closely together; more often, their actions lead in the same direction because they share similar political interests. In the U.S. political system unusual and contrived efforts to protect elites' power and authority—conspiracies—are rarely needed; and in many of the cases when they have been tried, they have backfired, as Richard Nixon discovered when the Watergate scandal unfolded. Watergate was silly precisely because it was so unnecessary; the president was in no political danger. Such is the case more generally for elites in America. When the political system operates according to design, democratic participation is channeled in such a way as to efficiently preserve existing power relationships.

The book is divided into three sections, each dealing with a separate mechanism employed by elites to preserve their political control within an ostensibly democratic system. The three chapters in Part I describe the "arenas of legitimation"

* *The Politics of Aristotle,* trans. Ernest Barker, London: Oxford University Press, 1958, p. 116.

used by elites for political socialization and communication. For elites, it is crucial that mass publics learn particular versions of political and economic reality: that, for instance, ours is the "best" democracy and that capitalism is a just and efficient economic system. The three arenas utilized to impart such cultural verities are made up of schools, media institutions, and electoral institutions and processes.

The chapters on schooling and elections call attention to the crucial processes of socialization that all Americans have experienced. Schooling and elections are essential for legimating the political system. Even in critical books, the overt function of elections normally focus on elections as mechanisms for selecting governmental leaders. As an alternative to this perspective, we consider elections as legimating events; we assert that elections are as important for socializing citizens as for choosing governmental leaders or keeping elites in check. For citizens they are the principal symbols of democracy. For elites, they provide frequent, sanctioned opportunities to communicate with mass publics and they are pivotal to elites' claims to legitimacy.

The chapters comprising Part II describe the ways that elites have rigged democratic processes to produce outcomes that they find acceptable. Throughout our national history, elites have manipulated the size and composition of the electorate and structured electoral processes so as to strictly limit voters' choices and control political debate. The founders artfully combined symbols of democratic government with a variety of mechanisms that were expressly anti-democratic. Elites have fine-tuned this system ever since.

In Part III we describe how elites have sought to remove government policies from the influence of electoral decisions. Elites in all political systems seek some room to maneuver in making policy. However, elites in the U.S. have succeeded all too well accomplishing this objective. A substantial portion of the domestic policy in the U.S. is made by subgovernments that operate beyond the public's view. An expanding literature in political science documents the nature and workings of these subgovernments, composed primarily of congressional committees, federal administrators, and interest groups. In the realm of foreign policy, policy has been removed from democratic processes altogether. A covert presidency has evolved to make decisions in secret, and the volume of state secrets has expanded in step with the proliferation of institutions specifically devoted to keeping them.

Though American democracy operates to preserve elites' power and class privilege, how can we be sure that this is the political system that most of them prefer? Is American democracy in any sense a "model"? We address this question in chapter 10. Though at first glance it appears to be simply an essay on U.S. policy in the Caribbean and Latin America, our purpose in writing it is to demonstrate that elites in the U.S. have evinced little attachment to democracy, except as a device for legitimating their political control. Again and again, the U.S. has intervened to topple democracies based on mass participation; and as the opposite side of the coin, the U.S. government has repeatedly supported or sponsored repressive regimes that are legitimated through rigged elections that are meant to bestow a veneer of democracy on ruling elites. The litmus test for U.S. elites is straightforward: the democratic ideal prescribes that democracy should protect but never endanger their wealth, privilege, and political domination.

This book is accessible to students in beginning courses and to interested citizens who have no formal background in political science. There is no jargon here, and although our account of American democracy is detailed and rooted directly in contemporary political science scholarship, our thesis is straightforward. Indeed, its starting point is the textbook interpretation of politics that all American have been exposed to through their many years of formal schooling.

The book is, in part, designed to be used as a supplement to a standard textbook in American politics and government courses. Its theme lends itself to a debate format, and we expect that it often will be used by instructors who disagree with us, but who want to provoke students to think carefully and critically about the state of American democracy. This book can also supplement point-of-view or thematic American government texts. It would be particularly appropriate to use this book as a counterpoint to Thomas R. Dye and Harmon Zeigler's *The Irony of Democracy,* which also is published by Brooks/Cole. Whereas Dye and Zeigler forcefully assert that elites protect democracy in America, we argue that the elites that have governed in America have shown little attachment to democracy except as a device to legitimate their political control.

This theme is timely because there are experiments in democracy taking place all over the world. It is urgent that people develop a clear understanding of its present status in the U.S. and elsewhere. In our view, the version of democracy that exists in the U.S. is not an appropriate model, for example, to the people in eastern Europe. However, a close examination of how democracy in America has evolved can usefully reveal the pitfalls and roadblocks to creating genuinely democratic institutions. We hope that the democratic regimes that are now being forged will evolve in such a way that democratic processes will not only legitimate government, but also keep it accountable. If this wish comes true, then perhaps Americans can borrow from other nations' experience to make their own system more fully democratic and less of a facade.

It is a pleasure to acknowledge the contributions of the many people who helped as we researched and wrote this book. The book was several years in process, and we are extremely fortunate to have been surrounded by supportive colleagues and friends, many of whom freely gave their time and energy to various facets of the project. We thank them very, very much.

Gwyneth Williams, a faculty colleague at Webster University, offered incisive, helpful comments on the manuscript. Jane Rune, at the time an undergraduate student at Webster, gathered extremely important data on elections and campaign finance. At the University of Missouri-St. Louis, Jackie Judd Udell provided editing assistance on portions of the manuscript. Jan Frantzen, Sandy Overton-Springer, Lana Vierdag, and John Kalinowski typed and produced manuscript at various stages. These four were enthusiastic supporters throughout the several drafts. If they ever winced at typing still another version, they were too polite to show it.

David Robertson, the author of chapter 9, provided helpful comments and criticisms on other portions of the manuscript. Roland Klose, coauthor of chapter 3, helped us refine the theme throughout. Lynne Silverman, coauthor of chapter 11, read several drafts and made many recommendations regarding research materials and intellectual theme. These people had a substantial influence on the development of the project.

A circuitous path wound from the beginning to the conclusion of this book. Matthew Lippman helped to develop the original project in the early 1980s and continued to provide comments on the various drafts. He has had a very substantial impact on the final product. We are grateful for the help of Jerry Pomper, Rutgers University, who guided our initial selection of the literature on parties and voting behavior. Dan Berman read two versions of the manuscript and provided trenchant comments, which are here incorporated.

We want to make it clear that the editors we worked with went well beyond the usual assistance authors expect to receive. Leo Wiegman of The Dorsey Press helped develop this manuscript in all its early stages, including providing important, incisive analysis of the intellectual themes. He was extremely patient when the project took much longer than anticipated. His nurturing, we hope he will agree, has paid off. David Folmer, at the time the president of Dorsey, also provided encouragement even after deadlines were missed. In their time at Dorsey, these two individuals contributed in important and visible ways to the development of social science scholarship.

In 1988, when Brooks/Cole bought the Dorsey list, we felt a great deal of trepidation, which we freely expressed to our new editor, Cindy Stormer. The project still needed a lot of development, a fact that successive waves of professional referees carefully documented. We want to thank the referees whose very perceptive reviews were essential for developing this book. They were: Richard Bush, Southern Illinois University; Kenneth M. Dolbeare, Evergreen State College; Peter Eisinger, University of Wisconsin, Madison; Philip Green, Smith College; James Klonoski, University of Oregon; Joseph Lepgold, Lawrence University; Peter A. Remender, University of Wisconsin, Oshkosh; Peter Steinberger, Reed College; and Robert Toburen, Louisiana Tech University.

Daniel Hellinger
Dennis Judd

Contents

Chapter 4
Candidates, Elections, and the Propaganda Apparatus 62

Part Two
Rigging Electoral Processes

Chapter 5
Voting As a Symbolic Act 84

Chapter 6
Political Discourse and the Electorate 111

Chapter 7
The Best Elections Money Can Buy 129

Part Three

Protecting Government From Democracy

Chapter 1

American Democracy As a Legitimating Device

The Oldest Democracy

Thomas Jefferson was serving as ambassador to France for the new nation when he heard about Shays' Rebellion. In the fall of 1786, Daniel Shays, a former fighter in the Revolution, led a rag-tag army of several hundred farmers and debtors into Springfield, Massachusetts, to stop foreclosure and debt trials presided over by the Supreme Judicial Court of Massachusetts. Confrontations between the rebellious farmers and state authorities dragged on for several weeks, provoking anxiety among rich merchants and landowners.[1] Jefferson's initial assessment, offered in a letter sent from Versailles, was that

> a little rebellion now and then is a good thing....It is a medicine necessary for the sound health of government....God forbid that we should ever be twenty years without such a rebellion....The tree of liberty must be refreshed from time to time with the blood of patriots and tyrants. It is its natural manure.[2]

Jefferson's aristocratic contemporaries who were closer to the action reacted with considerably less equanimity. Alarmed at the prospect of "mob rule" as well as by the bickering among the states over trade, taxes, and other matters, the Continental Congress called for a convention to meet in Philadelphia in May 1787 "for the sole and express purpose of revising the Articles of Confederation." The convention went far beyond its mandate, producing a national constitution in the "miracle at Philadelphia."[3]

The Constitution is often considered a miraculous achievement because it has endured for more than two hundred years. The histories of most nations suggest that political longevity of this sort is extraordinarily rare. America has the oldest written constitution in the world. There have been no coups d'etat, and since the Civil War there have been no general rebellions. How has such remarkable continuity been achieved?

Generations of Americans have been exposed to a precise, learned-by-rote answer to this question. The answer, contained in a multitude of civics and history textbooks, is that the "Founding Fathers" created democratic institutions that faithfully represent "We, the people." The following passage from a high school government text published in 1982 should sound familiar to most Americans:

> In its immense capacity to accommodate change, the American political system may be one of the wonders of the modern world.[4]

Alternatively, from a government textbook published in 1987:

> In our nation, political power reflects the will of all the people, not the will of a few at the top.[5]

From the early nineteenth century to the present, school textbooks have functioned as catechisms to teach a civic religion whose central article of faith is that America's government is the most perfectly functioning democracy humans have thus far devised.

College students quickly discover that their formal civics education is far from over. Most colleges and universities require a course in American government and, in Texas and several other states, in state government as well. Students in a few of these courses may be confronted with a shocking about-face that contradicts their previous twelve years of patriotic instruction: Perhaps they will be assigned one of the five "leftist" textbooks, like Michael Parenti's *Democracy for the Few* [6] or Edward Greenberg's *The American Political System: A Radical Approach*.[7] For students in most courses, however, no startling surprises are in store. The textbook will be mainly descriptive; the students' old assumptions may require, at best, some slight modification. If, for instance, they are assigned the college text *Toward a More Perfect Union,* the book and its title will feel familiar and comfortable, like old clothes, as will these passages about the "living Constitution":

> Adoption of the Constitution...pointed up American belief in reform, American acceptance of political change as an effective course.[8]

> The Constitution is a remarkable expression of the American political tradition. Its flexibility made it a workable constitution as the United States underwent the extraordinary transformation from a small, largely rural national community to a huge urban industrial society.[9]

The advocates of the "flexible Constitution" idea often freely admit that the original document was not particularly democratic. Their argument is that the Constitution has allowed democracy to evolve gradually in step with, for example, the expansion of the electorate during the Jacksonian period and electoral reforms in the twentieth century, such as women's suffrage and voting rights for blacks. A document appropriate for an age when aristocratic rule was the norm became the instrument that facilitated the gradual evolution to a full-fledged democratic republic.

A carefully crafted scholarly argument based on this view was put forward in 1963 by the eminent sociologist Seymour Martin Lipset. According to his account, violent change has generally been avoided in American history for two principal reasons: Charismatic political leaders successfully constructed a cultural consensus that the government was legitimate because it was democratic; and political elites have been willing to adopt reforms to respond to demands put forth by broadly based political movements.[10] Lipset traced this tendency toward reform and accommodation, as opposed to uncompromising conflict, to the "uniquely egalitarian" nature of American culture, which explained such phenomena as the failure of socialist and revolutionary labor parties in the United States. According to Lipset, the political system devised by the Founders has been able to accommodate popular demands even though the constitutional structure was explicitly designed to check the ability of popular movements to influence government policy. Political discontent could be satisfied within such a system because "Since progress is part of America's national self-image, progressive movements have been able to induce change without becoming radical."[11] This theme lent itself to unabashed patriotic sentiment. Accordingly, Lipset's book became a frequently cited source for textbook writers, and his name is still invoked today, often in college texts.

The textbook explanation of America's political longevity has significant problems. It is, to begin with, founded on myth and fable about the origins of the Constitution and the intentions of its writers. Lipset asserted, for example, that in the constitutional period "American social structure did not possess those great 'gaps' which...'conspire to separate the ordinary people from their government'."[12] This claim is absurd. In colonial America the top 20 percent of wealthholders owned 68 percent of total assets, and inequality in wealth distribution was about the same in New England as in the slave-holding South.[13] In 1771, the top 10 percent of Boston's population held 63 percent of the wealth—and the lowest three-tenths held less than one-tenth of one percent of taxable assets.[14] On the frontier, in contrast to the cities, a considerable equality prevailed, but this was because almost no wealthy people were living there.[15]

The founders were an aristocratic group; several of them were the richest individuals in all the colonies. The merchant and landowning elites gathered in Philadelphia were keenly aware of the threats that faced them. Many white Americans had been brought, often forcibly, to the British colonies as indentured servants (three out of four persons in Pennsylvania, Maryland, and Virginia at the time of the Revolution).[16] They had filled the ranks of the revolutionary armies, risked their lives, and were armed. For elites, it was urgent that a new government be founded that would elicit a widespread sense of legitimacy. Democratic symbols were crucial for accomplishing this purpose. But it was equally important to the founders that their own wealth and political power be preserved. This is not to say that most of the founders were antidemocratic per se, or that they were cynical about the limited democracy they were creating. They were, however, unable to distinguish the preservation of their own property from the establishment of democratic principles. Thus it should occasion little surprise that, as Charles Beard observed, "The overwhelming majority...were to a greater or less extent economic beneficiaries from the adoption of the Constitution."[17]

Elites and Their Strategies

Elites in every society employ strategies to keep themselves in power, but it is not necessary to think that they must, or ordinarily do, engage in conspiracies for this purpose. At times, of course, elite groups do act conspiratorially: The founders did so when they drafted the Constitution and plotted to get it ratified; Richard Nixon and his advisors did so in the 1972 presidential campaign (but then all election campaigns are partially, by their nature, conspiratorial). Corporations constantly engage in conspiracies; the term accurately describes a strategic plan or a product advertising campaign. But it is usually more accurate to consider the political strategies employed by elites as instinctive responses to threats to their political power and economic privilege rather than as conspiracies. It would be illogical to expect elites not to try to maintain their position in society. And it also would make little sense to believe that elites would respond to threats to their power in completely chaotic, ineffectual fashion. Elites share common interests, and they likewise share perceptions about how to respond when these interests are threatened.

The composition of elites has changed markedly during the nation's history, reflecting changes in the American economy and social structure. Consequently, the challenges to elites' autonomy and power, and the political options available to them, have changed. In the past two hundred years three elite "constellations" have dominated the U.S. economy and polity.[18] The constitution of 1789 constituted a compromise between merchant elites in New England, who derived their wealth from banking, trade, and land speculation, and the owners of large estates in the South whose wealth depended on a slave economy based on agricultural products—principally cotton, rice, and tobacco—that were traded on the world market. The delicate balance struck among the elite factions involved, among other things, an agreement by the merchant elites to count slaves in calculating representation in Congress (the three-fifths compromise), and an agreement not to abolish the international slave trade until 1808. Westward expansion eventually strained the compromise to the breaking point, at which point Southern elites tried to secede from the union.

By the 1870s, a new class of industrial capitalists consolidated their grip on economic and political institutions. The Industrial Revolution fundamentally transformed the nation's social composition and economic structure. Soon after the Civil War, the value added from industry exceeded that of commerce and agriculture. The nature of business organizations also changed. By the late nineteenth century, corporations accounted for 60 percent of value in manufacturing.[19] In 1896, twelve firms were valued at more than $10 million, but by 1903 fifty of them were worth more than $50 million.[20] The giant corporations that formed between 1896 and 1905 included (among others) U.S. Steel (now USX), International Harvester, General Electric, and American Telephone and Telegraph. These firms concentrated legal expertise, accountants, a growing army of white-collar workers, and finance capital into huge enterprises.

Over the past half century, another elite "constellation" has replaced the industrial capitalists. The idea of the "postindustrial" economy describes several phenomena: Individual wealthy industrialists have been replaced by professional managers and executives who run far-flung multinational corporations, though some families still control great wealth and institutional power, such as the du Ponts in Delaware and the Bushes and Danforths in Missouri. Families in the top 10 percent income bracket own 72 percent of all stock holdings and 65 percent of all bonds; the top 2 percent of families own 50 percent of stocks and 39 percent of bonds.[21]

Corporate institutions control an overwhelming proportion of America's productive, financial, intellectual, and governmental resources. The executives of the one hundred largest industrial corporations controlled 58 percent of all industrial assets in 1984, and the fifty largest banks held half of all banking assets. The three television networks produced 90 percent of television news, and the fifty richest foundations presided over 40 percent of all foundation assets.[22] The 7,300 persons holding the top positions in the institutions of the economy, government, and private foundations and in research and higher education institutions were in a position to make the key decisions about "war and peace, wages and prices, consumption and investment, employment and production, law and justice, taxes and benefits, education and learning, health and welfare, advertising and communication, life and leisure."[23] A few hundred individuals with leverage in the largest private and public institutions make the decisions that decide the well-being and life chances of all Americans.

All of the elite constellations that have dominated American life have been confronted with challenges, and in response they have employed a variety of strategies to maintain their political control. From time to time they have resorted to repression. The application of repression however, is costly and full of risk. The brushfires of rebellion must be constantly put out. Intrigues and divisions within the ranks of the rulers are more or less built into repressive regimes, and thus they are frequently short lived. It is far preferable for elites to find a way to elicit the voluntary acquiescence, loyalty, or, if possible, positive support of groups that are not in power. America's elites have always attended closely to the processes that nurture and build legitimacy, and they have been remarkably successful. Otherwise, repression would have been more frequent and more violent than it has been in our national history.

For elites, it is imperative that citizens embrace their rule as necessary and just. In a polity with democratic political processes, legitimation is necessarily based on the idea of the consent of the governed (as opposed, for example, to the "divine right of kings"). Therefore, elites must ensure that the institutions of socialization carry the message that the government in power represents "the people." Schools, media institutions, and elections themselves have been crucial socializing mechanisms organized and run by America's elites. We discuss these three arenas of socialization in Part One.

Despite the application of huge political and economic resources to the institutions of legitimation, America's elites have evinced a chronic anxiety about their position. Therefore, they have employed a panoply of strategies to manipulate democratic processes. They have successfully controlled the composition of the electorate and restricted political discourse, with the consequences that elections concern "safe" political issues and voters are able to decide only between candidates who represent elite preferences. In Part Two we detail the intricate strategies used by elites to ensure that democratic processes remain firmly within their control.

Since the Second World War, elites have invented a new set of strategies to supplement and amplify the effect of those inherited from the past. Whereas elites historically resorted to tinkering with the electoral system to keep it operating within narrowly circumscribed limits, in the past decades they have taken decisive steps to insulate government policy making from elections altogether. In Part Three we discuss these efforts. Government officials now possess an unprecedented capacity to manipulate information and shape public opinion, both at election time and in the periods between. The presidency and the executive agencies have vastly expanded their ability to define and control the public agenda, with profound effects. Most domestic policy is now made within the confines of hidden "subgovernments" made up of congressional career incumbents, key executive branch agencies, and relevant industries and corporate lobbyists. In a sense, government policy has become privatized, a state of affairs that has proceeded even further in foreign policy making than in domestic policy. Postwar foreign policy has been moved behind an impenetrable veil of secrecy and deception insulated almost completely from democratic processes.

It may be useful to summarize the various elite strategies in more detail. In the next section we consider the uses of repression and the political contexts that have triggered it.

Repression As a Political Strategy

The fact that repression is always available to elites, even as a last resort, exerts a powerful influence on the political activity of ordinary citizens. From time to time it has flared to ominous levels, rising during wars and periods of popular discontent, receding into the background when elites have felt more secure. When other strategies have proven insufficient, repression has always been readily available, and elites have made much more liberal use of it in American history than the mainstream textbooks will ever reveal. Coercion and the threats of force against political enemies were used as instruments for keeping elites in power even before the Constitution was drafted. During the American Revolution, the estimated one-third of the population that opposed the revolt faced retribution from supporters of independence. Those who sided with the British faced confiscation of their property and physical violence, including lynching, and they either fled to Canada or retreated into silence. In the eighty years between independence and the Civil War, slavery laws were enforced, Native Americans were annihilated, and labor organizers were fired, harassed, and sometimes murdered. Today these events normally are treated as unfortunate episodes that have little or no connection to the present. Never would a term like *genocide* be introduced in a school textbook, regardless of the appropriateness of the term as applied to the experience of indigenous Americans. To use such an expression would be to raise troubling thoughts about America's identity and obligation to the victims; better to treat such events as sidebars in a history whose main plot involves the extension and consolidation of freedom and democracy for all.

Likewise, episodes of repression of workers are represented in official history as unusual deviations from a democratic heritage. Of course, such an interpretation ignores the inconvenient fact that America's history of violence against workers is one of the bloodiest among Western nations. Between 1880 and 1900, there were almost 23,000 strikes in the United States,[24] and even more over the next several decades. Repeatedly, federal troops, state militias, and hired thugs were used to break strikes. In 1877, railroad workers across the country called a strike rather than accept a second 10 percent cut in wages imposed within an eight-month period. The national and state governments mobilized 60,000 troops against the workers; in less than two weeks, almost one hundred strikers were killed. A few years later, in 1886, a national strike for an eight-hour day led to a police massacre of union organizers in Chicago, then prosecution, trial, and death sentences for several unionists.[25] In the Homestead, Pennsylvania, strike against Carnegie Steel in 1892, a gun battle broke out between Pinkerton agents and strikers in which nine workers and seven agents died. Ten thousand state militia were mobilized. Two years later, during the Pullman railroad strike, state militias were sent against workers in seven states and federal troops poured into Chicago and Pullman, Illinois. Thirty-four strikers were killed. In 1914, in a dawn massacre near the coal fields at Ludlow, Colorado, state militia soldiers fired into the tents of striking workers and their families and killed twenty-six men, women, and children.

The government also targeted political radicals in the labor movement without waiting for strikes. Workers who joined the Industrial Workers of the World (IWW) were singled out for furious repression. In the years before the First World War, vigilante mobs organized by corporations and state politicians attacked IWW members ("Wobblies") all across the country.[26] The level of repression escalated when the United States entered the war. Congress used the war as a pretext for passing the Espionage Act of 1917, which was nominally aimed at spying activities. Relying on this legislation, the government sent more than 900 people to prison in one year for their political views, including the entire leadership of all the socialist organizations in the United States, as well as hundreds of labor union leaders. The states and the federal government worked with employers to ferret out "traitors." In 1917, the Department of Justice founded the American Protective League; within a year there were local chapters in six hundred towns and cities.[27] The Post Office Department refused to handle magazines and newspapers it considered politically unacceptable. The repression continued for years after the war had ended. In 1920, raids coordinated by Attorney General A. Mitchell Palmer rounded up hundreds of Wobblies. Government agents ransacked IWW offices and confiscated or destroyed their records. In scores of trials, some lasting only a few minutes, defendants were tried en masse and convicted for conspiracy, treason, and other "crimes." After midnight raids and secret deportation hearings, the federal government deported more than 4,000 people in less than a year. There is little question that a well-orchestrated government repression from 1915 to 1920 effectively destroyed the socialist movement and almost eradicated militant labor leadership in the United States.

World War II provided the pretext for a new wave of restrictions on civil liberties. Hundreds of pacifists were jailed for their political beliefs. Newspapers and movies were censored. Over 100,000 Japanese-American citizens were rounded up and interned in detention camps sprinkled throughout the western states. In the years after the war, congressional committees, federal agencies, state governments, and private employers hounded thousands of citizens in search of the "enemy within." The litmus test for disloyalty was defined as previous membership in any of several dozen civil rights, union, or left-of-center organizations that had flourished in the 1930s—or family or friendship connections to suspected individuals. In less than five years, the American left was decimated.

During the civil rights campaigns of the 1950s and 1960s, FBI agents infiltrated civil rights organizations and harassed and intimidated activists. All groups identified as "leftist" were similarly targeted. During the 1960s, for example, at least 10 percent of all members of the Socialist Workers' Party and about 8 percent of the Young Socialist Alliance actually were FBI informants.[28] The FBI's activities continued until the late 1980s, possibly ceasing in 1988 as a result of a federal court injunction (though, more plausibly, these activities continue but have become, once again, wrapped in a cloak of secrecy). The FBI infiltrated meetings; photographed people attending demonstrations; searched the household garbage of individuals working for peace in Central America; ran checks on license plates of cars parked near meetings and demonstrations; confiscated personal notes and books from people returning from visits to Latin America; and interviewed family members, landlords, and employers.[29] The investigation embraced dozens of organizations, including the Southern Christian Leadership Conference, Amnesty International, the American Civil Liberties Union, and the American Federation of Teachers.

Repression and threats of repression remain important guarantors of elite rule and governmental power. Too much or too blatant a use of violence, however, may provoke protest and opposition from elites more willing to accommodate change, more committed to democratic ideals, or fearful of the backlash that frequent resort to violence might generate. Such a backlash occurred in the early 1960s, when state and local law enforcement authorities brutalized civil rights marchers in the South, and again in 1968, when Chicago police went on a rampage against demonstrators at the Democratic National Convention. Repression has helped to preserve elites and governments in power in America because it has been applied selectively within the context of a political system that is widely regarded as legitimate.

Legitimacy and the Democratic Facade

Strategies for creating a popular sense of legitimacy have been far more important to America's elites than have strategies of repression. However, legitimation through a democratic ideal of rule "by the people" has often posed serious problems for elites because populist groups have repeatedly tried to use the electoral system to change the political balance of power. When confronted with such threats, elites have adjusted the rules of the game: They have expanded or reduced the size of the electorate, pushed for new campaign and election laws, and regulated the political parties. Invariably, reforms have been justified as necessary for improving democratic processes. Elites have expended a great deal of energy to fine-tune the day-to-day rules and procedures of the political system to protect their interests. If they are so troublesome to elites as to require constant tinkering, why have democratic processes been tolerated at all?

The delegates who convened in Philadelphia during the summer of 1787 agreed that there was an urgent need for a central government strong enough to contain popular discontent and protect property. Though it was not clear to all of them that democratic symbols were the answer, they faced the problem of creating a new government that would not soon be overturned. The landowner and merchant elites had just enlisted farmers and workers to overthrow British rule. The citizenry was now well armed and, as was so convincingly shown by Shays' Rebellion, it was capable of challenging the indigenous aristocracy. The Constitution was a brilliant solution to a practical problem. It legitimated aristocratic control by articulating a language of democratic participation.

The idea of democracy is immensely powerful. The measure of its symbolic value can be seen everywhere in the world: in the habit of dictators who hold rigged elections to prove their popularity (e.g., Ferdinand Marcos in the Philippines), in the one-party elections that prevailed until recently in Eastern Europe and in the Soviet Union, in the U.S. State Department's routine application of the label "democratic" to authoritarian regimes and military juntas that happen to be allied with the United States. The idea of democracy is irresistible. It would be odd indeed—even perhaps impossible—for American politics to proceed without the manipulation of the symbols of democracy by all who take part in it. These symbols are essential to elites as a means for preserving their political hegemony.

The term *hegemony* comes from the Greek word *hegeisthai,* meaning to guide.[30] To speak of the hegemony of the elites means to speak of their capacity to "guide," in particular to have the rest of us accept as "common sense" that the economic and political system that perpetuates their rule is the best and most just. This production and reproduction of what people come to think of as truth and common sense is not carried out through some grand, well-organized conspiracy, but by a variety of institutions, controlled by elites, that specialize in the production and distribution of ideas.

Political socialization takes place in a wide variety of settings, including the family, workplace, and church. But there are three principal arenas used by elites for the express purpose of political communication and socialization. The first arena is comprised of the institutions presiding over the process of schooling. These institutions assume the crucial task of inculcating in each new generation a political ideology that legitimates the state. This is accomplished in a straightforward, expensive, overt, meticulously organized manner: approved curricula, civics and history courses, textbooks, class discussions, and exams. By the age of eighteen, an American student has run an impressive gauntlet of political indoctrination. Schools have been regarded by elites as essential institutions for teaching Americans that their democracy is the "one best" system and that capitalism is essential for its success. Every generation of schoolchildren has been taught loyalty to the flag and the nation. More specifically, for most of our national history a great deal of energy has been expended to teach schoolchildren that America is governed by "We, the people," that all groups can easily assimilate into American life (if they want to), that Americans are prosperous and free, and that America is the beacon of freedom for all the world.

A second crucial arena of socialization is made up of institutions of the mass media. Americans are literally bombarded by images and words carried by the electronic media. Because most of our information, ideas, and opinions are derived from these media sources, the mass media industry has become a principal arbiter and interpreter of mass culture and political opinion. A survey conducted by the Roper Organization in 1983 asked Americans what appliance they enjoyed owning the most. More than half of the respondents mentioned their television sets. Which activity did they enjoy or look forward to during a day? Nearly one-third answered, "Watching television."[31] The average American is exposed to 1,000 commercial messages each day—about 190 on television alone.[32] Per capita media consumption in the United States exceeds that of almost every other nation on earth.[33]

How do Americans cope with this information flood tide and what role do media play in shaping political behavior? The question is not easy to answer because there is a key difference between exposure and consumption. People screen information. On average, people read only about half the stories they notice in a newspaper, and many of these only partially. They read less than one-fifth of the stories in full. Similarly, of the fifteen to eighteen stories reported in a typical television newscast, viewers retain only one "sufficiently well so that it can be recalled in any fashion shortly afterwards."[34] But the details are less important than the abstract messages. The media sustain and reinforce cultural values and political beliefs. Media institutions are pivotal for socializing mass publics into accepting sanctioned versions of political and economic reality.

Electoral processes make up a third crucial arena used by elites for political indoctrination and communication. Campaigns and elections have become elaborate pageants experienced by most citizens vicariously through television. The "key linkage now in American democracy is the spectacular presentations of the electronic media," which mediates national politics and culture as "sound bites and film clips on the screen."[35] As a result of this development, a lucrative industry of media consultants, pollsters, advertising agencies, and professional campaign managers has evolved, skilled at applying the techniques of persuasion borrowed from product advertising and applied to political campaigning. In the United States elections do not mainly serve the purpose of allowing voters to choose their political leaders. Rather, they are invested with the crucial legitimating symbols of democratic rule. They provide ritualized opportunities for people to participate, as individuals and as members of a collective citizenry, in the political process. When people vote, they reaffirm their belief that the political system listens to their voice.

Manipulating Democratic Processes

If socialization were a perfectly efficient process, elites would comfortably allow democratic processes faithfully to represent popular preferences about leadership and public policies because all political expression would be entirely predictable. Dissent would be literally unimaginable. However, as evidenced by the political turbulence that has characterized U.S. history, the values, opinions, and actions of ordinary people have been far from predictable. Populist movements have repeatedly been mobilized to challenge ruling elites, and in each historical period elites have responded to these challenges by taking steps to ensure that the political system cannot be used to upset existing social, economic, and political relationships. In short, democratic processes have been rigged to produce acceptable outcomes.

The Constitution can be regarded as the new nation's first successful attempt to rig the rules of government and democratic participation in favor of elites. Having won the war for independence, the creditors, merchants, and landowners now faced serious threats. State taxes imposed to pay the debts incurred to fight the war were resented by farmers and workers. In New England, farm foreclosures were common and the courts made matters worse by frequently jailing farmers who could not pay their debts. Between 1784 and 1786, almost one-third of the farmers in one Massachusetts county had been hauled into court to force them to pay their debts as well as the new taxes imposed by the Massachusetts government. Shays' Rebellion was a reaction to these conditions.

Had the delegates to the Constitutional Convention been representative of the people instead of the merchants, bankers, and plantation owners who composed it in secrecy in 1787, a much more democratic document would have emerged. In 1776, for example, backwoods farmers, laborers, artisans, and small tradesmen had taken control of Philadelphia and drafted a constitution that extended popular control to an extent "beyond any American government before or since." It created a single-house legislature and a weak executive (composed of twelve elected members of a Supreme Executive Council). Representatives had to stand for election every year before an electorate made up of anyone, propertied or not, who paid taxes. Compared to this plan, the Constitution should be regarded as a conservative, even counterrevolutionary document.[36]

American history and civics texts reflexively praise the ingenious structure of the government that the Founders produced, yet the result was hardly democratic. Only the members of the House of Representatives were directly elected by the people. With each legislator representing a small geographic constituency, an effective check was placed against what James Madison called the "sudden passions and impulses" of the mass electorate. Senators were chosen by the states. Electors who chose the President were selected by state legislatures. Aside from the checks on popular democracy written into the Constitution, electoral participation was strictly controlled. From the constitutional period to the late 1820s, the states imposed property restrictions that limited the number of eligible voters, which had the effect of excluding from the electorate riffraff like Daniel Shays and his ilk.

Jacksonian democracy, which resulted in the dropping of property restrictions and the vast expansion of the electorate, eventually presented problems to a new generation of elites. By the last decades of the nineteenth century, giant industrial corporations dominated the economy. After the 1860s, an agrarian and labor rebellion against the new capitalists waxed and waned, keeping time with economic cycles.

The Democratic party channeled protests against "big money" into the electoral arena by constructing a fragile coalition of midwestern farmers, southern white populists, and laborers. In the presidential campaign of 1896, William Jennings Bryan led the Democrats in a campaign against the "money interests" symbolized by such financiers and industrialists as Andrew Mellon, Andrew Carnegie, James Fisk, and J. P. Morgan. The Democratic platform advocated a reduction of tariffs to force eastern businesses to lower prices and compete with imported goods. Bryan called for a paper currency backed by silver as well as gold that would, it was presumed, benefit indebted farmers and small businessmen. The Democrats also proposed a graduated income tax, a government takeover of land grants previously given to the railroads, and public ownership of telegraphs and telephones. In the campaign of 1900, when he was once again the Democratic nominee, Bryan assailed trusts and monopolies, urged the direct election of senators, opposed court injunctions against strikes, and favored the creation of a Department of Labor.

Elites in the South reacted to populism by disenfranchising much of the electorate. The South's defeat in the Civil War had given blacks the vote, but by the early years of the twentieth century voter registration laws, literacy requirements, and poll taxes had effectively taken it away. Working-class and poor whites were discouraged from voting by these same reforms. In the North, voter registration and other reforms adopted during the Progressive Era reduced voting participation by foreign immigrants and by people on the lower end of the social scale. The consequences of these reforms are still felt; compared to other democratic nations, voter turnout in the United States is abnormally low. Proposals to increase electoral participation by easing voter registration requirements still meet with resistance from political elites. We examine why this is the case when we review the politics of electoral participation in chapter 5.

Elites also have successfully managed democracy by manipulating voter choice and political debate. Political scientists have often blamed the objects of this manipulation—the voters—for the sorry state of political discourse in American politics. In chapter 6 we demonstrate that voters are quite adept at linking their votes to issues they consider important—despite being presented with very little concrete information in campaigns, which in any case are conducted within very restricted ideological confines.

We show in chapter 7 that campaigning has become a significant growth sector of the American economy, and its ostensibly public function—to give the electorate a choice among candidates—has substantially been eclipsed. Elections have been privatized. Candidates employ a campaign industry of consultants, pollsters, and media specialists. The escalating cost of these kinds of campaigns have cast wealthy individuals and corporate interests as arbiters of the electoral process. By their contributions they winnow out candidates in the "hidden primary" that precedes the official nomination primary contests. Favored candidates who survive this stage then use money to buy the powerful technologies of modern campaigning. Thus, election campaigns have been made a straightforward extension of corporate America, a growth sector of the capitalist economy.

Historically, the political parties served as mechanisms for mediating political competition among elites and for facilitating political communication between elites and the mass electorate. The parties also engaged in coalition building on behalf of political candidates and political agendas. In chapter 8 we assert that the political parties have been eclipsed as the gatekeepers of the electoral process by professional campaign specialists and financial contributors. The fact that parties no longer serve their historic functions means that elections have been reduced to media-managed passion plays for the voters by professional campaign specialists and financial contributors.

Insulating Government from Accountability

In chapters 9 and 10 we show that America's policy-making institutions have become remarkably isolated from electoral decisions. Presidential power has expanded partly because the presidency has become the center (or object) of a continuous, sophisticated image-making industry. Presidents do not now campaign only for election and reelection. Pollsters and image makers work full time between elections to sell presidential policies to the public. No other institution has such a capacity for organizing such a well-organized, sustained public relations campaign. When selling policy does not work, presidents are able to insulate themselves from public accountability through covert, ad hoc agencies and groups that define and implement policies without the consent or knowledge of Congress, the courts, or the public. Since the Second World War, there has been a tendency for all presidents to expand their power in this way by exaggerating threats to national security.

Congress also has become remarkably insulated from electoral decisions, an outcome of the fact that elections have become less and less competitive. More than half of the representatives in the House elected in 1870 were serving their first term. By 1900, only about one-third were newly elected, and this proportion fell to about 15 percent by the 1970s.[37] In the 1986 congressional elections, 98 percent of incumbents who ran were reelected, and 99 percent were returned in 1988. Most representatives and senators have served for several terms, a fact that is virtually institutionalized in an era of high-cost media campaigns, when incumbency confers a decisive advantage in fundraising.[38] Congressional representatives and senators derive most of their campaign funds from political action committees (PACs) representing corporations and large interest groups; and they spend their money on expensive media campaigns. Senators and congressional representatives have become accustomed to conducting much of their business outside the public's scrutiny, through hidden subgovernments in which they can more or less continuously negotiate with executive agencies and corporate and interest-group lobbyists.

Elites and the Democratic Ideal

Except as a device for legitimating their control, elites in the United States have little attachment to democracy. At first blush, this assertion may seem indefensible. There are no cases in which these elites have abrogated democracy through resort to a coup d'etat. The Constitution has never been suspended (though during the Civil War and the Second World War some of its provisions were ignored). It would appear that America's elites have convincingly demonstrated their support for democratic processes; they seem to have met a two-hundred-year loyalty test.

Actually, however, on many occasions America's elites have demonstrated a distrust and disdain for democracy to the point where they have been willing to destroy it when it seemed inimical to their interests—that is, when it threatened their political hegemony and control over wealth-producing institutions. In chapter 11 we compare the governments opposed by the U.S. with those it has supported. The comparison is illuminating. In its self-proclaimed sphere of influence, the Caribbean and Latin America, the United States has repeatedly destroyed democracy and protected repressive regimes. Democracies based on mass participation have consistently been opposed, often violently, by U.S. political and corporate elites. Conversely, political systems pasted over with a transparent patina of democracy have been both supported and sponsored. These ostensible democracies are often as far removed from popular influence as are the military dictatorships that they often replace, but they are enthusiastically embraced as "democratic" by U.S. foreign policy elites. These cynical manipulations of democratic symbols can be used as a mirror that faithfully reflects the ideal of democracy embraced by America's elites. They tolerate democratic processes only if these processes pose no significant danger to their autonomy and political hegemony.

Must Democracy in America Be a Facade?

In his textbook written for college students enrolled in courses on American government, the political scientist Robert Dahl suggested several principles that may be used to judge whether a political system is genuinely democratic. He asserted that every citizen must have "unimpaired opportunities" to formulate political preferences. For these opportunities to exist, a formal educational process and a communications (media) system must present significant political alternatives so that citizens can make informed judgments by engaging in lively political debate. Second, according to Dahl, citizens must be able to express their preferences. This takes place in the voting booth but also in other contexts, such as demonstrations and associational activities. And third, citizens must have their expressed preferences "weighed in the conduct of government."[39] Electoral procedures must provide access to alternative sources of information and genuine competition among candidates. Incumbent officeholders must always be at risk of replacement when citizens' preferences are at variance from their own.

Citizens in the United States have neither an education system nor a media system that provides "unimpaired opportunities" for them to formulate and signify preferences. Neither liberal/conservative nor the Democratic/Republican spectrum of alternatives is sufficiently broad today to merit much confidence that competition among leaders for votes provides either meaningful political debate or a mechanism for mass influence over government. The decay of political parties and their replacement by a private-sector campaign industry has transformed elections into exercises in electronic advertising and information management. And, in any case, most of the government institutions that make both domestic and foreign policy now operate outside and beyond the reach of electoral politics.

The American political system amounts to a democratic facade. It is important to note that this label should not be equated with dictatorship or the kind of authoritarian government in which participation is prohibited, governmental power is concentrated into one institution or person, and only a few people are allowed a political voice. The American system does respond to well-funded and highly organized mass-membership interest groups. When energetic social movements emerge, whether or not they are encouraged by some elite sectors, they can wrest important concessions. In some circumstances, elections have taken on considerable significance. But recent national elections have become little more than symbolic exercises. They function mainly as mechanisms for conferring legitimacy on the elites that "win."

This situation need not persist. American politics is not and never has been quiescent. Beyond the world of the textbooks, American history is the story of political struggles. The symbols of democracy manipulated by elites inspire ordinary people to work for political change. The most significant reforms in our time would open up the political system so that democracy would not only legitimate government, but also keep it accountable.

Notes

1. See Jerry Fresia, *Toward an American Revolution: Exposing the Constitution and Other Illusions* (Boston: Southend Press, 1989), pp. 23-66. Fresia draws heavily on David Szatmary, *Shays' Rebellion: The Making of an Agrarian Insurrection* (Amherst: University of Massachusetts Press, 1980).

2. Quoted in Howard Zinn, *A People's History of the United States* (New York: Harper Colophon, 1980), p. 94.

3. Catherine Drinker Bowan, *Miracle at Philadelphia* (Boston: Little, Brown, 1966).

4. Armen Rosencranz, James B. Chapin, Sharon Wagner, and Barbara Finley Brown, *American Government* (New York: Holt, Rinehart & Winston, 1982), p. 680.

5. William H. Hartley and William S. Vincent, *American Civics: Constitution Edition* (Orlando, Fla.: Harcourt Brace Jovanovich, 1987), p. 434.

6. Michael Parenti, *Democracy for the Few*, 5th ed. (New York: St. Martin's Press, 1988).

7. Edward S. Greenberg, *The American Political System: A Radical Approach*, 5th ed. (Glenview, Ill.: Scott, Foresman and Co., 1989). See also the following texts: Kenneth M. Dolbeare and Murray J. Edelman, *American Politics: Policies, Power and Change*, 4th ed. (Lexington, Mass.: D. C. Heath, 1981); Ira Katznelson and Mark Kesselman, *The Politics of*

Power: A Critical Introduction to American Government, 3rd ed. (New York: Harcourt Brace Jovanovich, 1987); Robert Sherrill, *Why They Call It Politics,* 2nd ed. (New York: Harcourt Brace Jovanovich, 1974).

8. Samuel C. Patterson, Roger H. Davidson, and Randall B. Ripley, *A More Perfect Union: Introduction to American Government,* 3rd ed. (Homewood, Ill.: The Dorsey Press, 1985), p. 20. These authors rely heavily on Lipset's book, as do a number of others.

9. Ibid., p. 33.

10. See Seymour Martin Lipset, *The First New Nation: The United States in Historical and Comparative Perspective* (New York: Basic Books, 1963).

11. Ibid., p. 342.

12. Ibid., p. 92. Lipset is quoting Edward Shils, "The Military in the Political Development of the New States," in John J. Johnson, *The Role of the Military in Underdeveloped Countries* (Princeton: Princeton University Press, 1962), p.29.

13. Edwin J. Perkins, *The Economy of Colonial America* (New York: Columbia University Press, 1980), p. 157.

14. Gary B. Nash, *Red, White and Black: The Peoples of Early America,* 2nd ed. (Englewood Cliffs, N.J.: Prentice-Hall, 1982), p. 217.

15. Ibid.

16. Philip Foner, *History of the Labor Movement in the United States,* vol. 1 (New York: International Publishers, 1975), pp. 13-18.

17. Charles A. Beard, *An Economic Interpretation of the Constitution of the United States* (New York: The Free Press, 1965), p. 149. Originally published 1913.

18. See Edward Greenberg, *Capitalism and the American Ideal* (Armonk, N.Y.: Sharpe, 1985).

19. U.S. Department of the Interior, Census Office, Census Reports of 1900, vol. 7, *Manufacturers,* pt. 1, "United States by Industries" (Washington, D.C.: U.S. Government Printing Office, 1902), pp. 503-509.

20. William Miller, "American Historians and the Business Elite," *Journal of Economic History* 9 (1949): 184-208.

21. Robert B. Avery et al., "Survey of Consumer Finance, 1983," *Federal Reserve Bulletin* 70 (September 1984).

22. Thomas R. Dye, *Who's Running America? The Conservative Years,* 4th ed. (Englewood Cliffs, N.J.: Prentice Hall, 1986), pp. 12, 267.

23. Ibid., p. 1.

24. Stuart D. Brandes, *American Welfare Capitalism, 1880-1940* (Chicago: University of Chicago Press, 1976), chap. 1. Two concise histories of labor conflict in the United States are Milton Meltzer, *Bread and Roses: The Struggle of American Labor, 1865-1914* (New York: Alfred A. Knopf, 1967), and Edward C. Kirkland, *Industry Comes of Age: Labor and Public Policy, 1860-1897* (New York: Rinehart and Winston, 1961). The sources on labor history are voluminous. A very good bibliography is James C. McBrearty, *American Labor History and Comparative Labor Movements: A Selected Bibliography* (Tucson: University of Arizona Press, 1973).

25. For an excellent discussion of this history, see Sidney Lens, *The Labor Wars* (New York: Doubleday-Anchor, 1974).

26. Alan Wolfe, *The Seamy Side of Democracy: Repression in America* (New York: David McKay, 1973), pp. 25-29.

27. Zinn, *People's History,* p. 360.

28. "We have won a historic victory for political rights and constitutional freedoms," in *A Fight for Political Rights* (New York: Political Rights Defense Fund, 1986), pp. 3-6.

29. Mike Zielinski, "CISPES, other victims of witchhunt sue FBI," *The Guardian* (March 5, 1986), p. 1.

30. "Hegemony" is discussed by Antonio Gramsci, "The Intellectuals" and "On Education" in *The Modern Prince and Other Writings,* ed. and trans. by Quinton Hoare (New York: International Publishers, 1971).

31. "The Fact of (Everyday) Life," *Public Opinion,* August/September 1984, p. 25.

32. Barbara Seuling, "Inside: The Best Loved Myths about TV," *The Press,* August 1982, p. 21.

33. Herbert Altschull, *Agents of Power: The Rise of the News Media in Human Affairs* (New York: Longman, 1984), pp. 209-212.

34. Doris A. Graber, *Processing the News: How People Tame the Information Tide* (New York: Longman, 1984), p. 202.

35. Timothy W. Luke, *Screens of Power: Ideology, Domination, and Resistance in Informational Society,* unpublished ms, 1988, p. 200.

36. Kenneth Dolbeare, *Democracy at Risk: The Politics of Economic Renewal,* rev. ed. (Chatham, N.J.: Chatham House, 1986), p. 24.

37. Samuel Huntington, "Congressional Responses to the Twentieth Century," in David Truman, ed., *The Congress and America's Future* (Englewood Cliffs, N.J.: Prentice-Hall, 1965), pp. 8-9; and Mark Green, James Fallows, and David Zwick, *Who Runs Congress?* (New York: Bantam Books, 1972), pp. 226-227.

38. Gary C. Jacobsen, *Money in Congressional Elections* (New Haven: Yale University Press, 1980).

39. Robert Dahl, *Democracy in the United States: Promise and Performance* (Chicago: Rand McNally, 1972), p. 39.

Part One

The Arenas of Legitimation

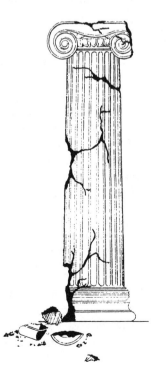

Chapter 2

American Schooling and the Cultural "Consensus"

"The Foundation of a Democratic Society"[1]

American schools always have been vested with an enormous political responsibility. The Puritans organized schools to counteract what they believed to be the influence of Satan on their children. Later, colonial schools were established for the purpose of forging a national culture and teaching "fidelity to the common wealth."[2] The campaigns that succeeded in creating a system of publicly funded education in the mid-nineteenth century were motivated by an often-expressed urgency to Americanize the immigrants. In the 1980s, schools still were regarded as the principal institutions for socializing each new generation of citizens. A national educational commission report issued in 1986 commented on the pivotal role of the schools in building cultural consensus: Education, said the commission, "must provide access to a shared cultural and intellectual heritage if it is to bind its citizens together in a commonweal."[3]

The teaching of a shared cultural and intellectual heritage always has been at the center of schooling in America. This characteristic hardly makes education in the United States remarkable or unique. In all societies, the driving impulse for formal education relates to the teaching of cultural values, and because of this agenda, education often serves as a lightning rod for conflict. As Aristotle observed more than two thousand years ago,

> People do not all take the same position about what should be learned by the young, either with a view to excellence or with a view to the best life; nor is it clear whether their studies should be directed mainly to the intellectual or to moral character.[4]

What is remarkable about schooling in America is the degree to which, in a country with so many ethnic and racial groups, it has imposed a consistent set of values over several successive generations. Though at times the schools have served as lightning rods for cultural conflict, more often they have functioned as institutions that preserve existing economic and political relationships. Generation after generation, American schools have helped to mold a compliant and quiescent citizenry.

Forging a National Culture

In the years following the American Revolution, formal education was seized on as the principal mechanism for creating a uniform national culture. The U.S. population was composed of a rich mixture of nationalities and religions, a source of considerable anxiety to the aristocrats of British and northern European origins. The revolutionary leader Benjamin Rush advocated the formation of an educational system that would impose Protestant doctrines on students, using the Bible as a basic text. Equal to this objective, which he stressed because he thought it necessary that America should remain a Christian culture, he thought that the schools ought to teach students "A SUPREME REGARD TO THEIR COUNTRY."[5] These two themes, religion and patriotism, together constituted Rush's notion of a "moral education." Similar definitions of the purposes of schooling were adopted by most of his contemporaries who advocated a system of universal education.

Thomas Jefferson, for instance, wrote that the object of a system of universal public education should be the creation of a "perfectly homogeneous" citizenry, to be forged through the use of standardized textbooks that taught a patriotic version of the American Revolution. He argued against the upper-class practice of sending children abroad for their education, on the ground that dangerous European ideas might be brought back into the country.[6] Noah Webster likewise emphasized the political function of the schools, arguing that

> our national character is not yet formed; and it is an object of vast magnitude that systems of education should be adopted and pursued...[that] may implant, in the minds of American youth, the principles of virtue and of liberty; and inspire them with just and liberal ideas of government, and with an inviolable attachment to their own country.[7]

Like Jefferson, Webster proposed a universal system of schooling based on standardized primers teaching the principles of republican government—an indirect, representative democracy guided by an educated elite—not, he took pains to point out, direct democracy based on participation by the masses.

Despite such concerns, the process of building a comprehensive school system was delayed for several decades. An assortment of institutions made up the educational system that evolved in the postrevolutionary period. Some were public schools supported by tuition-paying parents, where a few children from poor families were allowed to attend free. There were religious and parochial schools run by the Presbyterians, Lutherans, Congregationalists, and a few other Protestant sects, and by Roman Catholics and charitable organizations. Private schools educated the children of the rich. In the big cities, from 20 percent to 40 percent of children attended elementary schools. Any attempts to require school attendance brought protests from immigrant parents as well as from the manufacturers and mill operators who relied on child labor.

Crusades to build a comprehensive educational system picked up steam in the 1840s and 1850s, this time in response to the waves of foreign immigrants pouring into the cities. To "native" Americans—those who had come earlier from England and northern Europe—the new immigrants threatened to overwhelm Protestant morals, religion, and culture. Urged on by such concerns, by the late 1830s educational reformers began to press for "common schools" that would make education universally available to, or required for, all children. Within twenty years, they had succeeded in persuading state legislatures and cities throughout the northeastern and midwestern states to finance public schools through property taxes. In the process, the majority of nonreligious private schools were put out of business. By the 1880s, almost all states provided for publicly funded and compulsory education. In less than half a century, the school reformers had overcome persistent opposition to compulsory property taxes to support local schools, not only in one state and locality, but in many.

Campaigns to create a publicly financed system of education were energized by massive foreign immigration and the explosive growth of cities. Almost 90 percent of the nation's population was still rural in 1840, but by 1860 nearly 20 percent of Americans lived in cities.[8] Individual cities grew at a startling pace: Between 1840 and 1860, New York City tripled its population, from 369,000 to more than 1.1 million people. St. Louis's population increased tenfold, from a town of just over 16,000 to a city of over 160,000. In the same twenty-year period, Chicago was transformed from a village of 4,500 to a city of 110,000.[9] Foreign immigrants poured into the cities: a half-million in the 1830s, 1.4 million in the 1840s, 2.7 million in the next decade. The concentration of immigrants into crowded, grimy neighborhoods; the rising incidence of crime, disorder, disease, and ethnic and racial strife—all these conditions were traced by the public school reformers to a breakdown in public morality. Imbued with the idea that they were engaged in a historic struggle to save the Republic, most of them would have agreed with this assessment:

> Let us now be reminded, that unless we educate our immigrants, they will be our ruin.

> It is altogether essential to our national strength and peace, if not even to our national existence, that the foreigners who settle on our soil, should cease to be Europeans and become Americans...it is necessary that they become substantially Anglo-Americans.[10]

In the four decades leading up to the Civil War, Irish immigrants comprised almost 40 percent of all immigrants. The jump in Irish immigration began in the mid-1840s, when a disastrous failure of the potato crop pushed thousands of Irish peasants each month to American shores. Most of the Irish had never lived in cities. Almost all of them were illiterate. They carried heavy loads on the waterfront, wielded shovel and pick to build streets and roads and to lay track; they killed cattle and hogs in slaughterhouses and made sausages in packing plants. Living in squalid, crowded conditions, they symbolized the chaos and fragility of American culture. Established elites considered them to be unclean, alcoholic, criminal—and worst of all, they were Roman Catholic in the midst of a culture that equated Protestantism with heavenly salvation and moral virtue.

Only by forcibly removing children from their homes and placing them in schools, the educational reformers warned, would it be possible to protect "society against the vices which now invade and torment it; against intemperance, avarice, war, slavery, bigotry, the woe of want and the wickedness of waste."[11] An article published in an 1849 issue of *The Massachusetts Teacher* articulated the school reformers' especial enmity toward the Irish:

> Our chief difficulty is with the Irish...for the most part the simple virtues of industry, temperance and frugality are unknown to them.

> With the old not much can be done; but with their children, the great remedy is education. The rising generation must be taught as our own children are taught. We say must be because in many cases this can only be accomplished by coercion....If left to [parents'] direction the young will be brought up in idle, dissolute, vagrant habits, which will make them worse members of society than their parents are; instead of filling our public schools, they will find their way into our prisons, houses of correction, and almshouses.[12]

In its annual report of 1858, the Boston School Committee reported on the difficult task of taking Irish children, with "the inherited stupidity of centuries of ignorant ancestors," and transforming them "from animals into intellectual beings." Among other things, teachers would have to force Irish children to learn "agreeable and finished speech" by eradicating the Irish brogue.[13]

The school reformers also took on the responsibility of teaching the children of the immigrants the skills and habits necessary for the industrial work force. Employers needed workers who would be punctual, attentive to machinery, and responsive to discipline. Above all, factory workers had to possess an inexhaustible tolerance for repetition and boredom. In speech after speech, report after report, school reformers advised that the public schools should teach these traits by becoming, in effect, model factories where regimentation and unquestioning obedience would be instilled.

The reformers' strategies for remaking immigrant children relied, in part, on generous doses of political indoctrination. Spellers and readers, as well as history and geography texts, were crafted to exalt American political institutions and, above all, the Founders. According to school primers, American history was peopled by white, Anglo-Saxon, Protestant, upper-class aristocrats like George Washington and members of the Adams family. In the school texts the Revolution was inspired by God, and accordingly the revolutionary leaders took on the status of saints. George Washington was "immortal," "God-like," a "savior." One textbook author wrote: "We forget for a moment that he was a man. We regard him as some propitious divinity, sent from a better world than this, to take America by the hand, and lead her to independence, freedom, and happiness."[14]

In all the texts—and no class could proceed without rote learning from textbooks—the American people were uniquely patriotic, always Christian, early rising and working from sunup to sundown. American society was described as classless and homogeneous. When mention was made of Catholics, immigrants, or Jews, the message was always: These people are aliens, in need of assimilation to American values. McGuffey's Reader, the most popular school text of the nineteenth century, had this to say about immigrants in the cities:

> his playground a pavement, the scene of his juvenile rambles an arcade of shops, his young eyes feasted on the flags of a hundred alien governments, the streets in which he wanders crowded with foreigners.[15]

The reformers' zeal to build a system of schools to remodel society was rarely matched by a similar enthusiasm from the public-at-large. The fight for publicly funded common schools was protracted, and it took decades for the school reformers to win it. Citizens often resisted the idea of a mandatory property tax reserved exclusively for schools. In the past, education had been the responsibility of the family; free public education, if it existed, was treated as a philanthropic gesture to give a few children from poor families "a tolerable proficiency in reading, writing, and sometimes a slight acquaintance with geography."[16] Poor families could not easily take advantage of free schooling even in the few cities where it was offered, because the school-age children of the poor often had to work in factories and in the home to help support the family.

Manufacturers, mine and mill owners, and warehouse and retail store managers initially opposed universal education because it threatened to reduce their supply of cheap child labor. But gradually businessmen were converted to the idea that formal schooling was a means of producing a steady supply of skilled, disciplined workers. When school reformers won over the business community, the fight for a system of tax-supported schools gained an irresistible momentum. By the 1850s and through the ensuing decades, businessmen supplied much of the money and political support for public education. Because the reformers came from the upper strata of American society, the political alliance of public education with business proved to be enduring.

The Schools' Mandate

Educational reformers played on a sense of cultural and political crisis to build political support for compulsory schooling. In the half-century following the Civil War, they found a congenial environment for their agenda. Between 1865 and the First World War, unprecedented societal tensions strained America's social fabric. Small businesses were replaced by rigidly hierarchical and authoritarian industrial organizations that relied on the cheap and plentiful labor supplied by new waves of immigration. When millions of Italian, Eastern European, and Russian immigrants flooded to American shores between the 1880s and the 1920s, the school reformers' strident rhetoric urging assimilation through forced schooling rose to an hysterical pitch.

The post-Civil War immigrant surge spawned a rabid racism that swept the nation and filtered into the schools. Racist literature raised the alarm that white Anglo-Saxons were threatened by dark-skinned "races". Novels, plays, and social science literature played on themes of Anglo-Saxon superiority. After the turn of the century, racist ideas and theories were increasingly accepted as scientifically valid by scholars and the public. In 1916, Madison Grant, the curator of the Natural History Museum in New York City, published *The Passing of the Great Race,* in which he expressed dismay that Aryan blood was being diluted by the dark-skinned immigrants from Eastern Europe and the Mediterranean. His book was soon elevated to the status of a scientific work along with Lothrop Stoddard's *The Rising Tide of Color Against the White World-Supremacy* (1921).

In the midst of this escalating cultural xenophobia, school administrators and teachers believed that they possessed a manifest mandate to recast immigrant children to a new mold. According to the educator Ellwood Cubberly (writing in 1909), the recent immigrants were "illiterate, docile, lacking in self-reliance and initiative, and not possessing the Anglo-Saxon conceptions of law, order, and government."[17] Only through extreme measures, he said, could this generation of immigrant children be educated. A critic of the New York City schools in the 1890s described classroom instruction as including a prohibition against students' moving their heads or arms and added that "time is economized in the act of rising or sitting during the recitations, the children being so drilled that the child who recites begins to fall back into his seat while uttering the last word of a definition, the next succeeding child beginning his ascent."[18] Students were allowed only to look straight ahead, at the teacher. In the classroom and in the silent lines of students preparing to leave or enter classes, corporal punishment was freely used to punish misfits and laggards. Racist views about immigrant children provided the justification for such extreme authoritarianism, and this tendency was further magnified by the schools' mission to instill the discipline and habits suitable for the industrial work force. The training of future workers remained an important object of education, as it had been in an earlier time:

> Military precision is required....Great stress is laid upon (1) punctuality, (2) regularity, (3) attention, and (4) silence, as habits necessary through life for successful combination with one's fellowmen in an industrial and commercial civilization.[19]

The schools continued to shoulder the burden of teaching obedience and loyalty to political institutions. History and civics texts instructed students that America was uniquely religious among nations; that the Constitution was sacred and inerrant; and that, unlike elsewhere in the world, class and ethnic divisions did not exist in America. These were already well-worked themes in school curricula, but they became more elaborately embellished in the first decades of the twentieth century. The anti-immigrant passions produced new textbooks that extolled the Anglo-Saxon backgrounds of American heroes. Simultaneously, authors of these books expressed increasingly pessimistic views about the possibility of assimilating new immigrants into American life. According to one writer, foreigners would reduce everyone to a "common level of misery" unless they were kept out of the country.

Another textbook author noted that "great racial groups, especially such as speak foreign languages, or belong to races with which we do not readily intermarry, do add to the difficulty of solving certain social problems."[20]

The Challenge to Old Themes

In her influential book, *America Revised,* Frances Fitzgerald showed that twentieth-century history textbooks have been frequently revised so that historical "truths" change for each generation of schoolchildren. Even so, some themes have run like a thread through the textbooks of all periods. History textbooks in every generation peopled American history with a succession of white male heroes. The Founding Fathers, as they were invariably labeled, were sanctified, along with the presidents. As a nation, America was always described in chauvinistic tones as the best, most democratic country on earth, whose foreign policy ventures were innocent of economic motives. Not only were American economic interests absent in descriptions of foreign policy, but corporations were never mentioned at all in accounts of national history. Capitalism was, evidently, an economic system without specific business organizations or workers. In the 1930s, in the midst of an economic calamity, a few textbook authors mentioned income inequality and acknowledged the existence of poverty. These texts, however, had a short shelf life. Despite its pro–free enterprise stance, in 1938 a leading textbook written by Harold Rugg was subjected to a national campaign orchestrated by the National Association of Manufacturers, after which his book and other "liberal" texts were revised. Any discussion of inequality or poverty, however tentative, was once again forbidden. No school board or administrator would dare adopt such a book.

For more than one hundred years, American history and civics texts had expressed anxieties about the immigrants. But by the 1940s, Fitzgerald discovered, the texts began for the first time to promote the idea of American society as a "melting pot" of national cultures. This shift allowed more favorable attitudes to be expressed about immigrants (made possible, no doubt, by the strict immigration quotas that Congress had adopted in 1921 and 1924). A few accomplishments by individual immigrants were praised, and the cultural legacy of some immigrant groups were cast in a positive light. Until the 1960s, however, immigrants still were distinguished from "we Americans," and an anti-immigrant sentiment—though less shrill than before—still could be found in school textbooks.[21]

Black people did not appear at all in schoolbooks before the 1960s, except in passing references to slavery. These passages tended to be overtly racist, as illustrated by a discussion in a 1937 text that said that the slave "sang at his work....If his cabin was small, there were shade trees about it, a vegetable garden nearby and chickens in his coop."[22] The first mention of individual African Americans appeared in the late 1940s when pictures of the educator Booker T. Washington or the baseball player Jackie Robinson were inserted to illustrate the "progress" black people had made.[23] In the 1960s, a few more black leaders such as George Washington Carver and Ralphe Bunche were mentioned, but the textbook authors did not know what to make of the civil rights movement. Because it would be unthinkable to portray genuine cultural conflict, the civil rights movement was described as a few protests that quickly led white people to extend equal rights to all blacks.

Women were described, if at all, strictly in the context of stereotyped domestic roles, the only exception being an occasional sentence or paragraph on the suffragette movement of the Progressive Era. Of course, the male pronoun was used to refer to all people, a habit of language that still infects some textbook writing. That young women were pressed into labor in the textile mills of the eighteenth and nineteenth centuries, that women often fought for and secured public funding for schooling and universities and had to fight doubly for admission to these institutions, and that women were important labor leaders were nuances of history not learned by school-children.

Civics texts have tended to be even more fervently patriotic than the history textbooks that Fitzgerald reviewed. Because civics instruction always has been expressly designed to instill patriotism in schoolchildren, the American nation has been presented in texts as "the greatest," with the word *freedom* repeated over and over but never defined. National chauvinism has long been a rigid prerequisite for textbook writing, as demonstrated in a book published in the 1950s that asserted, "No other people on earth enjoy as many rights and privileges as Americans," and,

> Countries which favor liberty are friends of the United States. Those countries which favor communism and other forms of dictatorship consider the United States their greatest enemy. It is a great thing for a free people to be known as the champions of liberty.[24]

Of course, textbooks had always extolled the United States as a "bastion of the free nations,"[25] but in the apocalyptic visions of the 1950s America became, in the texts, "locked into a struggle with another powerful world leader...the Soviet Union."[26] Now absent was the optimism that earlier textbooks had expressed about the ultimate global triumph of democracy. With the purpose of preparing "young people" to resist communism, the 1955 edition of *The Story of Democracy* "compared" U.S. and Soviet institutions and life. The Soviet Union was portrayed as a leviathan on the verge of overwhelming the world—a three-color map (showing the "red" communist nations, the "pink" endangered nations, and the "white" free world) depicted most of the Middle East and Latin America as "endangered" (pink).

Even the United States was described as being subverted from within.[27] Students were encouraged to look for communists among their teachers, fellow students, neighbors, and at home. Some textbook writers suggested that the students' parents might be spies, and thus this advice:

> The FBI urges Americans to report directly to its offices any suspicions they may have about communist activity on the part of their fellow Ameri-cans....When Americans handle their suspicions in this way...they are acting in line with American traditions.[28]

The American tradition, apparently, was that citizens informed on one another—and why not? According to a leading high school text of the mid-1950s, Soviet agents had infiltrated every walk of life: "Unquestioning party members are found everywhere. Everywhere they are willing to engage in spying, sabotage, and the promotion of unrest on orders from Moscow."[29]

In such an atmosphere, it goes without saying that the "American dream" of equality for all was described as already fully realized. Students were advised, "Any man may rise to his best," "You may choose any kind of work or aim for any job," or, "Of all the modern industrial nations ours comes the closest to being a classless society."[30] The view that American government is a "government of the people" served, in the textbooks, as an adequate description of the processes of democracy:

> In our nation government has been organized to serve the people and to pro- vide for the general welfare of all the citizens. We will learn very shortly that all levels of government are responsive to the wishes of the people.[31]

What was omitted from a civics education? There was no mention of interest groups, political elites, or the influence of the media or money in politics, and no information about voter turnout levels or voting behavior among different groups, or about political socialization. These omissions are not surprising because the textbooks were designed to convey well-defined values and interpretations, not to encourage critical or independent thinking. Viewed from this perspective, the purpose of textbooks had changed remarkably little in over one hundred years.

By the mid-1960s this fact created problems for educators and text publishers. The civil rights movement exposed systematic racial discrimination in the South and racial bigotry in the North that could not possibly be explained by the old stereotypes of a conflict-free and classless society. The protests against the Vietnam War made it more difficult for textbooks and schoolteachers to sell the simple-minded idea that America was always engaged in noble causes in defense of freedom. New clothing styles, music, and lifestyles expressed a general questioning of cultural and political authority. The schools were not impervious to these developments.

Textbook authors scrambled to insert discussions of blacks in new editions, which meant that almost overnight texts were revised to recognize a few of the contributions of blacks to American society. For the first time textbook authors also were forced to recognize women, and, to a very slight degree, rarely more than a paragraph, Latinos and Native Americans. The changes were obvious, but much of the old message remained. By the mid-1970s, texts described America as a multiracial society, but one that was basically homogeneous, because, it was said, all Americans, regardless of background, had the same essential wants, desires, and opportunities.[32]

The "recognition" accorded to blacks, Latinos, and women took the form of mentioning important names, such as Martin Luther King, Cesar Chavez, and Susan B. Anthony, with little or no context provided so that the activities and motivations of these people could be understood. Text publishers and educators remained uncom- fortable with any material that might provoke opposition from parents or political groups. Thus any recognition that protests and violence had often accompanied demands for social change in the United States, or any information that pointed to a systematic oppression of a whole group (such as blacks), was studiously avoided. A student could read the books without ever learning about slums, crime, or poverty. History and civics texts of the 1980s still avoid such topics. It must be confusing for an inner-city child or a child living in the Mississippi Delta to look at the photos in these books; they make it appear, as noted by Fitzgerald, that "all non-white people in the United States took happy pills."[33]

Current controversies about the schools could leave the impression that a minor revolution occurred in civic education during the 1960s and 1970s. The term *revolution* vastly overstates the degree of change that was introduced into school curricula, but old-style civics education was, indeed, subjected to a strong challenge. Textbook publishers became sensitive to ethnic, racial, and sexual stereotypes, with the result that virtually all texts and teaching materials underwent scrutiny to ferret out stereotypical language. Even so, most history and civics texts continued to avoid controversial interpretations. Caught in the dilemma of having to acknowledge new groups and a few social "problems," but not willing to risk controversy, textbook authors wrote watered-down and insipid prose—or found that publishers performed the task for them. Perhaps the aversion to controversy explains why contemporary textbooks devote so little space to the discussion of minorities. A history text published in 1982 reserved four pages for a discussion of the civil rights struggle, three pages for a statement on Hispanics, and two pages for some words on Native Americans (ironically, this section is labeled, "Indians refuse to accept the role of 'vanishing Americans.'"[34] Another recent history text is more efficient; it devotes just one page inclusively to all minorities and to women's rights (including one paragraph on blacks, one on Native Americans, and three paragraphs on whether women can be drafted).[35]

Despite the slight changes in the textbooks, new perceptions about the identified purposes of social studies exerted a strong influence on school curricula. The New Social Studies, a label given to curricular materials drawn up by leading educators in the late 1960s, emphasized (like the New Math also then in vogue) "concepts," independent analysis, and "values clarification," in place of memorized facts and values imposed by teachers. The values approach broadly infiltrated the social studies curriculum across the nation, in part because it was promoted by a set of lesson plans and books funded by the National Science Foundation. A new course of study called "MACOS" *(Man: A Course of Study)* relied on "inquiry" texts and values clarification material that asked schoolchildren to examine their own values by reference to cultural beliefs and practices elsewhere in the world.

A backlash quickly erupted, led by people who were appalled that moral or cultural "relativism" would be taught in the schools. Book burnings, attempts to ban books and remove materials from school libraries, and demonstrations swept the nation, increasing in intensity all through the 1970s and accelerating in the 1980s. Summed up by the phrase "back to the basics," the reaction was founded on the idea that "old-time education" must be reestablished in the schools. But what appeared to be a popular mass movement was amplified and utilized by conservative and right-wing political elites that pressed their own agenda.

Back to the Basics

The "Back to the Basics" movement should be understood not merely as an isolated reaction to the New Social Studies, sex education, and other curricular material. The schools have been subjected to waves of religious fundamentalism and nationalistic fervor at many times in the past. In the 1920s, for instance, fundamentalists sought to outlaw the teaching of evolution in the public schools, and by 1935 thirty-seven states had adopted anti-evolution statutes.

According to Burt Pines, author of *Back to the Basics,* the first principle of basics schooling is a "God-centered education."[36] Religious issues make up a "pro-family" catechism opposing abortion, the Equal Rights Amendment, homosexuality, premarital sex, pornography, and sex education in the schools. For the New Right, the schools bear a heavy responsibility for upholding traditional roles in the family. Textbooks "suffer from an anti-God, anti-religion, anti-patriotism, anti-capitalism and anti-homemaker slant." Particularly alarming "is the disappearance from school books of traditional images of men, women and families."[37]

Civics education is the cornerstone of the back-to-the-basics edifice. Students are to be told about the evils of government regulation, government spending, deficit financing, welfare programs, national health care, and wage-price guidelines; about the sanctity of private property and profits; and about the importance of tax incentives for business expansion. Pines enthusiastically reviews "pro–free-enterprise" activities in schools, universities, and colleges: "In a testimonial to corporate America's mounting determination to do something to support capitalism, specifically endowed or funded chairs in free enterprise are proliferating rapidly."[38] Through institutes for free enterprise, high school teachers enroll in (or are required to take) pro-business seminars and workshops subsidized through corporate dollars, and local school districts are benefited by the injection of "economic/free enterprise concepts into the entire curriculum, from kindergarten through twelfth grade."[39] According to Pines, a junior high school textbook financed by business contributions is used in school districts in twenty-seven states, and business-sponsored instructional materials are used in economics classes all over the nation.

The New Right civics education stresses a brand of patriotism that requires allegiance to the New Right's position on a very long list of political issues. To Pines, the overall aim is to praise "America's unique meritocratic tradition that for generations has rewarded achievement and fostered social mobility."[40] History and civics instruction are supposed to show the unstinting generosity and freedom-loving motives of American foreign policy. In all cases, the imminent Soviet threat is destined to occupy center stage.

At the end of her book intended to document the horrors of "liberal" and "humanistic-inspired" education, Phyllis Schlafly published a twenty-five-point checklist that parents could use to evaluate whether their schools were engaging in heretical education practices. Among the twenty-five items listed are these three questions:[41]

Does it blur traditional concepts of gender identity...? Does it induce role reversals by showing women in hard physical-labor jobs and men as househusbands?

Does it describe America as an unjust society (unfair to economic or racial groups or to women) rather than telling the truth that America has given more freedom and opportunity to more people than any nation in the history of the world?

Does it propagandize for domestic spending programs, while attacking defense spending and economy in government? Does it lead the child to believe that disarmament rather than defense can prevent a future war?

By 1981, at least ten national organizations were attempting to rid schoolbooks of material on evolution. One such organization was the Parents' Alliance to Protect Our Children, which circulated to its subscribers a newsletter that analyzes school materials and recommends local action. Possibly the most influential organization was The Eagle Forum, organized by Schlafly on the principle that "parents have the right to expect schools" to "use textbooks and hire teachers that do not offend the religious and moral values of the parents" and to "use textbooks that teach the truth about the family, monogamous marriage, motherhood, American history and Constitution, and the private enterprise system" (among other expectations).[42] The targets of these groups were humanism, ideas promoting participatory democracy, the Equal Rights Amendment, sex education, global education, and a limitless number of other topics. These groups exerted substantial influence on school curricula—one example is that the average biology text used in high schools in the early 1980s contained only fifty lines on evolutionary theory.[43]

Groups like Schlafly's have not been able to gain control of many schools, but they have exerted enough influence to intimidate teachers and school officials. One measure of their clout was the resurgence of censorship of school materials following the 1980 presidential election. Hundreds of school districts excluded books from school libraries or went through protracted, bitter fights over censorship demands. According to the American Library Association, fifty-two books were banned in various schools across the United States during 1986 alone. A sample of titles included *The Diary of Anne Frank* ("sexually offensive passages"), *Cujo,* by Stephen King ("profanity and strong sexual content"), *The Color Purple,* by Alice Walker ("troubling ideas about race relations"), *I Know Why the Caged Bird Sings,* by Maya Angelou ("preaches bitterness and hatred against whites"), *The Living Bible,* by William C. Bower ("perverted commentary on the King James Version"), *To Kill a Mockingbird,* by Harper Lee ("undermining of race relations").[44]

The Reagan Administration's Educational Agenda

For eight years the Reagan administration enthusiastically lent authority and guidance to the education agenda of the New Right. The administration staffed the

Department of Education with people who were closely involved in back-to-basics campaigns. As Secretary of Education, William Bennett declared that the education system's deficiencies were responsible for the public opinion polls that revealed opposition to U.S. intervention in Nicaragua. Regarding social studies in the schools, he said:

> Surely one explanation for the fact that democratic values no longer seem to command the assent they once did is that for many years now the teaching of social studies in our schools has been dominated by cultural relativism. The notion that the attempt to draw meaningful distinctions between opposing traditions is a judgment which all virtuous and right-minded people must sternly condemn.

> One social studies series for elementary schools, for example, advises the teacher that the materials aims to "decrease inclination toward egocentrism, ethnocentrism and stereotyping." But what this means, it turns out, is more than teaching children that all cultures and traditions are not the same. It means teaching that all cultures and traditions are equally valid, that there are not real criteria for good and bad, right and wrong.

Bennett's conclusion was that the schools should teach that ours is the best system. To him, teaching that lesson was the only valid purpose of social studies.[45]

"Global education" became a particular target of the Reagan administration. In June 1984, an official in the Denver regional office of the Department of Education circulated a report castigating the University of Denver for using global education materials in teacher training courses. The materials committed the arch sin of describing world events and issues as often ambiguous, in contrast to the "accepted moral absolutes" that ought to be applied.[46] The Reagan official described the moral absolutes as "truths that are true for anybody, anywhere, at anytime,"[47] and noted that students need to be taught a "healthy skepticism" about "tolerance" for different points of view. His report castigated the "redistributionist ethic" in global education materials that encouraged students to think about how food and other resources could be distributed more equitably among nations.[48] According to the report, a "countervailing network of organizations" was needed to produce "*objective* curriculum materials" that would echo Secretary Bennett's description of America as "the last best hope on Earth."[49] The correct global education would teach children "patriotic love of country and commitment to this nation's leadership responsibility."[50]

The Reagan administration pressed its agenda in school districts all across the country. Soon after the controversy over the University of Denver's program erupted, a school district in Colorado was persuaded by a Department of Education employee to reject a state grant that would have paid teachers to attend a seminar on global education.[51] Encouraged by the Reagan administration, local right-wing groups mobilized against global education programs because they saw in them a threat to patriotic values. To some degree, these groups were no doubt correct; Americans who are educated about global problems are probably less likely to accept uncritically their nation's role in world affairs.

Still the Basics

The historic function of American schooling—to instill a sense of patriotism and shared culture—has never been lost. The schools still teach that America is a land of the free, prosperous, and peaceful. It is inconceivable that any schools would allow any systematically critical perspective about U.S. history or democracy to dominate the curriculum, simply because all schools are necessarily embedded in and dependent on mainstream culture. Try to imagine, for instance, this book being assigned in a high school classroom.

What, therefore, motivated the New Right's assault on the schools? In part, the attack was based on a solid foundation of widespread disenchantment with the quality of the schools: declining national test scores in reading and mathematics, the well-publicized illiteracy of high school graduates, and the fear that America is losing economic vitality to other nations. A great many Americans who do not consider themselves conservative share these concerns. Without doubt, public education in America is often inadequate, or worse. At a deeper level than this, however, the Back-to-the-Basics movement is not new. The schools have always acted as a magnet for social and cultural conflict. National ills are invariably traced back to the schools, for that is where, it is widely assumed, a national culture is supposed to be molded. During times of social or cultural turmoil, people often want the schools to impose discipline, authority, and patriotism:

> Complaints about the decline of education due to modern permissiveness go back at least to the nineteenth century. As a national mood, it often coincides with the ends of wars and with periods of economic downturn. Conservative, pessimistic, nostalgic, it seems to be some kind of quest for certainty in an uncertain world.[52]

The New Right has influenced education all across the nation. Publishers are careful not to include "controversial" discussions of evolution in biology textbooks; millions of dollars in revenues are at stake.[53] School boards, administrators and teachers are subjected to campaigns of harassment and expensive litigation involving the teaching of "secular humanism" (evolution) or civics material.[54] As a result of the obvious risks, publishers edit their texts on the basis of market surveys; authors do not control the editing procedure.[55]

Dozens of conservative think tanks and policy organizations take an interest in the education debate. These organizations receive money from corporations and corporate foundations (a leading Reagan supporter, Joseph Coors, was a big contributor). The triangle forged among federal administrators, conservative organizations such as the Heritage Foundation, and right-wing fundamentalist groups virtually guarantees that public schools will continue to promote a mythical American culture and politics (and a mythical biological curriculum as well).

The national government does not run America's schools. But this fact does not mean that education varies significantly from one community to another. A child attending an urban school in California will be exposed to curriculum materials and values almost identical to the instruction received by a child in rural Pennsylvania. Some might say that such uniformity is the glue that binds a culture together. It should also be pointed out that if the cultural bond is constructed from shared myths about a past that never existed; if ethnic, racial, cultural, and political differences and conflicts are papered over with a veneer of consensus and harmony, then an intolerance for differences is promoted or, just as likely, a fatalistic cynicism emerges when students discover that what they are being taught in schools bears no relation to their actual lives.

It is hardly surprising that students often find history, geography, and social studies to be dull and alienating. The safest way for teachers and textbook writers to escape censure from the right is to promote conventional patriotism and to leave critical analysis out of the classroom. This approach is producing citizens whose emotional buttons can be pushed by flag-waving politicians reciting the Pledge of Allegiance or blaring Neil Diamond's hymn, "Coming to America," but it is not likely to produce citizens capable of understanding the world. This worries some educational elites, who fear that such ignorance will contribute to the overall decline of American influence in the world economy. The National Commission on Social Studies concluded that students who can name all the American colonies, but who cannot understand what a colony is, are not well educated. To remedy this situation, the commission recommends, among other things, that teachers highlight connections between historical subjects and present content, not as something to be memorized, but as information that can be used to explore and confront "open and vital questions" about the world.[56] But what if the definition of a colonial relationship proves to be an apt description of U.S. relations with Latin America?

Opposition to critical history and social science comes principally from well-funded groups like Schlafly's Eagle Forum and Reed Irvine's oddly named "Accuracy in Academia." AIA claims to promote the right of college and high school students to think for themselves, but its principal activity is to encourage students to send copies of syllabi, exams, and classroom handouts from professors deemed ideologically unacceptable. To AIA, the freshman year in college is analogous to an Army boot camp where the right-thinking student learns to survive in a hostile environment. AIA warns college freshmen that teachers who espouse support for national liberation movements struggling against U.S.-backed governments are "most likely Marxist or left-leaning academics" who are about to subject "your mind...[to an] intense assault." According to Irvine,

> The goal of the classroom indoctrinator is to transform you into an ideological radical, so you'll serve his or her political cause. His strategy is to destroy your faith in the political-economic system—and the values that undergird that system—of the United States. Once you've become disillusioned with America, then you'll be introduced to an alternative system, based on different values, which will be touted as the cure-all for America's social evils.[57]

One example of what AIA regards as "indoctrination" is its objection to teaching students that racism was a motivating factor for the internment of 110,000 American citizens of Japanese ancestry into camps during World War II. Specifically,

AIA objects to a California State Assembly resolution declaring that the U.S. government

> wrongfully rationalized the internment on ground of national security and military necessity....The broad historical causes which shaped these decisions were race prejudice, war hysteria and a failure of political leadership....The current textbooks used by California's public school students do not accurately portray the internment experience as a violation of human rights.[58]

Irvine wants textbooks to continue to describe the "relocation" of these American citizens (as in current texts in California) "as a precaution taken for national security reasons."[59]

A false sense of cultural consensus serves political elites well. Dissent appears as unpatriotic and threatening to those people who have come to believe in the myths taught in the school curriculum. People who are relatively privileged will tend to accept stereotypical description of an America that is affluent and full of opportunity. Such a description confirms their life experience. For others, the schoolbook stories ring false. There is a tendency for these people to embrace cynicism, which translates into the habit of dropping out of the political system altogether. As we will demonstrate in the next several chapters, elites in the United States count on such nonparticipation as essential for preserving their political hegemony.

Notes

1. "Carnegie Forum's Task Force on Teaching As a Profession," excerpted in *The Chronicle of Higher Education* 32, no. 12 (May 21, 1986): 44. The complete quotation is: "...the first foundation of a democratic society for the nation and the individual alike."
2. The Works of Thomas Jefferson, ed. Paul L. Ford; Jefferson's "Bill for the More General Diffusion of Knowledge," excerpted in David B. Tyack, ed., *Turning Points in American Educational History* (Waltham, Mass.: Blaisdell, 1967), p. 111.
3. "Carnegie Forum's Task Force," p. 44.
4. Aristotle, *Politics VIII,* quoted in preface to *Reform on Campus* (New York: Carnegie Foundation for the Advancement of Teaching, 1972).
5. Benjamin Rush, *A Plan for the Establishment of Public Schools,* 1786, excerpted in Tyack, *Turning Points,* p. 105.
6. Tyack, *Turning Points,* p. 85.
7. Quoted in ibid., p. 86.
8. U.S. Department of Commerce, Bureau of the Census, *Historical Statistics of the United States, Colonial Times to 1970,* pt. 1, Bicentennial ed. (Washington, D.C.: U.S. Government Printing Office, 1975), p. 8.
9. Blake McKelvey, *American Urbanization: A Comparative History* (Glenview, Ill.: Scott, Foresman, 1973), p. 37.
10. *Transaction of the Fifth Annual Meeting of the Western Literary Institute and College of Professional Teachers* (1836), excerpted in Tyack, *Turning Points,* p. 149.
11. Quoted in David Nasaw, *Schooled to Order: A Social History of Public Schooling in the United States* (New York: Oxford University Press, 1979).
12. "Immigration," *The Massachusetts Teacher* 4 (October 1851), excerpted in *School Reform: Past and Present,* ed. Michael B. Katz (Boston: Little, Brown, 1971), pp. 169-170.

13. *Boston School Committee, Annual Report*, 1858; excerpted in Katz, *School Reform*, pp. 171-172.

14. Quoted in Tyack, *Turning Points*, p. 183.

15. William Holmes McGuffey, *Eclectic First Reader*...(1853), excerpted in Tyack, *Turning Points*, p. 210.

16. Lawrence A. Cremin, *The American Common School* (New York: Teachers College, Columbia University, 1951), p. 35.

17. Quoted in Tyack, *Turning Points*, p. 233.

18. Joseph M. Rice, *The Public School System of the United States* (1893), excerpted in Tyack, *Turning Points*, p. 329.

19. "A Statement of the Theory of Education in the United States of America as Approved by Many Leading Educators," excerpted in Tyack, *Turning Points*, p. 326.

20. Quoted in Frances Fitzgerald, *America Revised: History Textbooks in the Twentieth Century* (Boston: Little, Brown, 1979), p. 79.

21. Ibid., pp. 80-82.

22. Quoted in Fitzgerald, *America Revised*, p. 83.

23. Ibid., p. 84.

24. Frederick R. Smith and John J. Patrick, "Civics: Relating Social Study to Social Reality," in C. Benjamin Cox and Byron G. Masialas, eds., *Social Studies in the United States* (New York: Harcourt, Brace and World, 1967), pp. 113-114.

25. Fitzgerald, *America Revised*, pp. 117-118.

26. Ibid., p. 119.

27. Ibid., pp. 119-120.

28. Quoted in ibid., p. 121.

29. Quoted at ibid.

30. Smith and Patrick, "Civics," pp. 113-114.

31. Byron G. Masialas, "American Government: We Are the Greatest!", in Cox and Masialas, *Social Studies in the United States*, pp. 180-181.

32. Fitzgerald, *America Revised*, p. 105.

33. Ibid., p. 100-101.

34. Lewis Paul Todd and Merle Corti, *Rise of the American Nation, Liberty Edition* (New York: Harcourt Brace Jovanovich, 1982).

35. John Edward Weltz, *Modern American History: The Search for Identity* (New York: Harper & Row, 1981).

36. Burton Yale Pines, *Back to Basics: The Traditionalist Movement that Is Sweeping Grassroots America* (New York: William Morrow, 1982), p. 303.

37. Ibid., p. 177.

38. Ibid., p. 60.

39. Ibid., p. 61.

40. Ibid., p. 22.

41. Phyllis Schlafly, ed., *Child Abuse in the Classroom* (Alton, Ill.: Pere Marquette Press, 1984), pp. 436-437. Reprinted with permission.

42. Eagle Forum, pamphlet and membership application, n.d.

43. Stephen Arons, *Compelling Belief: The Culture of American Schooling* (New York.: McGraw-Hill, 1983), p. 19.

44. "Complete Title List, Banned Books Promotion," Office of Intellectual Freedom, The American Library Association, from *Resource Book for Banned Book Week 1986* and *Newsletter on Intellectual Freedom*, xerox, 1986.

45. Quoted in Gregg L. Cunningham, "Blowing the Whistle on 'Global Education,'" Preliminary Draft, prepared for Thomas G. Tancredo, Secretary's Regional Representative, Region VIII, U.S. Department of Education, June 1984, pp. 10-11.

46. Ibid., p. 7.

47. Ibid., p. 8.

48. Ibid., p. 13.

49. Ibid., p. 22; emphasis in the original.

50. Ibid.

51. "Fundamentalists Maintaining Scrutiny of Textbooks, Teaching," *Rocky Mountain News*, June 23, 1986. One of the authors, Dan Hellinger, has had a direct experience with the politics of global education through his participation in the St. Louis–based International Education Consortium.

52. Fitzgerald, *America Revised,* p. 207.

53. Karen O'Connor and Gregg Ivers, "Creationism, Evolution and the Courts," *PS: Political Science and Politics* (Winter 1988): 10-17.

54. Marsha Nye Adler, "The Politics of Censorship," *PS: Political Science and Politics* (Winter 1988): 18-24.

55. Diane B. Paul, "The Market as Censor," *PS: Political Science and Politics* (Winter 1988): 31-35.

56. Virginia Hick, "Understanding Studies Is More than Good Grades," *St. Louis Post Dispatch* (November 12, 1983).

57. "Welcome to Campus" and "Classroom Indoctrination: How It Works," *Campus Report from Accuracy in Academia* (September 1988).

58. "California Moves to Rewrite History," *Campus Report from Accuracy in Academia* (October 1989).

59. Ibid.

Chapter 3

Political Elites and the Media*

The Ideal of "A Multitude of Tongues"

Many voices have expressed the idea that democracy relies upon the un-impeded flow of ideas, and it has often been said that the vehicle for the public dialogue is a media free from government control. In this vein the head of the American Newspapers Publishers' Association has said that newspapers

> serve the diverse needs of their readers by providing the kind of information all of us need to make those important decisions we all face in our day-to-day living....They are a staying power for freedom and a mighty force in helping make our democracy work.[1]

American democratic theory accords preeminent status to the idea that the press and the media must be independent agents in political life. Judge Learned Hand wrote: "The First Amendment presupposes that right conclusions are more likely to be gathered out of a multitude of tongues than through any kind of authoritative selection. To many this is, and will always be, folly; but we have staked upon it our all."[2]

The notion of the "free press" has been a compelling idea since colonial times, when newspapers constituted the principal media institutions. Though newspapers have never been utterly free to express unpopular political ideas, the range of political debate in the nineteenth-century American press was considerable, compared to its constricted voice since the turn of this century. Newspapers reflected the views of their owners. Ownership of newspapers began to concentrate in the Progressive Era, a trend that has accelerated in the past two decades. Most significant newspapers and nearly all radio and television stations are now owned by multinational corporations. The image of an independent, free media is rooted in an understanding that the media in America are privately owned in contrast, for example, to formerly communist countries, where the mass media were controlled by government. But there is a considerable degree of deception in such comparisons, as illustrated by a discussion of media in a leading college-level textbook on American politics. According to the

* Coauthored with Roland Klose.

authors of the text (published before *glasnost*), "The only recognized function of the mass media in the USSR is political persuasion." Ideological dissent is not tolerated, although there may be criticisms of "slow progress on projects, sloppy workmanship, long food lines, poorly made goods, and the like." The only legitimate objective of broadcasting "is to advance Communist policies and improve the 'socialist state.'"[3] By implication, unlike the Soviet Union, media in the United States have been free to engage in fundamental ideological debate and to criticize government at will. (The reader is left to draw this conclusion since the authors offer no actual contrasting discussion of U.S. media in this section of their book.)

It needs to be emphasized that the absence of overt government censorship does not by itself produce an "independent" and "free" media. Media in the United States convey a remarkably uniform view of the world, and it has been a politically specific one: anticommunist, pro-corporate, and nationalist. It is hard to imagine any criticism of capitalism by a U.S. reporter or broadcaster. Perhaps the contrast with a media such as the USSR's should be drawn partly in this way: Until *glasnost,* theirs hewed to an ideology prescribed by government censors. In the United States, a different ideology is followed with equal reliability and consistency, but the most important mechanism of censorship is corporate ownership and management rather than government oversight. Like their Russian counterparts, the American media are adept at exposing "slow progress on projects, sloppy workmanship...poorly made goods, and the like," but the privately owned media is no more likely to attribute such lapses to capitalism than the communist-controlled media was likely, before *glasnost,* to attribute such problems to communism. When political discourse over fundamental political issues occurs in the United States, it proceeds in spite of, rather than because of, a technologically sophisticated, privately owned mass media that reaches into every home.

The Corporate Media

Television is the key link between elites and masses today. It shapes mass attitudes because we have become a nation of watchers rather than readers. A Roper Organization poll in 1984 found that 20 percent of Americans received most of their news from both newspapers and television; 24 percent from newspapers but not television; and 49 percent from television alone.[4] Readership of daily newspapers, measured by sales per one hundred households, has steadily fallen over the past fifty years. In 1930, one hundred households bought 132 newspapers per day. By 1940, that figure had dropped to 118, rising ten years later to 124. In 1960, consumption slipped to 111 newspapers for every one hundred households, and it has declined steadily since, to ninety papers in 1970 and seventy-nine in 1980.[5]

The decline in newspaper readership can be traced to the development of commercial radio in the 1930s and television in the 1950s, and also to concentrated ownership and dwindling competition among newspapers.[6] In 1900, there were 2,226 dailies published in 1,737 urban places,[7] and almost all of them were owned by an independent company or publisher.[8] By 1985, 80 percent of the 1,676 U.S. dailies in

8,760 urban places were owned by 149 chains.[9] Ten corporations controlled 40 percent of daily circulation and accounted for 60 percent of total newspaper revenues.[10] In almost all U.S. markets, the local newspaper has ceased to operate in competition with other local dailies. In the three biggest markets, New York City, Los Angeles, and Chicago, the second daily is financially weak compared to the dominant paper. In half the twenty cities with two daily newspapers, the papers pool their advertising income and staffs under Joint Newspaper Operating Agencies so that genuine competition is absent.

Ownership of other media institutions has become even more concentrated. Of about 11,000 advertiser-supported print and electronic media in 1982, twenty corporations accounted for more than half of total sales. There were 2,500 book publishers, but the majority of the companies published only one to five titles a year, and seven companies published the vast majority of paperback books. Approximately 9,000 radio stations were on the air in 1982, but ten corporations owned stations that reached over one-half the nation's radio audience.[11] At the beginning of the 1980s, even before a rash of mergers in 1985 and 1986, almost all American movies were made by eight or nine studios.[12]

Ten corporations earned more than half of all U.S. media revenues in 1984: ABC, CBS, Time Inc., RCA Corp. (which owned NBC), Times Mirror Corp., Gannett Co., Advance Publications, Knight-Ridder Newspapers, Tribune Co., and Dun & Bradstreet. These companies earned more than $22.4 billion dollars in revenues,[13] and they were tightly linked with nonmedia firms, including major airlines, defense contractors, oil companies, and retailers. Every leading media company has directors representing international banks, investment, and insurance companies. A Senate study in 1978 reported that:

> All four broadcasting organizations [ABC, CBS, NBC and Westinghouse] were represented on the board of the country's largest international banker, Citicorp, and the network companies linked with each other on the boards of other financial companies and industrials. These facts raise fundamental isues....They can bear on social issues and possibly control the shape and direction of the nation's economy.[14]

Media corporations are almost inseparable from nonmedia companies. CBS Inc., subject of a takeover attempt in 1985 by a right-wing group led by Jesse Helms, accepted a friendly "takeover" by Loews Corp., a diversified company involved in cigarette production, hotel development, and insurance. RCA Corp., which owns NBC, was acquired in 1985 by General Electric, a major producer of consumer goods, military hardware, and nuclear technology. The selling of media time is a major product and revenue source for the conglomerate corporate owners. By the late 1980s, one-hundred diversified corporations in the United States accounted for three-fourths of network television advertising, half of all magazine advertising, and a third of newspaper and radio advertising.[15]

In 1984, the Federal Communications Commission (FCC) significantly accelerated concentrated corporate ownership of the media industry by lifting a thirty-year-old rule that had limited group owners to a combination of seven FM stations, seven AM stations, and seven television stations—the so-called "rule of sevens." In 1989, that cap was lifted to twelve-twelve-twelve. Were it not for opposition from Congress and the motion picture industry (which feared reduced prices for films sold to the networks), the FCC would have removed ownership regulations altogether, effective in 1990. FCC chairman Mark S. Fowler, a political conservative and apostle of deregulation, lost the battle for complete deregulation, but he won the war. He successfully ended FCC regulations that prohibited the cross-ownership of news-papers and broadcast properties in the same market. In Fowler's view, financially troubled media outlets could be "saved" by their sale to corporations that had an interest in maximizing their own media dominance in a local market.[16]

The immediate effect of this partial deregulation was to reduce the number of companies in the media business. In 1985, broadcast mergers were valued at nearly $30 billion, up from $2.1 billion in 1984 and $1.8 billion in 1983.[17] General Electric paid $6.3 billion to take over RCA; Capital Cities paid $3.5 billion to acquire ABC. In 1986, to frustrate a takeover bid from Turner Broadcasting, CBS sold almost 25 percent of its stock to Loews Corp. Deflected from his attempt to take over CBS, Ted Turner bought one of the major motion picture companies, MGM/United Artists. Australian-born Rupert Murdoch, who had put together a chain of American papers that included the *New York Post, Chicago Sun-Times,* and *Boston Herald,* acquired half of 20th Century Fox in 1985, then acquired seven major television stations from Metromedia.

Media companies look good to investors because of their incredible profita-bility. From 1983 to 1984, the three networks recorded a revenue increase of 21.5 percent and net profits of 15 percent.[18] Unlike other industries, the media were able to weather the recession of 1983 and 1984 simply by raising prices. Wall Street was impressed. Louis Rukeyser, a syndicated columnist, wrote in mid-1986: "Wall Street's new enthusiasm for media properties...[is] not rooted in any fresh devotion to the First Amendment or the thrill of front-page competition. What appeals to investors is the scent of monopoly."[19]

Typically, chains did not acquire newspapers that operated in competitive markets. Papers that were failing in the early 1980s—the *St. Louis Globe-Democrat,* the *Philadelphia Bulletin,* and the *Cleveland Press*—were not acquired by the major media chains. Thus, FCC chairman Fowler's strategy of saving dying newspapers by allowing concentrated ownership actually rescued very few newspapers; instead, it prompted a frenzy of takeovers and mergers. Chains like Gannett preferred to acquire profitable monopoly companies such as the *Louisville Courier-Journal and Times* and the *Des Moines Register.* Times Mirror bought the *Baltimore Sun* for $600 million the day after its Hearst-owned competitor, the *News-American,* folded. Investment bankers enthusiastically financed the considerable media acquisition activity. As one media broker noted, "The banks take a look at these stations and find that the cash flow warrants the return on their money. It's here to stay and more and more banks are getting involved."[20]

After the merger activity of 1985 and 1986, stations directly owned by Capital Cities Communications/ABC reached 24 percent of the nation's 85 million television households; General Electric/NBC reached 21 percent; CBS, 19 percent; the Tribune

Co. (which owns the *Chicago Tribune* and *New York Daily News*), 19 percent, and 20th Century Fox (owned by Rupert Murdoch and oilman Marvin Davis), 18 percent.[21]

The Influence of Advertisers

Besides corporate ownership, commercial advertisers also potentially limit the diversity of news and entertainment programming. The influence of advertisers, like that of owners and high-level management, is not usually direct. The way James Gordon Bennett dealt with one of his prominent advertisers in New York City's *Herald* is often cited by media critics as an example of the pressure advertisers and publishers can wield. In 1835, one of Bennett's main advertisers was a Dr. Brandreth, who sold quack medicines. Bennett filled the *Herald* with news stories describing cures achieved by users of Brandreth's pills. When other pill makers complained about the *Herald's* favoritism, Bennett responded: "Send us more advertisements than Dr. Brandreth does—give us higher prices—we'll cut Brandreth dead—or at least curtail his space."[22] Nine months later, after the *Herald* raised its price by a penny, Brandreth cancelled his advertising contract, complaining that the paper was no longer reaching his audience. Bennett immediately decided the *Herald* had no room for quackery and denounced Brandreth as a charlatan. Years later, Brandreth returned to the *Herald* as an advertiser, and the negative stories about him once again stopped.

The blatant quid pro quo between Brandreth and Bennett has given way to subtler means of influence. Today's media simply omit or color information critical of their advertisers. In 1978, Chicago dailies refused paid full-page advertisements by a local union explaining why its members were picketing the city's largest retail advertiser, Marshall Field Company.[23] Stanford University students released a study in 1970 naming the generators of air pollution in the Bay Area, but fourteen of seventeen newspapers that carried the story deleted references to local company names.[24]

The greatest health problem in the United States today, addiction to tobacco, was studiously ignored for years by American newspapers, which receive 15 percent of all their advertising income from the top five tobacco companies. In 1939 and 1949, two medical studies, both presented in New York, linked smoking to serious health problems, including lung cancer. They were ignored by the entire New York press (eight dailies) except for one paper, which published a story in the back of its theatrical page. A prominent media critic of the time attributed this treatment to the power of the cigarette advertisers. In the 1950s, while NBC's news programming was sponsored by Camel cigarettes, all news tape showing a picture of a "no smoking" sign was banned.[25]

The relationship between advertisers and media policy may be even closer in the case of radio and television than in newspaper coverage, because every program or show must successfully pull its own weight in generating revenues. Until the early 1920s, most broadcasting was noncommercial. In 1922, colleges and universities held licenses for seventy-two radio stations, the majority of stations then broadcasting.[26]

But within a decade, most educational stations had gone off the air. What changed radio was the completion in 1928 of a coast-to-coast network of stations able to carry simultaneous programming. The telephone company–owned New York station, WEAF-AM, experimented with carrying national commercial messages as early as 1923. When the National Broadcasting Co., a subsidiary of the Radio Corporation of America, issued its prospectus in 1926, it endorsed the concept of advertiser-supported broadcasting, saying that "if broadcasting is to be a success, it must stand on its own legs."[27] Commercial sponsorship on a national level quickly led to programming expressly tailored to selling advertising. By 1928, sixty-five nationally sponsored programs were on the air.[28] Advertisers not only underwrote programming that promoted their products; their corporate names were linked directly to programming (the "Lucky Strike Orchestra," the "Swift [Ham] Hour," the "A&P Gypsies").

Such practices have not disappeared, and it is hard to imagine a corporate media that would not protect its owners and advertisers. Except in rare cases, however, it is difficult to demonstrate the influence of advertisers on programming, in part because it would be anathema for the media ever to admit to such influence, and advertisers would no longer be as crass as Dr. Brandreth (or Camel cigarettes) in trying to overtly buy favorable media treatment. If an advertiser made such an attempt outside the closed doors of a corporate boardroom, the attempt might well backfire, and the advertiser conceivably might be held up to ridicule, because the media has a huge stake in preserving an image as an objective source of information.

The "Objective" Media

Media institutions go to great lengths to maintain a public perception that they are accurate, fair, and objective in news coverage. The idea that the press ought to be objective found expression in the development of journalism schools at major universities in the first decade of the twentieth century. The schools had been inspired by Joseph Pulitzer, who in 1903 endowed a journalism program at Columbia University. By the early 1920s, more than twenty schools and departments had been founded.[29] The development of journalism as a discipline with an emphasis on professionalism quickly led to a carefully articulated ideology about the role of the press. This ideology consisted of four tenets: The press must be free from outside interference, it must serve the public's right to know, reporters must seek to find and report the truth, and the press must present facts objectively and fairly.[30] These principles were elevated to professional canon in 1923, when the American Society of Newspaper Editors (ASNE) issued their guidelines, including the dictum that American journalists must practice "impartiality," which ASNE defined as making a "clear distinction between news reports and expressions of opinion."[31]

The expressed ideal of "objective" reporting is designed to insulate the media from charges of bias.[32] A reporter who accurately reports the statements of an individual, although those statements may be obviously false or inaccurate, nonetheless has conformed to journalistic conventions. "We don't tell the truth, we report what people say," a newspaper editor once quipped.[33] Thus, "under the conventions of journalism prevailing today," contends Tom Wicker, associate editor of the *New York Times,* "[it] is impossible...for a reporter to step in and refute a false statement in his own voice."[34]

In the 1980s, conservative groups decided that media "objectivity" actually amounted to a liberal bias, and they launched a well-organized and well-financed campaign to pull the media to the right. Among the leading proponents of the "media as liberal" thesis were a number of activists with close relationships to the corporations and the military-defense establishment. Among these activists was Reed Irvine, a North Carolina conservative who founded Accuracy In Media (AIM). AIM publishes a biweekly report that examines the largest media organizations, with a particular emphasis on the *Washington Post,* the *New York Times,* the news weeklies, and the networks. Another organization, the American Legal Foundation (ALF), was organized by Daniel Popeo in 1980. The ALF involved itself in a number of regulatory and legal challenges to media companies. For example, it challenged minority and women's "citizen's agreements" with broadcast license owners and served as a resource center for businesses and politicians suing for libel. At the same time, the ALF petitioned the FCC to deny licenses to a group of nonprofit alternative radio stations carrying programs from the independent Pacifica Foundation.

Two other well-financed groups active in countering the allegedly liberal bias of the media included the Institute for Educational Affairs (IEA) and the U.S. Industrial Council Educational Foundation (USICEF). IEA, cofounded in 1978 by former Nixon Treasury Secretary William Simon and neoconservative author Irving Kristol, attracted funding from several foundations and corporations, including General Motors, Northrup, Nestlé, Dow Chemical, and Boise-Cascade. IEA and USICEF funded more than seventy student-run conservative newspapers from 1979 to 1985. USICEF helped launch the conservative *Yale Free Press* and the *Harvard Sentinel,* and it provided syndicated services to about fifty student papers.[35] Conservative organizations also organized programs to train and place journalists. The National Journalism Center trained reporters "within a context of traditional values."[36]

Fairness in Media (FIM) was organized in 1978 by a Raleigh, North Carolina, attorney named Thomas Ellis, a political ally of Senator Jesse Helms. According to Ellis, the liberal media was thwarting the will of the electorate: "We won the election, but we lost the battle afterwards because of the media....Every time the conservatives start to move, the liberal media is able to change that agenda."[37] Ellis said the idea to organize FIM was hatched as early as 1967 when, angered by network coverage of the Vietnam War, he bought one share each in CBS, ABC, and RCA. This example was cited in 1985 when FIM, Senator Jesse Helms, and conservative activists encouraged their supporters to buy shares in CBS Inc. in order to "become Dan Rather's boss."

Urged on by the Reagan administration, conservative critics launched an assault on journalists and broadcasters. Reagan's science adviser, George A. Keyworth, summed up the administration's charge of liberal bias when he said, "Much of the press seems to be drawn from a reactively narrow fringe element on the far left of our society...and...is trying to tear down America."[38] The networks responded to these attacks by mounting public relations campaigns. ABC initiated an ad campaign in the fall of 1985 entitled "American Television and You." According to explanations by ABC executives, the campaign was designed to allay public concerns about the effect of multibillion-dollar takeovers of the networks. After thirteen weeks of spot ads and concurrent newspaper advertising, ABC researchers noted an increase in the number of viewers "who felt more positive toward television than they did before they saw the message."[39] As a follow-up, ABC inaugurated *Viewpoint,* an irregular series featuring a live discussion format designed to provide an ostensibly objective forum for public criticism of the media.

Claiming that he knew of a "no more patriotic group than television journalists," in 1986 NBC's anchor Tom Brokaw took a "loyalty oath" to prove his own patriotism.[40] In the same summer CBS began running a series of advertisements promoting its evening news program. Using black-and-white stills of individuals, the voiceover on the spot said: "Americans, we know who we are. And when it comes to news, we know who we trust. Dan Rather, CBS News."

The networks also aired documentaries on the press. For example, NBC aired a "white paper" in June 1985, called *A Portrait of the Press: Warts and All,* written and hosted by commentator John Chancellor. In a closing segment, Chancellor said, "The most important thing we learned in covering the story of journalism in America today is this. The problems the press does have would be much easier to handle if there were more attention paid to the craft of journalism."[41] Indeed, the "craft of journalism" underwent profound changes in the 1980s that have had the effect of making the media an active partner in the neoconservative revolution. The pressures that brought this about were not only applied by political groups. In the end, news lost all possibility of a critical or investigative role (what its critics called "left leaning") because of corporate pressures.

As the networks became more economically integrated with other corporations, the news divisions were subjected more and more to "bottom-line" pressures of profit-and-loss analysis and ratings and audience shares. Increasingly, professional journalists were replaced with news personalities chosen for their appearance and delivery. With the pressure on to produce more news programming in cost-effective ways, news divisions began to rely on verbal and visual images provided by public relations experts rather than on information gathered by autonomous news staffs. News became packaged for its entertainment value.

The most important change in climate was induced by the replacement of executives with long experience in news production with those whose experience was producing sports and entertainment. The decade opened with ABC News under control of Roone Arledge, creator of *Wide World of Sports* and *Monday Night Football.* CBS News, having lost its trump card when Walter Cronkite retired in 1981, likewise turned its news division, the largest and most prestigious in the industry, over to its sports director, Van Gordon Sauter. In 1984, NBC's news operations were placed under the control of Lawrence Grossman, a career advertising man who had made his mark in the entertainment division. These ratings-conscious executives took control just as the networks were encountering challenges from cable television and were financially bleeding after warding off hostile takeovers—an especially important factor in the CBS case. In this atmosphere, the corporations that ran the networks welcomed the laissez-faire attitude of the Federal Communications Commission, which not only viewed multiple ownership favorably but rejected the philosophy that broadcasters had a public responsibility to provide public affairs programming in exchange for access to the public airwaves.

Not surprisingly, in the 1980s there were massive firings of research staff, a drastic reduction of documentary reporting (from twenty programs per year for each network in the 1960s to an average of fifteen each year from all three networks during the Reagan years), and greater dependence of news organizations on prepackaged information, like photo opportunities and staged news events. White House Director of Communications David Gergen and other top advisers to President Reagan openly acknowledged that they successfully manipulated the media, especially television, by serving up news on a platter to reporters. When writer Mark Hertsgaard suggested to Gergen that he seemed to feel that the administration had increased its power over the press as effectively as it had increased the U.S. military advantage over the Soviet Union, Gergen answered, "Yeah, I agree, that's a good point. It's a very relevant analogy."[42]

In the new environment of news-as-entertainment, corporate executives exerted a considerable direct influence over news content. Mark Hertsgaard found that corporate executives rarely ordered stories to be changed directly, but reporters were "encouraged" to rethink the tone and content of stories that seemed objectionable or controversial. Among many cases: CBS softened a documentary showing the impact of Reaganomics on the poor; the *New York Times* removed Raymond Bonner from his Central American beat after he was criticized by the White House; Leslie Stahl of CBS, the most tenacious White House reporter, was pressured to give the administration "fairer" treatment between 1982 and 1984; and in 1985 the Associated Press questioned two of its reporters over stories that laid out many of the pertinent facts about illegal aid to the Nicaraguan *contras* more than a year before the story showed up in a foreign newspaper.

The failure of the media to serve its watchdog role during the 1980s was often attributed to Ronald Reagan's genial personality and his alleged ability to manipulate the media. But it was the media itself, not the government, that manufactured the "Teflon" coating for Reagan, in part because the values of the corporate executives who own news organizations were the same as those that put Reagan in the White House:

> the press took its definition of what constituted political news from the political governing class in Washington. Thus while the press shaped mass opinion, it reflected elite opinion; indeed, it effectively functioned as a mechanism by which the latter was transformed, albeit imperfectly, into the former.[43]

In the 1980s, it was inevitable that the corporate media would amplify conservative voices in news and news commentary. George Will was named the lone commentator on ABC News in 1984, reaching the largest audience of any journalist in the country. Using this position, Will editorialized for the overthrow of the government of Nicaragua, the deployment of the MX missile, and military intervention against Libya; and he opposed sanctions against the Republic of South Africa. Two newly created news operations, Turner Broadcasting's Cable News Network in 1980 and Gannett's *USA Today* in 1982, were distinctly conservative in orientation. And since 1980, the *New York Times,* which provides a significant source of syndicated editorial material to other media, swung decisively toward neoconservative ideas and writers.[44] In other newspapers, the most widely distributed syndicated columnists by the late 1980s were conservatives like James J. Kilpatrick, George Will, Rowland Evans and Robert Novak, and Joseph Kraft. Liberals, such as Mary McGrory and William Raspberry, each were able to distribute their columns to less than one-third the number of newspapers reached by Kilpatrick. Of course, no syndicated "left" columnist was published in the national daily press.[45]

The Media's Political Slant

The idea that the media evince a liberal bias usually relies on evidence showing that a large proportion of news executives and reporters lean "left" in their personal political views.[46] But does this mean that their views become translated into news with a liberal bias? There is room for a considerable tension within news organizations, since the owners of media institutions, the corporate directors and stockholders, certainly are inclined to the ideological right. Whose views prevail?

It is illogical to suppose that ownership, combined with the financial leverage of corporate advertisers, does not exert an overwhelming influence. And indeed it does. Over the long haul, media institutions have served as consistently conservative organizations that represent the political interests and viewpoints of the elites that control them. On questions of ideology—the defense of capitalism and the "free market," and patriotic defense of American interests, as defined by corporate elites—the media always was unwavering. Media institutions were especially sensitive to charges that they were "soft on communism." Their status as business institutions made such sensitivity inevitable. Accordingly, the U.S. media always served as reliable mouthpieces for government officials who justified U.S. foreign policies by referring to the Red Menace. The close alliance between the media and government on this topic goes back a long way. For at least seven decades, the media interpreted the Soviet Union as an imminent threat to American democracy—except for the brief time during the Second World War when the Soviets were allies.

Journalists Walter Lippmann and Charles Merz analyzed press coverage of the Soviet Union in the three years following the abdication of the czar, from March 1917 to March 1920. Their study, which focused on articles published in the *New York Times,* found that the "news" overtly justified rather than "reported on" U.S. military intervention in Russia following the defeat of Germany. The U.S. press ran story after story about imminent Bolshevik military adventures. The *New York Times* published scare headlines like "LENIN THREATENS INDIA" and "REDS SEEK WAR WITH AMERICA."[47]

There were many reasons why editors magnified the power and threat of bolshevism. In the years following the First World War, American industry was beset by strikes: In a two-year period, 2 million workers walked off their jobs, including half a million coal miners and 350,000 steel workers. Attempting to explain worker unrest, the press linked strikes to communist agitation. Sensational headlines warned of the danger: "RED PERIL HERE," "PLAN BLOODY REVOLUTION," and "WANT WASHINGTON GOVERNMENT OVERTURNED."[48] In 1920, the U.S. Department of Justice arrested thousands of leftists and trade unionists in raids conducted in twenty cities.[49] Press coverage was uniformly enthusiastic.

The press's anticommunist fulmination continued as a staple throughout the 1930s and was muted only during the last four years of the Second World War, when the United States and the USSR were allied in the fight against Nazi Germany. Anticommunism was reinvigorated during the administration of President Harry Truman, and the press acted as enthusiastic partners in the cause. In what many regard as the media's first shot of the Cold War, *Time* magazine published an article on "Communist Contagion" on April 1, 1946. The article was accompanied by a map that divided the world into regions labeled "exposed," "infected," and "quarantined."[50]

The atmosphere of hysteria whipped up by the press exerted tremendous influence on politics within the United States. The near-universal editorial opposition to the 1948 presidential campaign of the short-lived Progressive Party presaged the press's collaboration in the hunt for internal subversives in the 1950s. The party's candidate, former Vice President Henry Wallace, offered voters a liberalized version of the New Deal. Wallace found himself excoriated in the press as "the centerpiece of U.S. communism's most authentic looking facade."[51] The anticommunist hysteria sustained a rollback in many of the rights that labor unions had won in the 1930s. The press did its part by painting the labor movement as a "communist front." Business's breakthrough against labor, the Taft-Hartley Act of 1947, was supported by almost all the major newspapers in the country. The act empowered the courts to issue injunctions against strikes and to levy heavy fines for violations. Mass picketing and secondary boycotts were outlawed. States were permitted to pass "right-to-work" laws allowing nonunion employees to work in unionized plants. Owners were allowed to lock out workers and to refuse to bargain. Union officials were required to sign oaths certifying that they were not Communists.[52] The press did not report on the conflict between industry, government, and labor so much as it acted as an active and powerful participant in the struggle. It played the crucial role of mobilizing public opinion sufficiently so that labor could be beaten: "Under the pressure of the combined forces of industry, government, and the press, the major strikes had been broken, wages driven down, the open shop restored and the ranks of the unions decimated."[53]

By 1950, the Soviet Union had detonated its first nuclear warhead, the Chinese Communist party had ousted the U.S.-backed government of Chiang Kai-shek, and the United States was sinking into an unpopular war in Korea. Alger Hiss, a State Department official, had been convicted in January of perjury, following a barrage of hysterically negative press reports that ensured he could not get a fair trial.[54] Julius and Ethel Rosenberg were arrested six months later, accused of conspiring to pass the secret of the atomic bomb to the Soviet Union. Their subsequent death sentence was, to the Hearst press, an appropriate way to rid the nation of a cancer: "The trial...disclosed in shuddering detail the Red cancer in the American body politic—a cancer which the government is now forced to obliterate in self-defense. The sentences indicate the scalpel which prosecutors can be expected to use in that operation."[55]

The Government-Media Connection

The close cooperation between the media and economic and political elites did not end when the climate of political hysteria of the early 1950s ran its course. Indeed, the relationship has become closer and better organized, as perhaps illustrated most clearly by the case of Nicholas Daniloff. On August 30, 1986, Daniloff, a Moscow-based correspondent for *U.S. News and World Report,* was arrested by the Soviet Union's secret police and jailed. The Soviet authorities accused Daniloff of spying.

The Reagan administration and the press hotly denounced Daniloff's imprisonment. Typical of media reaction was an editorial in Gannett's *USA Today* that described the seizure of an American correspondent as evidence of the continuing perfidy of the Soviet Union.

Daniloff is no spy. Instead, he is a hostage, as certainly as the U.S. embassy employees in Iran were hostages, as certainly as the innocent people held in Lebanon are hostages, as certainly as our citizens hurt in hijackings are hostages....Until Daniloff is free, Mikhail Gorbachev stands with Ayatollah Khomeini and Moammar Gadhafi as a terrorist. Until he is free, the Soviet nation wears the terrorist's mask, and the terrorist flag remains planted in Soviet soil....There is a temptation, now, for our leaders to once more escalate the level of anti-Soviet rhetoric, to once more lash out and label the Soviet Union "an evil empire." No need to say it. Just leave it to the Soviets. With its acts of inhumanity like the unjust jailing of Nick Daniloff, the Soviet Union brands itself an evil empire.[56]

At the same time that Daniloff was in custody, a Gallup Poll disclosed that less than one-fourth of the public thought there was "no chance whatever" that Daniloff was "actually involved in spying on the Soviets."[57] *Editor & Publisher,* a trade journal of the newspaper industry, editorialized that public opinion must be "a testimonial to the effectiveness of Soviet propaganda."[58]

But the public's skepticism seemed to have a solid basis. After Daniloff was released, the administration acknowledged the details of an incident reported in the U.S.S.R. government newspaper *Izvestia* that thoroughly compromised Daniloff's claim to innocence. According to the account, Daniloff had served as an intermediary in early 1985 between a self-styled priest who called himself "Father Roman" and U.S. embassy officials, carrying a packet of information addressed to the embassy. Daniloff was apparently compromised when a Central Intelligence Agency (CIA) employee at the embassy contacted the priest, saying "I'm a friend of Nicolae" and acknowledged receiving the packet.[59]

One reason for the public's skepticism may have been frequent revelations about a close relationship between the U.S. intelligence community and the media. Reporters and CIA agents historically have been so close that *U.S. News and World Report's* chief foreign editor, Joseph Fromm, once told a congressional committee that "a foreign government could be forgiven for assuming that there is some kind of informal link."[60] The long-standing relationship was disclosed in a series of congressional intelligence committee hearings held in the mid-1970s. Those investigations revealed not only that hundreds of reporters had worked closely with intelligence agencies, but that some reporters were actually on the CIA payroll. A partial list of journalists who had collaborated with the CIA included *New York Times* columnist C. L. Sulzberger, syndicated columnists Joseph and Stewart Alsop, editors for CBS and ABC news, and reporters for United Press International.[61]

At one time the CIA ran at least fifty of its own media and 200 wire services and publications (the present number is unknown).[62] The agency also provided financial support to Radio Liberty and Radio Free Europe.[63] It induced Kenneth Love, a reporter for the *New York Times,* to cooperate with it in its successful effort to topple the constitutional government of Mohammed Mossadegh in Iran in 1953, and it successfully pressured the *Times* into pulling a reporter (Sidney Gruson) from a story about the CIA-inspired overthrow of the democratically elected government in Guatemala in 1954.[64] On many occasions it planted news stories abroad in order to have them picked up by wire services and U.S. newspapers. In one instance among many, stories about Cuban soldiers killing babies and raping women in Angola were concocted by the CIA in the early 1980s, and reported as fact in the U.S. press.[65]

The CIA is not the only government agency that has forged close relationships with the media. For decades, the Federal Bureau of Investigation maintained cooperative relationships with more than 300 journalists in more than twenty-five cities, including at least twenty-five "friendly" media contacts in the Chicago area alone.[66] Uncooperative media were treated differently. The FBI acknowledged that from 1956 to 1971 it carried out large-scale intelligence-gathering and disruption efforts against alternative and underground newspapers, reporting syndicates and individual journalists.[67]

Even if media reporters wanted to establish their independence, the news process makes it difficult or impossible for them to check on government sources. For foreign reporting, reporters must primarily use such sources or rely on news generated by the major wire services (Associated Press, United Press International and British-based Reuters) and by the elite press (the *New York Times,* the *Washington Post,* and the *Los Angeles Times*). For this reason, alternative sources of information are rarely available to the news consumer and news stories reported by different news organizations are remarkably similar.

News During the Reagan Years

As a consequence of their heavy reliance on the government for information, news organizations are loathe to offend "official sources" and they are subject to manipulation. Government officials use their monopoly over information to generate favorable coverage and to manage the news. All presidential administrations have tried to control the flow of information as much as possible, but news management became a fine-tuned art during the presidency of Ronald Reagan. The Reagan administration, operating under the umbrella of what it saw as its conservative mandate, paid close attention to the art of controlling information. One of its best successes came with its decision to exclude the press from covering the October 25, 1983, invasion of the Caribbean island of Grenada. The invasion was used by the administration as an opportunity to assert almost complete control over information. As a result of acquiescing to these new government policies, the media has substantially agreed since 1983 to censor itself when covering military actions.

Journalists had been permitted to cover military operations in every previous military engagement since the American Revolution, including the Civil War; twenty Caribbean expeditions between 1880 and 1924; the First World War; the Second World War; the wars in Korea and Vietnam; and the 1956 intervention in Lebanon.[68] But the media accepted new restraints on the publication of news about the Grenada invasion, including information embargos and voluntary "ground rules." The military limited the number of reporters who could accompany individual units during specific operations.[69]

The military also imposed censorship, as it has done before. During the Civil War, correspondents were required to submit copy to a provost marshal for approval, telegraph lines were put under military control, and a number of newspapers were censored or closed. During the First World War, seventy-five newspapers in the United States were closed or censored and the government's Committee on Public Information issued a voluntary censorship code. Reporters were accredited by the military during the Second World War and the Korean War.[70]

But coverage of the invasion of Grenada was different from previous military operations. The U.S. media were limited to official and secondary sources of information, and the military made no pictures of the invasion available. "Reporters were working under unprecedented U.S. restrictions," one journalist noted, "that kept them 150 miles away from the battle and totally dependent on the military itself for information."[71] General John W. Vessey, Jr., chairman of the Joint Chiefs of Staff, explained his rationale: "We didn't bring the media with us to Grenada because of the need for surprise in this operation. We were going in there quickly, and we needed surprise in order to have it be successful." This explanation soon was exposed as false when it became known that two days before the operation, Radio Havana had broadcast news about an imminent U.S. invasion of Grenada.[72]

On the second day of the invasion, again relying on official sources, the U.S. press reported that the U.S. soldiers were meeting substantial resistance from 1,100 Cuban troops on the island, with "4,340 more on the way." For a week after the invasion, the U.S. press reported that the U.S. action had been provoked by "a reign of terror" on the island that endangered U.S. medical students. But British reporters outfoxed the press blockage and quickly discovered that these accounts were based on false information concocted by the military for media briefings. The *Manchester Guardian's* correspondent contradicted the claim by the Reagan administration that the island had been in a state of violent anarchy:

The island's calm had returned...American medical students prepared to resume classes...and three U.S. diplomats appeared to have agreed on orderly departures for anyone wanting to go....The invasion shattered the calm that had returned after Monday's announcement of a return to civilian rule, the lifting of the curfew, and the reopening of Pearl Airport.[73]

The *Guardian* and the *London Observer* reported, again contradicting U.S. government claims, that the resistance to the invasion had come largely from Grenadans, not Cubans. The *Observer's* reporter wrote: "During extended observations of the battlefield, neither I nor any of my colleagues saw any Cubans....The myth of the Cubans being the real power was clearly groundless."[74] Because of these reports, on October 31, the U.S. State Department revised the military's figures, admitting there had been only 678 Cubans on the island and that 200 were soldiers. Cuban officials contended that only forty-three military personnel had been on Grenada.[75]

Three days after the invasion, when the island was secured, Reagan telephoned Secretary of Defense Caspar Weinberger, ordering him to loosen the media restrictions. Guided tours, which ranged in size from twenty-seven to forty-seven reporters, were conducted for groups of journalists. Reporters complained that the tours were too brief and obviously contrived. On the second day of the military-conducted tours, a freelance photographer working for *Newsweek* sneaked away. As a result, the magazine's photographers were barred from further press pool trips for 24 hours. Condemning his photographer but not the military's restrictions, editor Maynard Parker called his employee's action "unacceptable behavior, and absolutely not condoned by the magazine."[76]

Although media organizations protested their exclusion from the invasion and American occupation, they nevertheless faithfully reported the unsubstantiated assertions offered up by the government. Although a few British on-the-scene press reports were printed in a few U.S. newspapers, including the *Washington Post* and the *New York Times,* many dailies either lacked access to these reports or, more often, chose to ignore them. Not surprisingly, therefore, after a brief period of public skepticism, opinion polls soon revealed overwhelming popular support for the invasion and for the decision to exclude the press.

In the face of protests lodged by some media representatives, the Department of Defense appointed a commission to study ways in which media access could be granted at the same time that information could be controlled. The commission was chaired by General Winant Sidle, former Chief of Information for U.S. forces in Vietnam and head of Martin-Marietta corporate public affairs. Although media organizations declined to serve on the commission, they sought to influence the commission's recommendations. The Sidle Commission's report was released in August 1984, and it recommended the establishment of formal press pools for accredited news organizations. Sidle advised:

[The] optimum solution to insure proper media coverage of military operations will be to have the military—represented by competent, professional public affairs personnel and commanders who understand media problems—working with the media—represented by competent, professional reporters and editors who understand military problems—in a nonantagonistic atmosphere. The panel urges both institutions to adopt this philosophy and make it work.[77]

The military began testing the efficacy of the pools in 1985. On Saturday, April 20, heads of eight Washington news bureaus were told to send reporters, photographers, and technical crews to Andrews Air Force Base outside Washington, D.C., the next morning at 4 A.M. The bureau chiefs were not advised where their employees would be going. The pool included reporters from the *Wall Street Journal*, United Press International, Cable News Network, Copley News Service, the Associated Press, Mutual Broadcasting System, and *Newsweek*. Judged by the standard of controlling the American public's access to information, the pool was a success. The reporters were supposed to cover American military maneuvers in Honduras, but only after troops were already in place. The first published report about the maneuvers appeared in early editions of Monday's *Washington Post*. As in Grenada, however, it was hard to keep news about U.S. military operations quiet outside the United States. The *Post's* Managua correspondent had heard about the exercises a day before from a local radio reporter.[78]

The first real opportunity to test a war-zone press pool presented itself in July 1987, with the Reagan administration's decision to provide naval escorts for oil tankers operating in the Persian Gulf. In mid-August, media representatives complained that the military had failed to authorize a pool. *Editor & Publisher* complained that "there was no media pool on any of the U.S. Navy ships acting as escorts of American-flagged Kuwaiti tankers—despite dozens of media requests to accompany the Navy. In most instances, however, editors were reluctant to criticize the military or the Reagan administration openly for fear that should a media pool be called in, their news organization might be excluded."[79]

The system worked perfectly when President Bush decided to invade Panama in December 1989. For the first two days of the invasion, the only media reports came from reporters who were detained in a warehouse from which they were prohibited to roam. One hundred additional reporters who accompanied the military expedition cooperatively returned home when the military informed them that it lacked the facilities to service them. With no access to the areas of fighting, the only casualty reports came from U.S. military officers, who estimated 200 Panamanian dead. Days later, Panamanian human rights officials estimated that 700 had died in just one neighborhood. The National Council of Churches estimated that the total civilian deaths may have numbered 2,000, at a minimum. Spanish news services estimated that 3,000 to 5,000 Panamanian civilians had been killed in the invasion.[80]

Even after the U.S. media had fuller access to information, it faithfully followed the government's official version, however implausible or inaccurate. Though independent estimates of civilian casualties soon became available, they were rarely mentioned by corporate media outlets. The U.S. media also continued to report the invasion as a surgical exercise designed to accomplish one purpose: to remove from power and prosecute General Manuel Noriega, who was accused of heading a huge drug-running operation. He also had voided an election held a few months earlier and brutally suppressed his civilian opponents. Noriega embarrassed the administration by successfully resisting several months of highly publicized efforts to remove him through economic sanctions and diplomatic pressure. The limits of U.S. patience were finally exceeded, according to the government, when Noriega's soldiers in the Panamanian Defense Forces (PDF) shot and killed a U.S. military officer.

It is important to note, however, that Noriega had a long history of cooperation with the U.S. military and with intelligence agencies, notably while George Bush was head of the CIA during the Ford Administration. Until 1987, the United States attempted to put a good face on Noriega despite his connections with the drug trade. As late as May 1987, the U.S. Justice Department praised his cooperation with drug interdiction efforts as "superb" and claimed that Panamanians had completely cooperated with drug interdiction efforts. After fraudulent elections in 1984, Secretary of State George Schultz attended the inauguration of Noriega's hand-picked candidate for president, despite a call of other Latin American leaders to boycott the inauguration in protest of the obvious fraud.[81]

Why did the United States turn on its former friend? An important triggering event in the policy reversal occurred in 1986, when Noriega refused to cooperate with Oliver North's plan to use a shipload of arms originating in Panama to accuse the Sandinista government of smuggling arms to Salvadoran rebels. But perhaps the most important factor was the Panama Canal Treaties of 1977, which will pass control over the Panama Canal into Panamanian hands by the year 2000. An important milestone in the process, the appointment of a Panamanian to head the Canal Commission, was approaching its effective date of January 1, 1990. U.S. military bases in Panama, home of the Southern Command, were to be phased out by the year 2000. Since these bases often have been used as staging areas for military intervention in Latin American countries, closing them could have serious consequences for America's foreign policies.

Even though the Panamanian people, the U.S. population, and the rest of the world were told that the death of the U.S. officer was the immediate cause for the invasion, there is evidence that the invasion had been planned for months. In June 1989, General Marc Cisnaros, a psychological warfare specialist, took command of U.S. ground forces in Panama. Between that time and the invasion, in blatant violation of the Canal Treaties—which allow only "limited exercises" necessary for the defense of the canal—U.S. forces conducted provocative maneuvers designed, charged a leading Panamanian journalist, "to generate a feeling of terror and powerlessness in the civilian population and to accustom the people to U.S. troop presence." For example, on July 2, U.S. troops surrounded and occupied the two water-processing and purification plants that provide Panama City with water. U.S. troops regularly patrolled five civilian neighborhoods and established roadblocks through which Panamanians had to pass in order to reach their own beaches. These maneuvers dramatically raised tensions between U.S. and PDF forces, a climate that probably contributed to the death of the U.S. officer just before the invasion.[82] None of this was reported by standard news organizations.

The Propaganda Machine

Propaganda is an accurate term for describing U.S. information policy. Indeed, use of the term in this context was justified by the conservative newsweekly *U.S. News & World Report* in 1985, with the reasoning that "[Propaganda] does not always involve distortion of the facts...it can consist of disseminating the truth to help one's cause. For this reason, at various times distinguished journalists such as Edward R. Murrow and John Chancellor have agreed to do stints in key USIA [U.S. Information Agency] jobs."[83]

The Reagan administration played to win the propaganda game. It steadily enhanced the budget of the USIA, which reached nearly $800 million in 1986—a 74 percent increase since 1981. It inaugurated "WorldNet," a $15 million per-year project linking foreign journalists and American policy makers by satellite. In October 1985, it began, for the first time since the end of the Second World War, 24-hour Voice of America (VOA) broadcasts to Europe.[84] Under the mantle of VOA, the administration also created Radio Marti, staffed by many anti-Castro expatriates, which broadcast programs to Cuba. In the 1970s, the CIA financed opposition dailies in Jamaica during the socialist government of Prime Minister Michael Manley and opposition newspapers in Chile during the socialist government of President Salvador Allende Gossens. After the Sandinistas took power in 1969, it provided a large part of the financial support for *La Prensa,* the main opposition daily in Nicaragua. Before the invasion of Grenada, U.S. psychological warfare units had been broadcasting to the island via Radio Spice Island.

These activities illustrate a much broader phenomenon—the overwhelming dominance of U.S. governmental and media institutions over communications around the world. During the past decade, developing countries have complained about the role of the international media in controlling information about world affairs. Their complaints cited the effects of policies dating back to the Second World War and before. In 1946, William Benton, Assistant Secretary of State, outlined the U.S. government's position on the freedom of international communications:

> The State Department plans to do everything within its power along political or diplomatic lines to help break down the artificial barriers to the expansion of private American news agencies, magazines, motion pictures and other media of communications throughout the world....Freedom of the press—and freedom of exchange of information, generally—is an integral part of our foreign policy.[85]

The United States can be credited with making the "free flow of information" an article in the UNESCO constitution when the United Nations was organized in 1946. The United States originally had proposed that the organization establish a worldwide communications system. Great Britain protested, charging that the United States was attempting to use the organization "to blitz the world with American ideas." The proposal was shelved, but the United States continued to produce material for UNESCO radio programming that even sympathetic foreign newspapers labeled as propaganda.

At least seventy countries gained their independence from colonial rule in the 1960s, and by 1969, at a UNESCO meeting in Montreal, a reaction against U.S. media dominance surfaced. New members introduced the concept of "two-way circulation of news and balanced circulation of news." A report from the conference argued:

> The fact that the production of mass communications materials is largely concentrated in the hands of the major developed countries...affects the role of the media in promoting international understanding. Communication at the moment is a "one-way street" and the problems of developing nations are seen with the eyes of journalists and producers from the developed regions; moreover, the materials they produce are aimed primarily at audiences of those regions. As a result, not only is the image of the developing nations often a false and distorted one, but that very image is reflected back to the developing countries themselves.[86]

Roughly 90 percent of the world news disseminated by the media in Asia, Africa, and Latin America (excepting Japan and China) originates from centers in Paris, London, and New York City.[87] Despite its resources, media in the United States use very few foreign media products. A report by the International Communications Agency in 1979 noted that most foreign news reaches the United States through AP and UPI and that the U.S. television system is the second most closed to foreign programming in the world.[88]

Political Discourse and the Media

Despite concentrated corporate ownership of media, some alternatives to corporate programming are available: two television news programs, the Public Broadcasting System (PBS) and Pacifica News; a few magazines, including *The Nation, Mother Jones, The Village Voice, The Progressive, Z,* and various magazines sponsored by environmental organizations; and newspapers like *In These Times* and *The Guardian.* The viewpoints and information represented in these sources, however, are relegated to the margins because of their very limited circulation and audience. The exception is PBS, which strives for a tone of objectivity and even-handedness. Its right-wing critics label its coverage "liberal" because corporate owners and advertisers are not constantly present to pull news and commentary toward the right (though corporations contribute money to PBS, with a potentially similar effect).

The flowering of an alternative press came about during the Vietnam War, peaking during a period bracketed by the end of the Johnson (1968) and the Nixon (1974) administrations. These media outlets—self-described as "underground"—were responsible for breaking some of the most dramatic stories of the period, ranging from disclosures of covert U.S. intervention abroad to domestic spying by the FBI and CIA. A case in point is recounted by a reporter who coauthored a report linking drug trade to officials in the South Vietnamese government:

The May 1971 issue of *Ramparts* featured the story on its cover with the headline "Marshall Ky: The Biggest Pusher in the World."...The story was a well-documented block-buster, but the conventional media virtually ignored it. There were a few column inches about Congressional hearings being called for, and then the story vanished for months until Senator Albert Gruening of Alaska opened hearings. Suddenly the story was "discovered" by the *Washington Post* and NBC News. However, after the hearings, the story received continued coverage only through alternative sources such as the Dispatch News Service International.[89]

Economic exigency spelled the end for a large number of overtly partisan, political, and radical papers. Some survivors, like the democratic-socialist weekly *In These Times,* which emerged in the 1970s, and *The Guardian,* which was founded in the 1950s, have periodically turned to readers for emergency financial support. An editorial published in *In These Times* in 1980 underscored the dilemma faced by the alternative media: "Because its readership is relatively small, regionally dispersed, and from a Madison Avenue standpoint, heterogeneous, it has no chance of gaining substantial revenues from advertising. Instead, it has to derive its income from circulation. Its circulation income, is, in turn, largely limited to subscriptions, acquired primarily through direct-mail."[90] The magazines *The Nation, Mother Jones,* and *The Progressive* also are forced each year to make appeals to subscribers for donations.

Corporate ownership of media institutions has had the effect of limiting the availability of finance capital to support alternative media. As a consequence, many alternative publications have become largely adjuncts to the establishment media. In the process they have lost much of their distinct political message and now focus on middle-class concerns about environmental and lifestyle issues:

> [Some] alternative papers that survived the protest years have prospered, emerging from homespun publications to become slick, professional managed multi-million-dollar businesses with upscale readers in their mid-20s to late-30s....[Some] in an effort to cash in on the success of the alternatives, have adopted their bread-and-butter coverage in the arts, lifestyles, service listing and personal ads—but left out the meat, the tough editorial stand.[91]

The mere existence of "alternative" media institutions—meaning noncorporate, publicly owned or nonprofit, not necessarily "leftist"—is sometimes cited as evidence that there is a "multitude of tongues" in American public discourse. But of course this claim ignores the enormous, even controlling influence that money wields on media institutions. Alternative media are accorded a right to compete in the same way that minor party candidates are allowed to compete with Democrats and Republicans. They are only denied a key resource, money, which originates most abundantly from corporations and wealthy individuals. Corporate America does not finance its own opposition, either in information or in politics.

Notes

1. William C. Marcil, "The Real Meaning of the First Amendment," *Editor & Publisher,* October 8, 1983, p. 16.

2. John Hohenberg, *Free Press/Free People, The Best Cause* (New York: Columbia University Press, 1971), p. 498.

3. William C. Marcil, "The Real Meaning of the First Amendment," *Editor & Publisher,* 116 (October 8, 1983), p.16.

4. Everett Carll Ladd, *The American Polity: The People and Their Government* (New York: W. W. Norton, 1987), p. 552.

5. Ben H. Bagdikian, *The Media Monopoly* (Boston: Beacon Press, 1983), pp. 197-198.

6. Ibid., p. 201.

7. Ibid., p. 177.

8. James N. Dertouzos and Kenneth E. Thorpe, *Newspaper Groups: Economies of Scale, Tax Laws, and Merger Incentives* (Santa Monica, Calif.: Rand Corp., 1982).

9. "Groups Still Own Most U.S. Dailies," *Editor & Publisher,* April 28, 1984, pp. 76-80; Bagdikian, p. 179.

10. "The One Hundred Top Daily Newspapers in the United States," *Editor & Publisher,* annual (1986), p. xii.

11. Bagdikian, *Media Monopoly,* pp. 14-15.

12. Ibid., p. 19.

13. "The Top 100 Media Companies," *Advertising Age,* June 27, 1985.

14. Bagdikian, *Media Monopoly,* p. 28.

15. "One Hundred Leading Advertisers," *Advertising Age,* September 28, 1988, passim.

16. "Deregulation: The Chairman Gets A Second Wind," *Broadcasting,* September 30, 1985, p. 39.

17. "Fifth Estate's $30 Billion-plus Year," *Broadcasting,* December 30, 1985, p. 35.

18. Kelly Walker and Stephen Kindel, "Still the Strongest Games in Town," *Forbes,* March 25, 1985, p. 217.

19. Louis Rukeyser, "Media Offer 'Monopoly' to Investors," *The Tennessean,* July 27, 1986, p. 1I.

20. "Brokers Critique 1984, Look Ahead to 1985," *Broadcasting,* January 28, 1985, p. 74.

21. "Television's Top 20," *Broadcasting,* December 30, 1985, p. 39.

22. Hillier Krieghbaum, "The Impact of Advertising Pressure on the Press," in *The Commercial Connection: Advertising and the American Mass Media,* ed. John W. Wright (New York: Dell, 1979), p. 246.

23. Ibid., p. 247.

24. Ibid.

25. The critic was George Seldes in *Media Review in Fact.* See "Seldes Crusade on Smoking—in 1949," *St. Louis Journalism Review,* September 1983, p. 17. On NBC, see Bagdikian, *Media Monopoly,* p. 158.

26. John Shelley Rubin, "Swift's Premium Ham: William Lyon Phelps and the Redefinition of Culture," in eds. Catherine L. Covert and John D. Stevens, *Mass Media between the Wars: Perceptions of Cultural Tension* (Syracuse, N.Y.: Syracuse University Press), p.4.

27. John W. Spalding, "1928: Radio Becomes a Mass Advertising Medium," in Wright, *Commercial Connection,* p. 76.

28. Ibid., p. 78.

29. J. Herbert Altschull, *Agents of Power: The Role of the News Media in Human Affairs* (New York: Longman, 1984), p.113.

30. Ibid., p. 129.

31. "The Canons of Journalism: Ethical Rules Adopted by the American Society of Newspaper Editors on April 28, 1923, and Since Endorsed by Many State Associations and Other Groups of Journalists," *Editor & Publisher* (January 31, 1931).

32. Bernard Roshco, *Newsmaking* (Chicago: University of Chicago Press, 1975), p. 42. For a general discussion of the myth of objectivity and its relationship to the professional norms and training of journalists, see W. Lance Bennett, *News: The Politics of Illusion* (New York: Longman, 1983), pp. 75-92.

33. William Stage, "Jim Fox Walks a Narrow Line Between Reader and Editor," *St. Louis Journalism Review* (April 1984): 12.

34. "Can the Press Tell the Truth?" *Harper's,* January 1984, p. 42.

35. Fred Clarkson, "New Right Money Finances New Student Papers," *St. Louis Journalism Review* (May 1985): 19.

36. Altschull, *Agents of Power,* p. 118.

37. Bill Abrams, "Jesse Helms' Bid for CBS Might Not Succeed, But He Could Reap a Large Political Reward," *Wall Street Journal,* March 29, 1985, p. 46.

38. Herbert J. Gans, "Are U.S. Journalists Dangerously Liberal?" *Columbia Journalism Review* (November-December 1985): 29.

39. "ABC's Duffy: Fifth Estate Is Much in Public Eye," *Broadcasting,* September 16, 1985, pp. 86-87.

40. Fred Barnes, "Why Did the Reporter Cross the Road? Media Realignment," *The New Republic,* May 6, 1985, p. 15.

41. John Chancellor, *An NBC White Paper: A Portrait of the Press, Warts and All,* broadcast June 15, 1985, National Broadcasting Co. Transcript.

42. Hertsgaard details these developments and Gergen's role (among others) in *On Bended Knee: The Press and the Reagan Presidency* (New York: Farrar Strauss Giroux, 1988), pp. 152-183. The quote is on p. 237. Richard Deaver, White House deputy chief of staff, made similar comments on the administration success on the Moyers' program, *The Public Mind,* produced by former Johnson press secretary Bill Moyers for the Public Broadcasting System in 1989.

43. Ibid., p. 347.

44. Barnes, "Why Did the Reporter...," pp. 12-16.

45. Edwin Diamond, "New Wrinkles on the Permanent Press: The Mass Media in Campaign '84," *Public Opinion* (Washington: American Enterprise Institute for Public Policy Research, 1985), p. 70.

46. See, for example, Dye and Zeigler, *American Politics in the Media Age,* pp. 136-138.

47. Michael Parenti, *Inventing Reality: The Politics of the Mass Media* (New York: St. Martin's Press, 1986), p. 114.

48. Ibid.

49. Ibid., p. 115.

50. "When World-Views View the World," *NACLA Report,* July-August, 1983, p. 24.

51. James Aronson, *The Press and the Cold War* (Boston: Beacon Press, 1970), p. 45.

52. See Parenti, *Inventing Reality,* pp. 119-120.

53. Aronson, *The Press and the Cold War,* p.29.

54. Ibid., pp. 56-57.

55. Ibid., p. 59.

56. "Daniloff Is No Spy; He's Helpless Hostage," *USA Today,* September 11, 1986, p. 8A.

57. James E. Roper, "Media Get Good Grades," *Editor & Publisher,* October 4, 1986, p. 19.

58. "Gallup Poll," *Editor & Publisher,* October 18, 1986, p. 12.

59. Roy Gutman, "CIA Inadvertently Implicated Daniloff," *Nashville Banner*, October 2, 1986, p. 1A. [syndicated *New York Newsday* story]

60. Frank Greve, "Reporters, the CIA and the Soviets," *Editor & Publisher*, October 18, 1986, p. 76.

61. Ibid.

62. Ibid.

63. Jeremy Tunstall, *The Media Are American* (New York: Columbia University Press, 1977), p. 227.

64. Parenti, *Inventing Reality*, p. 233.

65. Ibid.

66. Harold C. Relyea and Suzanne Cavanagh, "Press Notices on Disclosures Made Pursuant to the Federal Freedom of Information Act, 1972-1984: A Compilation," Washington, D.C.: Congressional Research Services, August 9, 1984. [Republished in *Hearings Before a Subcommittee of the Committee on Government Operations, House of Representatives, 98th Congress, 2nd Session, on S. 774* (May 24, 30; Jun. 20; and August 9, 1984), p. 732.

67. Ibid., p. 733.

68. Jack Landau, "Media Law Today," *Editor & Publisher*, December 10, 1983, p. 10.

69. Peter Braestrup, "Terms of a Truce," *The Quill* (September 1985): 16.

70. Peter Downs and Daniel Hellinger, "Censorship or Legitimate Self-Defense?" *St. Louis Journalism Review* (July 1982): 15.

71. Peter Downs, "How the British Media Saw the U.S. Invasion of Grenada," *St. Louis Journalism Review* (February 1984): 22.

72. ABC News, *Nightline*, transcript no. 643, October 26, 1983.

73. Cited in Downs, "How the British Media Saw the U.S. Invasion of Grenada," p. 22.

74. Ibid.

75. Stuart Taylor, "In Light of Invasion," *New York Times*, November 6, 1983, p. 20.

76. Otto Fredrich, "Anybody Want to Go to Grenada?" *Time*, November 14, 1983, p. 72.

77. "Key Sections of Panel's Report on the Military and the Press: Final Comment," *New York Times*, August 24, 1984, p. 6. Emphasis added.

78. "Media, Military Unhappy with Secret Pool," *News Media & The Law* (Summer 1985): 46.

79. George Garneau, "Media Combat Pool: How Effective?" *Editor & Publisher*, August 15, 1987, p. 9.

80. See "Panama: More on Invasion Death Toll," *Central America Update* (Latin American Institute, University of New Mexico), January 26, 1990. "Panama: More on U.S. Invasion Death Toll, Activities by Occupation Troops," *Central America Update*, January 31, 1990. "Perspectives on the U.S. Invasion of Panama," *Central America Update*, February 2, 1990. Central American Human Rights Commission, "Panama Crisis: General Findings," February 5, 1990.

81. Raul Leis, "The Cousins' Republic," *NACLA Report on the Americas*, 22 (July-August 1988), pp. 21-22.

82. Based on a Report from the Mexican news agency, NOTIMEX, summarized in Daniel Hellinger, "Panama, Behind the U.S. Invasion," *Update on the Americas* (St. Louis: Latin America Solidarity Committee), February 1990. See also Raul Leis, "Panama: The Other Side of Midnight," *NACLA Report on the Americas*, 23 (April 1990), pp. 4-6.

83. "The War of Words," *U.S. News & World Report*, October 7, 1985, pp. 34-42.

84. Ibid.

85. Francis N. Wete, "The U.S., Its Press, and the New World Information Order," *St. Louis Journalism Review* (July 1984): 20.

86. Herbert Schiller, "Exporting American Media: Effects on National Development," *Media Ecology Review* (March 1983): 13-14.

87. Mervyn de Silva, "The Third World Quarrel with the Western Press," *Sunday Observer,* Sri Lanka, August 15, 1976 [cited in "Toward a New Information Order—The Times They Are A'changing," *NACLA Report on the Americas* (July-August 1982): 12].

88. Wete, "The U.S., Its Press, and the New World Information Order," p. 23.

89. Chip Berlet, "How the Muckrakers Saved America," *Alternative Media,* 1 (1979): 5-7.

90. "Recession Imperils Small Press," *In These Times,* July 16-29, 1980, p. 14.

91. George Garneau, "Are the Alternatives Still Alternative?" *Editor & Publisher,* August 15, 1987, pp. 12-13, 28.

Chapter 4

Candidates, Elections, and the Propaganda Apparatus

Politics As a Media Commodity

The day after his defeat in 1984, Walter Mondale observed, "Politics requires television....I don't believe it's possible to run for president without the capacity to build confidence and communications every night. It's got to be done that way." Ronald Reagan and the Republicans so convinced the Democrats of the importance of using communications artfully that the Democrats virtually put their 1988 convention in the hands of professional television producers. Now candidates in both parties treat voters less like citizens of the polity than like product consumers. There is much disagreement about the overall effectiveness of political advertising, but nobody argues that candidates for national office can be successful without access to voters through mail and media, resources that consume huge amounts of money.

Campaigns have become an adjunct to the media industry principally since the presidential election of 1980. Ronald Reagan's run for the presidency in 1980 relied on an advertising campaign adapted directly from corporate product advertising. Many individuals who had made their careers by selling Pepsi-Cola and other products turned their talents to packaging the candidate. The image-packaging techniques were substantially refined for President Reagan's reelection campaign of 1984. George Bush's campaign managers fine-tuned these techniques further in 1988. In all three elections, the Democrats had yet to learn how to apply the technology of persuasion as skillfully.

The political consequences of these developments are far reaching. The technology of persuasion used in American electoral politics makes campaigns into vehicles for elite "guidance." Modern elections can be understood as agents of legitimation and social control. This may explain why presidential election results in 1980, 1984, and 1988 went directly against the electoral decision that might have been predicted on the basis of the public's views on important issues. According to polls, on a wide range of issues—*contra* funding, abortion, spending for social programs, gun control—the Reagan administration was on the wrong side of public opinion. Interestingly, though the "L" word seemed to work against Michael Dukakis in the 1988 presidential contest, as high a proportion of Americans considered themselves liberal or moderate as in 1975, the year before Jimmy Carter won the presidency.[1] The voters' preferences have changed much less than the ability of professional campaign consultants to manipulate the images of the candidates.

Advertising Politics

Some critics are skeptical that media marketing of candidates is effective. One study of the campaign ads aired in 1984, for example, concluded that they exerted little influence over voter choice.[2] The public may be alert to contradictory information and suspicious of simple messages. After more than three decades of exposure to television commercials, viewers are skeptical. Certainly the political landscape is littered with candidacies launched with media hype that failed. A good example was John Glenn's campaign for the Democratic nomination in 1984. His spots were regarded as skillfully packaged by his competitors and by Madison Avenue. But his dull appearance on the news and reports of inadequacies in his campaign organization contradicted the dynamic, successful image portrayed in his ads.

It would be absurd to suppose that all candidates can be sold equally well, even with the most sophisticated technology. The same observation can be made about consumer products. But this does not mean that advertising of either cars or candidates is soon going to be abandoned. Mass marketing doesn't always work, but its absence is almost a guarantee of failure. Candidates who survive *must have* good access to media technology. Candidates who cannot effectively be packaged usually fall by the wayside. This observation also applies to candidates who refuse to be packaged. In the 1980s, the measure of a good candidate for national office was one who learned to stand at the chalk line and mouth the words composed by campaign professionals.

Advertising surely has the effect of creating the political and ideological context for voter decisions. Like product advertising, political ads contain not only manifest but latent messages. Manifest messages communicate the candidate's name, personal characteristics, party affiliation, and (much less often) views on issues. But latent messages are much less likely to be critically evaluated by voters than overt ones. The public tends to place advertising of all sorts, including political commercials, into a schema based on prior learning, including that derived from other media sources.[3] Campaigns help to create a version of political reality that is all encompassing, even if the specific information that makes up the whole picture is often lost or ineffective.[4]

Consider, for example, the 1984 Republican party's effort to shift party loyalties in its favor. This sophisticated campaign sought, in part, to erode the Democratic party's majority among registered voters by encouraging young people from traditionally Democratic backgrounds to question the partisan leanings of their parents. The best example was one ad in which a burly, young, white male walking with his father asks if "we" are still voting Democratic this year. He reminds his father that the Democrats control the House and want to pass a tax increase. He doesn't want things "to go back to what they were," so he repeats, "Are we still voting Democratic?" His father seems to be vacillating himself as he reassures his son that once in the voting booth, no one knows how you vote.

On the manifest level this ad is about party loyalty. It associates the Democrats with an issue, taxation, that is assumed to be unpopular. The public is easily able to recognize the partisan nature of the ad. Partisanship, however, comprises only the overt message. There is also an important latent message: Americans are overtaxed and the problems of the country today are caused by a government that has overtaxed its citizens in the past. No Democrat is likely to reply to this message in counteradvertising, so "common sense" notions about taxation in America are reinforced in a way that makes it even more difficult for any candidates, Democrat or Republican, to propose new taxes in the future, even in the face of huge budget deficits.

Like Pepsi's call to the "new generation" to switch from Coca-Cola, the Republican appeal to change party loyalties will not work if the public sees no reason for change. But even if skeptical viewers are not convinced that one soft drink or one party is superior to another, the ad reinforces an overall point of view. The Pepsi ads of the 1980s were set within a context—youth, energy, excitement, sex appeal— meant to project images of American culture. In the process, cultural values were subtly molded. Political advertising exerts a similar effect.

Part of the genius of the Reagan campaign of 1984—a product of its thorough integration into the advertising industry—was its exploitation of the "pride in America" theme then trumpeted in commercials ranging from cola, to hamburgers, to beer, to automobiles, to solicitations to join the military. Walter Mondale's attempts to contradict this image by suggesting that the future was less than rosy failed not only because the economic recovery of 1984 made people feel more optimistic, but—one can speculate—because through endless repetition commercial advertising had helped to create an optimistic national mood. In the 1988 presidential campaign George Bush capitalized on similar images,[5] coupled with negative attacks on his opponent.

Advertising should be seen as an "extended message rather than a series of discrete units."[6] Attitudes are projected by corporate elites through the advertising industry; their themes are aired in the mass media constantly, repeatedly, in a collage of images. With almost every major advertiser from brewers to automakers proclaiming in one form or another in 1984 that "the pride is back; born in America," it seems understandable that the political messages with the most persuasive appeal would have embraced military aggressiveness, rugged individualism, fewer social programs, and cultural chauvinism. The same images sold products and candidates in 1988 as well. George Bush's campaign ads featured crowds of flag-waving Americans and showed him visiting a flag factory and bragging about the bombing of Libya and the invasion of Grenada. The abstract images, designed to elicit emotional reactions from viewers, were the point of these ads. They were devoid of any actual informational content.

Electronic Elections

Elections are high stakes contests to politicians and to the profitable industry supported by campaign spending. Individual politicians battle to keep their careers alive by manipulating media coverage. Though they often complain about the media's impact on politics, politicians and their handlers forge a close symbiotic relationship with the media industry. The two sides are involved in an intricate dance. Neither politicians nor media professionals thrive on risk. Like the candidates they cover, media executives and newscasters prefer to emphasize image over substance because such an emphasis resolves a nagging dilemma—how to generate audience interest without raising controversies about the medias' own role. Media professionals are extremely defensive about charges of "bias." Coverage revealing an overtly political point of view is certain to alienate some portion of the intended audience, and even a slight drop in ratings may cost millions of advertising dollars, which are as important to televised political events as they are to sports contests. Hence news organizations eagerly embrace seemingly neutral definitions of news that they can apply to electoral contests.

The strength of candidates according to polling organizations is the perfect "neutral" news item, for it allows reporters to avoid commenting on or summarizing contentious or complex issues. The presidential campaign season, at both the nomination and general election stages, is characterized by "horserace" reporting. Day after day, newscasters and newswriters chart the speed and position of the various candidates, as revealed by the polls. Horserace reporting of this sort seems to produce "real" or "factual" information in the form of polling results, and a news organization that conducts its own polls can, in addition, take credit for generating "the news."

Despite appearances, horserace reporting is far from neutral. Even before the first caucus has been held or primary vote cast, networks utilize polls to determine which candidates to cover most heavily. Before the first event of the delegate selection process (the Iowa caucus in January), the amount of coverage on the major television networks is closely correlated with poll results. Candidates who do best in the polls are scheduled for interviews and special feature stories. All through the process, polls provide the guidance: A study of the 1972 presidential election found that 73 percent of the coverage focused on standing in the polls rather than on what candidates were saying.[7]

Unlike a real horse race, in electoral contests the speed of the horse depends considerably on how much it is watched. Because they are watched the most, incumbents tend to run the best, with the "sure winners" among them attracting the most attention. According to a study of 104 House races in 1978, "sure winner" incumbents received an average of fifty-two mentions in their (respective) district's major newspapers, but their challengers averaged only twelve mentions.[8] Challengers averaged many more mentions, an average of 107 news items, when they faced vulnerable incumbents. But they still received far less coverage than the incumbents they faced, who were mentioned an average of 161 times. There is a "catch-22" aspect to this media bias in favor of incumbents: Challengers have little chance of winning unless they attract good media coverage, and yet they will not receive as much coverage as incumbents unless polls show that they already have unusual strength. When an incumbent is vulnerable, about one-third of campaign stories about both candidates are negative.[9] But when the polls show the incumbent far ahead, as is usually the case initially, critical stories about the incumbent appear half as often. Of course, this translates a media assumption that the incumbent is safe into a self-fulfilling prophecy.

Politicians and their managers understand the horserace nature of media coverage, and they accordingly try to manipulate perceptions of their candidate's position and momentum in the race. Events in the 1976 presidential nomination season illustrate how this is done. On the Republican side, campaign strategists for President Gerald Ford astutely prepared the media for Ford's narrow victories over challenger Ronald Reagan by playing up Reagan's supposed early strength. Otherwise, the close results might have been interpreted as indicating remarkable weakness for a sitting president. Ford's campaign managers seized the opportunity when Reagan's handlers predicted victory in the New Hampshire primary. When Reagan lost by a razor-thin margin, Ford's media strategists fed reporters a stream of "information"—often presented to the public as leaks from "party insiders"—claiming that unless Reagan carried Florida, he would be forced to withdraw. When Reagan narrowly lost Florida, his financial resources began drying up. Reporters in the next primary state, North Carolina, barraged Reagan with questions about when he would withdraw. One national reporter wrote that "Ronald Reagan brought his fading presidential candidacy into North Carolina with...a defiant refusal to quit."[10]

On the Democratic side, frontrunner Jimmy Carter still was facing challenges from several candidates as his campaign staff prepared for three major primaries on June 8. Everyone conceded the California primary to the state's governor, Jerry Brown. In Ohio, Arizona Senator Morris Udall, a fading candidate whom Carter had already twice beaten, was Carter's only serious threat. But in New Jersey, all of Carter's major opponents were entered, including Hubert Humphrey, a leading contender who had barely lost the presidential race to Richard Nixon in 1968. Objectively, New Jersey constituted the critical test of the three primaries, but Carter's advisers knew from the polls that he would likely lose there and in California. They went to work to convince the media that Ohio was actually the crucial contest. They called Chicago's Mayor Daley, who controlled eighty-six convention votes, and asked him to announce that the key primary race was in Ohio. The resulting media splash exerted its desired political effect when Carter, careful to underestimate in advance his strength in Ohio, won a convincing victory while losing the other two states. Asked how Ohio had become the critical primary, Patrick Caddell, Carter's pollster, admitted, "We orchestrated that."[11]

The Technology of Persuasion

Throughout the nineteenth century, political parties and newspapers closely tied to them were responsible for mobilizing voters. By the 1920s, however, mass circulation newspapers and wire services had changed the nature of campaigning by making nonpartisan media, rather than the political parties and the partisan press, the principal instruments for mobilizing the electorate. Radio reinforced this tendency (the first national convention carried on radio was the Democrats', in 1924). Franklin Roosevelt knew how to use the medium to maximum effect. When television was introduced into campaigns, it changed the nature of campaigning even more dramatically.

Political advertising on television began in 1952, when Dwight Eisenhower's campaign managers decided to hire two advertising agencies to design a series of television ads. The purpose of the ads was to play on popular discontent about the Korean War and the economy and to associate Eisenhower with the anticommunism crusades led by Senator Joseph McCarthy and others. The ads were primitive by modern standards, mostly showing Eisenhower talking into the camera. It is impossible to know whether they significantly enhanced Eisenhower's appeal, for he was already an enormously popular war hero who had been courted by both parties as a presidential candidate.

John F. Kennedy is generally thought of as the first "television president." In the 1960 campaign, both the Kennedy and Nixon campaigns made extensive use of television spot ads. But the most notable new twist was the face-to-face televised debates. Kennedy came off very well on television: angular and tall, strong-jawed, youthful, handsome. Nixon, in contrast, seemed to scowl, and the make-up artists who prepared him for the debates neglected to soften his deep-sunken eyes and five-o'clock shadow (some Republicans even speculated that the make-up team had made him look bad on purpose). Most political pundits identified the debates as the crucial events leading to Kennedy's close victory in November.

The 1964 and 1968 campaign ads were distinguished by the winning candidates' attempts to manipulate voters' emotions. Perhaps the most famous spot ad of all time was shown on behalf of Lyndon Johnson only once in the 1964 campaign. It depicted a young girl picking daisies in a field, with a voiceover counting down from ten to zero, followed by the image of a nuclear explosion and mushroom cloud. Johnson's distinctive Texas drawl ended the ad with the message, "We must love each other or we must die."

The ad provoked an instant controversy, so much so that all three television networks ran it on their evening newscasts. Republicans claimed that it maligned Goldwater by suggesting he might start a nuclear war. Johnson's campaign offices were deluged with phone calls, but according to his press secretary, Bill Moyers, most of them were favorable. Moyers said that Johnson called him and exclaimed, "Holy shit, I'm getting calls from all over the country." After a while, the president calmed down and admitted, "I guess it did what we Goddamned set out to do."[12] Johnson's campaign advisers withdrew the ad after only one showing, but it left an indelible imprint on the public mind.

Goldwater's managers also used spot ads, but in an incredibly inept way. In a painfully long half-hour campaign film called *Choice,* the Republican candidate tried to associate his rival with a long list of social, economic, and foreign policy problems. But Goldwater's charges were so exaggerated and sensationalized that the film moved perilously close to self-parody. In Goldwater's ads, President Johnson epitomized everything "evil" in America. "Evil" in Goldwater's universe ran the gamut from pornography to the new dance craze, the Twist. Even when Goldwater used appeals that would soon prove fruitful for Republicans, the message was too crude. In Goldwater's depiction of blacks in Johnson's America, they were rioting. When the film presented the image of the American past he would like to restore, they were shown picking cotton.[13]

But only four years later, the principle was firmly established that emotional ads appealing to public fears and prejudices were not necessarily ineffectual. The challenge assumed by Richard Nixon's propaganda team was to rehabilitate the image of a politician with a popular reputation for deception and spite—to make appealing the candidate who had lost the 1960 presidential debate with John F. Kennedy partly because of the sinister image he conveyed on television; a candidate who had baited media reporters after his 1962 loss in the California gubernatorial race by remarking that they would not have him "to kick around anymore." As described in Joseph McGinniss's classic book *The Selling of the President, 1968,*[14] Nixon's pollsters and media specialists made innovative use of survey and marketing techniques (for example, trying out ads and campaign themes on test groups) designed to remedy negative public perceptions about Nixon and to reinforce negative impressions of the Democrats' candidate, Hubert Humphrey.

Nixon's media approach involved manipulating emotions without making proposals of his own, and in this sense the modern age of electronic campaigning was launched in 1968. Several spots devised by media consultants almost made Johnson's daisy ad seem like a model of high-minded probity. One video depicted a sole policeman at a call box, followed by a rapid-fire collage of images—a bullet-shattered automobile window, a rifle and switch blade, a mugging, a drug sale, a youth gang fighting police, interspersed with the faces of anxious Americans. Nixon's voiceover claimed that the crime rate was rising nine times faster than the population. Another spot showed an anxious woman walking at night along a deserted street, with the announcer reciting statistics about muggings and robberies. In still another, scenes of urban riots carried a Nixon voiceover calling for "some honest talk about the problem of order."[15]

By employing the most advanced techniques of the advertising industry, Nixon's propaganda team avoided the errors committed by the Goldwater campaign. The new breakthrough was to allow the ads to be designed solely by the ad agencies and to minimize the candidate's influence. Ads were tested with "focus groups" before being released. The content of ads would be determined by the media consultants, not by the possibly misguided (from an advertiser's perspective) views of the candidate and his managers. In many ways, the 1988 Bush campaign employed the same approach, but only after the most successful media candidate in American history had exited the stage.

The 1980 Campaign

Ronald Reagan's media campaign in 1980 took place in the context of a conservative and Republican resurgence that, if not coordinated to the last detail, certainly was not spontaneous. In 1978, the Republican party spent $2 million on ads designed to repair the party's image. The GOP knew that in a race where all other things were equal, their candidate started fifteen percentage points behind just on the basis of the party identification of the voters, and they were determined to change that situation.[16]

A poll commissioned by the Republicans had shown that their party was identified in the public's mind with two disastrous presidential administrations, Herbert Hoover's and Richard Nixon's. To repair this image, a series of 5-minute ads were aired depicting Republican congressional figures speaking mostly on nonpartisan types of issues. Follow-up research showed that although the ads were successful, they were actually selling the public a positive image of both parties. The intent had been to spruce up the image of one brand; instead, the entire politics industry was getting a face lift. The GOP continued its search for ways to get its specific brand-name message across.

A 1979 poll commissioned by the Republican National Committee and the National Republican Congressional Committee identified significant dissatisfaction with the state of affairs in the nation and found that people were ready to agree that Republicans might have some good ideas. Eighty percent of the respondents said that Congress was a major cause of the problems, but few of them were aware that Democrats had controlled both houses of Congress for the previous twenty-five years. Armed with this information as well as with money raised through direct-mail fundraising, the GOP launched three waves of commercials to identify the Democrats with the country's economic problems. A car driven by a (Democratic Speaker of the House) Tip O'Neill look-alike ran out of gas in the middle of nowhere—just like the Democrats, said the voiceover. A child grew older during the twenty-five years of Democratic congressional control while the audience was reminded of an alleged rise in taxes and governmental spending during the child's life. Working-class people in appropriate job settings complained about inflation, taxes, and unemployment.

Ronald Reagan was a quintessential creation of public relations specialists, who had to help him recover from a near-fatal blunder early in the 1980 campaign season. His campaign had wasted a great deal of money in Iowa on expensive spot ads produced by the C. T. Cline ad agency of New York, trying to deliver a knockout blow to his main rival, George Bush. When Bush won the primary races, Reagan was in trouble.

A key event in Reagan's resurgence was the firing of Cline and hiring of Elliott Curson, a right-wing advertising wizard who had come to the attention of the Reagan campaign because of his impressive work in selling "supply-side" economics to New Jersey voters. In a single day, Curson shot eleven ads that constituted the entire radio and TV media arsenal of the Reagan campaign for the rest of the primaries—and for only $18,000. The ads were comprised of simple shots showing Reagan talking with a sincere voice into a camera. Media commentators disputed some of the facts used in the ads, but not with the kind of tenacity necessary to overcome the repetitious elegance of the Curson approach. Tougher criticisms would have risked charges of media "bias."

Curson did not plan the general election advertising strategy, but his influence carried over. With President Carter replacing Bush as the principal target, and with a replenished budget, the ads became more sophisticated. The new media team, assembled from people who had served in Nixon's 1972 campaign, put together what one observer labeled a "calculated dullness."[17] Madison Avenue experts criticized Reagan's ads as uninspiring, but the Reagan team adhered to a strategy of avoiding slick-looking ads, which, polling research told them, might irritate the public.

Of course, there is nothing new about polling itself; polls have been used in campaigns for fifty years. Since 1968, however, they have been combined with public relations techniques developed by the advertising industry for selling consumer goods in a mass market—for example, focus groups (testing an ad on a small selected audience in a studio) and test marketing (trying out an ad in selected geographic areas). Such techniques are expensive, but with their huge financial resources Republicans were able to provide Reagan's pollster, Richard Wirthlin, and his media strategists the resources to support a faithful adaptation of Madison Avenue techniques to political campaigning. All major spots were run in test markets and screened before focus groups. Wirthlin found that what the public wanted was the image of a sincere candidate. After playing sincere characters in fifty-nine movies, Ronald Reagan already had learned how to play the role to the hilt.

Projecting sincerity, however, was a somewhat tricky business. The public, more cynical and suspicious than ever about politicians, wanted a straightforward presentation of what the candidate believed. It did not want the appearance of image-building advertising. Nevertheless, even if the pitfalls of a slick, manicured "sincerity" were avoided—the danger was that the public might see through the facade of contrived sincerity—the approach was not an automatic formula for success. After all, Barry Goldwater had been "sincere," and Ronald Reagan was as conservative as Goldwater and much more prone to misstatements of fact. But Reagan's task was made easier by the sophistication of his media advisors, the proven technologies of the advertising industry, and the ineptitude of Jimmy Carter's reelection team.

Carter's ads were handicapped less by the complexity of the political issues at the time than by his own convoluted language, attacks on Reagan's character, and the admission that things had not gone well during his administration. Reagan's ad team tried out Carter's commercials on test groups and found them to be ineffectual, so they decided not to respond to them. The Democrats did not even use test groups for their own ads!

Reagan's 1980 campaign spent $18,476,000 on television advertising, and more than $18 million was additionally spent by "independent" PACs and by the Republican party. The "independent" groups, some of which were formed specifically for the 1980 campaign and subsequently dissolved, launched harsh attacks on Carter that saved both money and political capital for the Reagan campaign. The National Conservative Political Action Caucus (NCPAC), for example, spent nearly

$2 million, concentrating their media blitz in Alabama, Louisiana, Mississippi, and the Florida panhandle.[18] The wisdom of its choice was demonstrated when Reagan carried Alabama and Mississippi by less than a 1 percent margin.

Carter's campaign allocated only about half as much for television advertising as Reagan's, and spending by independent PACs on behalf of Carter was minuscule, in comparison to the financial muscle exerted by "independent" groups for Reagan. Spending by *all independent groups* on behalf of Carter totaled approximately $50,000. This was the same amount spent by *a single PAC*, the Christian Voice Moral Government Fund, on TV time in the South to spread the idea that Carter was advocating acceptance of homosexuality. This kind of advertising might have alienated some important blocs of voters in other parts of the country, but targeted in the South, it reached the intended group, fundamentalist Christians.[19]

Another right-wing PAC organized by Americans for Change spent a little over $700,000 in media markets where polls showed Carter and Reagan separated by less than two percentage points. The Fund for a Conservative Majority bought over $2 million in spot ads, aimed at parts of the northeast and Florida, with a special pitch made to anticommunist Cubans in Miami. In one ad, actors dressed as a Russian general, an Arab sheik, Fidel Castro, and Ayatollah Khomeini pushed around another actor dressed as Uncle Sam. Americans for an Effective Presidency spent nearly $1.3 million for ads stressing economic problems under the Democrats, targeted at the working class in swing states.[20]

There is always a danger that activities by "independent" groups can backfire on their intended beneficiaries, but this did not happen in 1980 or in 1984. Conservative groups that operated around the edges of Reagan's campaigns shared the ideological perspective of Reagan and his advisors. This enabled them to coordinate sophisticated propaganda blitzes without directly communicating or conspiring with the advisors directing the official campaign. In this way they were thereby able to evade federal election laws limiting campaign expenditures by the candidates and parties. While Carter flailed away at Reagan and tried to cast him as an extremist of the Goldwater ilk, Reagan projected an amiable "nice guy" image by responding with humor and grace. Right-wing groups did the dirty work for him.[21]

The 1984 Campaign

By 1984, the Democrats had mastered many of the techniques pioneered by the Reagan team, but Reagan's reelection campaign still retained an enormous advantage in party and "independent" expenditures. Reagan now had incumbency and economic recovery to add to advantages carried over from 1980—that is, ideological disarray among the Democrats and support from most of the corporate business community. With Madison Avenue convinced and on board, the Reagan team embarked on the most sophisticated propaganda campaign ever launched up to that point in American politics. In contrast to 1980, Reagan's managers opted for slickness over contrived simplicity. Its essence was to "frame" the president within a vision of a resurgent, optimistic America. There was little need and no desire to raise issues.

The president was framed inside a constellation of themes that had been echoed in four years of standard commercial product advertising—national chauvinism (presented as patriotism), militarism (presented as response to aggression), and order (depicted as rugged individualism and adherence to the work ethic). According to Mark Hertsgaard,

> The formal re-election campaign...was explicitly designed to insulate the President from serious scrutiny on the part of the press and to equate any criticism of him with criticism of America. It relied on the same news management principles that the apparatus had so skillfully applied over the previous three years: devise, on the basis of meticulous opinion polling, a long-term communications plan that emphasizes certain politically favorable themes, such as "America is Back"; provide one handsomely packaged photo opportunity story per day that reinforces the chosen theme of the day; repeat your message many times and in many ways; and, to assure control of the agenda, restrict reporters' access to the President and avoid whenever possible questions on unfavorable topics.[22]

Reagan's 1984 campaign was directed by a group of Madison Avenue executives called the "Tuesday Team."[23] The best and the brightest image makers—top executives and copywriters from the most successful firms on Madison Avenue—took paid leaves of absence to work for the Reagan effort. Star ad men on the Tuesday Team included propagandists responsible for Gallo Wine commercials, the Meow Mix singing cat, and Michael Jackson's Pepsi-Cola videos. With $20 million at their disposal, they set to work applying the high-power persuasion techniques of their business.

Besides their own expertise, they drew on the marketing job done on behalf of Conservative Prime Minister Margaret Thatcher in her 1983 landslide victory in Britain. Her media director, Sir Christopher Lawson, had come to study Wirthlin's 1980 polling operation, and he now returned to repay the favor. In Britain, where he was known as "the Man from Mars" for successfully refurbishing the image of Mars Candy, Inc., Lawson had sold Mrs. Thatcher like candy bars to the British public. The Tuesday Team decided to borrow from Pepsi-Cola and Coca-Cola commercials to achieve the same effect for Reagan.

Pepsi ads inspired an 18-minute "waving field of flags docu-spot," which premiered at the Republican Convention. Pepsi sales had soared after its commercials associated it with images of ordinary, happy people at work and at play. Drawing on this motif, a series of "Morning Again" spots conveyed the same bubbling optimism. In early ads Reagan hardly appeared—a striking contrast to the 1980 strategy, in which ads showed him addressing the audience simply and directly. This time, the ads were orchestrated to create a national mood: convince voters that times were good and distract attention from the issues that might have worked for Mondale, such as concerns about nuclear proliferation, the environment, and the budget deficit.

Research to guide the Reagan propaganda blitz consisted of a $2 million operation to monitor public opinion via a massive telephone survey research program implemented at both the national and state levels. Called "PINS" (Political Information System), the system permitted simulation of various campaign themes in order to select the most effective. Each morning of the campaign, beginning on June 1, reports were analyzed with as many as 300 tables of data generated by twenty-one specialists. Armed with these data, Reagan's pollster, Richard Wirthlin, revised the media strategy. If some negative factor began to emerge (for example, concern about the president's age), the reports would identify it almost immediately and indicate which groups in the electorate were being affected. As in 1980, television commercials were monitored for impact and tested on focus groups before being cleared for broadcast.

The first step in the PINS system involved purchasing a list of household names and telephone numbers bought from a consumer research firm. Next, Wirthlin and his team randomly chose from the list four "waves," or panels, of 250 names. Telephone interviews of the people comprising each wave began in June. In early October, the sample number in each wave was increased to 500, and in the last two weeks it reached 1,000. Toward the end of the campaign, instead of national tracking, the team focused the PINS system on twenty to twenty-five key states.

To run the mammoth operation, the campaign used the facilities of Wirthlin's own company, Decision/Marketing/Information, and other large marketing agencies. These companies provided the campaign with 520 interviewing stations around the country, each equipped for computer-assisted interviewing. Each interview took fifteen minutes. The first began each night at 5:15 P.M. in the East and finished seven hours later on the West Coast. Computer technology was critical to the team's ability to generate, store, and analyze the data and to print the reports within twelve hours of the start of interviewing.

The marketing technology reached far beyond polling. Two members of the Reagan propaganda team supervised intensive, in-depth interviews with more than fifty focus groups to help them compose effective "issue development" messages and to search for the strongest "Unique Selling Proposition" (a phrase borrowed from product marketing). This intensive research was responsible for two highly effective slogans: "Leadership that's Working" and "Prepared for Peace." One spot ad that emerged from this process was titled "The Bear." Produced by the Gallo Wine ad man, Hal Riney, the commercial, as described in *Public Opinion* magazine, subtly attacked Mondale's courting of the peace movement and endorsement by The Nuclear Weapon Freeze organization while simultaneously defending Reagan's military buildup. The president never actually appeared or spoke in the ad, which featured a bear as the symbol of the Soviet Union.

> (Camera up on a grizzly, lumbering across a hilltop, crossing a stream, forging through underbrush. A drum plays incessantly, like a heartbeat, over ominous chords.)
>
> *Announcer* (Hal Riney): There's a bear in the woods. For some people, the bear is easy to see. Others don't see it at all. Some say the bear is tame. Others say it is vicious and dangerous. Since no one can really be sure who's right, isn't it smart to be as strong as the bear?

(The bear walks slowly along a ridge, silhouetted against the sky; it looks up, stops suddenly and takes a step backward. The camera pulls back to show a man standing a few yards away, facing the bear. A gun is slung over his shoulder. He too is silhouetted.)

Announcer: If there is a bear.

Closing graphic: "President Reagan: Prepared for Peace."

The spot cost $80,000 to produce, including the cost of a trained bear. It was tried on more than one hundred focus groups and in three test markets. To be sure the spot would create the intended effect, public reaction was monitored via the "Viewer Response Profile," a system developed by the advertising industry to ensure that no unintended negative messages are conveyed by an ad.[24]

Not content with measuring voters' responses through surveys, the image makers next turned to biofeedback technology, an eerily appropriate Orwellian innovation considering that the year was 1984. During the presidential campaign debates, the Reagan team used the "TRACE copy-testing equipment/methodology" to measure audiences' second-by-second responses. In TRACE, people in a focus group register their reactions to what is being said through hand-held devices. By this method, the research team learned that the public responded negatively to Mondale's attack leveled at Reagan's promise to share Star Wars technology (once developed) with the Soviet Union. Mondale tried to portray the president as irresponsible for offering to share high technology with the Soviets. When Mondale's advisors made a commercial by excerpting the incident, the Tuesday Team was delighted, aware that their rivals were inadvertently making commercials that benefited Reagan.[25]

Another device used for monitoring the campaign, though not new, was vastly improved with the help of computer technology. Under the code name "Voices for Victory," 208 volunteers monitored local press and media coverage and funneled the information nightly back to Reagan-Bush headquarters. Less than 24 hours later, local contacts were supplied with material that they could send to local media. Everything said in public by Mondale as far back as 1961 had been entered in advance into a computer data base, enabling the team to check for contradictions between past and present issue positions. This "Rapid Response" program was adopted from Margaret Thatcher's 1983 campaign.

Perfecting the Techniques in 1988

The 1988 Republican presidential campaign combined and fine-tuned the accumulated experience of campaigns between 1968 and 1984. By 1976, all candidates in both parties had learned to play the "spin" game and to attempt to lower expectations for the primaries, and George Bush proved particularly adept at doing so before his crucial victories in New Hampshire, South Carolina, and the South on Super Tuesday—the first time ever that all southern states, save one, conducted their primaries on the same day. Bush's campaign manager, Lee Atwater, had been responsible for Gerald Ford's remarkable comeback, which fell just short in 1976.

Once the general election campaign got rolling, Bush's ads borrowed heavily from the 1984 themes of "Peace and Prosperity" and struck a tone meant to associate the vice president with the highly popular Reagan. From 1980, the campaign borrowed the device of making extensive use of "independent" committees to produce and distribute ads that might be politically damaging if officially associated with Bush's campaign.

The national nominating conventions of the two parties symbolized the degree to which politics had become packaged as a market commodity. Both conventions were remarkably sterile and dull, closer in tone to the Miss America pageant than to a political event. For the Democrats, with the party's various contending and often contentious groups, the atmosphere, as it was projected on television, seemed especially contrived. Their convention was choreographed down to the last detail. The mass-produced, officially approved placards were distributed and gathered up on cue. The networks were handed the script in advance so they could inform viewers about the next scheduled "demonstration." Michael Dukakis's consultants were so anxious to portray a happy, peaceful convention that they virtually turned over one evening of prime time television coverage to the only genuinely charismatic figure in attendance, Jesse Jackson. The main story of the convention became the networks' coverage of the behind-the-scenes maneuvers between the Dukakis and Jackson camps to keep the televised proceedings orderly.

Immediately following the Democratic convention, polls showed that Dukakis was benefiting from the usual favorable "bounce" that the presidential nominee receives from the carefully orchestrated coverage that a convention generates. It should have surprised no one that Bush closed the seventeen-point (Harris Poll) gap after the Republican convention, but the speed and extent of the comeback was unprecedented in presidential campaign history. It began a week before the GOP convention with a Republican media blitz consisting of "teasers" intended to boost the size of the audience by reminding voters of the sense of economic and international crisis that had prevailed during Jimmy Carter's administration. Even before the Republican convention began, a Gallup Poll showed that Bush had closed the gap to seven points.

The Republicans' convention was as orchestrated as the Democrats', but this seemed consistent with the party's image: affluent, satisfied, conservative. The networks spoke openly about the "choreographers" in charge of keeping things moving along. At one point, a network commentator announced that there would be a scheduled 5-minute demonstration for Nancy Reagan, "unless she cuts it short." The conventions epitomized what political campaigns have become in the 1980s. Professional pollsters and ad men choreograph campaign appearances and TV spots. The job of the candidate is to stand at the chalk line when instructed to do so, smile and frown on cue. George Bush proved adept at it; in the face of similar demands, however, Michael Dukakis projected a wooden and lifeless image.

The networks relied on "spin doctors" to generate news about the conventions, presidential debates, and campaign advertising. In a typical program several political analysts or pollsters would sit around offering interpretations about the day's events. The decided tilt toward conservative "spin" was evident, with George Will, David

Gergen, and Patrick Buchanan typically providing the conservative spin. News commentators and pollsters posed as neutral spin doctors to convey a sense of objectivity. Leading office holders in the Democratic Party represented the "liberal" or opposition party's point of view, when it was represented. Of course, leftist spin was invariably absent.

The George Bush campaign constituted a perfect model for high-technology application of advertising techniques to politics; indeed, the *Wall Street Journal* called it "a triumph over the open discourse of old-time politics."[26] The image makers working for Michael Dukakis were, by comparison, far less skilled—or perhaps less able completely to encase their candidate in a cocoon, shielded from direct contact with reporters and the public. Michael Dukakis was widely criticized for waiting so long to counterattack the negative advertising orchestrated by Bush's team. Indeed, Dukakis had overruled his advisors, who urged him to become more aggressive right after the Republican convention. Such an error could not have occurred in the Bush campaign, because the candidate appreciated that an effective high-technology election campaign requires disciplined obedience to the professionals.

Bush's campaign began each morning at 7 A.M. with a study of the polling data from the night before. Daily national polls based on 1,000 telephone calls, supplemented by statewide polls and polls of special groups, provided the basis for that day's campaign message. The message, whether about crime or taxes, was then packaged into snappy lines and witty phrases, to create the "sound bites" that are useful for network television news. Bush was kept at a distance from reporters; any spontaneous comments might "clutter the message,"[27] or the candidate might make a mistake.

Once again, TV ads were developed using polling results, then tested in focus groups. The members of these groups sat in a theaterlike room and used hand-held meters to register their positive or negative reactions to various messages. A positive ad about Bush was usually selected to run in tandem with a negative one about Dukakis. The ads could be changed frequently and on short notice. According to Roger Stone, a Bush advisor, "We are running a campaign that is designed for network TV. That means only one message a day, and getting it out early enough to get on the networks and major media markets that night. It means not allowing anything unplanned."[28]

The 1988 general election race often was described as the dirtiest presidential campaign in recent history. The commercial that portrayed Michael Dukakis in the most unfavorable light featured a police photograph of Willie Horton, who had raped a woman in Maryland and stabbed her fiancé while on a weekend pass from a Massachusetts prison. Dukakis had been governor at the time.

The ad opened with side-by-side photographs of the candidates, with an announcer intoning, "Bush and Dukakis on crime." A picture of Bush then flashed across the screen with the words, "Bush supports the death penalty for first-degree murderers." Cut to a picture of Dukakis, with the announcer voiceover: "Dukakis not only opposes the death penalty, he allowed first-degree murderers to have weekend passes from prison." Then a grainy mugshot of Willie Horton, glowering at the camera, followed by a blurred black-and-white photograph of Horton being handcuffed by police, with a voiceover to detail his various crimes. The words "kidnapping," "stabbing," and "raping" flashed across the screen. The last photo showed Michael Dukakis with the voiceover, "Weekend prison passes. Dukakis on crime."

Willie Horton is black, his victim was white. The overt racism of the message could hardly be missed, which is doubtlessly why the Bush campaign went to some pains to distance itself from the ad, which was sponsored by the National Security Political Action Committee. The committee had collected more than $7 million through mass mailings labeled "Americans for Bush," enough money to run the ad for twenty-eight days in September and October. The ad team that did the commercial had worked closely with the Republican party for a long time; indeed, the ad was shot by a former employee of a consulting firm then working for Bush's campaign. The committee's founder gushed, "Officially the campaign has to disavow themselves from me. Unofficially, I hear they're thrilled about what we're doing."[29]

While officially disavowing the Willie Horton ad, the Bush campaign was able to reap benefits from it by running its own negative TV spot about the Massachusetts furlough program. On the basis of focus group test results, a black-and-white ad was selected over a color version. The ad showed actors going through a revolving door in front of a prison (in fact, the Utah State prison). The voiceover announced that Dukakis's "revolving-door prison policy gave weekend furloughs to first-degree murderers not eligible for parole. While out, many committed other crimes like kidnap and rape, and many are still at large."[30] Of course, the spot failed to point out that all states and the federal government have similar furlough programs.

Racism was not the only emotionally coded theme used by the Bush campaign. By stressing that Dukakis was a "card-carrying member" of the American Civil Liberties Union, Bush was not merely quarreling with his opponent's endorsement of that organization's beliefs. "Card-carrying member" is a cultural symbol for Communism, and by extension anything smacking of Communism implies antipatriotism. Bush reinforced this theme by reciting the Pledge of Allegiance, suggesting that Dukakis's veto of a Massachusetts bill mandating its recitation in classrooms was motivated by disloyalty to the country rather than respect for civil liberties. Bush did not raise this issue in a sudden rush of patriotism. His handlers noticed that in the Republican primaries Pat Robertson had successfully sold himself by reciting the Pledge and blasting the American Civil Liberties Union. Before he tried it himself, Bush's public relations people tried both ideas on focus groups.[31] Had these groups reacted negatively, Bush would have left his patriotism in the closet, but he discovered that it would be an asset to wear it on his sleeve.

Elections As Mechanisms of Social Control

The most important messages sold by public relations specialists may not be, in the end, about the candidates or political parties. The most enduring messages convey impressions of American culture and politics. Katherine Hall Jamieson, a specialist on political advertising, has concluded that ads serve as a "safety valve" that "by underscoring the power of the ballot," teaches people that "your vote makes a difference." With unbridled admiration, she extols the virtues of media campaigns:

Political ads affirm that the country is great, has a future, is respected. The contest they reflect is over who should be elected, not over whether there should be an election. The very existence of the contest suggests that there is a choice, that voters' selection of one candidate over the other will make a difference. Ads also define the problems we face and assure us that there are solutions. If there are no solutions, a candidate would speak that truth at great risk.[32]

In *The Symbolic Uses of Politics,* Murray Edelman observed that elections are ritualistic acts that legitimize the political system. They could not serve this function "if the common belief in direct popular control over governmental policy through elections were to be widely questioned."[33] Another political scientist has also noted the symbolic purpose of elections:

> What voters decide, and thus how they come to vote as they do, is far less consequential for government and politics than the simple fact of voting itself. The impact of electoral decisions upon the governmental process is analogous to the impact made upon organized religion by individuals who obey the injunction to worship at the church of their choice. The fact of mass electoral participation is generally far more significant for the state than what or how citizens decide once they participate.[34]

In his analysis of the outcome of the 1984 election, Wilson Carey MacWilliams argues that media dominance marks the death of the pluralist style of campaigning. Modern presidential elections entail the manipulation of public opinion, and the "gatekeepers" for these elections are professionals in the media industry.[35]

The manipulation of mass publics by media professionals continues between elections, and when it was in office the Reagan administration was well aware of how the process worked. Public relations specialists in the White House used the media to draw attention to issues and mobilized grass-roots support through right-wing networks and direct mail advertising and fundraising. The same media experts that made the Reagan campaigns so effective also managed public opinion between elections.

After Reagan's second inauguration, the PINS technique and the "strongest Unique Selling Proposition" were applied on a week-to-week basis by a team of presidential advisers called the "Blair House Group." Their job was to position the president against telegenic backdrops symbolizing the themes in his remarks, accomplishing what they called "a visual approach that ties in with the spoken words." This use of television may be a relatively new propaganda tool, but the idea of repetition is not. According to one presidential aide, "The notion absolutely is that you establish themes through repetition. You've got to establish unanimous agreement on the part of those who have to put it forth; then you have to say it, resay it and figure out different ways to say it."[36]

Over the course of his eight years in office, Reagan's propaganda team in the White House carried out 500 national surveys of 500,000 voters. Monthly surveys of 1,000 to 2,000 interviews each were conducted, much more than the number reported by the leading polling organizations such as Gallup, Yankelovich, and Roper and Harris. During seventeen periods identified as "crises," such as after Libya was bombed, daily "brushfire surveys" of 800 respondents each were done every two days. Profiles of voters in key congressional districts were undertaken so that effective "grass-roots" campaigns could be organized to swing public opinion in those districts. Profiles on key celebrities, especially television news anchors, also were maintained. A July 1987 study on Tom Brokaw of NBC News yielded ten pages of computer printout.[37]

Considering the huge resources devoted to managing information, it is remarkable that the American public is ever able to arrive at opinions that contradict the government's agenda. But despite a carefully orchestrated media blitz utilizing fabricated stories and calling the *contras* "freedom fighters" and comparing them to the Constitution's Founders, for example, the Reagan administration failed to convert the public to its policies on Nicaragua. In fact, it is likely that only the weight of public opinion restrained the administration from launching an invasion of Nicaragua.[38]

Elections are necessary but not sufficient to produce democracy. The reality in America is that the spectrum of choices available to voters is narrow. The information presented to voters is circumscribed by the homogeneous, superficial, and unimaginative coverage of elections in the news media. The propaganda apparatus of the advertising industry is used to manipulate and manage, not to enlighten. American electoral politics not only fails to provide for the accountability of government to the people, it has become a principal tool for elites to manage politics and political choices.

Notes

1. Barry Sussman, *What Americans Really Think and Why Our Politicians Pay No Attention* (New York: Pantheon, 1988), esp. p. 252.

2. Edwin Diamond and Stephen Bates, "The Ads: How Madison Avenue Fought the Election," *Public Opinion* 7 (December-January 1985): 57.

3. Doris Graber, *Processing the News: How People Tame the Information Tide* (New York: London, 1984).

4. See Graber, ibid., pp. 123-177. For a good summary of the vast literature on audience response to political advertising, see Dean E. Alger, *The Media and Politics* (Englewood Cliffs, N.J.: Prentice Hall, 1989), pp. 37-72 and 185-230.

5. Kathleen Hall Jamieson, *Packaging the Presidency: A History and Criticism of Presidental Campaign Advertising* (New York: Oxford University Press, 1984).

6. Robert Goldsborough, "The '84 Ads: High Gloss, Low Blows," *Advertising Age*, November 5, 1984, pp. 3, 82.

7. Jamieson, *Packaging the Presidency*, p. 448.

8. Thomas Patterson and Robert McClure, *The Unseeing Eye: The Myth of Television Power in National Elections* (New York: G.P. Putnam, 1976), p. 41.

9. Edie N. Goldenberg and Michael W. Traugott, *Campaigning for Congress* (Washington D.C.: Congressional Quarterly Press, 1984), pp. 128-130.

10. Ibid.

11. F. Christopher Ahterton, *Media Politics* (Lexington, Mass.; Lexington Books, 1984), pp. 178-180.

12. Ibid., pp. 180-182.

13. Jamieson, *Packaging the Presidency*, pp. 202-203.

14. Ibid., p. 212.

15. Joseph McGinniss, *Selling of the President, 1968* (New York: Trident Press, 1969).

16. Benjamin I. Page, *Choices and Echoes in Presidential Elections* (Chicago: University of Chicago Press, 1979), pp. 199-200.

17. Jamieson, *Packaging the Presidency.* Our description of political advertising efforts between 1978 and 1980 relies on her account on pp. 378-445.

18. Ibid., pp. 417-428.

19. Ibid.

20. Ibid.

21. The idea of having "private" individuals and groups carry out public initiatives was a contributory factor in the Iran scandal. Barred by Congress from directly soliciting funds for the *contras,* government operatives formed a network of private supporters who raised millions of dollars from domestic sources, some of which was used to lobby Congress and perhaps to influence the 1986 congressional elections. To a certain extent, this activity was probably a cover for vast amounts of aid collected, in violation of the law, from foreign governments for the *contras* and for ignoring *contra* drug racketeering. The facts needed for the media to shed light on this activity were known well in advance (See NACLA's *Report on the Americas,* July-August 1986), but the political circumstances were not right. This situation changed when the administration's dealings with Iran were exposed. The administration also was weakened by Reagan's lame duck status and the GOP setback in the 1986 congressional elections.

22. Mark Hertsgaard, *On Bended Knee: The Press and the Reagan Presidency* (New York: Farrar Straus Giroux, 1989), p. 251. Hertsgaard's account of the 1984 elections is on pages 238-270.

23. The Tuesday Team and the Reagan-Bush media campaign are well described by the bible of the public relations industry, *Advertising Age,* November 5, 1984; by Kevin J. Kelly, "Mad, Mad (Ave.) Election," *The Guardian,* October 17, 1984; by Diamond and Bates, "The Ads." See also interviews with Richard Wirthlin and Peter Hart in the same issue of *Public Opinion* and in *Advertising Age* (December 10, 1984).

24. The Viewer Response Profile and other devices described later in the chapter are described in articles in *Advertising Age* (November 5, 1984).

25. As to why many people reacted negatively, we believe that by trying to outflank Reagan on the right Mondale was sending conflicting signals to the public, attempting to appear as the "peace" candidate while taking a hard line against communism.

26. James M. Perry and Monica Langley, "Bush Thrives on One-A-Day TV—Message Capsules Prescribed by His Skilled Poli-Tech Image Makers," *Wall Street Journal,* October 27, 1988, p. A16.

27. Ibid.

28. Ibid.

29. Stephen Engleberg, "Bush, His Disavowed Backers and a Very Potent Attack Ad," The *New York Times,* November 2, 1988, pp. 1, 16.

30. Perry and Langley, *"Bush Thrives on One-A-Day TV,"* p. A16.

31. Allen D. Hertzke, "Pat Robertson's Crusade and the GOP: A Strategic Analysis," paper presented at the Annual Meeting of the Midwest Political Science Association, Chicago, Illinois, April 13-15, 1989.

32. Ibid., p. 453.

33. Murray Edelman, *The Symbolic Uses of Politics* (Urbana: University of Illinois, 1964), p. 94.

34. Benjamin Ginsberg, *The Consequences of Consent: Elections, Citizen Control and Popular Acquiescence* (Reading, Mass.: Addison-Wesley, 1982), p. 5.

35. Wilson Carey MacWilliams, "The Meaning of the Election," in *The Election of 1984*, ed. Gerald Pomper (Chatham, N.J.: Chatham House, 1985), p. 161.

36. See Dick Kirschten, "A New Team of Stage Managers Maximizes Reagan's Star Quality," *National Journal*, January 18, 1986, pp. 162-163.

37. John J. Hanomichl, "How Reagan Took America's Pulse," *Advertising Age,* January 23, 1989, pp. 1, 25, 32.

38. Sussman, *What Americans Really Think,* pp. 8-9, 60-63.

Part Two

Rigging Electoral Processes

Chapter 5

Voting As a Symbolic Act

The Voting Behavior Puzzle

In the United States, citizens are told from an early age that democracy depends on every person's vote. Schoolchildren read textbook passages like the following, from one of the most popular high school civics texts of 1984:

The most common reason for not voting is a person's belief that her or his vote will not make a difference in the outcome of an election. Of course this is not true. The vote of every individual helps determine who wins or loses an election. Only by exercising our right to vote can Americans influence the laws and policies that greatly affect our lives.[1]

As adults, too, Americans are inundated with the message that every individual vote is essential for the democratic system to work. At election time it is hard to avoid the drumbeat of rhetoric by candidates, political parties, and civic organizations that promote the vote. In one of its pamphlets, for example, the League of Women Voters has said that:

The vote is a fundamental political right in a self-governing country.
The vote is a symbol of equality.
The vote is a weapon for self-protection.
The vote is a tool to get things done.
The vote assures that the voice will be heard even after election day.[2]

With a litany of such messages pouring forth in election years, it would be logical to presume that voter participation in the United States must be extremely high. This expectation is, however, far from the reality. A very high proportion of the potential American electorate stays home on election day. In 1982, 36 percent of the voting age population went to the polls to choose representatives in Congress. And despite unusually well-organized voter registration and get-out-the-vote drives, only 53.5 percent of the eligible electorate went to the polls in the 1984 presidential election, barely above the 1980 percentage (53.2%). In November 1988, turnout fell to its lowest level (50.2%) in a presidential election since 1924.

As table 5-1 indicates, high rates of turnout were common from 1840 to the turn of the century, when 70 percent to 80 percent of voters regularly went to the polls. Since 1900, however, turnout has declined, falling sharply from the election of

Table 5-1 **Voter Turnout**
Estimated Turnout among Eligible Voters in Presidential Elections,
1840–1924

Year	South	Non-South	National
1840	75	81	80
1844	74	80	79
1848	68	74	73
1852	59	72	69
1856	72	81	79
1860	76	83	82
1864	Civil War	76	76
1868	71	83	81
1872	67	74	72
1876	75	86	83
1880	65	86	81
1884	64	84	79
1888	64	86	81
1892	59	81	76
1896	57	86	79
1900	43	83	74
1904	29	77	66
1908	31	76	66
1912	28	68	59
1916	32	69	62
1920	22	55	49
1924	19	57	49

Source: Walter Dean Burnham, "The System of 1896: An Analysis," in Paul Kleppner et al., eds., *The Evolution of American Electoral Systems* (Westview, CN: Greenwood Publishing Group, Inc. 1981), table 1, p. 100. Copyright 1981 by the authors. Reprinted with permission.

1904, when 66 percent of eligible voters went to the polls, to 49 percent in 1924 (see tables 5-1 and 5-2). By the 1928 presidential election participation began to rise again, reaching 65 percent of eligible voters by 1960. Since then, it has fallen steadily.

Voter participation in the United States is abnormally low in comparison to turnout in other Western democratic nations. As table 5-3 indicates, only in Switzerland do a smaller proportion of voters cast their ballots than in the United States—but probably because its citizens are asked four or five times each year to vote in national referenda. Voter turnout in the United States is even lower than in most Latin American nations, where electoral processes are commonly interrupted by military coups and civil wars (see table 5-4).

One consequence of low voter participation is that in recent history no presidents or congresses have been sent to Washington by a majority of the potential electorate (which includes eligible citizens who failed to register). Despite his landslide victory in 1984, for example, President Ronald Reagan received less than 30 percent of the votes of the potential electorate. The largest party in American politics is neither Democratic nor Republican; it is the party of nonvoters. There is

Table 5-2 **Voter Turnout**

Presidential Turnout among Eligible Voters in Presidential Elections, 1928–1988

Year	South	Non-South	National
1928	23	66	57
1932	24	66	57
1936	25	71	61
1940	26	73	62
1944			
1948	25	62	53
1952	38	71	64
1956	37	70	62
1960	41	73	65
1964	46	69	63
1968	52	66	62
1972	46	61	57
1976	49	58	56
1980	50	57	53
1984			53
1988			50

Source: Updated and adapted from Walter Dean Burnham, "The System of 1896: An Analysis," in Paul Kleppner et al., eds., *The Evolution of American Electoral Systems* (Westview, CN: Greenwood Publishing Group, Inc.). Copyright 1981 by the authors. Reprinted with permission.

Table 5-3 **International Voter Turnout**

Ranking of Countries by Turnout, Most Recent Elections through 1981

Rank Country	Percent	Rank Country	Percent
1. Italy	94.0	12. New Zealand	78.5
2. Austria	89.3	13. France	78.0
3. Belgium	88.7	14. United Kingdom	76.0
4. Sweden	86.8	15. Japan	74.4
5. Portugal	85.9	16. Spain	73.0
6. Greece	84.9	17. Canada	67.4
7. Netherlands	84.7	18. Finland	63.0
8. Australia	83.1	19. Ireland	62.3
9. Denmark	82.1	20. United States	52.6
10. Norway	81.8	21. Switzerland	39.4
11. Germany	81.1		

Source: Adapted from David Glass, Peverill Squire, and Raymond Wolfinger, "Voter Turnout: An International Comparison," *Public Opinion* 6 (January/February 1984), p. 50, table 1. Reprinted with permission.

an obvious contradiction between actual voting behavior and the barrage of messages telling everyone to vote, but this anomaly has not emerged in American politics by accident. It has been functional for elites in the twentieth century to sell the message

Table 5-4   **Latin American Voter Turnout**
Percentage of Adult Population Voting, Selected Recent Latin American Elections

Country	Year	Adult Population Voting (percent)
Nicaragua	1984	91
Venezuela	1983	90
Argentina	1983	89
Costa Rica	1982	87
Brazil (legislative)	1982	81
Honduras	1981	79
Mexico	1982	75
El Salvador	1984	69
Colombia	1982	68

Source: U.S. Department of State, Bureau of Public Affairs, "Democracy in Latin America and the Caribbean," Current Policy Statement No. 605 (August 1984), table 1, p. 1. Estimate for Nicaragua based on estimation in "Report of the Latin American Studies Association Delegation to Observe the Nicaraguan General Election of November 4, 1984," *LASA Forum* 15 (Winter 1985): 21.

that voting is an essential act of citizenship, and it has been equally functional for them to make the act of voting relatively difficult in practice.

The Symbolic Meaning of the Vote

The act of voting is invested with immense symbolic meaning. Elections are, in part, an exercise that ties the masses to political leaders by giving ordinary citizens the feeling that they can influence government and its policies. At election time, citizens take part in an elaborately orchestrated pageant that invests officeholders with the aura of legitimacy. By reference to this one means of participation, government officials claim the right to govern and to make policy. The act of voting also serves as an emotional catharsis essential for reaffirming the individual's participation in a political community. Elections

> give people a chance to express discontents and enthusiasms, to enjoy a sense of involvement....Like all ritual...elections draw attention to common social ties and to the importance and apparent reasonableness of accepting the public policies that are adopted.[3]

A remarkable feature of the American political system is that elites have managed to retain all the benefits of ritualistic participation despite low voter turnout.

Exposed to the ritual, drama, and circuslike panorama of election night returns and interviews, even the potential voters who stayed at home on election day are hard put not to feel that they, too, have participated. Low turnout might seem to make it difficult for a politician or media analyst to read a policy mandate into election results, but election winners nevertheless always claim a mandate. In 1980, 70 percent of the potential electorate did not vote for Ronald Reagan. Still, Reagan's pollster offered the following analysis shortly after the President's election:

> The nineteen eighty election provided a mandate for change. That mandate was not clearly defined beyond the electorate wanting a strong leader to deal with inflation, but it was a rejection of the New Deal agenda that had dominated American politics since the mid-thirties.[4]

Reagan's opponents disagreed with the claim that the 1980 election constituted a mandate for abandoning programs that benefit the economically disadvantaged. They cited polls showing that the most common reason that people voted for Reagan in 1980 was that they were dissatisfied with Jimmy Carter's administration. Even in the wake of the president's landslide victory in 1984, it could be shown that on only a very few issues did a majority of the electorate agree with specific positions adopted by the President or included in the Republican platform.[5] For candidates, though, it matters little if mandates can be objectively read into election returns. What they seek is the legitimacy to govern.

Elections provide this legitimacy, but they are always problematic, because elections can be won, in principle or potentially, by popular majorities that may wish to overturn existing property and social class arrangements. Throughout U.S. history, elites have expended considerable resources trying to walk a fine line: They persuade citizens that elections are meaningful political events, but they also try to make sure that the political choices made in the electoral arena are acceptable to elites.

Controlling voter participation has been an important means that elites have used to accomplish two objectives—legitimation and social control. In the nineteenth century, participation rates were high partly because voting was easy to do and the political parties had an interest in mobilizing the electorate. In the late nineteenth and early twentieth centuries turnout rates began to fall when elites made it much more difficult for ordinary citizens to register to vote. New restrictions on the franchise were proposed, in large part because elites became convinced that the electoral process might produce unacceptable results.

The "Problem" of Mass Suffrage

The delegates who gathered in Philadelphia to draft a new constitution during the summer of 1787 agreed that there was an urgent need for a central government strong enough to contain popular discontent against wealth and property. In response to Shays' Rebellion in Massachusetts, George Washington exclaimed, "Good God! there are combustibles in every state, which a spark might light a fire to."[6] By late 1786, the army of farmers and debtors led by Daniel Shays had seized several towns in Massachusetts and threatened to overrun the Springfield military garrison. An army assembled by the state's merchants finally routed Shays' volunteers, and the insurrection collapsed.[7] But the threat of civil turmoil existed elsewhere, too. Debtors rioted in Maryland in 1786; a year later, farmers in Vermont tried to stop foreclosures.[8] In this atmosphere, the Founders drafted a constitution that established a democratic form of government, a daring step at a time when European nations were still ruled by hereditary monarchies and rumors of rebellion filled the air. But it was a cautious step as well. The Founders established a republic that simultaneously allowed democratic expression and contained effective safeguards against popular majority rule.

The Founders were divided on the question of how narrowly the franchise should be restricted. Though he was the principal architect of "checks and balances," James Madison believed that additional safeguards were needed. Convinced that a property qualification should be written into the Constitution, he told delegates to the convention: "In England, at this day, if the elections were open to all classes of people the property of the landed proprietors would be insecure." Roger Sherman of Connecticut feared that the people "are constantly liable to be misled." And George Mason of Virginia argued that "it would be as unnatural to refer the choice of a proper character for [president] to the people as it would be to refer a trial of colors to a blind man."[9]

In the aftermath of the Revolution, however, political elites urgently needed a way to legitimate the new government. The entire white male population was armed, a condition that had been indispensable to victory over the British. But many of those who had served in the revolutionary armies were poor and in debt, and capable of turning their fighting experience against the rich and well born. Extension of the right to vote was an important instrument for institutionalizing the Revolution and calming political unrest.[10] In the end, the Founders left the regulation of the vote to the states. Because all the states imposed property qualifications, only about 5 percent of the male population was eligible to vote.

The concern that popular majorities might use the vote to threaten property rights remained an issue whenever the states adopted voting regulations, and this concern persisted long after the constitutional period. In Massachusetts, delegates to the state constitutional convention of 1820-21 were warned that they should take a lesson from Great Britain, where elites were resisting pressure to extend the right to vote to males who did not own property: "All writers agree, that there are twenty persons in Great Britain, who have no property, to one that has. If the radicals should succeed in obtaining universal suffrage, they will overturn the whole kingdom, and turn those who have property out of their houses."[11]

Following the Revolution, the states making up the original colonies continued to restrict voting to property-owning white males. Such restrictions helped eastern patricians to maintain a stranglehold on national politics for more than forty years after the Constitution was adopted. In the 1824 presidential race, John Quincy Adams of the Old Guard defeated Andrew Jackson despite the fact that Jackson carried the popular vote. The more populous eastern states delivered a solid block of Electoral College votes for Adams, ensuring his victory.

States that joined the Union after the Revolution did not generally impose property restrictions on voting because social relations in frontier cities and small towns were far more fluid than in the East. As more states joined the Union, it did not take long for voters in the new states to tip the balance of power in the Electoral College. Property or tax-paying restrictions were applied to voting in fourteen states in 1828, but they were dropped rapidly in the next few years. Five states still imposed them in 1840. Connecticut, Louisiana, and New Jersey dropped their restrictions in the 1840s, and Virginia followed suit in 1851. The last state to retain property restrictions, South Carolina, lost its right to impose them at the end of the Civil War.[12]

The Old Guard of the revolutionary period finally was forced to give way to a new generation whose fortunes were tied to westward expansion. In 1824, 355,000 voters participated in selecting the president. Only four years later, turnout more than tripled, to 1,155,000 people, and the "new" Jacksonian Democratic party became the first mass-based political party in the country. Jackson's opponents, including the emerging "Whigs," had to learn to play the mobilization game as well. Stimulated by keen competition between the parties, turnout levels in the nineteenth century rose well above levels known in Europe, where the right to vote was still tightly restricted or completely denied.

The Decline of Participation: The South

In the six presidential elections from 1840 to 1860, national rates of voting turnout in the non-southern states varied from 72 percent to 83 percent. In the states outside the South, turnout rates remained high until the turn of the century, then began a steady decline to 55 percent by the election of 1920 (see table 5-1).[13] Turnout rates in the South were always somewhat lower than elsewhere, and they fell somewhat after the Civil War. Voting participation dropped precipitously after the election of 1896, when 57 percent of the electorate voted. In the presidential election of 1912, 28 percent of the South's potential electorate went to the polls. By the election of 1924, only 19 percent of the southern electorate voted.

It is not difficult to identify the reasons for the sharp decline in voting participation throughout the southern states. Property-owning southern elites lost their grip on electoral policies for a brief time after the Civil War, but when the northern occupation ended following the 1876 election, they quickly began searching for ways to drive blacks and poor whites out of the electoral system. In this effort they were remarkably successful.

The political control exercised by propertied southern elites was shattered by the outcome of the Civil War. Backed by military occupation, Reconstruction Republicans flooded into the South and guaranteed an expansion of political power for blacks, and also incidentally for poor whites, by extending the vote to the former slaves. Hundreds of blacks were elected to state and local public offices, and a few were elected to Congress. With the withdrawal of federal troops from the southern states in 1877, however, southern white elites organized to reverse the enfranchisement of black and white voters. By the late 1890s, they had achieved their objective.[14]

In 1877, Georgia imposed a mandatory poll tax that prompted an immediate decline in turnout, and Georgia's example was soon followed elsewhere. The poll taxes levied by Georgia and other states required voters to pay one or two dollars annually, a considerable amount for sharecroppers and agricultural workers whose annual income was measured in tens of dollars. Estimated per capita income in the

South, including the value of crops and goods produced at home, was only $100 in 1900.[15] In 1882 South Carolina passed the "eight-box" law, and Florida adopted this procedure in 1889. This law required voters to place their ballots in separate boxes labeled for each candidate.[16] The intent, and the effect, was to make it impossible for illiterate voters to cast their ballots accurately. But such a complicated system proved to be unnecessary because most states pioneered in more direct methods to disenfranchise their illiterate citizens. Mississippi adopted a poll tax and a literacy test when it revised its state constitution in 1890. In Mississippi's literacy test, a black voter would be asked to read a passage from the state constitution and then was required to give a "reasonable demonstration" of its meaning. The judgment about whether the voter passed the test was left entirely to the registrar. By 1900, overall voter turnout in Mississippi had dropped to 17 percent.[17]

Additional insurance against black political influence was secured by instituting the all-white primary. The legal rationalization for this device to remove blacks from the nomination process relied on the argument that political parties were akin to private clubs with a right to make their own rules, and that as a consequence they could not be regulated by the government. White primaries withstood federal court challenges until 1944.

Terror was employed to achieve the final destruction of political influence by blacks. The Fourteenth, Fifteenth, and Sixteenth Amendments had been enacted by the post–Civil War Congress to empower blacks politically, but before long the U.S. Supreme Court moved to limit federal enforcement of blacks' voting and civil rights. In 1876, for instance, the Supreme Court dismissed one hundred federal indictments against the perpetrators of sixty political murders of blacks, on the ground that Congress could not make murder a crime prosecutable under federal law *(U.S. v. Cruickshank).*[18]

The many strategies to disenfranchise black voters were effective. Within a few years, the southern black electorate was "expeditiously destroyed." In Louisiana, registered black voters fell from 130,334 to 1,342 between 1896 and 1904. In five other southern states it was halved.[19]

Many of the efforts to reduce the political influence of blacks were aimed at poor whites as well. Proponents of election "reform" understood that restrictions on voting by blacks could be used to undercut whites who might challenge oligarchic control by big landowners and employers. A white politician in Virginia stated: "It is not the negro vote which works the harm, for the negroes are generally Republicans, but it is the deprived and incompetent men of our race who have nothing at stake in government, and who are used by designing politicians to accomplish their purposes, irrespective of the welfare of the community." An Alabama lawyer observed in 1905: "How to get rid of the venal and ignorant among white men as voters was a far more serious and difficult problem than how to get rid of the undesirable among the negroes as voters."[20]

In the North as well as in the South, elites were concerned that workers might close ranks to forge a political movement aimed to regulate corporations and financial institutions. Agrarian populism was on the rise at the same time that the industrial and trade unions were growing in strength. In cities, socialist parties were attracting an increasing number of followers, and the party machines seized power by mobilizing immigrant voters. Such developments prompted elites to seek reform of election processes.

Restricting the Vote: The Progressive Reforms

In the North, changes in voting laws that reduced participation by poor and working-class people were defended by Progressive reformers as a means of restoring "good government." Corruption and election fraud were the ostensible targets of the reformers, but the result of reforms was to reduce political influence by urban workers, foreign immigrants, and less-educated rural dwellers.

It might seem contradictory that a movement seeking to rid elections of corruption should be regarded as instrumental in making the United States a less participatory democracy, particularly because Progressives also sought to regulate industry, end child labor, curb the growth of monopolies, and establish a graduated income tax. Progressives also championed the Sixteenth Amendment, providing for election of senators by direct popular vote, and supported the movement for women's suffrage. How, then, can they be held responsible in any sense for a decline in electoral participation?

The answer to this question is that the Progressives did not oppose voter participation per se, but they were highly disturbed about the political influence of foreign immigrants who, they felt, were corrupting American culture and politics. Most leading Progressives were upper-class descendants of northern European and English immigrant stock, though they thought of themselves as "native Americans." They dominated government, business, and social institutions and sought to impose Protestant cultural norms and religious traditions that historians have labeled "pietist."[21]

The immigrants brought with them new cultural customs and religious traditions. In the cities they constituted a pool of potential voters to be mobilized either by trade union movements or by machine politicians. In a coalition with rural populists, they might have brought class conflicts over wages, working conditions, prices, unionization, and control over factories and transportation solidly into national electoral politics.

Socialism emerged as a new political force early in the century. The first Socialist party representative to Congress was elected in 1910. Seventy-three Socialist mayors were elected in 1911, and in the same year 1,200 Socialists won state and local elections. Eugene Victor Debs received almost 6 percent of the vote for president in the 1912 election. The Industrial Workers of the World (the "Wobblies") enrolled workers all across the country. Socialists won still more state and municipal contests in 1917, 1918, and 1919.

The combination of socialism, prairie populism, the union movement, and urban machine politics caused anxiety among business elites. Bloody conflicts between federal troops and state national guard, local police, and company goon squads on one side and workers on the other often escalated into national protests. For example, in 1914 National Guardsmen, called out by the Colorado governor and paid by the Rockefeller family, broke a strike in Ludlow. First there was a machine gun massacre that killed thirteen miners, two of their wives, and eleven children; in less than a week, sixty-six people were killed. Protests erupted all over the country; demonstrators stormed Rockefeller offices on Broadway in New York. To solve the problem, the *New York Times* editorialized that President Woodrow Wilson should dispatch troops to subdue the miners. He promptly did.

Control of private institutions and of the national government remained in the hands of business elites. But, at least in the cities, control of electoral politics had slipped from their grasp. Powerful, centralized urban machines ran politics in New York, Boston, and most other cities with concentrated immigrant populations. Machine politicians came from the immigrant wards; they wore scruffy clothes, spoke in heavy accents, and often enough met their constituents in saloons. Their style of politics affronted the sensibilities of upper-class Protestant reformers. They provided small services for their constituents in exchange for the vote; sometimes they bought the vote outright. Reformers were blind to the services that machine politicians delivered to their immigrant constituents. What they saw was the corruption of democracy. And, indeed, electoral corruption was pervasive in big city elections:

> This was the period of massive voting frauds. In the elections of 1868 and 1872, 8 percent more people voted in New York state than were registered. In 1910, when the New York City vote was challenged and recounted, 50 percent of the votes were found to be fraudulent. In New Jersey, glass ballot jars had to replace the wooden boxes to prevent vote stuffing. In Pennsylvania and Michigan, gangs of mobsters moved from polling place to polling place beating up the opposition and voting at will. Indeed so numerous were the instances of fraud that practically all voting statistics from this period are suspect.[22]

Progressive reformers introduced several measures to control election fraud. Though most of these reforms were aimed at eliminating corruption, they also had the effect of reducing electoral participation by the people the reformers sometimes labeled the "Great Unwashed." The key reforms aimed at individual voters included:

- *Voter registration and literacy requirements.* These requirements reduced repeat voting and stopped the practice of importing voters in for an election. These reforms were aimed principally at urban machines, and thus were implemented first in several big cities. Before 1920 virtually all the states had imposed registration laws.

- *The Australian ballot.* This was a ballot that could be marked only by the individual voter and cast in secrecy. Before its introduction in the 1880s, ballots were printed by the parties and often cast publicly, or even handed already marked to voters. Use of the Australian ballot became universal after the turn of the century.

◆ *Nonpartisan elections.* Reformers fought hard to remove party labels of any kind from many state, and most municipal, election ballots. Where they succeeded, voters had only one clue as to how they should vote: the name of the individual candidate. At the same time, the number of elected offices proliferated, so that very long ballots listed "nonpartisan" candidates for judgeships, city clerk circuit judge, even dog catcher.

The effect of these reforms was to reduce voting turnout among recent immigrants and less educated voters. Twenty-five percent of the white males of voting age in the United States in 1900 were first-generation immigrants, and two-thirds of the immigrants had come from non-English-speaking countries. In the cities, the proportion of foreign-born immigrants was much higher, comprising often well over half of all voters. Before reform they might ask for help in filling out the ballot or even cast a premarked one. When they showed up to vote, their eligibility was assured. Now they had to register to vote in writing, often months before an election. And when they went to the polling station, they now faced an election judge, a secret voting booth, and a printed ballot they might not be able to read.

Recognizing the party symbol on the ballot had been infinitely easier than reading candidates' names. By removing the party symbol as a reference for lower-class voters, the nonpartisan ballot represented class interests in its effects as well as in its conception. Working-class candidates had few personal resources to expend on political activities. The party organization supplied campaign money and workers and freed the candidate from the necessity of holding a normal job, which of its own accord would have denied a working-class candidate time for participation in politics. Few politicians in the cities could have started or stayed in politics without a party organization's help. If there were no party organization to pool the resources among coalitions of politicians, each with limited resources, people of wealth and social standing could more easily dominate local elections. This result was, in fact, the objective of the nonpartisanship crusade—to make politics once again an "honest" calling appropriate to the educated and cultured classes.[23]

The effect of these reforms in the southern states was even more extreme, for few immigrant-based party machines existed to fight reform and voters did not receive help from precinct captains or ward committeemen in registering to vote or in looking over a sample ballot. In the South there was an explicitly racist motive for adopting the Australian ballot, as revealed by a Democratic campaign song popular in Arkansas in 1892:

> The Australian Ballot works like a charm,
> It makes them think and scratch,
> And when a Negro gets a ballot
> He has certainly got his match.

Illiteracy among southern white males varied between 8 percent and 19 percent; for black males, it varied between 39 percent and 61 percent. The Australian ballot drastically reduced voter participation by both blacks and poor whites even before other hurdles for voters were erected, such as poll taxes and literacy tests (see table

Table 5-5 **Voter Participation**
Turnout Rates before and after Registration Laws and the Secret Ballot,
Two Southern States

State	Election	Estimated Turnout		Male Illiteracy, 1900	
		White	*Black*	*White*	*Black*
Alabama	1892, Governor	80	64	13.6	59.5
	1896, Governor	68	49		
Arkansas	1890, Governor	75	71	10.4	44.8
	1892, Governor	67	38		

Source: Adapted from J. Morgan Kousser, *The Shaping of Southern Politics* (New Haven, Conn.: Yale University Press, 1974), tables 2.1 and 2.2, p. 55.

5-5). Voter participation fell drastically in the South in the first years of the twentieth century, and less steeply, but nevertheless significantly, in the North (see table 5-1). In the 1896 presidential election, 79 percent of the national electorate cast a vote. By 1920, only 49 percent of voters went to the polls.

Changes in electoral rules were sought by upper-class reformers who saw no advantage to be gained by making it easier for ordinary citizens to get to the polls. The middle-class public also supported these reforms because the problems that beset elections in the United States, especially widespread fraud, were manifestly important political problems. To reformers who wanted to reduce immigrant and working-class influence, electoral changes designed to reduce fraud—such as annual registration, ballot reform, secrecy in the voting booth, and laws against vote buying and repeat voting—were piggy-backed onto reforms that had little or nothing to do with corruption, such as nonpartisan ballots and at-large elections. By cloaking all reforms in the same language of "cleaning up" politics, reformers were able to portray themselves as nonpolitical fighters of corruption. In this way, "the demobilization and antipartisanship of the post-1900 era was achieved by a common mass consensus."[24]

The Contemporary Politics of Voter Registration and Turnout

The best testimony to the continuing importance of the politics of turnout is the response when proposals are put forth to relax voter registration requirements. In 1971, the League of Women Voters completed a study of registration laws and practices in 251 counties in various states. After noting a pattern of inefficiency and delay in the system of registration, the league reported an oft-expressed fear by election officials that any easing of registration laws inevitably would lead to voter fraud. The league's response: "More noteworthy...is the fraud perpetuated on the American people by a system which excludes millions of eligible voters from the electoral process in the name of preventing a few dishonestly cast votes."[25]

The league found that "long lines, short office hours, inaccessible registration and polling places, and registration periods remote from the date of election are common experiences to many Americans." Election officials were "generally insensitive" to these problems, evincing "an attitude...which tends to obstruct rather than encourage the efforts to expand the electorate." The result was that three out of every one hundred people who showed up to register left without enrolling. Analyzing the league's report, a political scientist concluded: "The question arises that if the government can find a citizen to tax him or draft him into military service, is it not reasonable to assume that the government can find that same citizen to enroll him as an eligible voter and include him in the active electorate?"[26]

Despite election day rhetoric, voters are often discouraged from going to the polls. For example, in New York City a voter registration drive in 1984 bogged down after registration officials built a backlog of 50,000 registrations. It was estimated that 62,000 voters were turned away on election day because they were not yet listed on the rolls.[27]

Inefficient registration procedures reduce voter participation. The lack of uniformity in electoral laws exerts a similar impact. Registration requirements differ from state to state, or even from county to county within a state. Americans are a mobile population; about one-third of the respondents in a recent election study had lived at their address less than two years.[28] Probably half of voters change addresses in the four years separating presidential elections.[29] After each move they are expected to reregister. A few states and counties still require double registration—once for local and separately for national elections. In some places, voters are expunged from the rolls for failing to vote in a single election. Several Georgia counties require a citizen to drive up to fifty miles to register at a courthouse. In some counties in Alabama, registration offices are open only two to three days a week for limited hours.[30] Across most of the country, offices are rarely open except during working hours.

In the last few years, registration by mail has become more common; by 1988 twenty-five states allowed it. But the registration forms are not easy to get because they are not available to people outside registration offices. Locating the registration offices' phone numbers is not always as simple a task as it might seem because the elections boards are listed under various names in different counties and states. In some states, forms must be notarized before they can be returned.[31] When a prospective voter returns the form, election officials may find a multitude of ways to classify the forms as faulty, because the "forms themselves are booby-traps":

> In New York City, the board of elections routinely discards forms that are completed in pencil, or signed only on one side, or signed with a middle initial on one side but not the other, or with Mr. or Mrs. on one side only.[32]

The hurdles to registration are many; there is no guarantee of success once they are negotiated, and they must be jumped over and over again in the life of the ordinary citizen. Better-educated people accustomed to bureaucratic processes find it easier to negotiate the registration process. They know what to ask of the officials, who also tend to feel more comfortable with people who act and dress like themselves.

As a consequence, the administrative complexities of voter registration are far from neutral: "Contemporary voter registration obstacles thus function as de facto equivalents of the poll tax, literacy test, and other class- and race-oriented restrictions on the suffrage of an earlier era."[33]

Most Western democracies operate on the principle that it is the government's responsibility to solicit or even enforce voter participation. Italy's registration system is administered locally, but all citizens older than eighteen are automatically enrolled. Germany enrolls citizens and requires under penalty of a fine that citizens notify registrars when moving. Austria requires registration as a matter of law; Belgium and Australia go further and mandate voting. Sweden registers voters through its national tax collection bureaucracy, and in Britain local officials are required to register voters once each year. In Canada, registrars are required to prove that a citizen is ineligible to vote, unlike the United States, where the voter must prove eligibility to a registrar if challenged.

In the months before the 1984 presidential election, various efforts were undertaken to register new voters.[34] Some were carried out by organizations that claimed to be nonpartisan; other registration drives targeted segments of the population favorable to a particular party or candidate. The NAACP tried the novel approach of organizing marches to register voters. One Richmond to New York march netted 8,000 registrations, but this was only a small fraction of the 2.5 million unregistered voters along the route. Another registration project, called Human SERVE, tried to get seventy national organizations to put 100,000 activists into the field in an attempt to register 1,000,000 new voters in a single day. Only 125,000 were actually enrolled. Another organization, Project Vote, sought to enroll voters with deputized volunteers. By September 1984, it had put only 350,000 new voters on the rolls by its own count.

Why did these efforts come up short? Project Vote was hampered when election officials in many areas refused to deputize volunteers. Some deputy registrars were actually arrested. Some of the problems stemmed from infighting among Project Vote, Human SERVE, and various registration organizations targeting African-American voters. In New York City, groups gearing up for a challenge to incumbent Mayor Koch did not like the nonpartisan approach to registration taken by Human SERVE. The efforts were hampered further by inexperience and scarce resources. But bureaucratic impediments to registration, especially refusals to deputize new registrars or train them, were overwhelmingly important.[35]

Not the least of the problems confronted by those seeking to register poor people and minorities was the lack of interest evinced by the Mondale campaign, which put less than $6 million of the $15 million it promised into voter registration. The campaign also failed to target efficiently what money it did spend. Many of Jesse Jackson's supporters charged that the Democratic party failed to register voters in 1984 because of fears by party officials that this would only aid Jackson four years down the road in 1988.

In contrast, the Republican party poured $11 million into voter registration campaigns in 1984. The GOP utilized computers, phone banks, analysis of census data and mailing lists from upper-class–oriented magazines and catalogs to target unregistered voters who were likely Reagan supporters. Republicans expected the conservative Christian community to register at least two million voters on its own.[36] By November, the GOP could report an exact count on how many new voters it had registered: 4,036,378.[37] At the same time, attempts to institutionalize voter registration in welfare and other social service agencies met with stiff resistance from Republicans, including a court challenge in New York State.[38] (Registration in public agencies was allowed, though not necessarily encouraged, in eighteen states by 1988.)

Groups supporting President Reagan spent $30 million on registration drives. Approximately 40,000 churches in the Moral Majority network were mobilized for the effort. In its letter to local conservative activists the National Conservative Political Action Committee warned, "even now as you read my letter, Jesse Jackson and Big Labor are leading a massive liberal democratic drive to register 3 to 5 million new voters. They may be trying to register many voters in your area." Americans for Responsible Government raised $2 million in tax-exempt donations, half of which went to the El Cajon (California) American Coalition for Traditional Values, which in turn organized a voter registration drive in conservative California churches.

The American Defense Foundation mobilized military personnel, anti-gun control forces, and anti-abortion groups. In Illinois, Rotary Club and Chamber of Commerce members offered to be deputized as registrars to help GOP registration efforts. In 1983, the California GOP offered to pay $1 for each newly registered voter to any county or Republican organization that set up a registration drive. In June 1984, the party paid an independent company to register Republicans at $1.75 each. Democrats joined the bounty-hunting game, although they offered only $1.20 for each new voter. They expected to be outspent three to one by the GOP.[39]

There were few registration drives in the 1988 elections, except on behalf of one candidate, Jesse Jackson. In the primary season Jackson's supporters tried to recruit new poor, working-class, and minority voters. No other candidates for the Democratic party apparently felt that expanding the size of the electorate would benefit them. After securing the nomination, Michael Dukakis's handlers evidently felt the same. Despite early promises to spend $5 million to register new voters, the National Democratic Committee spent only a little more than $2 million.

In contrast to 1984, voter registration drives of all kinds attracted little attention and few resources in 1988. Independent groups found that financial support had all but dried up: Foundations contributed a total of $3.5 million to the drives in 1988, compared to $5 million four years earlier.[40] Perhaps because groups that would benefit the Democrats were less active, the GOP and conservative groups also cut back their efforts. The Republicans spent about $2 million for voter registration efforts, compared to almost $11 million in 1984.[41] The overall effect of sharply reduced voter registration drives translated into lower registration levels. A survey by the Committee for the Study of the American Electorate found that 70.9 percent of eligible voters were registered for the 1988 presidential election, compared to 73.1 percent in 1984.[42] The decline for self-identified Democrats was far steeper than for Republicans. Democratic registration fell in thirteen states and increased in only two. In the South, the registration of blacks dropped by 0.5 percent, but rose 0.2 percent for whites.[43]

Efforts by interest groups to bring new voters into the electoral system cannot substitute for new registration laws that would make it easier for voters to get onto the rolls—or registration procedures that, as in several other nations, might put the burden for registration on the government rather than on individual citizens. Two bills have been introduced in Congress that would fundamentally change registration procedures. The Universal Voter Registration Act would impose day-of-election and mail-in registration on all states and require state and local governmental agencies that receive federal funds to help people register. Another bill would require the states to couple voter registration with drivers' license applications.[44] It has been suggested that if the government took responsibility for registering voters, registration would rise by as much as fourteen percentage points.[45] Leaving voter registration efforts to independent partisan groups makes registration, and turnout on election day, into an overtly partisan process.

What If the Electorate Were Mobilized?

The stability of American electoral politics depends, to a considerable degree, on low participation. Hurdles to registration potentially deter all voters, but some are more handicapped than others. The potential impact if current nonvoters were brought into the electorate can be understood by observing that the present electorate is disproportionately made up of higher-income voters.

This pattern has become more accentuated election by election since the 1960s. Though turnout has declined for all income and occupational groups, the drop for lower income and lower occupation voters has been steepest: 83 percent of white-collar voters went to the polls in 1968, but 78 percent did so in 1980. But for blue-collar workers, turnout in the same period fell from 59 percent to 45 percent. The difference in participation rates between white-collar and blue-collar voters thus widened from 24 percent in 1968 to 33 percent by 1980.[46]

The skewed pattern of turnout heavily favors the Republicans. Democrats have historically relied on the poorest third of the electorate and on blue-collar workers and union members. There are distinct differences between Democratic and Republican voters. Studies of voters exiting the polls in the 1988 presidential election showed that for the 1980, 1984, and 1988 elections, the Republican vote was very closely related to the family income of voters. Thirty-seven percent of voters from families making less than $12,500 a year voted for George Bush in 1988 (compared to 45 percent for Reagan in 1984). But 62 percent of voters from families with incomes over $50,000 cast their votes for Bush.[47]

In 1983, Kevin Phillips, a conservative writer, sounded the alarm that a mobilization of poorer and minority voters could threaten Republican electoral gains. He based his view on the fact that the group composition of the electorate is not representative of American society as a whole:

> The American electorate is disproportionately white and prosperous. Blacks constitute 11 percent of the national population, but cast only 7 percent of the

total ballots in 1980. Hispanic turnout rates are even lower. One can reasonably suggest that the economic bottom third of the country cast only 20-25 percent of the total vote, while the top third cast perhaps 40-45 percent. This is a much greater imbalance than exists in any other major Western industrial nation, and could easily begin to change as the effects of...a conservative-dominated zero-sum economics [in which upper-strata groups prosper at the expense of lower-strata groups] become fully felt. To protect transfer payments and government spending programs, low-income and minority turnout has the potential to surge. These voters could come to the polls to protest conservative economic policies tailored to redistribute income toward upper rather than lower income groups. Of all the trends that will affect the 1980s, this could be the most important.[48]

The potential impact of voter turnout by various groups is particularly obvious in the case of blacks, in part because significant participation by blacks has been possible in the South only since the mid-1960s. The manipulation of registration and turnout is a standard feature of the American electoral system. For black voters, such manipulation has historically been, and continues to be, especially transparent.

The Twenty-Fourth Amendment to the Constitution, adopted in 1964, eliminated the poll tax and literacy tests in both primary and general elections. A year later, Congress enacted the Voting Rights Act, which for the first time since 1876 returned federal registrars to southern states to protect blacks' right to vote. Southern counties where less than half of the voting age population was registered, or where less than half the electorate had voted in the 1964 presidential election, were subject to scrutiny by federal registrars and poll watchers. In 1970, Congress extended the Voting Rights Act (but also removed provisions allowing federal examiners to register voters) by making the 50 percent triggering clause applicable to all states rather than exclusively to the southern states known to have a notorious history of racial discrimination. Federal officials were now sent to counties in several nonsouthern states, including Arizona, Wyoming, New York, and Michigan, to oversee registration of African Americans and Hispanics.[49]

Beginning in 1961, the Student Non-Violent Coordinating Committee (SNCC) mobilized black voters in Macomb, Mississippi. SNCC and the Southern Christian Leadership Conference organized the Mississippi Summer Project in 1964. These and other activities helped bring about the Voting Rights Act the next year. Following passage of the Voting Rights bill, the Voter Education Project sent hundreds of young adults into southern states to register blacks. By 1967, the percentage of blacks registered to vote in eleven southern states had risen to 54 percent, up from 35.5 percent in 1960. In Mississippi, the state with the nation's highest percentage of African-American residents, registration by blacks rose to 60 percent, up from less than 7 percent in 1960. A study of five states where selective counties were subject to federal intervention found that registration of blacks increased from 11 percent to 61 percent in the counties with federal oversight, but in counties that were not subject to federal intervention, registration rose more modestly from 30 percent to 52.5 percent.[50]

Turnout patterns were affected by the increased registration of blacks. The Voter Education Project estimated that two-thirds of southern blacks voted in 1980, and they gave 90 percent of their votes to Jimmy Carter. African-American voters provided Carter's margin of victory in many states in 1976.[51] Outside the South, registration and turnout rates also climbed. By the 1984 election, the percentage of blacks registered nationally exceeded the percentage for whites (73% to 72%) for the first time ever.[52] The increase in black voters, however, also served as a catalyst to drive up registration by whites, especially in Alabama and Mississippi, where by 1970 the percentage of registered whites rose to 90 percent and 91.5 percent, up from 1960 rates of 69 percent and 70 percent, respectively.[53]

The most obvious effect of increased voter participation by blacks has been a dramatic rise in the number of public offices held by blacks. Before 1965, there were fewer than one-hundred elected black officials in the South. By 1982 this number had risen to 2,601, and by the end of the decade there were more than 3,000 black officials. Blacks have been elected mayors in such major cities as Atlanta, Detroit, Los Angeles, New Orleans, Newark, Washington, D.C., and Chicago. In 1989 black mayors won in New York City, Seattle, and New Haven, and a black governor was elected in Virginia.

In the 1984 presidential election, turnout by black voters reached 56 percent, compared to an overall national voter turnout of 53 percent. For the first time, a black presidential candidate carried a campaign to the Democratic party convention. When Jesse Jackson made his second run for the presidency in 1988, blacks turned out in unprecedented numbers in the primaries, exceeding 70 percent in most southern states. In the general election, however, turnout for blacks plummeted to new lows, helping to account for turnout rates of 36.9 percent in the District of Columbia, 38 percent in Georgia, 38.4 percent in South Carolina—in fact, turnout of less than 45 percent in all but two southern states (it was 45.5% in Alabama).[54]

African-American voting power is seriously diluted by the "race-conscious" electoral behavior of whites. Blacks are accustomed to voting for white candidates, but whites are extremely sensitive to the presence of a black candidate. One study showed that in the twenty-two Democratic primaries held in 1988, an increase of 1 percent in the percentage of black voters was associated with a decline of 1 percent of white voters who supported Jackson.[55] Biracial electoral coalitions are very difficult to build and this has been the case at least since blacks joined the Democratic party in large numbers in the 1930s.[56] This is one reason why Dukakis's handlers refused to participate in an aggressive voter registration drive advocated by Jesse Jackson, and this reticence was almost certainly responsible for low turnout by blacks on behalf of Dukakis.

In the South, white voters have defected from the Democratic to the Republican party in droves. In 1937, 78 percent of whites in the southern states identified themselves as Democrats. This percentage fell to 56 percent by 1960, but Republicans still constituted only 21 percent of the southern electorate. By 1984, white desertion from the Democratic party in the South reached the point that the party's advantage had narrowed to eight percentage points (37% to 29%). The declining Democratic prospects have been even more evident in presidential elections than these numbers might suggest. Forty-seven percent of southern whites voted for Jimmy Carter in 1976, compared to 35 percent in 1980. Only 28 percent voted for Mondale in 1984, and 32 percent for Dukakis in 1988. The southern white vote for Democratic congressional candidates slid from 60 percent in 1976 to 38 percent by 1984.[57]

These changes have occurred, in part, because of a specific strategy by Republican candidates to attract white southern votes. This "Southern Strategy" was first developed by advisers for Barry Goldwater's 1964 presidential campaign, but it was more effectively implemented by Richard Nixon in 1968 and 1972, and again by Ronald Reagan's supporters in the 1980s. Most analysts have been reluctant to classify the new Republican appeal as racist, yet it is obvious that GOP candidates have been playing on white fear of African-American political power, and sometimes their approach has been less than subtle. At a stop in Macon, Georgia, during the 1984 campaign, President Reagan used the traditional segregationist cry, "The South will rise again," in justifying his advocacy of the line-item veto, and he approvingly invoked the name of Jefferson Davis, leader of the Confederacy.[58] In 1988, the Republicans deftly used the crime issue as a surrogate for race by advertising Willie Horton's crimes.

Rising electoral influence by blacks stimulated deliberate efforts to disenfranchise poor and minority voters, and ironically the Voting Rights Act was employed for this purpose. Edwin Meese, Reagan's attorney general, invoked the 1965 Voting Rights Act to prosecute southern registrars who were too vigorously recruiting black voters (they were accused of accepting illegal absentee ballots). In a similar vein, in 1981 New Jersey Republicans hired off-duty policemen and stationed them, armed, with official-looking insignia, at polling places located in black neighborhoods, which prompted a lawsuit by the Democrats.

In the fall of 1986, the Republican National Committee launched a coordinated strategy to challenge black voters in Louisiana. A Chicago firm, "Ballot Integrity," was hired to send out 350,000 first-class letters with "Don't Forward" on them to eleven heavily Democratic districts with large numbers of blacks. The addresses of returned letters were then turned over to the state GOP, which filed 30,000 challenges, the overwhelming majority of them against blacks. In response to a Democratic lawsuit, a federal judge issued an injunction against the plan, calling it "an insidious scheme to remove blacks from the rolls." Republicans had been planning to implement the scheme in five more states before their project was unmasked.[59] It goes without saying that the GOP planned no comparable schemes to check registration in white neighborhoods.

Although Democrats fought these tactics in the courts, they hardly had their own house in order. As voting power by blacks increased, changes were adopted to limit its impact in Democratic primaries and caucuses. In Missouri, for example, party officials had been at loggerheads for years over proposals to replace the caucus system with a primary. The Jackson phenomena in 1984 helped put the pro-primary forces over the top when party regulars saw blacks flood into caucuses in north St. Louis and parts of Kansas City in support of their candidate.

Aggregated to the national level, it seems certain that voter registration drives have had little effect on competition between the two parties. But the registration of blacks, coupled with their high turnout rates in some elections, have exerted a dramatic impact on party competition in some congressional districts, especially in the South, and in northern cities where blacks comprise a large proportion of the population. The 1983 mayoral race in Chicago is at once a case study of how turnout can be affected by the stakes and the degree of competition in an election, and of the potency of racism in American electoral politics. When black Democratic Congressman Harold Washington defeated incumbent Mayor Jane Byrne and Richard M. Daley (the son of the late machine boss Mayor Richard J. Daley) in the Democratic party primary, Washington proclaimed to a black rally, "It's our turn now." He claimed the quote was taken out of context, but in any case the suggestion that the mayor might reward his supporters and direct more city services and contracts to African-Americans should not have been shocking in a city accustomed to machine politics.

Immediately following the primary, eight of fifty Democratic ward committeemen did something that would have been unthinkable in any other circumstance. They switched their support to the Republican candidate, millionaire Bernard Epton. Epton alluded to Washington's remark with his campaign slogan, "Epton, before it's too late." The underlying racism of the campaign was made manifest when some Epton supporters wore buttons with watermelon drawings and sang campaign songs to the tune of "Bye-Bye, Blackbird." As the campaign progressed, Washington saw his lead steadily shrink. It became clear that he would need 15 percent of the white vote, which he expected to derive from the affluent white liberal wards along the lakefront, and also that he would need a massive turnout by blacks. Speaking to one African-American audience, the mayoral candidate pleaded, "If you don't vote, I don't make it. Momma, don't let anybody stay home on Tuesday. If that man don't vote, don't let him put his foot under that table. And you young people...you know Momma's tired. But remind her, too....Do it firmly, but gently. Get out there and vote."[60]

Washington won with 52 percent of the vote, composed of more than 90 percent of the black and more than half the Hispanic vote. He received 18 percent of the white vote. Eighty-five percent of the city's electorate went to the polls, an astonishing turnout for a municipal election, and unprecedented in Chicago. Almost 150,000 new voters participated. A newspaper columnist asserted,

> Now *this* is participation! Chicago in 1983 was a political system in which whites thought they could lose something they valued, whereas blacks believed they could gain something of value. Both whites and blacks believed that their participation would make a difference, and that the political game itself was far from trivial.[61]

Washington's allies won control of the city council when he was reelected in 1987. He was consolidating his political power at the time of his death in December 1987.

The Ideological Bias of Low Participation

The comparative study of election systems suggests that turnout is related to the nature of the party system. One study compared the level of electoral participation by citizens from lower social and economic strata in several countries to the degree of activity in the United States. It found that less affluent groups were twice as active in campaigns in Austria than in the United States; two to seven times more active in Japan; and five to twenty times more active in the Netherlands.[62]

Many nations with higher turnout rates use proportional representation systems, which in principle means that parties are awarded legislative seats "proportionate" to the percentage of the vote they receive in the election. Thus, even parties winning only 5 percent of the vote typically send members to Parliament. In contrast, the winner-take-all method used in the United States nearly ensures that a vote cast for a new party will be wasted, in the sense that even a sizable proportion of votes, such as 25 percent, will not send anyone to Congress or to a state legislature. Studies of elections in the American states show that the degree of competition between parties is a major factor is determining voter turnout,[63] suggesting that a system of representation that would increase party competition would also increase turnout. An electoral system that facilitated the organization of new parties would presumably have the same effect.

It may seem contradictory, but studies show that more voters in the United States have firm loyalties to a political party than do voters in Europe. It is important, however, to distinguish identification with a political party from the function that parties serve in presenting policy options. Voters more frequently change loyalties to parties in Europe than in the United States, in part because there are a larger number of parties arrayed on a broader ideological spectrum in Europe.[64] Voters in European nations are presented with a much larger range of options on election day.

Consider, for example, two leaders of the right and left wings of the two parties in the U.S. Senate: Republican Jesse Helms and Democrat Ted Kennedy. A right wing exists in Europe that corresponds to Helms's position in the United States. But in the Western European political context, Kennedy would at best qualify as a moderate leader in one of the labor-based parties, like the Social Democratic parties of Germany, Britain, or Scandinavia. He would find himself outflanked on the left by several large Communist parties, the German Green party, most of Britain's Labor party, the Greek Socialists, and several other small parties. The parties on the left mobilize voters who otherwise might not participate in elections at all. It is clear that the Democratic party in the United States does not fulfill this function:

> The Democratic party is not remotely to be confused with a left party in organizational structure, or in terms of serious motivation to mobilize the 'party of nonvoters'. Accordingly, the party of nonvoters as a whole corresponds comparatively to the place...that a genuinely left party would occupy if it had been historically possible to organize it in this country.[65]

The United States is the only major industrialized country that does not have an influential socialist party. Ideological competition in electoral politics is almost nonexistent in comparison to other Western democracies. From the perspective of political elites, however, this is an entirely good thing because a higher level of competition in the electoral arena, especially if it involved significant ideological debate, might threaten control by the few.

Why Elites Prefer Low Participation

Pessimism about participation by the masses in the political life of the nation did not end with the Progressive reformers. The belief that democracy survives best when participation is carefully regulated has survived to the present day. There are plenty of contemporary advocates for the idea that eligibility to vote should be tied to a demonstration of responsibility or worthiness. Consider, for example, the argument advanced by some politicians who oppose the idea of registering people in social services agencies instead of requiring them to go to designated sites on their own. Carl F. Gnodtke, a Republican member of the Michigan House of Representatives, said in 1984: "Someone like that would have more free time to do that than a working individual....I think it would mean more to the individual, too, [if] they had to do something a little extra to be eligible to vote. Anything you get for nothing, you take for granted."[66]

Liberals tend to view voting as a device to channel participation and to keep it manageable. In the 1960s, the civil rights movement and Vietnam War preoccupied many politically active young people. Liberal politicians paraded before a congressional committee in 1968 to testify that the vote should be extended to eighteen-year-olds, several of them arguing that the advocates of civil disobedience on campus "would find themselves with little or no support if students were given a more meaningful role." Students needed the "right to make a positive choice as an alternative to a negative protest"; in the absence of an acceptable outlet, student energy might "dam up and burst and follow less-than-wholesome channels"; they might even "join the more militant minority of their fellow students and engage in destructive activities of a dangerous nature."[67] The National Student Association favored extending the franchise to eighteen-year-olds, but there were no demonstrations or campaigns organized by youth to get the vote. Still, a constitutional amendment went through to lower the voting age.

If conservatives are concerned that the riffraff might disturb politics as usual, liberals evidently fear that if enough people do not vote, they may express themselves politically in more dangerous ways. The view that abstention poses a threat to democracy has been eloquently stated by Arthur Hadley, in an aptly titled book, *The Empty Polling Booth*:

> As there is a critical mass of nuclear material necessary to trigger an atomic explosion so there appears to be a critical percentage of nonvoters necessary to produce rapid political change. Historically that percentage has been close to the 50 percent we now approach. They sit out there, the great mass of refrainers, disconnected from the process of democracy, but able at any moment to dominate our future. Our future is their future. To start them back now as

voters is important. Not because our country will necessarily be governed better if they return, but because their growing presence menaces any government.[68]

When the question is posed about whether low voter turnout is problematic or not, one's answer will depend on whether elections are viewed as instruments of elite control or as the means by which citizens control their government. In treating this issue, the authors of a leading college textbook on American government assert that all forms of apathy among the masses are a good thing:

> The irony of democracy is that democratic ideals survive because authoritarian masses are generally apathetic and inactive. Thus the lower classes' capacity for intolerance, authoritarianism, scape-goatism, racism, and violence seldom translates into organized, sustained political movements.

The authors' fear of popular participation is founded on a belief that formal education, and possibly some other characteristics that elites share (they are not clear on this point), make them more protective of individual freedoms than the common citizen. They assert that *democracy requires that the masses not participate* very much:

> Reflecting the masses' antidemocratic, extremist, hateful, and violence-prone sentiments, [their] activism seriously threatens democratic values....Any genuine "peoples revolution" in America would undoubtedly take the form of a right-wing nationalist, patriotic, religious-fundamentalist, antiblack, anti-intellectual, antistudent, "law and order" movement.

They regard as "demagogues those leaders who would mobilize the people," and claim, "Elites give greater support to democratic values than do masses. Elites are also more consistent than masses in applying general principles of democracy to specific individuals, groups, and events."[69]

In a similar vein, during the 1970s a prominent international group of business leaders, politicians, and intellectuals associated with the Trilateral Commission expressed a conviction that capitalist countries are better off when citizens refrain from or are discouraged from extensive participation.[70] The events of the 1960s and early 1970s unsettled political and economic leaders. The Trilateralists feared that rising demands from unions, consumers, minorities, women, and environmentalists had created a "crisis of governability" in Western democracies and in Japan. They warned that the American, Western European, and Japanese political systems would not be able to satisfy all of the demands placed on them. They urged that steps be taken to reduce these demands by concentrating more power in governmental institutions.

Throughout American history, elites have tended to become alarmed when mass participation in politics has reached "excessive" levels. During such times, elites have initiated reforms to reduce and channel participation. In the case of electoral reforms, the result has been to turn elections into legitimating devices for elite control. The electoral process in the United States has progressively lost its historic functions of mobilizing new groups into the political system and creating broad-based coalitions of diverse political interests. Legitimacy, however, cannot be divorced from

these purposes. When elections become little more than occasions for elite manipulation, they may even fail to confer legitimacy, because the political community may
itself be weakened:

> It...seems plausible that low participation and voter apathy may damage social
> cohesion in American life. The democratic political system is supposed to bind
> citizens, communities, and social groups together. Choosing not to participate
> in the common activity of governance weakens those ties.[71]

Consultants to the Trilateral Commission like political scientist Samuel
Huntington walk a fine line when they advocate lower levels of participation because
above all they want ruling elites to be blessed with the aura of legitimacy—but not
at the cost of accountability.

Notes

1. William H. Hartley and William S. Vincent, *American Civics,* 4th ed. (New York: Harcourt
Brace Jovanovich, 1983), p. 229.
2. League of Women Voters, *Is Politics Your Job?* (Washington D.C., 1966), p. 12.
3. Murray Edelman, *The Symbolic Uses of Politics* (Urbana: University of Illinois, 1964), p. 3.
4. "Moving Right Along? Campaign '84's Lessons for 1988," *Public Opinion* (December-
January 1985), p. 8.
5. Thomas E. Cronin, "The Presidential Election of 1984," pp. 57-59, and Walter Dean
Burnham, "The 1984 Elections and the Future of American Politics," pp. 212-232, in *Election
84, Landslide Without a Mandate?* ed. Ellis Sandoz and Cecil V. Crabb, Jr., (New York: New
American Library, 1985).
6. George Washington to Henry Knox, letter, December 26, 1786, in *The Writings of George
Washington* ed. John C. Fitzpatrick (Washington, D.C.: U.S. Government Printing Office,
1939), p. 122.
7. Page Smith, *The Constitution: A Documentary and Narrative History* (New York: Morrow,
1978), pp. 71-85; David P. Szatmary, *Shays' Rebellion: The Making of an American Insurrection* (Amherst, Mass.: University of Massachusetts Press, 1980).
8. Joseph L. Davis, *Sectionalism in American Politics,* 1774-1787 (Madison, Wis.: University
of Wisconsin Press, 1977), pp. 151-152.
9. All three quotes are cited in Arthur T. Hadley, *The Empty Polling Booth* (Englewood Cliffs,
N.J.: Prentice-Hall, 1978), p. 53.
10. Ibid., pp. 19-22. On expansion of the suffrage in the United States, see William J. Crotty,
Political Reform and the American Experiment (New York: Thomas Y. Crowell, 1977),
pp. 11-16; and Howard Zinn, *A People's History of the United States* (New York: Harper &
Row, 1980), pp. 76-101 and 206-219.
11. Crotty, *Political Reform and the American Experiment,* p. 7.
12. Frances Fox Piven and Richard A. Cloward, *Why Americans Don't Vote* (New York:
Pantheon, 1988), p. 85.
13. Walter Dean Burnham, "The System of 1896: An Analysis," in *The Evolution of American
Electoral Systems* ed. Paul Kleppner et al., (Westport, Conn.: Greenwood Press, 1981), table 1,
p. 100.
14. See V. O. Key, *Southern Politics* (New York: Alfred A. Knopf, 1949), pp. 533-643, on
how this was accomplished. On post-bellum social and economic practices and their relation-

ship to politics, see C. Vann Woodward, *The Strange Career of Jim Crow* (New York: Oxford University Press, 1957) and *Reunion and Reaction: The Compromise of 1877 and the End of Reconstruction* (Boston: Little, Brown, 1966).

15. J. Morgan Kousser, *The Shaping of Southern Politics: Suffrage Restriction and the Establishment of the One Party South, 1880-1910* (New Haven: Yale University Press, 1974), p. 64.

16. W. A. Dunning, "The Undoing of Reconstruction," *Atlantic Monthly* 88 (1901), p. 443, as cited in Piven and Cloward, *Why Americans Don't Vote*, p. 81.

17. Kevin P. Phillips and Paul H. Blackman, *Electoral Reform and Voter Participation* (Stanford: American Enterprise Institute and the Hoover Institution on War, Revolution, and Peace, 1975), p. 8; as cited in Piven and Cloward, *Why Americans Don't Vote*, p. 82.

18. Ibid., pp. 31-32.

19. Crotty, *Political Reform*, p. 30.

20. Key, *Southern Politics*, pp. 542-543, and footnotes, p. 543.

21. Norman H. Clark, *Deliver Us from Evil: An Interpretation of American Prohibition* (New York: W. W. Norton, 1976).

22. Hadly, *Empty Polling Booth*, p. 61.

23. Samuel Haber, *Efficiency and Uplift: Scientific Management in the Progressive Era, 1890-1920* (Chicago: University of Chicago Press, 1964), pp. 99-101.

24. Walter Dean Burnham, *The Current Crisis in American Politics* (New York: Oxford University Press, 1982), p. 87.

25. League of Women Voters, *Obstacles to Voting* (Washington, D.C.: 1972), p. 5.

26. Crotty, *Political Reform*, p. 60.

27. John Trinkl, "Not a Million More Oct. 4, But Still New Voters, *The Guardian* (New York), October 17, 1984, p. 3.

28. Peverill Squire, Raymond E. Wolfinger, and David P. Gloss, "Residential Mobility and Voter Turnout," *American Political Science Review* (March 1987), also cited in Piven and Cloward, *Why Americans Don't Vote*, p. 179.

29. Piven and Cloward, *Why Americans Don't Vote*, p. 179.

30. Akinshiju C. Ola, "Left Foot, Right Foot, For Voter Registration," *The Guardian*, September 19, 1984, p. 5.

31. Piven and Cloward, *Why Americans Don't Vote*, p. 179.

32. Ibid.

33. Ibid., p. 180.

34. See Ola, "Left Foot," Trinkl, "Not a Million," p. 3, Trinkl, "What if They Held an Election and Everybody Came," *The Guardian*, September 19, 1984, p. 3, J. Rogers, "The Politics of Voter Registration," *The Nation*, July 21, 1984, p. 33.

35. Joan Walsh, "The Numbers Game," *In These Times*, September 26-August 3, 1984, p. 8.

36. "How Republicans Trumped the Democrats' Ace," *National Journal*, October 20, 1984, p. 1971. Maxwell Glen, "Republicans and Democrats Battling to Raise Big Bucks for Voter Drives," *National Journal*, September 1, 1984, pp. 1618-1622.

37. Ann Cooper, "Voter Turnout May be Higher on Nov. 6, but for the Parties It May Be a Wash," *National Journal*, November 3, 1984, p. 2072.

38. Ibid., p. 2073.

39. Glen, "Republicans and Democrats Battling to Raise Big Bucks," pp. 1620-1621. "How Republicans Trumped...," p. 1971.

40. Bill Lambrecht, "Sign-Up of Voters Suffering," *St. Louis Post Dispatch*, September 23, 1988, p. 1, 20A.

41. Ibid.

42. Richard L. Berke, "Study Finds Marked Drop in Voter Registration Since '84," *New York Times,* November 4, 1988.

43. Ibid.

44. Frances Fox Piven and Richard A. Cloward, "National Voter Registration Reform: How It Might Be Won," *PS: Political Science and Politics* (Fall 1988): 868-875.

45. Ruy Teixeira, "Will the Real Non Voter Please Stand Up?" *Public Opinion* (July-August 1988): 44.

46. Thomas Byrne Edsall, *The New Politics of Inequality* (New York: W.W. Norton, 1984), pp. 184-185.

47. *New York Times*/CBS News Poll, November 10, 1988 *(New York Times,* November 10, 1988, p. 18).

48. Kevin P. Phillips, *Post-Conservative America: People, Politics and Ideology in a Time of Crisis* (New York: Random House, 1983), p. 103; cited in Piven and Cloward, *Why Americans Don't Vote,* pp. 212-213.

49. Crotty, *Political Reform,* p. 8.

50. Ibid., pp. 61-67.

51. Richard Hudlin and K. Farouk Brimah, *What Happened in the South, 1980* (Atlanta: Voter Education Project, 1981).

52. *National Journal,* August 18, 1984, p. 1598.

53. Crotty, *Political Reform,* p. 64.

54. *New York Times,* November 10, 1988, p. 24.

55. Manning Marable, "Racism Pervades Campaign '88," *The Guardian,* September 21, 1988, p. 2.

56. Robert Huckfeldt and Carol Kohfeld, *Race and the Decline of Class in American Politics* (Urbana: University of Illinois Press, 1989).

57. Various poll results reported in *Public Opinion* (December-January 1985), p. 34.

58. Akinshiju C. Ola, "Racism Won Big in the Elections," *The Guardian* (November 28, 1984), p. 1.

59. Matthew Cooper, "Beware of Republicans Bearing Voting Rights Suits," *Washington Monthly* (February 1987): 11-15. John Judis, "Campaigning for Republican 'Black Out'," *In These Times,* October 15-21, 1986, p. 6.

60. Quoted in Nicholas Henry and John Stuart Hall, *Reconsidering American Politics* (Boston: Allyn & Bacon, 1985), p. 56.

61. Ibid., p. 57.

62. A key study here, covering not only Europe and the United States but thirty liberal democracies in all, is G. Bingham Powell, Jr., "Voting Turnout in Thirty Democracies: Partisan, Legal and Socio-Economic Influences," in *Electoral Participation: A Comparative Analysis,* ed. Richard Rose (London: Sage, 1980); also reprinted in Niemi and Weisberg, *Controversies in Voting Behavior,* pp. 34-53.

63. Two studies that relate degree of party competition to voter turnout across states and districts within the United States are: Stanley Kelley, Jr., Richard E. Ayres, and William G. Bowen, "Registration and Voting: Putting First Things First," *American Political Science Review* 61 (1967): 359-379; and Jae-on Kim, John R. Petrocik, and Stephen N. Knokson, "Voter Turnout Among the American States: Systemic and Individual Components," *American Political Science Review* 69 (1975): 107-123.

64. On the importance of ideology and the left-right dimension in other systems, see Annick Percheron and M. Kent Jennings, "Political Continuities in French Families: A New Perspective on an Old Controversy," *Comparative Politics* 13 (1981): 421-436, reprinted in Niemi and Weisberg, *Controversies in Voting Behavior,* pp. 377-389. Niemi and Weisberg summarize

and cite some of the relevant literature on ideology and the instability of party identification among European voters on p. 395.

65. Burnham, *Current Crisis,* p. 188.

66. Quoted in Ann Cooper, "GOP and Democrats Split over Public Agencies Signing Up the Poor to Vote," *National Journal of Politics* (June 6, 1984): 1176.

67. Quoted in Benjamin Ginsberg, *The Consequences of Consent: Elections, Citizen and Popular Acquiescence* (Reading, Mass.: Addison Wesley, 1982), pp. 11-12.

68. Hadley, *Empty Polling Booth,* p. 126.

69. Thomas Dye and L. Harmon Zeigler, *The Irony of Democracy: An Uncommon Introduction to American Politics* (Belmont, Calif.: Wadsworth, 1984), pp. 130-133, 135.

70. Michael Crozier, Samuel Huntington, and Joji Watanuke, *The Crisis of Democracy* (New York: New York University Press, 1975).

71. Teixera, "Will the Real Non Voter Please Stand Up?" p. 44.

Chapter 6

Political Discourse and the Electorate

Two Views of Elections

In a representative democracy, it is assumed that elections keep government and elites responsive to the popular will, broadly expressed. A two-party system, if nothing else, is supposed to ensure that elections produce a general majoritarian mandate for government policies. The civics textbook interpretation of the two-party system affirms that this is how American elections work:

> This *two-party system,* as we'll call it, has worked remarkably well. When one party fails to please a majority of voters, there is another strong party ready to take over. The newly elected party often tries different programs and policies in dealing with the nation's problems.[1]

In contrast to this view is the oft-repeated phrase that the Democratic and Republican parties are like Tweedle-dum and Tweedle-dee, impossible to tell apart. This view was given creative expression by self-styled "Gonzo" journalist Hunter S. Thompson, who covered the 1972 presidential election for *Rolling Stone* magazine. Thompson followed George McGovern's campaign for the Democratic nomination, which had mobilized thousands of previously inactive young people. On the strength of the youth movement's ability to deliver caucus and primary votes, McGovern wrested the nomination from the party's establishment powerbrokers. But as election day neared, Thompson felt that McGovern was abandoning the youth movement in a bid to gain support from politicians, the media, and wealthy donors. Awaiting the Nixon landslide, Thompson asked:

> How many more of these stinking, double-downer sideshows will we have to go through before we can get ourselves straight enough to put together some kind of national election that will give me and at least 20 million people I tend to agree with a chance to vote for something, instead of always being faced with that old familiar choice between the lesser of two evils?[2]

For elections to go beyond the "lesser of two evils," or for elections to reveal a popular mandate for government policies, at least four conditions must be met: (1)

voters must have clear alternatives from which to choose; (2) voters must be concerned with issues and interested in influencing future policies of government; (3) majority preferences must be ascertainable in the results; and (4) elected officials must feel bound enough by public preferences to carry out the appropriate policies.[3]

Do American elections commonly meet these criteria? In this chapter we focus on the first three of these four criteria—the party system and the character of the electorate, which have been the subject of intense scrutiny by political scientists for almost forty years. Until recently, almost all of this research has described voters as remarkably uninformed about candidates and issues to such a degree that elections could not be said to reflect much more than an emotional response from an ignorant electorate. Many political scientists believe that through their apathy, political ignorance, and contradictory opinions, voters have, in effect, voluntarily handed over control of the political system to elites. In their view, voters are normally unable to follow the debate even when parties and candidates express clearly divergent policy alternatives. If unqualified candidates and unpopular policies sometimes result from such a context, the voting public gets what it deserves.

Recently, this image has been challenged by new research that shows a more complex understanding of the interaction among political parties, candidates, the media and the electorate, the most important being the way political choices are limited and articulated by candidates and the media. Voters are far more rational and well informed than previously thought, despite the nature of election campaigns, which seem efficiently intended to place strict constraints on the range of issues injected into political debates. Though the media must share responsibility for this state of affairs, the two-party system is a crucial means for ensuring that elections will be run within a narrowly defined public discourse. It isn't so much that the voters get what they deserve; elites go to considerable lengths to guarantee that they can get nothing else.

How Ignorant Is the American Electorate?

Voter survey research conducted in the 1950s by political scientists at the University of Michigan would have shaken the faith of anyone who believed in popular democracy. A study published in 1960 under the title *The American Voter* reported that only 18 percent to 36 percent of the electorate were familiar with issues, knew the current government policy on key issues, and perceived differences in the positions adopted by the two parties. Most people voted on the basis of party loyalty, not knowledge of political issues. Issues were less important than candidate personality.[4] The image of the "rational" voter, who like the consumer in the marketplace assesses the relative costs and benefits of various alternative "products," was replaced in the scholarly literature by the image of a passive, uninformed dolt, blindly voting the party line without benefit of political awareness. A whole generation of political scientists (including the authors of this book) were trained to accept and to teach this interpretation.

Studies conducted at Columbia University in the late 1940s and reported in

The People's Choice showed that voters often made up their minds before campaigns even began.[5] Issues seemed to be almost irrelevant. In the 1948 election, for example, the Democratic party made opposition to the Taft-Hartley Act, a measure that weakened unions and limited the right to strike, a central component of their campaign against the Republicans. Yet a third of the electorate indicated in November that they had not heard of the act, and an additional third expressed no opinion. In reviewing this literature a few years later, the authors of *The American Voter* concluded that "almost seven out of every ten adult Americans saw the curtain fall on the presidential election of 1948 without knowing whether Taft-Hartley was the name of a hero or a villain."[6]

In 1945, only 21 percent of the public could identify the Bill of Rights or any of its features. In 1954, 19 percent of survey research respondents could name the three branches of government by their generic names—executive, legislative, and judicial. And there has been little improvement over time. In 1978, 52 percent of survey respondents could identify both of their senators, but only 23 percent could accurately report that the Soviet Union and the United States were the two nations then involved in the Strategic Arms Limitation Treaty (SALT) talks.[7]

The authors of *The American Voter* conceded that voters are forced to take short cuts because it is impossible for anyone to gather all of the relevant and often conflicting information on political issues. They suggested that even sophisticated voters might appear to be ignorant on a wide range of issues but nevertheless still possess a consistent, integrated belief system. Defining as "ideological" those voters having opinions consistent enough to form an "elaborate, close-woven, and far-ranging structure of attitudes," the Michigan researchers expected that ideological voting would be a more widespread phenomenon than issue voting. But they found that only about 11 percent of the electorate seemed to choose on this basis. Forty-two percent of voters seemed to make decisions more on the basis of whether or not a candidate or party was "good" for a particular social group (for example, unionized workers). Twenty-four percent decided on the basis of whether they thought the economy was in good or in bad shape, and on the basis of which party they blamed for economic problems. And incredibly (to the researchers), for 22.5 percent of the electorate, loyalty to one party or the other seemed unrelated to any issue content.[8] Many people were Democrats or Republicans solely because that had been their parents' preference.

Over the years, the Michigan voter surveys have seemed to document a consistently dismal portrait of the electorate. The survey results show that few voters hold logically consistent opinions about issues. And voters appeared to be mercurial, changing opinions and attitudes frequently. Using surveys he administered through the Michigan Survey Center in 1956 and 1960, Philip Converse concluded that a majority of voters shifted positions on issues and changed their evaluation of candidates over very brief periods. He found that elites (people with higher status jobs, more education, and higher incomes) were more likely to hold consistent and stable attitudes than the public as a whole.[9]

These findings provide evidence to support a view that mass publics cannot be trusted and that elites constitute the stabilizing element in electoral politics. Despite their apparently impressive consistency, however, voter survey findings are subject to more than one interpretation. For example, why should people who vote on the basis of ideology be regarded as more sophisticated than those who decide on the basis of "group benefits"? Is a worker who believes that the Democratic party represents the interests of wage earners less ideological for this conviction? What about the businessman who believes that the Republicans represent business and that what is good for business is good for the country?

Even where interpretation is straightforward, survey results can be deceptive. Subtle variations in wording or in the types of responses required can drastically affect the profile of public opinion. The Michigan pollsters asked respondents to recall the names and political views of candidates and parties. It has been shown that far more voters are able to recognize the names of candidates when these are mentioned to them. Though voters may have difficulty ascribing a position on a particular issue to a candidate or officeholder, they often are able to identify the general ideological orientation of candidates and to make judgments about important personal characteristics related to their fitness for office.[10]

The Michigan surveys maximize the possibility of discovering voters' ignorance. The questionnaires ask respondents to identify and express knowledge about issues that already have been listed by the researchers, and they are asked to identify the positions of the candidates and parties on these issues. Believing that the issues considered important vary from individual to individual, one scholar instead asked respondents first to name "the most important problems" facing the federal government. He found that respondents could accurately perceive party differences on the issues they (not the researchers) regarded as important, and were as likely to have voted (in 1964) on the basis of issues as by reference to party.[11] For example, almost 80 percent of the voters for whom medical care for the aged was a major issue were able to identify one party or the other as more favorable to their position on health care, *but they were not necessarily similarly informed on other issues*. Only 5 percent of respondents cited this issue as important to them, but overall more than 60 percent of the public was able to discern party differences on nineteen of twenty-five issues they (not the pollster) identified as the "most important" public problems.

When we examine public perceptions about the "most important" issues, as indicated by surveys conducted between 1937 and 1976, it is obvious that the salience of public issues changes constantly (see table 6-1). Would this not be the case? It is hardly surprising that economic issues dominated the public's mind during the Great Depression. Between 1953 and 1968, the era of the Cold War, Cuban missile crisis, and the Vietnam War, foreign affairs emerged as the issue most frequently cited by respondents as the most important public problem. During the recession of the 1970s, economic issues again gained ascendancy in the public mind. In the late 1980s, after being inundated by a drumbeat of government and media hysteria about drugs, the public ranked drugs as the most important problem.

The public's familiarity with issues is sensitive to media coverage, government action, and political debate. Though in 1964 nearly two out of three voters

Table 6-1 **Voter Perceptions**

Public Perception of "Most Important" Issue Areas,
1937–1976

Issue Area	1937–1944	1945–1952	1953–1960	1961–1968	1969–1976
Economic issues	60%	45%	30%	13%	35%
Foreign affairs	35	38	50	50	23
Social and welfare	5	17	20	37	42

Source: Compiled from Gallup Poll data and presented in Pierce, *The Dynamics of Public Opinion* (Glenville, Ill.: Scott Foresman, 1982), p. 135.

answered "Don't Know" to the question "What should we do about the war in Vietnam?", this percentage quickly dropped to about 25 percent within one year and fell to 10 percent by 1970. The reason? Escalation and rising casualties in Vietnam, growing congressional opposition, mass protests, and media coverage converged to make the issue salient.

Not only are voters quite knowledgeable about the issues they consider to be most important to them, they tend to be much more consistent on issues that are closest to their religious and personal value systems. In 1976, for example, only 2 percent of the public expressed "No Opinion" on abortion, but 32 percent said they had no opinion to offer on foreign aid. When their views were compared to the opinion profile of 1972, considerable consistency was discovered on the abortion issue, but opinions about foreign aid had changed measurably.[12]

In recent years it has become fashionable to decry the rise of "single issue voting." There is little indication, however, that the electorate is normally polarized around any single issue. Just before the 1984 election, the *New York Times*/CBS News poll asked voters whether there was one issue so important "that you would change your vote because you disagreed with a candidate's position on that single issue." Twenty-five percent answered "Yes." Such a large block of the electorate certainly could swing an election, perhaps providing a basis for reading a "mandate" in the results. No one issue, however, constituted the same determining influence for more than 4 percent of the electorate. Abortion had been identified as the key issue by 7 percent of voters in 1980, but this proportion dropped to 4 percent in 1984, the same level as for national defense. No other issues were identified as the sole basis for voting by more than two percent of people polled.

Finding a mandate even among those voters who make their choice on a single issue is difficult. During the Vietnam War era, as more of the public became convinced that American involvement was a mistake, many voters considered the war to be the most important issue, but they were divided almost equally on the question of what to do about it—to withdraw immediately, to withdraw gradually, or to escalate.[13] Likewise, "single issue voters" concerned about abortion in 1984 split almost evenly on each side of the question of whether it should be legal.[14]

Politicians and Voters

After reviewing the huge literature on electoral behavior produced over the previous quarter century, two leading political scientists concluded in 1984 that "voters are reasonably sophisticated—not budding analysts but far from the truly unsophisticated cretins portrayed earlier."[15] Though most of the individuals responding to various surveys may not have evinced a high degree of sophistication about political controversies, they nevertheless held parties and political leaders responsible for their overall performance and competence.

The view of voters as ignorant or irrational often assumes that informed, rational voting should be "prospective"—that is, based on an informed judgment about what candidates *would do* if elected. There is not much evidence that most voters do make this calculus. There is, however, considerable evidence that voters make "retrospective" judgments—that is, they cast ballots based on evaluations about the past performance of candidates and the parties. "Retrospective" voting requires less specific information than prospective voting, which requires that the voter make predictions about future performance based on current policy statements and promises:

> What does it matter if [the] voter is not familiar with the nuances of current government policies or is not aware of the precise alternatives offered by the opposition? He is not the professional policy formulator. He has not devoted a career to pursuit of public office nor sought such office on the basis of his competency to govern. Perhaps he can't "cognize the issue in some form," but he can go to the polls and indicate whether or not he likes the way those who can "cognize the issue" are in fact doing so. He passes judgment on leaders, not policies.[16]

When we consider the fortunes of presidents and parties over the past sixty years, some kind of system of electoral reward and punishment seems to be in effect. The Republicans were tossed out in 1932 as a result of the Great Depression. Democrats lost elections in the midst of unpopular wars (Korea and Vietnam) in 1952 and 1968. During periods of economic growth, Presidents Eisenhower, Johnson, and Reagan were able to win new terms. Republicans were punished in the 1974 and subsequent congressional elections for the Watergate scandal. Although Gerald Ford was not personally unpopular, he was handicapped in 1976 by a negative popular reaction to his pardoning of Nixon and by a lingering distrust for establishment politicians.[17] Jimmy Carter benefited from his image as an "outsider" campaigning against old-style politics. Carter was subsequently punished for failing to provide effective leadership on economic and foreign policy issues. In 1988, George Bush's winning margin may well have resulted from a perception that the economy was in generally good shape, and that Bush had substantial experience by virtue of having been vice president to a popular president.[18]

The public's perceptions of the parties arguably derive from real-world events, not from mass ignorance. After the 1930s, the Democrats were regarded as the party best able to handle economic issues, whereas the Republicans were viewed as best at dealing with issues of war and peace (see table 6-2). But as memories of

Table 6-2 Party Perceptions

Peace or Prosperity? Poll Data, 1952–1986

Year	"Looking ahead for the next few years, which political party do you think would be more likely to keep the United States out of World War III...?"			"Which political party...will do a better job of keeping the country prosperous?"		
	Republican Party	Democratic Party	NA	Republican Party	Democratic Party	NA
1952 (January)	35%	15%	49%	31%	35%	34%
1956 (October)	46	16	38	39	39	22
1960 (October)	40	25	35	31	46	23
1964 (October)	22	45	33	21	53	26
1968 (October)	37	24	30	34	37	29
1972 (September)	32	28	40	38	35	27
1976 (August)	29	32	39	23	47	30
1980 (September)	25	42	33	35	36	29
1984 (September)	39	38	23	50	33	17
1986 (October)	34	29	37	41	30	29

Source: Adapted from The Gallup Organization, *Public Opinion* (December-January 1985): 38 (updated by the authors).

the Great Depression faded, to be replaced by other concerns such as the high inflation rates and rising joblessness in the 1970s, these perceptions changed.

Indicators of economic prosperity and the outcome of presidential and congressional elections are so closely linked that the public's approval rating for presidents, together with key economic indicators, can be used to predict accurately the net percentage gain or loss of the two parties in presidential and off-year congressional elections.[19] One might be inclined to regard such a close correlation as evidence that the electorate is more attuned to short-run gratification than to the long-run health of the economy. But surveys indicate that voters do not vote simply on the basis of their own pocketbooks, but also according to their perception of what is best for the nation's economic condition: "The party in power suffers at the polls during hard times because voters act on their negative assessments of national economic conditions—quite apart from the trials and tribulations of their own economic lives."[20]

When unemployment in January 1983 reached its highest level since 1939, President Reagan's approval rating slipped to 35 percent, lower than the midterm rating for any of the six preceding presidents. But when the economy recovered, the president's popularity rating similarly recovered. His extraordinary popularity persisted until November 1986, when the Iran-*contra* scandal shook public confidence in this administration.[21] His popularity rebounded, although only partially, by 1988.

Initially, the 1988 electoral campaign seemed to contradict the traditional wisdom of political scientists. By most conventional economic indicators, George Bush should have been ahead going into the campaign, but in fact he trailed by margins as large as 17 percent before the two major party conventions, despite data showing that in May 1988 a higher percentage of people felt they were better off financially than felt so at the end of the Carter administration.[22] However, by election day the voters apparently were heavily influenced by the state of the economy, which barely outweighed the electorate's tendency to want a change of parties after a two-term president.[23]

The idea that voters hold parties and governments responsible in a general way does not lead us very far, for it focuses on voters without revealing anything about the mechanisms by which voters are informed about policy alternatives. It is obvious that voters require clear alternatives and lots of information if they are to be good at making informed decisions. As pointed out by V. O. Key,

> Fed a steady diet of buncombe, the people may come to expect and to respond with the highest predictability to buncombe. And those leaders most skilled in the propagation of buncombe may gain lasting advantage in the recurring struggles for popular favor.[24]

If parties and political leaders spend most of their energies attempting to manipulate the electorate rather than providing it with information, then it is manifestly absurd to blame voters for their own ignorance, though this does not deter a great many political scientists from doing so. A more balanced assessment is that

> voters are not fools. To be sure, many individual voters act in odd ways indeed; yet in the large the electorate behaves about as rationally and responsibly as we

should expect, given the clarity of the alternatives presented to it and the character of information available to it.[25]

The Poverty of Political Discourse

The two major parties conduct their political arguments within an extraordinarily narrow range, and the extent of their differences is reflected in the views of party loyalists. Political scientist Benjamin Page examined the magnitude of difference between Democratic and Republican partisans in 1967 and 1968, utilizing 119 questions asked by several polling organizations during that period. Altogether, the questions were combined into two clusters of issues; twenty-seven issues dealt with foreign policy, and thirty-six concerned domestic affairs. On 59 percent (that is, sixteen) of the foreign policy issues, the spread between the percentage of Democrats and Republicans expressing an opinion one way or the other was no more than 5 percent, which is statistically insignificant. This was also the case for 42 percent of domestic issues. In effect, the Democrats and Republicans largely agreed on nearly half (49 percent) of the issues put to them in polls. Despite the rising controversy over the war in Vietnam, which would force Lyndon Johnson from the presidency in 1968, there was not a single foreign policy issue on which Democratic and Republican identifiers diverged by more than twenty percentage points (e.g., a 60% to 40% split). The greatest differences in political opinions between Democrats and Republicans involved a few select domestic issues, especially federal assistance for medical care, employment, and education. Democratic respondents were slightly more likely (by a 21% to 18% margin) to support the rights of various kinds of employees to organize unions and to strike.[26]

By comparing speeches by presidential candidates Hubert Humphrey and Richard Nixon in the 1968 election, Page tried to determine how closely candidates' issue differences fit with the positions expressed by Democratic and Republican activists. He found that on 87 percent of the issues the candidates mirrored the difference between supporters, when these existed. Humphrey and Nixon, however, meticulously avoided strong positions on the most controversial issue of the day—Vietnam—and both attempted to project a centrist image on the occasion of their main image-making opportunity, their nomination acceptance speeches. By the most generous estimate, only about 10 percent of Nixon's acceptance speech and 8 percent of Humphrey's dealt with Vietnam. Both candidates strived for ambiguity and vacuity. Nixon, for example, promised to make a "complete reappraisal of America's policies in every section of the world" and to make it a high priority "to bring an honorable end to the war in Vietnam." Page concluded, "The voter could not hope to find much information here—or in the TV spots or stump speeches which echoed the acceptance speech: whether he would 'end the war' by massive escalation, by unilateral withdrawal, or by negotiation." Humphrey's statements were equally insipid. In the most specific references Page could find, Humphrey mentioned the "necessity for peace in Vietnam," and promised that he would "do everything within my power to aid the negotiations and to bring a prompt end to this war," adding on another occasion that the "policies of today need not be limited by the policies of yesterday."[27]

In contrast to such meaningless and contrived platitudes, George Wallace, running as a third-party candidate, made thinly veiled racist appeals for votes, complaining that the federal government was forcing people "to sell or lease your home or property to someone that they think you ought to lease it to" and "saying you folks don't know where to send your children to schools." These remarks were obviously aimed at fair housing policies and integrated schooling for blacks and whites.[28] Wallace's demagoguery sharpened the controversy over civil rights and framed the issues for voters. Four years later, a poll found that voters found it relatively easy to define their own positions on civil rights. On the other hand, the Vietnam War remained a very difficult issue for voters to define in 1972.[29]

It is important to ask why Eugene McCarthy's 1968 and George McGovern's 1972 campaigns failed to sharpen the Vietnam conflict for the electorate in the same way that Wallace's campaign helped to define the civil rights issue. McCarthy and McGovern both campaigned as peace candidates and were sharply critical of the war. Wallace was willing to attack directly the liberal consensus on civil rights, and thus the policy alternatives were clear. McGovern, although he consistently opposed the war throughout his campaign, was unwilling to attack the knee-jerk anticommunism that both parties long had embraced as the linchpin for their foreign policy positions. As a consequence, the policy alternatives were ambiguous: As in all previous post-war elections, in 1972 the candidates "mostly repeated the prevailing wisdom that national security must be sought through mutual armament; that 'freedom' must be defended abroad against socialism." [30] McGovern felt that Vietnam was not the appropriate place to defend American interests, but he defined these interests in a rather conventional way.

The 1988 Democratic platform and the nature of the campaign suggest that despite substantial public support for "liberal" positions on specific issues (as distinct from liberalism as an ideology),[31] most Democrats shunned the label. Dukakis was determined to avoid being branded a liberal, successfully using his majority of delegates at the convention to keep the platform deliberately vague, preferring to make the election turn on "competence" rather than on ideology or issues. The Democratic National Convention was carefully crafted to mute debate over issues, and political commentators repeatedly stressed the value of having Jesse Jackson criticize Dukakis from the left in the latter stages of the primary so that voters would perceive Dukakis as a centrist. What actually happened, however, is that George Bush put Dukakis on the defensive, and Dukakis began to articulate a vaguely populist campaign with only two weeks to go, too late to turn the tide. Voters who made their minds up in the last two weeks selected Dukakis by a 55 percent to 43 percent margin; but only one voter in seven decided so late in the campaign.[32]

The Republican platforms of 1980, 1984, and 1988 presented clearly conservative positions on the issues. The shift to the right in American politics, however, was not preceded by shifts in public opinion on most of the items composing the conservative agenda.[33] Conservatism has become the leading "brand name" ideology largely because liberalism has left the field of battle. In 1976 Jimmy Carter presented himself as a southern moderate, and in 1980 he offered what amounted to an apology for his first term and a promise to do better in his second. In 1984 Walter Mondale offered concrete promises to various interest groups, but voters contradicted the Michigan study findings by refusing to vote merely on the basis of membership in an interest group. Dukakis so successfully avoided saying anything concrete, especially about taxes, at the Democratic convention that George Bush's campaign researchers found that the epithet "stealth candidate" was one of the most popular phrases that Bush used to describe Dukakis.

Although the Republican platforms of the 1980s were quite issue oriented, candidates Reagan and Bush were cautious. What Ronald Reagan's campaigns succeeded in doing was to create an encompassing, coherent image based on "a powerful myth that a return to a single, carefree, omnipotent America could be reached through the magic of slashing big government."[34] Bush did not successfully convey such an image but instead was able to cast Dukakis as a threat to traditional American values: Liberalism was painted as "a general softness, especially on crime and defense; alien values; threats to the family; rampant permissiveness; anti-Americanism; and radicalism."[35]

The "L" word became a scarlet letter[36] because Dukakis offered no rejoinders that could frame the issues effectively. In media campaigns, when issues are replaced by "sound bites" and fleeting TV images, the absence of equally dramatic sound bites and images carrying a different or opposing message leaves a vacuum that only exceptionally informed or ideological voters can fill on their own. The day after the election, Michael Dukakis seemed to appreciate this when he said, "I think one of the lessons of this campaign is you have to respond, you have to respond quickly."[37] But respond with what? Dukakis was only the latest in a line of Democratic candidates so eager to find the "center" of political opinion that they dared not stake out solid ground of their own. Perhaps Dukakis carried this tendency the furthest, projecting an image of no convictions at all; he "whined about being labeled, confirming a sense that there must be something wrong with the politics that dare not speak its name."[38]

It is clear that in 1988 a majority of Americans favored "liberal" programs for more aggressive environmental policies, education programs, child care, gun control, access to abortion, deep cuts in nuclear weapons, and a rapprochement with the Soviet Union.[39] Yet the Bush campaign was able to use the Pledge of Allegiance, attacks on the ACLU, and Willie Horton's crimes to label Dukakis as a liberal. The images conveyed in these attacks on Dukakis were constructed of sacred cultural symbols of family, religion, and patriotism along with profane symbols of crime and radicalism.[40] The issues making up the liberal agenda could have been framed around the same images and symbols, as Jesse Jackson showed in the primaries. By fleeing from the fight, Dukakis "left huge sectors of the population frustrated, alienated and feeling as if they [had] no stake in the election. Worse, his flight...abdicated the middle ground of political discourse."[41] Voters were denied even the familiar choice between the lesser of two evils.

Of course, a political discourse that involves "two sides," identified as current American brands of liberal and conservative thought, is itself remarkably truncated and artificial, especially when compared to the panoply of ideologies represented in a competitive multiparty system. Liberals share so many assumptions with conservatives that the two cannot be accurately called oppositional ideologies. Accordingly, a study of the origins of ideological identification in the American public concluded that the liberal and conservative labels "have largely symbolic, nonissue-oriented meaning to the mass public," and that voters' self-identification as liberal or conservative is derived largely from evaluations of the labels that they take from their environment—that is, politicians' rhetoric and the media.[42]

Nonetheless, one must acknowledge that losing one of the "sides" in American political discourse exerts a significant effect on American politics. The ideological identification one assumes does affect one's position on an issue or a candidate. Obviously there is a complex interaction among voters, candidates, and political parties. Voters are generally blamed for being no more clear about issues than politicians seem to be.

A political process designed to obscure issues cannot produce or even tolerate an informed public. The most effective technique for a challenger is not to offer policy alternatives, but *to highlight and make more salient* (but not necessarily to define) those broad values that are deeply held by the national electorate. In 1968, Richard Nixon instructed his speechwriters to prepare a list of excerpts from his convention acceptance speech. He told them to choose phrases that were "meaty and quotable and...zero-in primarily on the four [*sic*] major themes," which he defined as law and order, spending and "the foreign policy respect for America theme."[43] His intent was to raise alarm while avoiding policy solutions.

The politician commonly known as "Tricky Dick" was no more deceptive than his peers. Carter, a politician often lauded for his candor, used a similar strategy, as was eloquently expressed in an April 1976 memo to candidate Carter from his pollster and advisor, Patrick Cadell, written at a point when people were beginning to ask who Carter really was. Did Cadell and Carter welcome the opportunity to discuss the issues, as candidates always say publicly? Cadell advised Carter:

> We have passed the point when we can simply avoid at least the semblance of substance. This does not mean the need to outline minute, exact details. We all agree that such a course could be disastrous. However, the appearance of substance does not require this. It requires a few broad, specific examples that support a point and it requires a better definition of these priorities and approach....We need to have set formal addresses—no matter how distasteful—...to satisfy the press, elites, and eventually the public that we are presidential and competent.[44]

John Kessel, a scholar who specializes in the study of presidential campaigning, has observed that the campaign speech most often given on the stump is not a principled, coherent statement of the candidate's views, so much as

> a pastiche of applause lines the candidate has discovered in previous months of campaigning. It is a "theme song" made up of phrases the candidate likes, and which have demonstrated their ability to spark crowd reaction....The repetition is tedious...but repetition helps develop a candidate's image in the same way that endless exposure to Alka-Seltzer or Pepto-Bismol commercials fix the names of these products in the minds of television viewers.[45]

The key is to repeat catchy lines, like John Kennedy's "It's time to get America moving again," Nixon's "It's time for new leadership," Carter's "I'll never lie to you," or Bush's "Read my lips."

Campaign speeches are usually aimed at national media, and therefore to broad audiences. When candidates make appeals to special groups, they tend to become more specific in addressing issues of particular concern to the constituency they are courting. Even in this case, candidates prefer ambiguous signals conveyed through symbolic words and actions. In a two-party system, candidates must appeal to groups arrayed all over the political landscape, and thus specific proposals or promises cause trouble. In 1968, Richard Nixon was forced by negative publicity to back off from an indication he had given in several speeches that he would not cut off federal funds to racially segregated schools. Instead, in an attempt to appeal to white Southerners he began to appear frequently in the company of politicians associated with resistance of the civil rights movement, such as Senator Strom Thurmond of South Carolina.

In 1960, John F. Kennedy tried to avoid alienating white voters by hardly referring at all to civil rights in his 1960 campaign. But to solidify his standing among blacks, he made a sympathetic phone call to the wife of Martin Luther King, Jr., when King was being held in a Georgia jail. Kennedy actually offered no comment on the situation that led to King's arrest. He merely called to express his "concern."[46] Just before election day, 2 million pamphlets referring to the call were distributed outside black churches.

Another technique used by candidates is to imply different positions when speaking to various audiences, relying on just enough artful obfuscation to avoid being caught in a contradiction if challenged. An example is Hubert Humphrey's attempts during the 1968 campaign to gain support from veterans' groups even as he adopted a vaguely "dovish" position on Vietnam in an attempt to secure support from people opposed to the Vietnam War. Addressing Catholic War Veterans in Minneapolis, he declared that the people of South Vietnam "won't get a sell-out." In front of the American Legion in New Orleans, he played down his reputation as a liberal friend of blacks and the poor by taking a very tough stand against crime. After having endorsed a proposal for reducing farm subsidies, he told a Sioux Falls, South Dakota, audience that he wanted basic farm programs made permanent, improved, and "adequately funded."[47] Nixon and Humphrey both made their strongest pro-Israeli appeals in front of Jewish groups and told workers in struggling industries, like textiles, that they favored protection in the form of higher import taxes. Humphrey explained his plan to expand social security to senior citizens in Los Angeles and Detroit; Nixon promised to maintain lucrative tax breaks for the oil industry when in Texas.

Obviously, in a multiparty system centrist candidates and parties may try to be as ambiguous and contradictory as candidates in a two-party system. Candidates on the left and right, however, sharpen the issues. They spell out specific policy alternatives. They have an interest in exposing the artful dodging of other candidates. Political discourse is, as a result, enriched. Research conducted in 1978 found that political elites in three European countries with multiparty, parliamentary democracies identified themselves to the left of the mass public.[48] It is interesting that this applied even in Britain, which most closely approximates the two-party system found in the United States. Even when conservative political leaders come to power, as they have in the 1980s (most notably Margaret Thatcher in Britain), parties on the left keep political dialogue alive. Probably as a result, voters find party labels more meaningful, in relation to programs and ideology, than do voters in the United States.[49]

The quality of political discourse engaged in by candidates and other elites inevitably trickles down to the electorate. Social scientists who are surprised and dismayed to find a low level of issue awareness among American voters are, one may surmise, assuming that the electorate ought to be able to reach well-defined issue preferences even in a political system in which candidates and parties meticulously avoid debating issues.

Manipulating Information in the Electronic Age

Recent developments in campaign technologies could be used to improve the level of political discourse in campaigns. For example, computers make it possible to retrieve information almost instantly about candidates and their activities. Well-financed presidential campaigns now put on computer records past votes and speeches by political opponents, constantly updating their data banks as candidates make statements around the country. In 1984, for example, when Ronald Reagan tried to project a concern for the poor by visiting a Buffalo housing project, Mondale researchers were able to quickly ascertain that he had opposed financing the program that made the project possible. Using technology to retrieve information in this way certainly carries the potential for raising the public's awareness of issue content and candidates' positions.

In reality, new communications technologies are not likely to make politicians less vague and more consistent in discussing issues. With more than thirty years of experience in manipulating consumer tastes and tailoring commercials for specific demographic groups, the advertising industry is skilled at targeting subgroups in the electorate while avoiding alienating other groups. "Selling," not "communication," is the object. This is evident in the way that candidates have handled televised presidential debates.

The tendency to avoid issues has become a central feature of American campaigning at all levels. In Senate, House, and gubernatorial campaigns, half the campaign ads aired between 1960 and 1976 sought to transmit messages about personal qualities ("honest," "hard-working," "new leadership"). About 28 percent of ads during the period from 1960 to 1968 contained any references to issues. For 1970 to 1976, the issue content was even lower, falling to less than 16 percent.[50]

Debates appear to offer a remedy to the lack of issue content in political campaigns; it would seem that they would force candidates to express clear positions because the entire electorate is being addressed through a "big event." Politicians understand this, and to avoid having to be specific they arrange a format that is more like a panel discussion than a debate. The news media does little to encourage them to be precise because reporters and commentators focus much more on how the candidates come across personally than how much they differ on issues. Even so, because the debate format forces candidates to respond to questions posed by reporters, one would expect more focus on issues than would be found in the public relations copy written for campaign advertising.

One study compared the content of televised presidential debates to the content of TV ads for the 1960, 1976 and 1980 campaigns. As expected, debates were found to be more issue oriented than spot ads, and candidates were less likely to use debates than ads to appeal to voters on the basis of personal qualities rather than issues. In every debate, however, ambiguous references to issues outnumbered specific statements sometimes more, sometimes less than in spot television ads. In no debate did as much as a third of all the statements contain specific positions on issues.

And unfortunately, the content of debates is not all that matters. The assessment of debates by the media, which many analysts feel is key to the public's perception of who won or lost, always focuses on the "performance" aspect of the encounter rather than on the issue content.[51] In this respect, the media's coverage of debates is very much like its coverage of campaigns—there is a reliance on "horserace reporting" that gives the impression of media neutrality. It should not be surprising, therefore, that the public's overall perception, like the medias', gravitates toward performance and candidate bearing.

Reagan's pollster Richard Wirthlin explained that the flight from issues was an intentional component of the 1984 campaign's media strategy:

> We know from our research that it was the soft Democrats [those who lean Democratic, but often vote Republican] who would disagree with some of the Reagan policies but who would not dispute Reagan's leadership or effectiveness. Therefore, the tone and thrust of much of our advertising played to those two themes almost exclusively in the early phases of the campaign....To contrast the Reagan administration's performance with what had gone before was a big political plus for us.[52]

To solidify the victory, Wirthlin went on, the campaign in later phases emphasized a "vision of the future." This vision was based on an idealized version of the American past, absent of content. The Mondale strategy was, in effect, a mirror image. Mondale pollster Peter Hart explained in a post mortem interview that the Democrats decided early on that they would try to make the election a referendum on the future, a wise enough choice in light of Mondale's association with the discredited Carter administration.[53] But this meant that the Democrats would not defend the party's past record, an inclination that also guided Dukakis in the 1988 election. Without a history, however, the Democrats could not hope to frame for the public a meaningful debate about policies.

Perhaps the most creative tactic for avoiding the issues while giving the appearance of openness was devised by the Reagan campaign staff in 1984. The crew of the helicopter used to ferry the president from the White House to the airport was instructed to rev the engines each time the president passed reporters on the White House lawn. The effect was to drown out the president's responses to any questions—an apt metaphor for the entire campaign. In 1988, George Bush's handlers did not have to go that far. They simply announced, with two weeks left to election day, that their candidate would not make any more policy statements because he held a comfortable lead in the polls.

Notes

1. William H. Hartley and William S. Vincent, *American Civics,* 4th ed. (New York: Harcourt, Brace Jovanovich, 1983), pp. 198, 202, 212.

2. Hunter S. Thompson, *Fear and Loathing on the Campaign Trail '72* (San Francisco: Straight Arrow Books, 1973), pp. 55-56. Thompson called his style "Gonzo journalism" to describe his combination of "creative fiction" and open partisanship—in contrast to the journalism practiced by most reporters, in which principals of "objectivity" and strict corroboration are practiced to the point where only the most superficial aspects of political campaigns are reported.

3. See the substantial agreement on these principals registered in three sources that adopt very different positions on the question of the meaning of elections: Dye and Zeigler, *The Irony of Democracy,* p. 159; Gerald Pomper, *Elections in America,* 2nd ed. (New York: Longman, 1980), p. 212; and Richard G. Niemi and Herbert Weisberg's summary of the position articulated by the "Michigan school" of voting research, in *Controversies in Voting Behavior,* 2nd ed. (Washington, D.C., Congressional Quarterly Press, 1984), p. 89.

4. Angus Campbell, Philip E. Converse, Warren E. Miller, and Donald E. Stokes, *The American Voter* (New York: John Wiley, 1960). The main results are summarized in the final chapter.

5. Paul Lazarsfeld, Bernard Berelson, and Helen Gaudet, *The People's Choice* (New York: Columbia University Press, 1948).

6. Campbell, Converse, Miller, and Stokes, *American Voter,* p. 172.

7. Thomas Mann, "Public Awareness of Congressional Candidates," in Niemi and Weisberg, *Controversies in Voting Behavior,* pp. 251-268. [Originally in Thomas Mann, *Unsafe at Any Margin: Interpreting Congressional Elections* (Washington, D.C.: American Enterprise Institute, 1978].

8. See the summary of findings in Niemi and Weisberg, *Controversies in Voting Behavior,* p. 319.

9. Philip E. Converse, "Attitudes and Non-Attitudes: Continuation of a Dialogue," in *The Quantitative Analysis of Social Problems,* ed. R. R. Tufte, (Reading, Mass.: Addison-Wesley, 1970), pp. 168-189.

10. Mann, *Unsafe at Any Margin.* A key chapter is reprinted in Niemi and Weisberg, *Controversies in Voting Behavior,* pp. 251-268.

11. David Repass, "Issue Salience and Party Choice," *American Political Science Review* 65 (1971): 389-400.

12. John Pierce, Kathleen M. Beatty, and Paul R. Hagner, *The Dynamics of American Public Opinion* (Glenville, Ill.: Scott Foresman, 1982), p. 152.

13. See John Mueller, *War, Presidents and Public Opinion* (New York: John Wiley, 1973), summarized in Pierce, Beatty, and Hagner, *Dynamics of American Public Opinion,* pp. 152-156.

14. David Rosenbaum, "Poll Shows Few Votes Changed by Abortion," *New York Times,* October 8, 1984, B8.

15. Richard Niemi and Herbert F. Weisberg, "Do Voters Think Ideologically?" pp. 319-320, in *Controversies in Voting Behavior*. See also, in the same volume, chap. 21, Edward Carmines and James A. Stimson, "The Two Faces of Issue Voting," originally in *The American Political Science Review*, 74 (March 1980), pp. 78-91.

16. Morris P. Fiorina, *Retrospective Voting in American National Elections* (New Haven: Yale University Press, 1981), pp. 10-11.

17. Barry Sussman, *What Americans Really Think and Why Our Politicians Pay No Attention* (New York: Pantheon, 1988), pp. 234-239.

18. Alan I. Abramowitz, "An Improved Model for Predicting Presidential Election Outcomes," *PS: Political Science and Politics* (Fall 1988): 843-847.

19. Edward R. Tufte, *Political Control of the Economy* (Princeton, N.J.: Princeton University Press, 1978); also ibid.

20. Political scientists like to give exotic names to newly discovered phenomena, like physicists give exotic names to newly discovered particles. The two researchers responsible for this conception of voting call it "sociotropic." See Donald R. Kinder and D. Roderick Kiewiet, "Sociotropic Politics: The American Case," *British Journal of Political Science* 11 (1981): 129-161, reprinted in Niemi and Wiesberg, *Controversies in Voting Behavior*, p. 212.

21. Sussman, *What Americans Really Think*, pp. 223-234.

22. *Public Opinion*, July-August 1988, p. 30.

23. Abramowitz, "An Improved Model," pp. 843-847.

24. V. O. Key, *The Responsible Electorate* (Cambridge, Mass.: Harvard University Press, 1966), p.7.

25. Ibid.

26. Benjamin I. Page, *Choices and Echoes in Presidential Elections* (Chicago: University of Chicago Press, 1978), pp. 66-68.

27. Ibid., pp. 153-165.

28. Ibid., pp. 204-206.

29. Carmines and Stimson, "The Two Faces of Issue Voting," pp. 80-83.

30. Page, *Choices and Echoes*, pp. 274-276.

31. Thomas Ferguson and Joel Rogers, *Right Turn: The Decline of the Democrats and the Future of American Politics* (New York: Hill and Wang, 1986), pp. 3-39. Sussman, *What Americans Really Think*, pp. 240-253.

32. E. J. Dionne Jr., "Voters Delay Republican Hopes of Dominance in Post-Reagan Era," *New York Times*, November 10, 1988, p. 18.

33. Ferguson and Rogers, *Right Turn*, pp. 3-39. Numerous polls in the mid-1980s document the gulf between public opinion and Reagan Administration policies. See note 20, chap. 8, of this volume for examples.

34. David Moberg, "How 'L' Came to be the Scarlet Letter," *In These Times*, November 9, 1988, p. 6.

35. Ibid.

36. Ibid.

37. Robin Toner, "Wistful Dukakis Sees No Bush Mandate," *New York Times*, November 10, 1988, p. 21.

38. Moberg, "How 'L' Came to be the Scarlet Letter," p. 6.

39. Daniel Yankelovich and Sidney Harman, *Starting with the People* (Boston: Houghton Mifflin, 1988), and Sussman, *What Americans Really Think*.

40. John Dillon, "Deep South 'Non-Issues' Hit Dukakis," *Christian Science Monitor*, October 25, 1988, p. 1.

41. Susan J. Douglas, "What He Should Have Said Was," *In These Times,* October 26–November 1, 1988, pp. 22, 24.

42. Pamela Johnston Conover and Stanley Feldman, "The Origins and Meaning of Liberal/Conservative Self-Identification," *American Journal of Political Science,* 25 (1981), pp. 617-645, also in Niemi and Weisberg, *Controversies in Voting Behavior,* pp. 354-376.

43. John Kessel, *Presidential Campaign Politics* (Homewood, Ill.: Dorsey Press, 1984), p. 123.

44. Cited in Richard Joslyn, *Mass Media and Elections* (Reading, Mass.: Addison-Wesley, 1984), p. 29.

45. Kessel, *Presidential Campaign Politics,* p. 122.

46. Page, *Choices and Echoes,* pp. 143-144, pp. 145-148.

47. Ibid., p. 272-273.

48. Giacomo Sani and Giavanni Sartori, "Frammentazione, Polarizzazione e Cleavages: Democrazie e Deficili," *Revista Italiana de Scienza Politica,* 8 (December 1978), pp. 339-362, cited in Howard Reiter, *Parties and Elections in Corporate America* (New York: St. Martins Press, 1987), p. 33. See also Russell J. Dalton, Scott C. Flanagan, and Paul Allen Beck, *Electoral Change in Advanced Industrial Democracies: Realignment or Dealignment?* (Princeton: Princeton University Press, 1984).

49. For a general discussion, see Reiter, ibid., pp. 31-36. Also, Robert Harmel and Kenneth Jander, *Parties and Their Environments* (New York: Longman, 1982), p. 29.

50. Joslyn, *Mass Media and Elections,* pp. 43-46.

51. See the commentary on press analysis of the 1984 debates in *National Journal,* October 27, 1984, p. 2042.

52. Quoted in Ben J. Wattenberg, "Moving Right Along? Campaign '84's Lessons for 1988: An Interview with Peter Hart and Richard Wirthlin," *Public Opinion* (December-January 1989), pp. 8-11.

53. Ibid.

Chapter 7

The Best Elections Money Can Buy

Money and Politics

In 1905, ex-Senator George Washington Plunkett of New York's infamous Tammany Hall machine expressed his philosophy about money and politics: "The day may come when we'll reject the money of the rich as tainted, but it hadn't come when I left Tammany Hall at 11:25 today."[1] The Progressive movement targeted the corruption of big city machines like Tammany, and today no politician would so boldly endorse the political influence of wealth. The Progressives, however, only succeeded in driving the problem underground. Seventy-five years later, columnist Elizabeth Drew warned,

> Until the problem of money is dealt with, it is unrealistic to expect the political process to improve in any other respect....The argument made by some that the amount spent on campaigns is not particularly bothersome because it comes to less than is spent on, say, advertising cola, or purchasing hair-products, misses the point stunningly....What is at stake is the idea of representative government.[2]

People understand that politicians beholden to powerful economic interests are incapable of representing the broader public interest, and politicians, therefore, go to great pains to avoid the image of being bought. But even if they are not personally corrupt, politicians must turn to private and corporate wealth to meet the stupendous cost of conducting modern campaigns in the age of media and public relations specialists. This practice inevitably provides contributors with political leverage, and it also undermines respect for elections as a legitimate expression of the popular will. Thus politicians are caught in a bind. They share a collective interest as a group and as individuals to avoid the appearance of being bought, and at the same time their careers depend on their skills as fundraisers.

Since 1974, when the seamy side of electoral politics was exposed by the daily soap opera about real political life called the Watergate scandal, several reforms have been instituted in an effort to control the flagrant corruption of politics with money. These measures have failed; more than ever, elections in the 1990s are subject to successful fundraising and the artful application of money. The political liabilities associated with such a system remain. The trials and tribulation of House Speaker James Wright illustrate these liabilities. In 1989, Wright found himself embroiled in a losing battle for his political life as he attempted to refute charges that he evaded limits on how much representatives can earn from outside activities. Among other things, he was charged with disguising honoraria from sales of a book he wrote and with receiving $145,000, including $18,000 in salary to his wife, as compensation for a phony investment scheme. A wealthy Texas real estate magnate, George Mallick, provided the money.

Wright's troubles may have reflected to some extent his personal greed, but they also show the vulnerability of our political institutions in some interesting ways. Mallick was not accused of trying to influence legislation because he was a lobbyist, but because he was rich. By this criterion, any politician who accepts contributions or gifts from wealthy individuals is subject to the same charges because rich people and corporations are able to influence policy more than ordinary citizens. This is why corporations open offices full of lobbyists and public relations specialists in Washington. The problem is not greed but the subversion of democracy by great concentrations of wealth.[3]

Private wealth has penetrated the halls of Congress in many ways that are not illegal but certainly seem just as injurious to the public welfare as any of Wright's indiscretions. For example, in 1986 Representative Tony Coelho (D. Calif.) won an election among his colleagues for the position of whip of the Democratic caucus partly on the strength of his ability to make a total of $570,000 in 245 contributions, including thirty at the maximum level of $5,000 each, to the campaigns of his fellow Democrats. Rep. William Gray, competing for the chair of the House Budget Committee, gave a dinner at Washington's opulent Occidental Restaurant on February 23, 1988, at which he gave each of ten colleagues $1,000 contributions, and then went on to form a political action committee specifically to raise money to support his quest to chair the committee. Rep. Les Aspin is reported to have raised about $43,000 from defense contractors to give to his colleagues on the Armed Services Committee. In at least two instances, liberal Democrats have organized political action committees ostensibly dedicated, respectively, to supporting disarmament and to opposing U.S. policy in Central America, only to turn around and use money collected to make contributions to fellow representatives known for their hawkish views on foreign policy.[4]

All these examples involve liberal Democrats—that is, just the portion of the political elite presumably most sensitive to the interests of those who can least afford to contribute to political campaigns. We show in this chapter that money and politics are intricately linked in American politics; this point applies to honest and dishonest politicians alike. The corruption of politics that results is rooted more in the structure of campaign finance than in personal greed.

What Money Can Buy

The Watergate scandal left a deep imprint on American politics. The centerpiece of the scandal was President Richard Nixon's attempt to hide the involvement of his Committee to Reelect the President (CREEP) in the burglary of the Democratic National Party headquarters at the Watergate Hotel in Washington, D.C. As it unraveled, the episode revealed a systematic pattern of illegal campaign contributions, and it also illuminated the enormous amounts of legal money given in implicit or explicit exchange for favorable policies.

To cover up their contributions to the Nixon campaign, corporations "laundered" funds, frequently with help from Nixon's advisers. In one instance, American Airlines sent money from a U.S. bank to Lebanon for the stated purpose of purchasing a plane. The money was returned through an intermediary to another bank in the United States, which then passed it on to the finance committee of the Nixon campaign. Other companies used secret slush funds, sold bogus airline tickets, or created phony bonus schemes for employees who then passed the money on to the campaign. Wealthy private and corporate donors viewed the operation as little more than a high-powered extortion scheme; they knew that big contributions of this kind were expected in exchange for influence with the administration.

The scandal came as a shock to the public, but in hindsight it is obvious that something like it was almost inevitable, considering the incredible escalation in the costs of campaigning. In the 1968 presidential campaign, Nixon outspent Hubert Humphrey $25.4 million to $11.6 million. Four years later, Nixon alone spent $61.4 million on his reelection campaign. Besides the illegal and hidden corporate contributions, the sources for this sum included wealthy individuals like W. Clement Stone of Chicago, who donated over $2 million in 1968 and again in 1972, and Richard Mellon Scaife, heir to a fortune from holdings in Gulf Oil, Alcoa, and Mellon banks, who chipped in another $1 million or so. Though Democratic candidate George McGovern's campaign expenditures of $30 million was less than half of Nixon's, it was close to three times more than Humphrey had spent four years earlier. Though more dependent on small donors than Nixon, McGovern's campaign relied on some large contributors, too—such as Stewart Mott, heir to a General Motors fortune, who weighed in with $400,000 for the campaign.

Campaign spending reform received a strong push forward when the Watergate scandal revealed that some individuals were more interested in buying jobs and favorable policy initiatives than in promoting their general political preferences or ensuring access to policy makers further down the road. For example, the Nixon administration in effect sold diplomatic posts in exchange for contributions. Actually, the practice is and was common, but Nixon's campaign committee made the process too gauche when it literally auctioned off the posts to the highest bidders. In testimony before the special Senate Committee to Investigate Campaign Finance, Ruth Farkas, a director of Alexander's Department Store in New York City, complained, "Isn't $250,000 an awful lot of money for Costa Rica?" She ended up giving $300,000 and becoming ambassador to Luxembourg. President Nixon's personal lawyer was convicted and jailed for his role in this aspect of the scandal.

With this close relationship between private wealth and political campaigning, corruption is endemic to the American political system. The relationship was more or less formalized in the election campaign of 1896, and it has flourished ever since. The key innovations in organizing business influence in elections were carried out at the turn of the century by Mark Hanna, a wholesale grocer from Cleveland, on behalf of the Republican party. Hanna's effort to systemize fundraising was facilitated by business leaders' fears of the populist movement. To defeat the Democratic candidate William Jennings Bryan, Hanna went so far as to assess contributions from businesses according to their size. Banks, for instance, were expected to contribute one-quarter of 1 percent of their capital. Republicans spent more than twice as much in the presidential election of 1896 as in 1892. Hanna was able to raise approximately five times the total finances available to Bryan in 1896 and seven times as much as Bryan in 1900 (see table 7-1).[5] The Republican advantage has continued right up to the present; the only exceptions before the Second World War occurred in 1912 and 1916, when some important business leaders supported Woodrow Wilson, the Democratic nominee and winner.

After the 1948 election, the new communications media, television, pushed expenditures rapidly upward. The ratio of dollars spent to votes cast was twice as high (in constant dollars) in 1980 as in 1952. In 1952, the two major candidates spent less than $3.6 million on television and radio. By 1980, television and radio absorbed more than $30.7 million ($4.1 million for radio), not including $4.2 million spent by the Republican Party on a media campaign supporting all Republican candidates generically.[6]

Campaign reform began with legislation adopted in 1971, even before the Watergate scandal. Another bill was enacted in 1974, followed by additional legislation in 1976 and 1979. These laws and some court decisions restricted the size of individual contributions, introduced the concept of public financing, limited spending for some types of races and candidates, and established the Federal Elections Commission (FEC). The FEC categorizes campaign receipts according to contributions and loans provided by private individuals and the candidates themselves; support from political parties; money from the government through a system of matching funds; and contributions from organizations called "political action committees," or PACs.

How successful have these reforms been? In neither congressional nor presidential elections have they curbed the influence of money for very long. It does appear that the 1974 law resulted in a less costly and more evenly contested presidential campaign in 1976 than in 1972. Indeed, if only the official campaign expenditures by the major candidates in the general election are considered, it seems as though the laws have been effective. Each candidate in 1988 officially spent $46.1 million, the limit imposed by the FEC. This was far less even in 1988 dollars than the amount Nixon spent in 1972; and in addition the historic Republican financial advantage appears to have been wiped out.

The official figures, however, are misleading. An obscure "reform" passed by Congress in 1979 allows the national parties to collect and spend unlimited funds as long as they earmark them for state and local parties, routine operating expenses, or "party-building activities." This provision has turned out to be a loophole that developed into what the *New York Times* called a "campaign sewer." Both parties quickly learned to define most of their campaign expenditures and contributions as falling into the unlimited categories. As reflected in table 7-1, this loophole resulted

Table 7-1 **Presidential Campaign Costs, 1860–1988**

Year	Republican		Democratic	
1860	$ 100,000	Lincoln[1]	$ 50,000	Douglas
1864	125,000	Lincoln[1]	50,000	McClellan
1868	150,000	Grant[1]	75,000	Seymour
1872	250,000	Grant[1]	50,000	Greeley
1876	950,000	Hayes[1]	900,000	Tilden
1880	1,100,000	Garfield[1]	335,000	Hancock
1884	1,300,000	Blaine	1,400,000	Cleveland[1]
1888	1,350,000	Harrison[1]	855,000	Cleveland
1892	1,700,000	Harrison	2,350,000	Cleveland[1]
1896	3,350,000	McKinley[1]	675,000	Bryan
1900	3,000,000	McKinley[1]	425,000	Bryan
1904	2,096,000	T. Roosevelt[1]	700,000	Parker
1908	1,655,518	Taft[1]	629,341	Bryan
1912	1,071,549	Taft	1,134,848	Wilson[1]
1916	2,441,565	Hughes	2,284,590	Wilson[1]
1920	5,417,501	Harding[1]	1,470,371	Cox
1924	4,020,478	Coolidge[1]	1,108,836	Davis
1928	6,256,111	Hoover[1]	5,342,350	Smith
1932	2,900,052	Hoover	2,245,975	F. Roosevelt[1]
1936	8,892,972	Landon	5,194,741	F. Roosevelt[1]
1940	3,451,310	Wilkie	2,783,654	F. Roosevelt[1]
1944	2,828,652	Dewey	2,169,077	F. Roosevelt[1]
1948	2,127,296	Dewey	2,736,334	Truman[1]
1952	6,608,623	Eisenhower[1]	5,032,926	Stevenson
1956	7,778,702	Eisenhower[1]	5,106,651	Stevenson
1960	10,128,000	Nixon	9,797,000	Kennedy[1]
1964	16,026,000	Goldwater	8,757,000	Johnson[1]
1968	25,402,000	Nixon[1]	11,594,000	Humphrey
1972	61,000,000	Nixon[1]	30,000,000	McGovern
1976[2]	23,186,641	Ford	24,600,000	Carter[1]
1980[3]	46,565,818	Reagan[1]	32,944,670	Carter
1984[3]	77,300,000	Reagan[1]	71,100,000	Mondale
1988[3]	104,200,000	Bush[1]	104,200,000	Dukakis

[1] Indicates winner.

[2] The figures for 1976, the first to involve public financing, include money spent by the national committees of each party.

[3] The figures for 1980 and 1984 include not only national committee expenditures but spending for and against candidates by local and state committees. Independent expenditures by PACs not included for any of the years. The 1988 figure includes official expenditures, national committee expenditures, and the estimated $50,000,000 spent by each national committee as contributions to state and local parties, but in reality used for the presidential campaign.

Source: Data for 1860 through 1972 are from Herbert Alexander, *Financing Politics: Money, Elections, and Political Reform* (Washington, D.C.: Congressional Quarterly Press, 1984), table 1-1, p. 7. For 1976 to 1984, see Herbert Asher, who cites Alexander and several FEC reports, *Presidential Elections and American Politics* (Chicago: Dorsey Press, 1988), table 8-1, p. 212. For

in a rapid growth of overall spending, particularly in 1988, when the amount of party spending for each presidential candidate exceeded the candidates' "official" campaign expenditures.[7] Significant expenditures are not included even in the $104 million-plus amount listed for each candidate in table 7-1. For example, Michael Dukakis chose Texas Senator Lloyd Bentsen as his running mate in part because Bentsen could also simultaneously run for reelection for U.S. senator in Texas, which meant that Bentsen's robust Senate campaign treasure chest was at the disposal of the Democratic national ticket in the nation's third largest state. This money, however, was not counted by the FEC as part of the presidential campaign.

The cost of pursuing the presidential nomination has escalated even more dramatically than expenditures in the general election. Walter Mondale spent $18 million and Gary Hart over $11 million before the 1984 Democratic convention. Dukakis and Bush each spent $23 million pursuing the major party nominations in 1988. With big primaries yet to come, the total cost of competing for the nomination through the end of March 1988 exceeded $166 million for all candidates, almost two and a half times the $60 million spent over the comparable period in 1984.[8]

By 1988, spending on House and Senate races was five and a half times greater than in 1972 (see table 7-2). The most expensive Senate campaign in history was conservative Jesse Helm's $16.5 million successful campaign in North Carolina in 1984. In that same year, liberal Alan Cranston in California spent $11.6 million—but still he was slightly outspent by his conservative Republican opponent. Successful races for the House of Representatives cost $38 million in 1975–76, compared to $155.4 million in 1985–86; in the same period, spending on successful Senate races increased from $20.1 million to $104 million. The bill for successfully challenging a House incumbent in 1986 cost, on the average, about $375,000. For 1988, preliminary reports by the FEC indicate that spending on all House races (including primaries) rose 7.2 percent over 1986, reaching $256.5 million. Senate spending fell 5 percent to $201.2 million in 1988, but the cost of campaigning really had not leveled out. Winning campaigns in the Senate actually increased 18.5 percent in a two-year period; winning House campaigns rose by 10.3 percent.[9]

Public financing of presidential campaigns began in 1974, and many states provide public money for Senate and House candidates. A system of matching funds is used, with a limit on the size of any one contribution that can be used for matching purposes. For presidential elections, this limit is $250. But public financing has totally failed to reduce the influence of wealth in elections and possibly has, in a perverse way, amplified its effect. Candidates need big contributions and loans early in a campaign to cover the costs of the direct mailings used to gather the multitude of small contributions required to qualify for public funds. One study found that in 1974, the first year that public financing was available, 60 percent of campaign contributions came from 11 percent of the highest income earners.[10]

1988, besides FEC reports on official spending, see the report of a national conference at which Bush and Dukakis campaign officials admitted to the estimated $50,000,000 additional funds spent in 1988 (Richard Berke, "Some Tales of Campaign Cash," *New York Times,* December 11, 1988.

Table 7-2 **Congressional Campaign Costs**

Campaign Expenditures, U.S. House General Election Candidates, 1972–1988

Year	Average, Each Candidate Democrats	Republicans	Total All Candidates
1972			$40.0 million
1974			45.0
1976	$74,757	$71,945	79.2
1978	108,502	107,011	110.6
1980	133,105	145,415	136.0
1982[1]	202,962	221,256	204.6[1]
1984	219,575	214,962	177.6
1986	265,225	254,243	210.6
1988[2]	287,560	258,441	222.3

[1] 1982 figures are inflated because money collected by one committee within a campaign and transferred to another in the same campaign were counted each time a transfer occurred.
[2] Preliminary estimates.
Source: For 1972 to 1984, data were compiled by the Citizen's Research Foundation from FEC reports, presented in Herbert Alexander, *Financing Politics,* 3rd ed. (WAshington, D.C.: Congressional Quarterly, 1984), p. 138. For 1986, FEC release, May 10, 1987; for 1988, FEC release, February 24, 1989.

When wealthy New York conservative James Buckley teamed with former Democratic Senator Eugene McCarthy to challenge limitations on campaign spending and contributions on grounds that they infringed on their freedoms of speech and assembly, the Supreme Court had to decide, as Justice Potter Stewart recognized, whether money and speech are equivalent.[11] On the whole, the court decided that money is speech. Limitations on contributions were found to be constitutional, but not limitations on expenditures unless candidates accepted public funding. Serious presidential contenders always accept such funding. However, the court ruled that expenditures for candidates made by groups operating "independently" of official campaigns cannot be restricted. Nearly all "independent" contributions are made by political action committees, which have proliferated over the past decade. PAC contributions to congressional campaigns reached $148.1 million in 1988, constituting more than seven times the total they contributed ten years earlier. In 1978, PAC contributions accounted for 17 percent of congressional campaign spending. By 1988, PACs contributed almost one-third of the money spent in congressional races (see table 7-3).

PACs, Property, and Privilege

Before Watergate, most important political action committees were connected to labor unions. One of the first successful such organizations was created in 1943 by the Congress of Industrial Organizations (CIO) in an effort to lend support to and gain influence with the Roosevelt administration. Business groups quickly responded.

135

Table 7-3 **PAC Contributions to Congressional Candidates**

Year	Total No. Office Seekers	Total Receipts (millions)	PAC Contributions (millions)	PAC Contributions (percent)
1978	1,909	$199.4	$34.1	17.1%
1980	2,288	248.8	55.2	22.2
1982	2,240	354.7	83.6	23.6
1984	2,036	397.2	105.3	26.5
1986	1,868	471.4	132.2	28.0
1988[1]	1,791	476.4	148.1	31.1

[1] Preliminary data.
Source: FEC releases, May 10, 1987 and February 24, 1989 (preliminary data).

Taking advantage of the sense of emergency created by the Second World War, and following the war with a campaign against "communism within," elites successfully rammed through Congress a number of laws in 1947 to prohibit the presumably left-leaning unions from providing financial support to politicians and parties.

By curbing the political clout of unions in the electoral arena, the balance of power between the working class and business was shifted decisively in favor of the latter. Corporations, it should be noted, had been prohibited since 1907 from contributing directly to candidates, but corporate executives and holders of stocks and bonds (who tend to be the same people) have wealth and income as individuals which they can use to exert influence. Only through collective efforts can workers hope to compete effectively against business interests, since individually they have few personal resources. Unions were a logical vehicle for this purpose. The 1947 prohibition on union political action committees therefore severely inhibited the ability of workers to compete with employers and corporations in the political sphere. Possibly more important, it helped keep the Democratic party from becoming a more labor-oriented party of the sort found virtually everywhere else in the capitalist world.

After 1947, unions founded PACs to promote "political education," and these PACs found ways of tendering support to favored candidates, usually Democrats.[12] But labor leaders more or less accepted their marginalization from the party system. This decision fundamentally shaped the relationship between the American party system and the labor movement. The Republican party is unabashedly pro-business, whereas the Democrats embrace both corporate and labor interests. Unlike business, labor has no party of its own.

Business PACs already were proliferating before the reform legislation of the 1970s. The number of business-oriented PACs increased from eleven in 1964, to 33 in 1968, to 200 by 1972.[13] Legislation in 1971 and 1974 had the effect of legitimizing and facilitating further development of corporate PACs. In 1971, PACs were formally recognized by law as organizations permitted to support candidates overtly, and their numbers mushroomed. PACs representing labor unions actually raised more for congressional candidates in 1978 than did business PACs, but only two years later, in 1980, business contributions to PACs exceeded labor's contributions by $19.1

million to $13.2 million, and the corporate advantage has increased steadily (see table 7-4). In addition, PACs representing trade membership and health professionals collect more, in the aggregate, than do labor union PACs. Many of these PACs, which represent physicians, realtors, lawyers, and other professional groups, are, essentially, business associations.

The majority of campaign money still comes from public financing, individual citizens, and candidates' personal resources. About one-third of the money raised in congressional campaigns comes from PACs. Still, PACs are the largest single source of money for congressional campaigns.[14] In 1988, PAC contributions accounted for 40 percent of the money raised by House candidates, and 24 percent for candidates in Senate races.[15]

PACs not only influence elections through their contributions to campaigns but through "independent expenditures"—on behalf of a candidate or cause. In 1980, independent committees expended nearly $12 million to promote Ronald Reagan— obviously a significant amount in a campaign where the total public financing for each presidential candidate was limited to $29 million.[16] PAC spending moves the ideological "center" in electoral politics to the right. The best-financed "independent" PACs have been organized by right-wing ideological groups and multinational corporations. Eight of the richest twenty corporate PACs in 1983–84 represented defense contractors. In that election cycle, the three largest trade PAC contributors to congressional candidates were organized by the American Medical Association, the realtors' political action committee, and a PAC representing construction companies. The National Rifle Association's PAC also ranked among the ten wealthiest.

Among ideological PACs, the best-financed three in 1980 included the National Conservative PAC (NCPAC), with an incredible $19 million war chest, the Fund for a Conservative Majority, and Jesse Helms's National Congressional Club. All these lobbied for New Right causes and candidates. Many ideological PACs expend large amounts of their money on the fundraising process itself, but this should not mislead anyone into thinking that such a practice necessarily reduces their effectiveness. Much direct-mail fundraising literature is highly propagandistic and thereby constitutes part of the electoral process, setting a tone that boosts or damages individual candidates.

The biggest winners in the contest for PAC money are incumbents, who received 74 percent of all PAC contributions in 1987–88, up from 68 percent in 1985–86. If PAC contributions to incumbents of each party are matched against their respective challengers (second column, table 7-5), the ratio in favor of Democratic incumbents to Republican challengers is more than 24:1; for Republican incumbents versus Democratic challengers, it is 3.7:1. Overall, then, Democrats rely more on PACs than do Republicans, partly because there are more Democratic incumbents (and all incumbents receive more PAC money than challengers, by a ratio of 7:1) and partly because Republicans benefit more from individual contributions by wealthy individuals (and thus rely proportionately less on PAC money). As might be expected, Republicans rely more on corporate PACs and attract very little labor support. The most significant development is that Democrats also attract significant corporate and trade contributions. Indeed, as shown in table 7-5, in the 1987–88 election cycle 29

Table 7-4 PAC Contributions

Breakdown of PAC Contributions to Congressional Candidates
1978–1988

Year	Total PAC Contributions ($ millions)	Corporate PACs ($ millions)	Percent	Labor PACs ($ millions)	Percent	Trade/Membership/ Health PACs ($ millions)	Percent
1978	$34,100,000	$9,500,000	27.8%	$ 9,900,000	29.0%	$11,200,000	32.8%
1980	55,217,291	19,182,122	34.7	13,211,725	23.9	15,873,908	28.7
1982	83,620,190	27,528,000	32.9	20,288,604	24.3	21,872,635	26.2
1984	105,330,090	35,475,630	33.7	24,830,637	23.6	26,739,293	25.4
1986	132,179,611	46,006,975	34.8	29,843,517	22.6	32,799,275	25.0
1988	147,897,641	50,457,316	34.1	33,934,846	22.9	38,888,003	26.3

Source: FEC releases: June 29, 1979; March 7, 1982; December 2, 1983; December 8, 1985, May 21, 1987, April 9, 1989 (interim report).

Table 7-5 PAC Contributions

Pattern of PAC Contributions to House Candidates, 1987–1988

Party/Status	Net Campaign Receipts ($ million)	PAC Contributions ($ million)	PAC Contributions Percent of All Receipts	Percent of Contributions from Various Sources [1]			
				Corp.	Labor	Trade	Ideol.[1]
Democrats	159.9	67.6	42	10	16	10	5
Incumbents	102.5	53.6	52	15	16	14	5
Challengers	29.5	7.7	26	1	17	3	5
Open seats	28.0	6.3	23	2	12	4	5
Republicans	116.6	34.6	30	13	2	10	3
Incumbents	73.0	28.8	39	18	3	14	3
Challengers	22.0	2.2	10	4	1	3	3
Open seats	21.6	3.6	17	6	1	6	4

[1] All PACs making campaign contributions: Corp. = Corporate PACS; Labor = union PACs; Trade = PACs listed by FEC as "trade/member/health"; Ideol. = PACs listed by FEC as "non-connected," which are in the majority of those organized around a specific issue, candidate, or general political philosophy, hence classified here as "ideological." PACs associated with corporations without stock are included in the category "corporate." PACs associated with cooperatives contributed $2.6 million but are not included here.

Source: For receipts, FEC release, February 24, 1989. For contributions, FEC release, April 9, 1989.

percent of the money flowing to Democratic House incumbents was contributed by corporate and trade PACs, compared to 32 percent of the contributions to Republican House candidates. This pattern has contributed significantly to the erosion of partisan differences in Congress.

In recent years, Democratic politicians, unions, and interest groups with liberal orientations have increased their PAC activities. Through March 1988, the top ten PAC spenders included a labor group and a pro-environmental organization. Also among the top ten, however, were real estate interests, trial lawyers (worried about tort reform, which would limit their business), and American Medical Association (opposing national health insurance), organizations linked to conservative political candidates, and American Telephone and Telegraph.[17] If only PACs that specifically promote conservative versus liberal ideologies (rather than existing to support particular candidacies or interests) are considered, the balance remains overwhelmingly tilted toward the right. As table 7-6 shows, in 1985–86, the top six right-wing ideological PACs outspent the top six liberal PACs by a ratio of almost seven dollars to one.

Labor unions are often singled out for criticism, but they exert far less financial leverage than do corporate and wealthy contributors (see table 7-4). In 1988, labor contributions accounted for 23 percent of all PAC contributions but only 10 percent of all the money received by House candidates. Labor's potential influence is substantially diluted because most Democratic candidates also receive corporate PAC money. GOP candidates rely almost exclusively on corporate, trade, and conservative PACs, and they attract much more money from individual contributions. Democrats, more dependent on PACs in the first place, rarely depend on labor PACs alone, and frequently their corporate contributions outweigh all other sources, including labor. This has the effect of moving Democrats to the right, which helps explain why corporations are so eager to defend PACs even though Democrats get more PAC money than Republicans. President Bush's principal media advisor, Roger Ailes, even made a propaganda film vigorously defending PACs.

The Enhanced Importance of Personal Wealth

The post-Watergate reforms did not so much reduce the influence of money in politics as they rearranged the relationship between politicians and their financial backers. The campaign finance laws still permit large contributions. Individual citizens may contribute up to $5,000 to national candidates, $5,000 to a political action committee, and $20,000 to the national committee of a political party. In addition, various loopholes permit an individual to contribute hundreds of thousands of dollars to influence elections in any given year. For example, nothing prevents multiple contributions at maximum amounts to one candidate through the simple device of having each donation come from different members of the same family. In any case, the campaign finance laws apply mainly to campaigns for national office. Donations unregulated by federal law can be made to state parties and candidates. Finally, contributions can be made to multiple PACs, which in turn contribute to campaigns or make "independent" expenditures on behalf of candidates.

The original reform legislation limited the amounts wealthy individuals could spend on their own campaigns and subjected all campaigns, whether or not the candidate accepted public financing, to spending limits. In *Buckley* v. *Valeo,* however, the Supreme Court struck down campaign spending limits on candidates who reject public financing. Hence it is still possible for aristocrats to attempt to buy themselves a seat in Congress. Liberal Democrat Mark Dayton, of Dayton-Hudson retail fame and married to a Rockefeller, dug into his personal fortune for $1.1 million in his unsuccessful 1982 bid to defeat a Republican incumbent in Minnesota. Both senatorial candidates in the 1982 New Jersey race were wealthy. The Republican lent or contributed $877,000, the Democrat nearly $4 million. The latter, Frank Lautenberg, made huge loans to his own campaign under the assumption that it could be recovered from contributors eager to jump on a campaign bandwagon already well financed. Hence Lautenberg successfully gambled $4 million of his $14 million fortune.

Can an election in fact be bought by a wealthy politician or successful fundraiser? All other things being equal, the candidate with the most cash has an important advantage. But money alone does not determine the outcome. There are many cases in which a candidate is outspent but emerges victorious. In seventeen of twenty-nine Democratic primaries in 1984, the largest spender was not the winner. And there have been some spectacular, costly failures. John Glenn spent more than all of his opponents in the New Hampshire presidential primary in 1984, but lost badly and after a few more disappointments dropped out of the race. John Connally, a former governor of Texas and Secretary of the Treasury in the Nixon administration, is notorious for his $13 million campaign that netted him one solitary delegate to the Republican nominating convention in 1980. Losers in 1982 Senate races included Lewis Lehman, who spent 8 million of his own dollars in a bid to become governor of New York; oilman William Clements, who blew $14 million trying to become governor of Texas (though he subsequently won in 1986); and Mark Dayton, who failed to buy a Senate seat in Minnesota for $7 million.

Being wealthy does not guarantee victory, but personal wealth confers a special advantage early in a campaign, when money is needed to make a candidacy credible and to provide the basis for additional fundraising. Several features of the post-Watergate legislation favored wealthy candidates. The right to public funds was made dependent on the ability to raise $5,000 in private contributions of $250 or less in at least twenty states. The legislation was designed to give small contributors more influence. But "early" money from big contributors is required to finance solicitation of these "small" contributions. Furthermore, a growing number of PACs and individuals act as brokers who solicit small contributions and bundle them together for delivery to favored candidates. This practice helps defeat the intent of laws requiring candidates to secure a minimum number of small contributors because they can best accomplish the task by bringing a few key brokers on line.

Table 7-6   **Ideological PAC Contributions**
Spending by Ideological PACs [1]
1985–1986

	Total Spending ($ million)	Contributions ($ million)		
		Total	Democrat	GOP
Liberal PACs				
Americans for Democratic Action	84,324	73,669	73,669	
Committee for America's Future	263,790	171,000	171,000	
Democratic Study Group	238,503	83,000	83,000	
Democrats for the 80's	963,149	314,250	314,250	
Hollywood Women's Political Committee	364,192	115,500	115,500	
National Committee for an Effective Congress	2,497,965	692,282	689,784	2,498
TOTAL	4,411,923	1,449,701	1,447,203	2,498

	Total Spending ($ million)	Contributions ($ million)		
		Total	Democrat	GOP
Conservative PACs				
Conservative Victory Fund	215,212	61,397	500	60,897
Free Congress Foundation	542,376	61,269	2,651	58,618
Fund for a Conservative Majority	2,717,612	81,559	3,315	77,960
National Congressional Club	15,571,698	63,594		63,594
National Conservative PAC	9,249,810	55,919	1,169	54,472
Republican Congressional Boosters Club	543,932	118,500		118,500
TOTAL	28,940,640	442,238	7,635	434,041

[1] Political action committees that exist to promote broad, ideological objectives.

Source: Ed Zuckerman, *Almanac of Federal PACs* (Washington, D.C.: Amward Publications, 1988).

The Hidden Primary

The net result of the American campaign system is that a disproportionate number of politicians either have great personal wealth or become dependent on the largesse of the wealthy. As a result, even before the first official primary of the long presidential campaign season, there is already underway a "hidden election," or "invisible primary"[18] in which money and the support of elites, rather than votes or popular support, determine who may compete. Two political scientists, Thomas Ferguson and Joel Rogers, have argued that the connection between elite sectors and presidential candidates is so close that political scientists would be better advised to study the contest among candidates for elite financial support than for the votes cast by the mass electorate. Studying the latter, according to Ferguson, is like trying to predict the movement of a cattle herd by examining the droppings (i.e., the votes) rather than studying the cowhands (the elites). The real election is "hidden."

The "hidden election" serves as an initial screening device, assuring that elites can pick the candidates before ordinary citizens are offered any degree of participation. The 1987-88 campaign of Missouri Democrat Richard Gephardt provides a good illustration of how the hidden primary season works. On the one hand, because he is a Democrat, Gephardt needed labor union support. Hence he introduced legislation to restrict imports in industries where jobs seemed threatened by foreign competition. In an attempt to appeal to farmers, he cosponsored a farm relief program. To build credentials as a populist reformer, he gave a speech to Wall Street brokers castigating them for a wave of scandals involving insider trading, emphasizing that American workers paid the cost of Wall Street corruption and financial speculation. To reduce opposition from the National Organization of Women, he reversed his previous position in favor of a constitutional amendment to outlaw abortion. The strategy worked. The media soon anointed him the "populist" candidate.

Though Gephardt may very well have believed in the positions he adopted, his campaign was inconsistent with his record in Congress, where he advocated budget cuts, replacement of the progressive income tax with a two-tier system, higher defense spending, and outlawing abortion.[19] Much of this record made Gephardt an attractive candidate to wealthy elites and to a specialized group of contributors who assume roles as brokers by soliciting support from others. The invisible primary campaign was much more consistent with Gephardt's past record than was his public rhetoric.[20]

Gephardt met a rich Texan, Milledge (Mitch) A. Hart, on a hunting trip in 1985. Owner of five Dallas-based companies that made products and provided services ranging from insulation to international trade, Hart promised in 1987 to tap into the pockets of his Texas friends. Needing to raise $5 million to $7 million at a time when he was the preferred choice of only 1 percent to 3 percent of Democratic voters in Iowa, site of the first delegate selection contest, Gephardt also turned to key politicians and corporate elites in his home state for a boost. St. Louis Mayor Vincent Schoemehl, August Busch III (chair of the Anheuser-Busch brewing empire), Louis B. Susman (a key corporate lawyer), and Mark Turken (chair of his own real estate development company) each promised to find $50,000 for the Gephardt campaign, magnifying their importance far beyond that implied by the $5,000 limit on contributions written into the campaign finance laws.

The hidden campaign took Gephardt to meetings with key elites across the country. In California, his backers included Michael Ray, a real estate developer who organized a PAC with one-hundred members who each contributed $1,000 per year to belong. Another early Gephardt backer was Steve Chaudet, a defense industry executive. In Michigan, Deborah Dingell was a key Gephardt fundraiser. She was an executive with General Motors and wife of a congressman. In Boston, Gephardt was backed by Peter Vermilye, chairman of an investment management company. The support by medical doctor Clifford Findeiss, of Florida, meant not only one more affluent contributor but access to money from a significant portion of the medical establishment; Findeiss was president of Emergency Medical Service Associates, which contracts to provide emergency room doctors to hospitals in ten states. Another Gephardt backer from New Orleans ran a consulting company that specialized in helping companies break existing unions and defeat attempts to certify new ones.

Gephardt's initial success with wealthy contributors and PACs did not mean that each of them was irrevocably and exclusively committed to Gephardt. For example, one important PAC located in the Sun Belt, Impact '88, decided to divide their contributions among several Democratic contenders. How important is Impact '88? One reporter on the Gephardt campaign trail said that it was "a group of about 50 people who have some of the biggest bank accounts and fattest Rolodexes in the party. The ticket to belong is the ability to raise $250,000." Scoring with this group was the "dream of this year's Democratic aspirants."[21]

Other candidates of both parties were working the same groups with varying degrees of success. Gephardt was completing a rite of passage that would ensure that, once in office, he would be broadly responsible to the interests of business, regardless of his populist rhetoric and legislative proposals. For this reason, even those whom he most vigorously attacked did not find his overall outlook unacceptable. One of his backers, a New York venture capitalist who could easily qualify as one of the principle targets of Gephardt's rhetoric about corruption and speculation on Wall Street, was not put off excessively by Gephardt's attack on brokers. He had already expressed a willingness to solicit a few dozen of his comrades to contribute $1,000 to Gephardt *even though* he disliked Gephardt's views on closing tax loopholes for business. He liked the idea of having someone in the White House whom he could talk to, someone he regarded as a serious student of taxes and trade.[22]

A recent innovation in the invisible component of electoral politics are the PACs specifically designed to enhance the aspirations of leading candidates. Ronald Reagan's vehicle was "Citizens for the Republic"; Rep. Jack Kemp of New York, a leader of the New Right, had his "Campaign for Prosperity." Soon after the 1984 election, George Bush, with the help of many of Reagan's former backers, formed the "Fund for America's Future." By mid-November 1985, the "Fund" had already amassed $2.3 million for Bush's future, most of it based on the vice president's lecture fees, before it had even launched its first direct-mail appeal. By mid-1986, Bush's campaign chest had accumulated an estimated $8 million.[23] Kemp and other GOP

145

hopefuls, such as former Senator Howard Baker and Senator Robert Dole, found their own PACs trailing far behind Bush's.

On the Democratic side, several presidential aspirants organized PACs closely linked to their own ambitions. Gephardt and Senator Bill Bradley of New Jersey founded "Citizens for a Fair Tax," an organization that promoted tax reform and tax simplification. The effort to collect backers on a national scale for a popular cause enabled them to attract national attention from media, important elites, and the public. Equally important, it left them with an invaluable list of citizens who had demonstrated an interest in their political agenda. Gephardt's presidential PAC, the "Effective Government Committee," undoubtedly benefited from the groundwork laid by the allegedly nonpartisan "Citizens for a Fair Tax."

These kinds of PACs permit some politicians to enhance their influence as political brokers even if they do not aspire to the presidency. One advantage of such PACs is that until a candidate declares formally for office, money contributed to his or her PAC need not be reported to the FEC, thus helping to keep the invisible election out of the public eye. And they have other uses as well, even for nonviable presidential candidates. The "leadership" PACs founded by politicians can be used to gain influence over their colleagues within the congressional committee and caucus system.[24] Contributions by politicians to one another through their PACs jumped from $207,728 in 1979–80 to $1.17 million in 1982–83. By the 1988 elections, such contributions soared to $4.1 million by October. Campaign money influences not only campaigns but the legislative process itself.

Many politicians take money left over from previous campaigns and transfer it wholesale into their presidential campaign coffers, even though much of the money raised in earlier races came from contributions larger than those permitted for the presidential sweepstakes. By December 1987, Robert Dole had transferred $250,000 from the $2 million surplus left over from this 1986 Senate race to his presidential campaign[25] and later tapped into the rest, even though his own PAC remained healthy; the FEC listed it as the top spender through the 1988 primaries.

The "nonprofit" foundation is another device for evading the financial reform laws. These foundations are established for ostensibly "educational" activities, and thus contributions to them are not only unregulated but tax deductible, even though they are used to boost the fortunes of the politician closely associated with the foundation. Gary Hart, who made a great point of opposing PACs and refused to establish his own, organized one of the most successful of these foundations, but virtually every candidate in the 1988 presidential race had such an organization.

The hidden primary for the 1988 race was well underway early in 1987. Vice President Bush had already raised $9.1 million by the end of June, followed by Senator Robert Dole and Representative Jack Kemp of New York, each with about $3.5 million. Three other aspirants had not yet collected $1 million. On the Democratic side, Massachusetts Governor Michael Dukakis had raised $4.7 million, including about $2 million from a single dinner in Boston. Gephardt and Senator Paul Simon each hovered around the $1 million mark, behind Senator Joseph Biden of Delaware and Senator Albert Gore, Jr. of Tennessee, each with about $1.5 million. Gephardt's defense of oil interests in Congress apparently paid off, since wealthy donors from

Texas and Louisiana, through the medium of PACs, were particularly generous to his campaign. Pat Robertson and Jesse Jackson had not yet filed reports, since neither had declared as official candidates by the June 1987 deadline. But Jackson was reported to have collected about $300,000, and Robertson claimed to have raised over $8 million.[26] In the FEC's September 30 listing, Jackson was reported to have raised $1 million dollars, a small sum compared to the $11.6 million raised by Robertson, who, like Jackson, had never held elective office.

The Jackson campaign showed that the "hidden primary" is not a foolproof device that elites can use to winnow out the candidates. Jackson collected more than 18 percent of the votes cast in the 1984 primaries, but he nevertheless found it extremely difficult to raise money for his 1988 presidential bid. The paltry $300,000 at his disposal by June 1987 put him at a severe disadvantage. Even with public funds, Jackson was forced to campaign, as in 1984, without paid television and radio commercials. He was almost completely dependent on grassroots organizations and whatever free news coverage he could generate.

Jackson's funding base improved as he became more successful, especially following his dramatic victory in the Michigan primary in February 1988. In the first four months of 1988 he raised $10.1 million, with a much higher return than normal for direct-mail fundraising. During this period, Jackson received $5.3 million in individual contributions and $2.7 million in federal matching funds.[27] Jackson established a goal of $2 million for his "Keep Hope Alive" PAC. With a good financial base laid for 1992, Jackson could be even more competitive than he was in 1988. If he becomes a leading candidate as a result, will the campaign finance system pull him toward the mainstream, or will he be able to mount a populist challenge that has enough funding to shake up the political establishment?

The Tilt to the Right

By curbing the kinds of extravagant and illegal donations that led to the Watergate scandal, reform legislation helped to preserve a degree of influence for those individuals with sufficient income to make modest contributions—the upper middle class. Although the GOP claims that the average contribution to its candidates is $25, the proportion of Americans contributing anything at all is very small. According to the Joint Center for Political Studies, only 6.8 percent of the electorate made direct contributions to political candidates in the 1970s.[28] The system of tax credits and deductions designed to encourage contributions is of little benefit to the working class and poor, who do not earn enough to make use of such benefits. And there are signs that middle-class influence is eroding as well. In 1984, only 19 percent of House contributions came from people who contributed less than $150 a year to campaigns. Ten years earlier, these donors accounted for half of all House campaign financing.[29]

Since few working class voters can afford to make substantial individual contributions, they must rely on union or mass membership PACs to balance corporate, wealthy individual and upper-middle-class influence. As we noted earlier, compared to corporate and trade PACs, the strength of union PACs has declined sharply. Furthermore, candidates find it far easier to build campaigns from the contributions of wealthy donors and corporate PACs. Only a handful of politicians have successfully raised enough money through a combination of union PACs, grassroots organizations, and small contributors.

The overwhelming Democratic congressional majorities resulting from the 1974 off-year election prompted the Republicans to redouble their efforts to improve their financial base. Two conditions were important to the new push: (1) conservative and business fears that the Democrats were about to embark on a new round of liberal economic and social policies, and (2) GOP fears of permanent minority status. The party's concern reached fever pitch after the Watergate hearings and President Nixon's resignation. Guy Vander Jagt, named chair of the National Republican Congressional Committee in 1975, grasped the nature of the perceived crisis and understood that it could be turned to advantage. Vander Jagt offered a summary of his activities.

> In 1975, I spent most of the year trying to get business and industries to establish PACs. I worked with the Chamber of Commerce and with the National Association of Manufacturers, and I travelled the country giving my Paul Revere speech: "Wake up, America, wake up. There's a war going on—a war that will determine the economic future of this country, and you aren't involved."[30]

That the call was heeded is reflected in the growth of corporate and trade PACs in the ensuing period.

The financial edge enjoyed by corporations, conservatives, and Republicans has a qualitative dimension not readily grasped from a superficial analysis of the data on contributions. Corporate capital has managed to organize itself in such a way as to maximize its influence at critical pressure points in the system. Business PACs have effectively targeted members of key congressional committees and subcommittees vital to their particular interests. A good example is the House Energy and Commerce Committee. In 1982, labor PACs contributed the sizable sum of $665,757 to members of this Committee. However, the combined PAC contributions solely from energy companies ($468,820) and from the real estate and construction industry ($223,223) surpassed total labor contributions. Additional contributions to committee members from PACs linked to banking and finance and corporations involved in food, automobiles, communications, doctors, hospitals, pharmaceutical, insurance, aerospace, and other firms together matched the labor contributions a second time over.[31] The situation was similar for other key committees, such as the Senate Finance Committee and the House Ways and Means Committee, where business PACs accounted for 68 percent ($11 million) of all PAC contributions made to committee members in 1984.[32]

The need to attract corporate PAC contributions has strengthened the hand of Democratic leaders who seek to cure the party's ills by loosening its ties to minorities, the unions, and the working class and poor. Stung by their loss of the presidency and control of the Senate in 1980, the Democrats decided to seek corporate PAC contributions aggressively. Rep. Tony Coelho (D–Calif.) persuaded big Democratic financiers to contribute to the party's congressional fund and at the same time helped the Democrats to organize more effectively to solicit corporate PAC donations. Both major parties and politicians within each party established "clubs" to facilitate interaction between wealthy contributors and politicians. (Richard Gephardt's "Democratic Leadership Council" is an example.) Major party figures gave speeches and held conferences for such clubs, but Coelho indicated that political education was hardly the driving motivation for joining. "Access. Access," he told columnist Elizabeth Drew, "that's the name of the game. They meet with the leadership and with the chairmen of the committees. We don't sell legislation: we sell the opportunity to be heard."[33]

Impressive signs of Democratic gains in fundraising lie in the comparisons of contributions to the congressional elections in 1984 and the off-year elections in 1986. In this two-year period, Democratic challengers and candidates for open seat races greatly increased their share of contributions from corporate, trade, and "nonconnected" PACs, while maintaining their near monopoly on labor PACs. Democratic candidates' share of corporate contributions rose from only 8 percent in 1984 to 28 percent in the 1986 off-year elections. In 1988, their share compared to contributions to Republicans rose to 27 percent.[34]

Despite (or because of) the Democratic gains in fundraising, it is clear that the ideological pendulum did not swing back toward liberalism. The Democrats' courting of corporate and trade PACs reflected a swing to the right in the congressional wing of the party. As the *National Journal* pointed out after the 1984 elections, business gave more to the Democrats because "there was a dearth of vulnerable Democratic incumbents with voting records that the business community opposed."[35] The American Enterprise Institute's Michael Malbin attributed shifting corporate funding to "congressional Democrats...speaking more about capital formation and other business issues."[36] Representative Coelho's attempts to attract corporate money prompted the chair of the PAC funded by Tenneco Inc., the third largest corporate PAC giver in 1984 and fourth largest in 1986, to comment that "the political climate has changed somewhat and is more [supportive of] the private sector."[37]

Corporate PAC money also helps keep the Democrats listing to the right because it helps more conservative candidates defeat liberals in Democratic primaries. Where liberal Democratic incumbents are relatively secure, corporations use PAC contributions to preserve access to them, as in the case of possible presidential contenders like Senators Ted Kennedy and Joseph Biden. But when liberals are confronted with a viable conservative challenger, they are likely to get short shrift from wealthy individuals and business interests. Liberal Bruce Morrison of Connecticut, for example, was touted by Representative Coelho as worthy of business support, but in the last few weeks of his close but successful 1984 race to retain his seat, he attracted only $7,000 from corporate PACs while his more conservative opponent received $37,000.

Though Democratic incumbents have been attracting more and more corporate support, few Democratic challengers have been similarly blessed. Lockheed Corporation, the biggest corporate sugardaddy in 1984, divided its contributions evenly among Democrats and Republicans, but only two of the 122 candidates it supported were nonincumbents. Tenneco contributed to thirty-seven Democrats, but only one was a nonincumbent.[38] If corporate PACs inadvertently fail to support the winning side, it is easy to show contrition. After several of their preferred Republican incumbents were defeated in 1986, corporate PACs made amends by contributing after the election to the victorious Democratic candidates. The latter welcomed this largesse, since all of them had substantial campaign debts to pay.

The Democratic drive to compete with the GOP for corporate money manifested itself at the 1988 Democratic convention in Atlanta. Dukakis's fundraiser Robert Farmer, determined that the Democratic treasure chest would not be lighter than the Republicans', went to work on the business community. Fat cats were pumped to join the party's Victory Fund Board of Trustees (which already numbered 200 members) for the modest amount of $100,000 each (through the medium of PACs). Farmer even envisioned seven-figure contributions reminiscent of the pre-Watergate days. Affluent potential contributors were treated to a midnight dinner with Dukakis and Bentsen in Atlanta, which of course was not included in a published list of official events provided by the party. One Dukakis fundraiser, Nikolas Patsaouras, was rash enough to say of the process: "We're given the names and we meet with them. We get them when they're warm, and we close the sale."[39] But Dukakis fundraisers were careful not to promise the contributors too much. They arranged a third party to witness the "closing" of the sale to ensure that there were no misunderstandings about "deals" being made.[40]

The Financial Realignment of American Politics

Changes in the campaign finance system are intricately entwined with the overall rightward drift in American politics underway since 1968. It is worth recalling, in this regard, that the first modern reform in campaign financing came in 1971, before Watergate and the worst abuses of the Nixon campaign. The influence of money was already rising to a degree that alarmed even career politicians, who were understandably reluctant to change the rules of the game that helped keep them in office. But they recognized that if they did not take action, they would be forced to ride the tide of political money to wherever it would take them.

In view of the continuing rise in the volume of political money, it may seem ludicrous to assert that campaign finance reform has greatly affected anything. Without reform, however, the system would have been even more blatantly offensive to the American public than it is today because the internecine battles among elite factions would have lacked sufficient internal restraint and regulation. Whereas wealth continues to translate into power, the new system reduces the kind of overt blackmail in which Nixon's campaign indulged, and it makes it more difficult (although not impossible) for any single corporate sector to "buy" a candidate.

Hence the relative autonomy of the state was enhanced for a while by campaign finance reform. Smaller contributors, including the upper-middle-class and less wealthy business owners, were given symbolic reassurance that the influence of wealth had been curbed. But campaign reform contributed to a drift to the right in American politics, and the influence of personal and corporate wealth was actually enhanced. The Democrats have learned to play the game by drifting rightward with the GOP. As private and corporate wealth finds new routes into the campaign system, more scandals are inevitable. Meanwhile, the political discourse that occurs in campaigns is more restricted than ever, dictated as much by the search for money as by the search for votes.

Notes

1. *Plunkett of Tammany Hall,* recorded by William Riordon (New York: E. P. Dutton, 1963), p. 73 (original publication 1905). Tammany Hall, the building housing the New York City Democratic Committee, became the name used to designate the Democratic machine in New York.

2. Elizabeth Drew, *Politics and Money* (New York: Collier Books, 1983), pp. 4-5.

3. John Judas, "Wright's Wrongs and Real Issues," *In These Times,* April 26–May 2, 1989, p. 2.

4. Ross Baker, "Leadership in Congress: Mutual Aid or Institutional Challenge?" paper presented at the Annual Meeting of the Midwest Political Science Association, Chicago, Ill., April 13-15, 1989.

5. Herbert Alexander, *Financing Politics,* 3rd ed. (Washington, D.C.: Congressional Quarterly Press, 1984), pp. 57-58.

6. Ibid., pp. 10-14.

7. FEC release, March 27, 1989; "The Campaign Sewer Overflows," editorial, *New York Times,* November 7, 1989; "Campaign Finance: Smell No Evil," editorial, *New York Times,* December 12, 1988; Richard L. Burke, "Some True Tales of Campaign Cash," *New York Times,* December 25, 1988.

8. Calculated from FEC release, May 2, 1988.

9. FEC release, February 24, 1989.

10. Gary C. Jackobson, *Money in Congressional Elections* (New Haven: Yale University Press, 1980), p. 65.

11. FEC release, November 4, 1988, pp. 41-42.

12. Larry Sabato, *PAC Power: Inside the World of Political Action Committees* (New York: W. W. Norton, 1984), pp. 4-7.

13. Alexander, *Financing the 1972 Election* (Lexington, Mass.: D. C. Heath, 1976), pp. 461, 504. See also the American Enterprise Institute study cited by Evert Carl Ladd in "As the Realignment Turns," *Public Opinion* (December-January 1985), p. 7.

14. Maxwell Glen, "Focus on Fund Raising," *National Journal,* December 7, 1985, pp. 2798-2799. Sabato, *PAC Power,* pp. 76, 89. In 1983–84, House candidates received 34 percent of their campaign funds from PACs, twice the percentage for Senate candidates.

15. FEC release, November 4, 1988.

16. Drew, *Politics and Money,* p. 142.

17. FEC release, June 22, 1988.

18. Arthur Hadley, *The Invisible Primary* (Englewood Cliffs, N.J.: Prentice-Hall, 1976).

19. Drew, *Politics and Money,* pp. 41-42, 44, 46, 49-51; Bill Lambrecht, "Southern Money Is Flowing to Gephardt," *St. Louis Post-Dispatch,* July 17, 1987, p. A10.

20. An excellent article on Gephardt's fundraising, and the basis for his account, is Bill

Lambrecht, "A-Hunting Gephardt Goes—for Money," *St. Louis Post-Dispatch,* January 18, 1987, pp. 1, 8.

21. Ibid.

22. Ibid.

23. FEC release, July 21, 1986.

24. Data cited by Baker, "Leadership in Congress," passim.

25. Lambrecht, "A-Hunting . . ."

26. Ibid. Robertson was later fined by the Federal Election Commission for unreported campaign expenditures made before his official announcement.

27. Bruce Stone, "In 1988 Jackson Money Trees Paid Off," *National Journal,* July 3, 1988.

28. Cited in Thomas Byrne Edsall, *The New Politics of Inequality* (New York: W. W. Norton, 1984), pp. 98-99.

29. Data cited in *The Guardian,* December 11, 1985.

30. Drew, *Politics and Money,* p. 11.

31. Ibid., p. 71.

32. *National Journal,* August 3, 1985, p. 1818.

33. Drew, *Politics and Money,* p. 49.

34. Everett Carl Ladd, "Campaign Spending and Democracy," *The Ladd Report* 4 (1986); FEC release, April 9, 1989.

35. Maxwell Glen, "Focus on Fundraising," *National Journal,* January 19, 1985, p. 156.

36. Ibid., p. 159.

37. Ibid., p. 158.

38. Ibid., p. 159.

39. Carol Matlack, "Democrats Love the Money Man," *National Journal,* convention special, July 23, 1988, p. 1928.

40. Carol Matlack, "Dropping By: A Top Fund Raiser's Daily Drill," *National Journal,* convention special, July 23, 1988, p. 1926.

Chapter 8

The Decline of the Parties

The Weakening of the Party System

Historically, the two dominant parties have been crucial instruments that elites have utilized to mobilize broad electoral coalitions. Competition between the parties and among groups within each party has helped elites arbitrate their differences. The parties also have worked as linking mechanisms between elites and the masses, though the relationship has been a hierarchical one in which elite factions have sought to swing mass sentiment or the electorate in one direction or another, or in which they have responded to mass discontent, especially during times of economic crisis like the Great Depression.

Over the past two decades, the parties have largely been supplanted by professional campaign staffs, media specialists, fundraisers, pollsters, political action committees, and other players as "gatekeepers" in the election process. Elections managed by a professional campaign industry possessing the technology to frame issues and candidates' images cannot fulfill the same function as elections conducted through a party system. Media-based elections do not provide an opportunity for mediation and bargaining among elites, and they do not forge a link between the electorate and the elites that win government power. Failing to fulfill their historic political functions, elections in the United States have become increasingly marginal to the governmental apparatus. They have become a part of America's television culture, peopled with media stars and contrived soap opera drama.

The New Deal Coalition and the "Liberal Alternative"

To understand the erosion of the two-party system, it is crucial to examine the structure and internal politics of the Democratic party. This is important because the Democrats have constituted the majority national party—defined by reference to voter preferences and congressional leadership—since the 1932 presidential election. Between 1901 and 1933, the Democrats controlled both houses of Congress only three times. Between 1933 and 1989, in contrast, the Democrats failed to control both houses only three times.

The Great Depression revolutionized the group composition of the U.S. party system. The center of gravity for the Democratic party shifted to northern cities, where large numbers of working class and poor people were concentrated. In addition to the cities and the solid South, so many people benefited from New Deal programs that the new voting coalition ensured that the Democrats would become ascendant. In 1936, a Gallup poll found that large blocs of voters benefiting from New Deal programs supported Roosevelt: 59 percent of farmers (Agricultural Adjustment Act, Farm Credit Administration, Farm Mortgage Corporation, abolition of the gold standard), 61 percent of white-collar workers (bank regulation, FHA home loans, savings deposit insurance), 80 percent of organized labor (government recognition of collective bargaining, unemployment insurance, work relief), and 68 percent of people under twenty-five years of age (Civilian Conservation Corps, National Youth Administration). Among lower-income groups, 76 percent favored Roosevelt, compared to 60 percent of the middle class.[1] In contrast, upper-income groups identified overwhelmingly with the Republican party.

Working-class urban voters constituted the center of the New Deal coalition in the North. Union members and their families, urban ethnics, and blacks voted more heavily for Roosevelt in the 1936 election than did any other groups in the country. Their tacit alliance with the one-party South, where Republicans rarely even fielded candidates for congressional, state, and local offices, created a national coalition of formidable electoral strength. But it was a fragile coalition, and racial divisions threatened constantly to break it apart. In the 1964 election, Republicans began to break the Democrats' grip on the South. In the North, demographic and economic changes eroded the strength of inner-city party organizations. Their constituents were moving to the suburbs, and the sons and daughters of union members were joining the ranks of educated white-collar professionals. In the process, attachments to the Democratic party weakened.

Following the Second World War, serious contenders for the Democratic presidential nomination traded on the rhetoric and symbols of the New Deal: a beneficent government that would help the underdog and downtrodden, a government that would promote equal opportunity in education and jobs. The liberals who sought the presidency ran on platforms that promised government programs to redress inequality even while they tried to preserve the Democratic hegemony in the conservative South. By the 1980 election, however, it was clear that the New Deal coalition had mostly dissolved, and as a consequence Democratic presidential candidates no longer knew how to package the issues. The Democrats' contenders were scarcely able to contribute to a public dialogue about policy and politics at all, as illustrated in 1988, when Michael Dukakis tried to assert that "competence" rather than "ideology" was the main issue in the presidential campaign.

The public philosophy of American liberalism that endured until the 1980s was created largely in the 1950s, but the electoral alignment that sustained it was forged earlier, in the 1930s and 1940s. During the Great Depression, liberals and social democrats like New York's Senator Robert Wagner and John L. Lewis of the

United Mine Workers mobilized workers, farmers, the poor, and blacks throughout the North. Left-wing socialists, religious radicals, independent progressives, and communists also were prominent in union and Democratic party politics.

Within the Democratic party, the 1948 election forced a definitive split between liberals and the Left. Left wingers formed the Progressive party, choosing former Vice President Henry Wallace as its presidential candidate to challenge Democrat Harry Truman and Republican Thomas Dewey. Many of the planks in the Progressive platform presaged legislation that would be enacted later by the Democrats—public housing (in 1949), civil rights legislation (1964), food stamps (1963). Other social welfare programs were never adopted: national health insurance, government assistance for cooperative middle-income housing projects, and a permanent public works employment program.

The Progressives (not to be confused with the "good government" movement just after the turn of the century) also favored nationalization of some of the largest banks as well as corporations that provided energy and transportation, as had been done in several Western European nations. They advocated negotiations with the Soviet Union to outlaw atomic weapons; supported the United Nations and proposed that the massive economic aid program, known as the Marshall Plan, be implemented under U.N. auspices rather than channeled only to governments and groups in Western Europe that the United States supported.

Wallace proposed these programs to 32,000 delegates and spectators assembled at the Progressive party's July 1948 convention in Philadelphia. But the Philadelphia convention marked the end rather than a beginning of a left alternative in American politics. Democratic liberals and the Republicans joined forces to label the Progressive party as a communist front. Inside the Democratic party, liberals organized to drive leftists out. One key figure in the effort was Minneapolis mayor Hubert Humphrey (the Democratic presidential nominee in 1968), who, along with Walter Mondale (the Democratic standard bearer in 1984), took the lead in purging the left from the Minnesota Democratic Farmer-Labor party.

A national anticommunist hysteria was whipped up by the inflammatory rhetoric of the 1948 campaign. The Smith Act of 1947 and the Internal Security Act of 1948 gave the government the legal tools to prosecute alleged Communists and "Communist-front" organizations. For almost five years, Senator Joseph McCarthy and the House Committee on Un-American Activities led a campaign to ferret out Communists from government bureaucracies, the movie industry, the universities, labor unions, and professions. McCarthy dragged hundreds of witnesses before his Senate committee in his search for Communists and their "dupes and sympathizers." Thousands of artists and intellectuals were fired and put on employment blacklists. To promote their own careers, some witnesses enthusiastically provided the names of suspected communists and their "sympathizers." The president of the Screen Actors Guild, a Democrat named Ronald Reagan, cooperated by providing the committee with the names of "security risks" in Hollywood. In Hollywood, as in other professions, to speak out against the witch hunts was a ticket to unemployment.

Beginning in 1947, liberals made themselves complicit with McCarthyism when the Department of Justice under President Truman undertook to prosecute

Communists and other leftists under the Smith Act and the Internal Security Act. To prove it was not "soft on communism" at home, the Truman administration required tens of thousands of federal employees to appear before loyalty boards to "prove" they were not "subversive." These boards asked employees questions such as, "Were you a regular purchaser of the *New York Times?*" "What do you think of female chastity?" "At one time or two, were you a strong advocate of the United Nations?" About 12,000 federal employees resigned under the pressure; another 2,700 were fired for giving wrong answers.[2] Thousands of public employees in state and local governments and in schools and universities were fired. Often, their sin was that they were Jewish, black, or had previously associated with civil rights organizations.

Finally, in 1954, some politicians and media figures began to speak out against the witch hunts. The nation's leading newscaster, Edward R. Murrow, played a critical role in turning the tide of public opinion against McCarthyism. McCarthy over-reached himself when he accused military officers of having communist sympathies. By then Dwight Eisenhower, a five-star general and war hero, occupied the White House. As a result of McCarthy's fall from grace, the pressure was eased, but the Left had already been effectively eliminated from American political life.

As a result, American political discourse was sharply truncated. Political alternatives identified as left of center in the ideological spectrum—such as national health insurance, public works, stronger protections for unions and government housing programs—were routinely labeled as communist. In the late 1940s, the American Medical Association launched a campaign against public health insurance on the ground that it was "socialized medicine." Public housing barely passed Congress in 1949, even though it enjoyed widespread popular support, because the president of the National Association of Real Estate Boards got a lot of mileage out of calling it "socialized housing." In such an atmosphere meaningful dialogue about domestic policies was difficult to sustain. On foreign policy, it was lost altogether and it has never been recovered. Democratic liberals embraced belligerent Cold War anticommunist rhetoric as enthusiastically as did Republican conservatives.

All social welfare programs were inevitably labeled as "creeping socialism" or as part of an international communist conspiracy to weaken the rugged individualism ascribed to Americans. Liberals who favored such programs were therefore always on the defensive, trying to avoid these labels themselves. And thus the crisis of modern liberalism emerged in full bloom. Any attempt to accomplish a domestic agenda of workable social welfare programs came up against the fact that the liberals had helped to destroy their best allies on the left who would have helped mobilize electoral support from blacks, working-class and poor people, small farmers, and union members. Liberals no longer occupied the center between conservatives on the right and socialists or welfare state advocates on the left. Now they *were* the left, such as it existed in the context of the American two-party system.

The Democrats' Loss of Labor

The marriage between labor and the Democrats was consummated during the New Deal. The National Recovery Act of 1932 recognized the right of workers to organize trade unions. The National Labor Relations Act of 1935 provided a legal basis to make that right a reality by specifying procedures that workers could follow to establish a union at their plant. Among the achievements of this movement were not only higher wages but protection from arbitrary treatment by employers. Promotion by seniority, grievance procedures, and other rights limited abuse of workers by management. "Unfair" labor practices, designed to intimidate workers trying to found unions or to undercut the unions' effectiveness in bargaining or enforcing contract provisions, were subject to penalties meted out by the Department of Labor. The labor movement also fought for such programs as Social Security, unemployment compensation, and public housing. Union membership shot from 2.9 million in 1933 to 8.9 million in 1940.

Southern Democrats opposed labor unions. President Roosevelt remained generally aloof. But influential northern congressmen and governors, such as New York's Senator Robert Wagner, sought to establish the labor movement as the basic foundation for the Democratic party. There was a strong communist and socialist presence in the labor movement, but even the most radical leaders, with very few exceptions, did not seek to replace the capitalist with a socialist economy.

Although almost all employers opposed the new labor relations system at first, many of them began to realize that unions were not necessarily anticapitalist and that, in fact, there might even be a benefit to signing a peace pact with labor. At the plant level, employers now had to adapt to the loss of some of their arbitrary power to hire and fire, promote and demote, and dictate working conditions. But at the same time, the union-management contract bound union members to follow some work rules and not to strike.

The Second World War was seized on by employers as an opportunity to reverse some of labor's gains. Although workers supported the war against fascism overall, they resisted the repeated attempts by employers to use the war as an excuse to speed up production, lengthen the work day, and take back control of working conditions. The result was a series of strikes in 1944 and 1945. The first year after the war saw intense labor conflict, but in 1947 an effective truce was achieved. Labor leaders accepted a bargain with employers under which wage increases and employers' acceptance of their right to exist were traded for concessions in other areas. Contracts restored management's right to control production on the shop floor, with unions giving up much of the leverage won during the 1930s. Most labor leaders opposed new legislation to curb union power, but they failed to use strikes or other measures to prevent the passage of laws like the Taft-Hartley Act in 1947, which (among other provisions) permitted states to enact right-to-work laws that allowed nonunion workers to work in union shops and that gave courts and the president the authority to issue injunctions against strikes. Increases in the numbers of supervisory personnel confirmed the new management control over workers. The number of management supervisors rose from fourteen per one-hundred workers in 1950, to twenty-one per one-hundred workers by 1965.[3]

Most unionized workers saw their real wages rise during the period of labor-management harmony, but in the long run the pact between capital and labor crucially favored capital. Labor gave up any meaningful representation on boards of directors or any ability to influence investment patterns, including whether profits would be reinvested locally to improve the quality of life in local communities and keep the industry competitive with firms elsewhere. Later, when corporations would use their complete control over investment decisions to move plants and jobs to cheaper, nonunionized production sites in the Sun Belt or the Third World, the tide turned decisively against labor. Corporations moved plants to "right-to-work" states and opened new nonunion shops even when they stayed in the United States. The unionized sector of the work force plummeted from 34 percent of the nonagricultural labor force in 1954 to 28 percent in 1970, and to 17 percent by 1986.[4]

With wages and benefits improving during the postwar economic boom, workers and their union leaders showed little interest in how management used profits, and even less in extending their unions into the southern and southwestern states. These were areas that held great attraction for corporations, for their cheap labor and absence of strong unions served as magnets to management looking for ways to cut costs. At the same time, the economy was changing. The two fastest-growing sectors were domestic labor and food services, both difficult to organize because many of the employees were minorities, women, very young or old, or illegal immigrants. These developments further undermined union strength.

The pact between organized labor and management relied upon economic expansion. When the recession of the 1970s hit, a crucial prop was pulled out from under labor-management relations. Productivity per person hour in the United States rose at an average annual rate of 2.8 percent in the 1960s, and as late as 1970 U.S. manufacturing was still about twice as productive as Japanese manufacturing, and a third more productive than manufacturing in Germany and France. But the other countries were catching up fast. They built new plants with the latest technology, made possible in part by government subsidies and a degree of joint government-corporate-labor planning that was rejected in the United States as "socialistic." Their economies were also not as heavily burdened by military spending. By the early 1980s, average output per hour in manufacturing in the United States trailed behind output in France and Germany and only slightly outpaced output in Japan.[5] In 1958, it took 27 hours to make a ton of hot rolled sheet steel in Japan, compared to 9 hours in the United States. By 1980, it took only 4.4 hours in Japan, and 5.3 hours in the United States. In 1965, it took 9 hours to produce a television set in Japan, compared to 7.6 hours in the United States. By 1980, it took 0.8 hours in Japan, but 2.6 hours in the United States. In machine tools manufacturing the Japanese were, in 1965, about 40 percent less productive than U.S. workers, but by 1985 they were about 25 percent more productive. In the critical industry of the postwar economy—automobiles—the Japanese lowered their average number of hours per car from 260 hours in 1970 to 140 hours by 1981. The U.S. automakers stayed right at 210 hours. Other industries in which the U.S. lost the productivity edge included watches, cameras, large electric motors, trucks, bulldozers, agricultural tractors, buses, and subway cars.[6]

Much of the reason that U.S. productivity lagged was because American firms had failed to invest in new plant, equipment, and technology. Instead, profits were used to build plants where labor was cheaper or to reach agreements with foreign firms. U.S. banks provided much of the capital for foreign companies to compete with American manufacturing. In addition, U.S. foreign policy helped provide the "right" kind of business climate (cheap labor, low taxes, little regulation) for the expansion of multinational capital into the Third World, even as the U.S. economy became less competitive.

A common myth in the United States is that the blame for falling U.S. competitiveness in the world economy lies with overpaid workers. But productivity rose much faster than salaries during the postwar boom. Between 1948 and 1966, the average production worker's hourly output increased by $2.68 per hour, but the average hourly wage increased by only 86 cents per hour, leaving a difference of $1.82. The government took 61 cents in taxes; only 35 cents of the remaining $1.21 generated by workers was reinvested in new or better plant and equipment. The remaining 86 cents went for higher dividends paid to investors, higher profits and executive salaries, and more management employees.[7]

To have insisted on a wiser use of the nation's wealth would have required a labor movement and leadership interested in the overall political position of labor. In an era of prosperity and anticommunism in the mass culture, and following the purge of the Left in the early 1950s, there was little chance of such a development. Labor had long given up its voice in corporate decision making and had purged the labor leaders who might have pushed hard for an influential voice in investment and production decisions.

In 1936, the Congress of Industrial Organizations (CIO) formed to represent those members of the industrial labor force that the more conservative, white, skill-and-craft-oriented American Federation of Labor (AFL) had long eschewed. Communists and leftists had been courageous and essential allies in the struggle to organize the CIO in the face of well-organized violence meted out by industry's hired thugs and state National Guards. Following the war, however, Phillip Murray, president of the CIO, joined with Walter Reuther of the United Autoworkers and James Carey of the United Electrical Workers to rid the unions of their leftist members.

The effect of removing militant and radical labor leaders was that many of the union leaders who remained were interested less in the political and economic influence of workers than in enriching themselves by pursuing full-time careers as union bureaucrats. The idea that labor had a distinct political interest antagonistic to or even separate from capital was completely lost. George Meany, president of the AFL-CIO after the merger of the AFL and CIO in 1955, exemplified the new generation of union leaders. Meany was a Cold War liberal to the core, and when some unions, such as the United Auto Workers, announced opposition to the Vietnam War in the mid-1960s, he forced them out of the AFL-CIO. Meany and the labor movement supported the civil rights movement as long as it stuck to the concept of equal rights under the law, but when it became clear that black leaders were going to challenge white political bosses in the cities and seek a more influential voice in the Democratic party, Meany resisted any further concessions—particularly since many affiliate unions were guilty of racial discrimination and were unwilling to cooperate with equal opportunity employment plans. Meany and his successor, Lane Kirkland, worked against any kind of quotas for minorities and women, both in employment and in delegate selection for national party conventions. When blacks, women, and the youth movement entered Democratic party politics in 1968 and 1972, Meany aligned with older, white male party leaders, like Mayor Daley of Chicago, to resist.

After Jimmy Carter's defeat in the presidential election of 1980, Kirkland and other labor leaders decided to make the Democratic party into a surrogate labor party, and they pushed hard to make an old labor ally, Walter Mondale, the party's candidate. But they were at least twenty years too late. The union leadership attempted to convert the Democrats into a vehicle for representing labor at a time when 70 percent of the public (according to one poll) agreed that the "high wages paid to American workers are primarily responsible for making U.S. products more expensive than imported products," and 51 percent of blue-collar workers agreed that "unions are not concerned enough with increasing productivity" (only 38 percent disagreed).[8] For at least three decades, Americans have seen big labor leaders repeatedly indicted for corruption, violence, and close associations with organized crime. Most of the labor leaders who were committed to worker democracy and workers' welfare were kicked out long ago, labeled as Communists or Socialists. For the Democratic party and its liberal leadership, the chickens had finally come home to roost. The basic foundation of their party hardly existed as a political force anymore.

The Defection of the South

The Democratic ticket won the 1964 presidential election with 61 percent of the popular vote and swept 486 electoral college votes to Barry Goldwater's 53. But the landslide concealed an ominous development for the Democratic coalition. Goldwater decided to "go hunting where the ducks are": to appeal for southern white votes by defending the concept of "states' rights"—a code phrase for opposition to civil rights. He received 87 percent of the popular vote in Mississippi, almost 70 percent in Alabama, and substantially more than 50 percent in Louisiana, Georgia, and South Carolina. Goldwater carried a majority of white votes in every former Confederate state except Texas.[9] After 1964, Republican candidates began to win southern state elections for the first time since Reconstruction.

In 1968, the Republicans capitalized on white resentment of blacks' civil rights gains by reviving the law and order issue, which had been Goldwater's favorite theme in the 1964 campaign. In November, the Democratic nominee Hubert Humphrey carried only one southern state, Texas. Across the South, he carried only 31 percent of the vote, running behind both Republican Richard Nixon (34.5 percent) and segregationist third-party candidate George Wallace (34.6 percent). Jimmy Carter of Georgia carried the South in 1976, but the Democratic presidential candidates since then have carried less than 40 percent of the Southern vote. The party's share of state and local offices fell from 80 percent in 1970 to 60 percent in 1982.[10]

The loss of the solid South might have presented national Democratic leaders with the opportunity to form a more unified national party, now that its conservative wing had defected. But the party was in disarray. Feminists and blacks pressed demands for a new round of social legislation to fund child care, expand welfare benefits, implement laws requiring equal pay for equal work, and improve affirmative action legislation. By the mid-1970s, a majority of Democratic House members from the North represented districts with substantial white middle-class constituencies. The political effects of four decades of suburbanization were far reaching. Cities were no longer a pivotal electoral constituency for the northern wing of the party. Jimmy Carter and Walter Mondale carried the big cities by sizeable margins in 1980 and 1984. But most of the votes were not to be found in cities. Only 12 percent of the national vote in 1984 was cast in large cities (over 50,000 in population), and 55 percent was cast in suburbs and small cities.[11] The majority of Democratic senators and representatives became beholden to constituencies outside the cities, and the political effects were far reaching. The big-city liberals of the Democratic party were replaced by a new generation of "neo-liberals" (if they used the "L" label at all), who tended to favor tax cuts and fiscal austerity, though they tended to be more "liberal" on social (not social welfare) issues than Republicans.

A Republican Realignment?

As early as 1964, some conservatives claimed that history was swinging their way and that conservative policies would soon be legitimated by electoral decisions. In 1969, this argument was articulated clearly and convincingly in *The Emerging Republican Majority,* by Kevin Phillips, a Republican conservative. Phillips foresaw a Republican realignment on the basis of a coalition uniting conservatives in the South and West with white suburban voters throughout the country.[12]

A new version of this theory, recognizing that it has not happened as thoroughly and abruptly as originally envisioned by Phillips, was christened "rolling realignment" by Richard Wirthlin, Reagan's media consultant in the 1980 and 1984 elections.[13] The term is meant to describe a gradual shift in popular opinion and partisan loyalties underway since 1964. According to the theory, realignment was occurring without a precipitating "earthquake" event like depression or war, which might bring about a sudden shift of partisan loyalties. Wirthlin claimed instead that previously Democratic working-class and middle-class voters were moving toward the GOP because they now rejected liberal social programs. Conservatives hoped to win over these voters as well as the younger voters, who had never been part of the New Deal alignment.[14]

Wirthlin showed that younger people were identifying as Republicans at a rate unprecedented in the postwar period.[15] If Republicans could sustain the loyalty of this group from election to election, the Democrats would eventually become a minority party. The Republican advantage among younger voters would produce a "rolling realignment" in the purest sense: Each generation of voters would fall more securely in the Republican camp. In 1986 young voters slightly favored the GOP over the Democrats, 33 percent to 31 percent—with 36 percent saying they had no party preference.[16] If the GOP can retain the loyalty of these new voters as they age and can continue to attract each generation of new voters, this will eventually result in a realignment favoring the Republicans.

Over the last forty years, national surveys have asked people whether they think of themselves as Republicans, Democrats, or Independents. If there has been a "rolling realignment" in favor of the Republicans, it has gathered momentum only since 1982 (see table 8-1). Before that, Democrats usually could count on the expressed loyalty of 42 percent or more of voters, compared to less than 30 percent for the Republicans. After the 1960s there was a pronounced rise in the number of self-identified Independents, (29 percent in 1972, up from 16 percent in 1937 and 22 percent in 1950) a fact that led the Minnesota Republican party to change its name to the "Independent-Republican Party" in the late 1970s.

In 1946, Democrats actually trailed the Republicans by 39 percent to 40 percent, but by 1950 they led by twelve percentage points, 45 percent to 33 percent. The Democratic advantage peaked in 1964, probably as a result of Barry Goldwater's disastrous presidential campaign, then fell back to more "normal" levels until the 1980s. There was some impressive movement toward the GOP between 1982 and 1985, peaking in 1985 when the GOP trailed Democrats in voters' expressed preference only by 33 percent to 38 percent. But even before the Iran-*contra* scandal broke in November 1986, there were signs that the tide was ebbing. An August 1986 Harris Poll showed that the Democratic lead had widened to 39 percent to 32 percent. The gap further widened in 1987 to a ten-point spread, 40 percent to 30 percent.

Of course, as the scandal fades from memory, Republican gains may be recouped. Indeed, George Bush's successful campaign showed that the scandal had

Table 8-1 **Political Party Affiliations**

Year	Republican	Democrat	Independent
1937	34%	50%	16%
1946	40	39	21
1950	33	45	22
1960	30	47	23
1964	25	53	22
1968	27	46	27
1972	28	43	29
1976	23	47	30
1980	24	46	30
1982	26	45	29
1983	25	44	31
1984	31	40	29
1985	33	38	29
1986	32	39	29
1987 (April)	30	40	30

Source: The Gallup Report, no. 260 (May 1987): 16–17.

not fatally affected the careers of Republican politicians, and both he and the Republican party showed substantial gains in public approval ratings in the wake of the invasion and occupation of Panama in December 1989. The Republican surge after 1974, however, has been built in part on the party's ability to woo working-class voters away from the New Deal coalition on the basis of conservative social policies (anti-abortion appeals, "law and order") and middle-class voters on the basis of greed (e.g., lower taxes). But the social polarization produced by Reaganomics threatens to erode GOP support among conservative working-class voters. And the politics of abortion threatens to swing some middle-class voters back toward Democratic candidates, who tend to run more pro-choice candidates.[17]

Though a wholesale partisan realignment has not occurred, there is little doubt that Republicans have made significant gains among several important groups (see table 8-2). If we take 1955 as the base year and compare it to 1985, such a shift is evident among white southerners (especially Protestants), skilled workers with some college education, Jews, business managers, and men. White southerners have been Democrats since the Civil War, and their defection to the GOP is historic, coinciding with the rise in black registration and voting. (Fifty-eight percent of southern whites identified themselves as Democrats in 1955; this figure fell to 36 percent by 1985, when 39 percent said they were Republicans.) Jews still express a heavy preference for the Democratic party, but their shift to the Republicans (from 10 percent in 1955 to 22 percent in 1985) is also historic. Tensions between blacks and Jews, two important blocks in the old New Deal coalition, were especially pronounced after Jesse Jackson's open espousal of human rights for the Palestinians in the 1984 presidential primary campaign (which was interpreted by some Jews as anti-Israel), controversy over his use of the epithet "hymie" in a private conversation overheard by a reporter, and the anti-Semitic speeches of one of his key supporters, the Reverend Louis Farrakhan. Jews, however, also have reason for distrusting the Republican right wing because of an embedded anti-Semitism and the aggressive stance of religious evangelical groups on issues such as prayer in the schools.

The size of the service sector, including the proportion of the work force employed at various levels of corporate management and as independent professionals, has been increasing at the same time that the size of the work force employed in manufacturing has declined. Hence, as an occupational sector grows that has traditionally voted Republican, a gradual realignment of voter loyalties may emerge.

Perhaps the shift in the partisan identification of Roman Catholics can be considered a barometer of realignment. Immigrant Roman Catholic workers and their descendants constituted a key component of the New Deal coalition. But the movement of many white Catholics from working-class neighborhoods in central cities to middle-class suburbs has changed the political behavior of this group. As table 8-1 shows, however, one of the most significant shifts in the past forty years is a movement of voters away from *both* parties. Before the 1960s, only about one-fifth of voters declared themselves as nonpartisan. But this proportion increased to 30 percent by 1976, and it has remained at about that level since, while the fortunes of the two parties ebb and flow.

Table 8-2 Party Identification

Change in Party Identification,
1955–1985

Group	1955		1985	
	Percent GOP	Percent Democrat	Percent GOP	Percent Democrat
All	32%	44%	34%	37%
Social Groups				
Protestants	35	42	38	36
Catholics	26	52	30	40
Jews	10	48	22	48
Northern white Protestants	44	32	45	26
Northern white Catholics	28	47	30	38
Southern white Protestants	22	59	41	34
Southern whites	21	58	39	36
Blacks	18	62	10	73
By Education				
Less than high school	29	50	26	49
High school graduate	34	40	34	37
Some college	32	42	39	30
College graduate	36	36	39	30

Group	1955		1985	
	Percent GOP	Percent Democrat	Percent GOP	Percent Democrat
By Occupation				
Professional	42	28	38	30
Manager	35	38	44	27
Clerical, sales	33	45	37	34
Skilled	27	46	31	33
Semi-skilled and unskilled	25	52	27	42
Farmer	38	43	32	44
Gender				
Women	34	44	34	40

Source: Gallup Poll data report by Everett Carll Ladd, "Alignment and Realignment: Where Are All the Voters Going?" (*The Ladd Report* no. 3, 1986), tables a, b, c, d, pp. 30–33.

An Ideological Realignment?

It might be argued that an ideological shift toward the Right in public opinion would be at least as important in legitimating new public policies as a partisan realignment favoring the Republicans. No such shift, however, has apparently taken place. The *New York Times* survey of voters as they left the polls in 1984 found 17 percent professing to be liberals, 35 percent conservatives, and 44 percent moderates—not much different from Harris Poll results reported since 1964.[18] The 1988 postelection *New York Times*/CBS News poll documented very little change: Eighteen percent of voters said they were liberals, 33 percent conservatives, and 45 percent moderates.[19] Though twice as many respondents identify themselves as conservatives than as liberals, the categories do not hold up very well when specific issues are examined. Across a wide spectrum of issues, including abortion, spending on social services, arms control, the Equal Rights Amendment, environmental regulation, military spending, and U.S. intervention in Central America, polls generally show majorities favoring positions in contradiction with the conservative policies of the Reagan and Bush administrations.[20]

Majorities continue to favor some key principles that derive from the New Deal. Seventy-five percent of the Democrats who voted for Reagan in 1984 agreed that "government should do more to protect ordinary Americans from the power of banks and big corporations." Eighty-five percent agreed that "government has a responsibility to see that every able-bodied person in the country has an opportunity to work."[21] In contradiction to the conservative doctrine that social welfare programs have done "more harm than good," a *New York Times*/CBS News poll conducted in early 1986 showed that less than one-fifth of the public believed that the government programs of the sixties had made things worse for poor people.[22]

It is easy to become confused by the avalanche of public opinion data that can be marshaled on either side of the argument that an ideological realignment has occurred. So much depends on how questions are put to the voters. If asked whether they wanted money to go to the Nicaraguan *contras,* most Americans in the mid-1980s said, "No." But if asked whether they wanted the government to stop "communism" in Central America, the majority answered "yes." Asked if they supported welfare for the poor, they answered "yes"; asked whether they would accept a tax increase to pay for welfare, they often said "no." This does not necessarily mean that the public is irrational. It is clear, rather, that public opinion is shaped and conditioned by how the media and politicians communicate policy alternatives. It is hardly surprising that public opinion reflects the rhetoric used by political leaders. When liberal politicians run from the label "liberal," as Michael Dukakis did in 1988, those voters who favor traditionally liberal positions find that the political differences among candidates are almost nonexistent.

One of the few prominent Democrats to recognize this development was Arthur Schlesinger, a former advisor to John F. Kennedy. He blasted Senator Bill Bradley of New Jersey and other Democrats who championed tax reform in 1986 because the "reform" reduced the number of tax brackets to only three rates.

Schlesinger pointed out that the principle of progressive taxation—that is, that those who earn more ought to pay more—constitutes a fundamental premise of a just taxation system. According to polls, a majority of Americans felt that the tax system was unfair. Schlesinger also noted that the Democrats' failure to offer a clear policy favoring a diplomatic rather than military solution to the crisis in Central America, an area in which public opinion overwhelmingly opposed the president's policy, permitted Reagan to win renewed funding for the Nicaraguan *contras* in 1986.[23]

Why have few political entrepreneurs in the Democratic party sought to stake out a clear "liberal" alternative to the Republicans? We have addressed this question in previous chapters where, in sum, we argued that the ties that bind politicians to elites are stronger than those that bind them to the public. The Democrats are as dependent on the new technologies of campaigning, on the media, and on corporate money as are the Republicans. A populist-style campaign appealing to discontented and disadvantaged voters works at cross-purposes to candidates' attempts to get early money for the "hidden primary." Voters in the bottom third of the income pyramid turn out for elections, and especially for primary contests, at a far lower rate than upper-income voters. A populist campaign must change this well-established pattern and mobilize the very groups that have stayed away from the polling booth. Recent Democratic candidates running for the presidency have attempted to win the presidency by leaning to the right and have failed in the last three elections. As a result, a tug-of-war over the Democratic soul is taking place. On one side are voices who argue for a populist reorientation; on the other are those who believe that a populist-style campaign simply would not work, that instead it would alienate too many white middle-class voters.

Democratic contenders have been almost schizophrenic about how to pitch their campaigns. Some have adopted populism as a style while offering little that is populist in substance. Richard Gephardt tried to project a populist image in his run for the 1988 presidential nomination. Relying on Gephardt's principal campaign strategist, Michael Dukakis took a similar posture in the closing weeks of the general election campaign. His brand of populism was composed almost entirely of code words like "compassion," "caring," and "hope," with a notable absence of content, but the new style was widely credited with narrowing the gap between himself and Bush by election day.

Can a Populist Movement Be Mobilized?

Each of the political parties had within its ranks of potential presidential nominees in 1988 an unorthodox candidate who presented a significant populist challenge. In the Republican party such a threat came from a right-wing Christian evangelist, Pat Robertson. Within Democratic ranks, Jesse Jackson posed the strongest challenge from the left since Henry Wallace's campaign of 1948.

Jackson put together a populist campaign in 1984 that showed that he tilted distinctly to the left of Walter Mondale and Gary Hart, the only other two candidates to stay in the race for the nomination up to the party's convention. American politics is so skewed to the right that it is odd, actually, that Jackson ever was labeled a leftist at all. Certainly he would have been considered a centrist in Europe, but in the American context he appeared as a radical because he tried to mobilize several discontented groups. Jackson's domestic program "was arguably the first social-democratic alternative seriously offered to the American electorate in a presidential campaign."[24] Jackson unabashedly advocated reform of labor laws; attacked open shops; stood up for the rights of undocumented workers; denounced plant closures and farm foreclosures; and promoted expansion of welfare, public works programs, and civil rights. In foreign affairs, Jackson's anti-interventionism and highly visible trips to Cuba, Nicaragua, and Syria and his recognition of Palestinian human rights not only challenged President Reagan's policies in particular, but the entire Cold War ideology that has justified American expansionism. His call to cut 20 percent from the arms budget would have hardly derailed militarism, but no other candidate in the 1984 election advocated even holding the line on defense spending, much less reducing it so drastically.

Four years later, the behind-the-scenes battle between Michael Dukakis and Jesse Jackson at the 1988 Democratic convention revealed a vast difference between Jackson's populism and Dukakis's search for the political middle (though the media, except for the cable network C-SPAN, treated the television audience only to the carnival on the main convention floor). Jackson was able to wring only one concession from Dukakis in Atlanta. At his insistence, the Democratic platform labeled South Africa as a "terrorist state" for its support of counter-revolutions in Angola and Mozambique. Jackson also favored sending U.S. military aid to the African front-line states bordering South Africa, and he wanted the United States openly to support the African National Congress, the anti-apartheid group then outlawed by the government of South Africa. Dukakis would go no further than advocating tougher economic sanctions against Pretoria.

Jackson wanted the Democrats to repudiate military intervention in Central America, but Dukakis would only accept a phrase making military aid to El Salvador conditional on its human rights record, and he rejected a clear statement opposing aid to the Nicaraguan *contras*. Jackson asked for a freeze on military spending at present levels (changing his stand from 1984); Dukakis refused. Instead, Dukakis advocated spending less on nuclear weapons but more on modernizing conventional weaponry. Jackson asked for termination of all money for research on the Star Wars program; Dukakis, though opposing deployment of space-based weapons, favored funding for continued research.

On domestic policy, Jackson favored a $10 billion increase for education and a massive new public works program. Dukakis refused to commit himself to any increase in the education budget and advocated only a $500 million increase in public works to bring down unemployment in depressed areas. He spoke of a "partnership" between the private sector and government but continued to regard the government only as the last resort for solving social and economic problems. Jackson advocated an industrial policy much like Japan's, where the government engages in economic planning and invests in specific industries.

Perhaps the clearest sign that Dukakis had no intention of reversing the domestic policies of the Reagan era was his rejection of Jackson's call to raise taxes on the rich and corporations. Since 1980, changes in the tax laws and other government policies have significantly widened the gap between rich and poor. Dukakis said that it was unnecessary to raise anybody's taxes to reduce the federal deficit. He took the unconvincing, even silly, position that enough new revenues could be raised if taxes were collected more efficiently.

Such positions as Jackson's are radical in the American political context. But Jackson asserted that a majoritarian alliance, a "Rainbow Coalition," could be assembled to provide the necessary political support. This coalition would draw from the growing populations of Hispanics, Asians, blacks, Native Americans, and other minorities and seek common ground with whites drawn from the ranks of the working class, farmers, peace advocates, feminists, and other groups with grievances against the system. Since blacks comprised only about 11 percent of the U.S. population, Jackson's strategy could be viable only with substantial support from other minorities and much of the white electorate.[25]

The contest for the 1984 Democratic nomination showed that traditional liberals like Walter Mondale could no longer monopolize the nomination process within the Democratic party. Jackson's electoral appeal, when combined with Gary Hart's, denied Mondale an electoral majority in the primaries in every region of the country. Jackson drew approximately 20 percent of his 3.15 million primary votes from whites, 5 percent of the total white vote cast in the primaries. Mondale won about 18 percent of the black vote, Jackson about 77 percent, and Gary Hart 3 percent.

Jackson's strength in 1988 was even greater. For weeks after "Super Tuesday" there was speculation that he might show up in Atlanta with enough delegates to deny Dukakis a majority. By the end of the primary season, and with less money than any other major candidate, Jackson finished with the second highest percentage of primary votes, over 30 percent. While a majority of Jackson's support continued to come from African-American voters, he was able to attract over 30 percent of the vote in several northern states with small black populations. On March 9, Super Tuesday, when every state in the South except South Carolina held its primary, Jackson won more primary votes that any other candidate. Dukakis spent $3 million on television advertising in the South. Two other Democrats, Sen. Albert Gore and Rep. Richard Gephardt, spent $2 million and $1 million, respectively. Jackson spent only $100,000. By the end of his campaign, Jackson had raised over $5 million, but this was only about one-third of the amount Dukakis had at his disposal. What Jackson had proven was that a candidate with a populist message could challenge the conventional candidates with fat campaign treasuries.

The Rainbow Coalition was a logical outcome of the entry of blacks into the political arena. As late as 1932, blacks supported Herbert Hoover because of their historical allegiance to the GOP as the party of abolition. The New Deal mobilized blacks into the Democratic party, but even so, in 1936, 1940, 1944, 1956, and 1960, more than 29 percent of the black vote, on average, went to Republicans.[26] Since 1964, however, 85 percent or more has gone to the Democratic candidate. In the 1984 election, according to the *New York Times*/CBS News exit polls, 89 percent of

Jackson's voters cast their ballots for Mondale in the general election. This figure fell slightly in the 1988 election when 86 percent of Jackson's supporters voted for Dukakis in November.[27]

More African Americans hold political office than at any other time since Reconstruction. But rising black electoral power has not been accompanied by a commensurate increase in black representation within the Democratic party—whether measured by number of elected officials, delegates to the national conventions, or influence within the state and national party committees. Manning Marable has summarized blacks' frustration with the Democrats:

> Blacks have their backs against the wall and are increasingly distressed by the erosion of past gains and the rapidly deteriorating conditions within Black and poor communities. As Black leaders have attempted to remedy these problems through the Democratic Party...too often they have been ignored or treated with disrespect.[28]

The fusion of black political interests and voting power with disenfranchised groups would be historic. But can this be accomplished? Marable argues,

> A Black candidacy could use an 18 million eligible Black voter base to put together a "coalition of the rejected," including appealing to six million Hispanics, women, more than 500,000 Native Americans, 20 to 40 million poor whites, and an appeal to the moral decency and enlightened economic self-interest of millions of rejected white moderates, liberals, and others.[29]

In April 1983 Jackson asserted that such a coalition would present an alternative in American politics capable of increasing "voter registration and political participation [that] would have a profound impact on the status quo of the Democratic party."[30]

The Rainbow strategy assumed a seamless web connecting class struggle in the United States and the Third World, especially where the stresses are most acute, as in South Africa, Central America, and Israel. Jackson interjected into American politics the idea that intervention in the Third World and racism at home are linked.[31] This opposition to intervention sharply distinguished Jackson from his Democratic rivals, who continued to support overseas intervention in the name of anticommunism and U.S. "national security." Jackson threatened to bring back into the political arena the leftist thrust that liberals expurgated from Democratic party politics shortly after the Second World War.

Jackson represented a radical challenge in the American political context, and because of this there was a tendency to exaggerate his radicalism. Jackson may have been "anti-imperialist," but there was nothing in his record to suggest that he saw capitalism as the root of either foreign or domestic injustice. Much of Jackson's rhetoric places emphasis on getting a larger slice of the pie for blacks and other disadvantaged groups. The target of one such campaign, Anheuser-Busch brewery, saw the light and not only provided more distributorships for blacks but picked up the tab for a celebration after the National Rainbow Coalition meeting in 1986.

The National Rainbow Coalition (NRC), founded in 1986, was organized as a nonprofit corporation with broad objectives of promoting social, racial, and economic reform. In 1988, it was ostensibly independent of Jackson's presidential campaign (which had its own organization), though it devoted most of its energies to collecting money and working on his behalf. Many leaders and members of the NRC want it to be a national political movement not tied too closely to Jackson. According to the cochair of the Vermont committee, "We don't see ourselves as the left wing of the Democratic Party. Instead, we see ourselves as an independent progressive movement."[32]

Jackson may run for the Democratic presidential nomination in 1992. But his relationship with the Rainbow Coalition may be strained if he stays in the Democratic party. After the 1988 elections, an NRC member and coalition organizer in Chicago predicted that "it's going to be very difficult to make a case for staying within the Democratic party after the way they treated their most loyal constituency. I'll be frank: Jesse has his work cut out for him during the upcoming board meeting. He'll have to be at his rhetorical best to convince folks to remain supportive of the Democrats."[33]

Any attempt by Jackson to try a third-party strategy is likely to be defined by the media as "sour grapes" and interpreted as proof that he cannot win by playing by the rules of the game. And such a move would surely divide even his black constituency, since there are now significant numbers of blacks who are Democratic officeholders. It is especially significant that in February 1989 the Democrats selected Robert Brown, a black campaign manager of Jackson's in 1988, as the head of their National Committee. Many on the Left see no alternative to working inside the Democratic party. They may concede that Democratic politicians pay more attention to corporations and the rich than to ordinary constituents, but they point out the formidable obstacles to third-party movements and the costs that ordinary people are forced to bear when more conservative candidates defeat liberals in elections because of factional strife and defections from the Democratic fold.

Despite the serious divisions that would occur over a Jackson candidacy in 1992, he will remain a formidable political force. His appeal in 1988 was not based on media hype or a huge financial budget but on the genuine excitement he elicited from various disaffected groups. These groups have little interest in intellectual debates among leftists about whether or not the Democratic party can be reformed. They are looking for alternatives to conventional policies. It may be that the Democratic party cannot survive an enlivened political dialogue. Before the 1992 presidential election, the party either will embrace the new populism or mainstream party leaders will try to reject the challenge from the left altogether. The Democratic party may well break apart in this struggle.

The Decline of Both Parties

A chapter on the two parties, such as this one, unavoidably overestimates the role of the parties in contemporary politics because it focuses upon intramural battles and strategies within the parties. It is important to reemphasize that both parties have been eclipsed in selecting candidates and in electoral campaigns by the campaign industry made up of consultants, advertising executives, the media, and corporate money.

By some measures, the parties appear to be gaining in strength. The national committees of both parties collect huge sums of money, and have learned to adroitly distribute funds to candidates in critical House and Senate races. Frank J. Fahrenkopf, the Republican National Committee chair, was quoted in 1984 as saying that his goal was to use the assets of the committee to rebuild his party right down to the county level. This would pay off in state and local victories, he predicted, but also, "the beauty of it is that we will be able to say to our presidential and vice presidential nominees [in 1988]...that we have in place a meaningful vote delivery system in the key electoral counties in each of 50 states."[34] GOP efforts aim to encourage a general shift in party loyalties among voters and among local politicians. The White House claimed that 140 local politicians had moved from the Democrats to the GOP by mid-1985.[35] The Democratic National Committee has also taken significant steps to build a solid financial base that will help state and local party organizations. Like the Republicans, the Democrats are able to help local organizations raise funds more effectively by sharing expertise, technology, and data.

The key question is: What do these "revitalized" parties do? They become important players in the campaign industry; they selectively send money to candidates, and they advertise the generic label (the party) in an attempt to help candidates who sell their own messages. But the parties most assuredly do not mobilize voters as parties once did. With their money they buy advertising and media spots, hire pollsters, organize phone banks and mass mailings, and sell themselves and their candidates with the same techniques of persuasion that would be used by candidates if the parties didn't exist at all.

When a popular candidate wins big, as Ronald Reagan did in 1980 and 1984, it appears that the party as well as the candidate carries a popular mandate. In fact, however, the parties fall in line *behind* strong candidates who have made it on their own already. (It is useful to remember that Reagan competed for the nomination in 1976 and 1980 *against* the party's would-be power brokers. They considered him too conservative to win a general election.) Candidates choose the parties; the parties very rarely are in a position to choose candidates. In the case of presidential nominees, the only occasion when a strong candidate's own agendas sometimes collide with the party's is at the national conventions, when fights over the platform may break out. Realizing that within reasonable limits the platform language is of no consequence except to a few excitable delegates, the candidates compromise or even concede major points. The business of negotiating the platform is hidden from the television-viewing audience. After the convention, the candidates go off to campaign according to the themes and strategies determined by their own media consultants and handlers.

In this vein, it is significant that some of Ronald Reagan's handlers actually preferred that the Republican party remain relatively weak, since their own skills could be best applied in isolation from a strong party with its own voice. And these advisors did not necessarily want a voter realignment that might result in a permanent Republican majority. In 1984, Reagan's chief of staff James A. Baker (George Bush's campaign manager in 1988 and after the election Secretary of State) and campaign manager Edward Rollins publicly rejected having Reagan campaign for Republican House and Senate candidates until the last stages of the 1984 campaign. Rollins said that this was not just a short-term electoral consideration but a strategic one when he told the *National Journal,* "My sense is that the Republican party today is Ronald Reagan and everything else is irrelevant." As for the prospect of a Republican realignment, he added,

> I don't think the Republicans are necessarily going to become a majority party. I personally don't care whether they do or not....[T]he bigger the independent vote gets, the happier I am. With a skilled candidate or what have you, I believe I can get a large enough majority of that segment to win over all. I just don't want the Democrats [to] creep back up into the 40's or 50's.[36]

Candidates who emerge with their own strong financial backing and campaign organization are happy to receive the blessings and resources from a political party, but they do not want the party that can insist on its own agenda. Party politics of any kind is an inconvenience to the professionals who specialize in packaging candidates and issues for mass consumption. Even though Republican Senator Robert Dole complained bitterly on election night in 1988 that the Bush campaign had done little to help the GOP congressional candidates, Dole himself would probably have committed the same sin had he won the nomination.

Indications are that things were going the way Rollins wanted—toward dealignment—a circumstance in which neither party can mobilize a reliable majority of voters. A Daniel Yanklevitch poll indicated that only 2 percent of Reagan-Bush supporters in 1984 considered identification with the Republican party as the principal reason for their choice. Rollins, Wirthlin, Baker and other engineers of the successful Republican presidential victories in the 1980s understood that a weak party system without enduring voter alignments enhanced their ability to pursue their own agendas and to exercise even more control over candidates and issues. Without partisan attachments, voters could be influenced on short notice by artful spot ads and catchy slogans, making electoral politics more manageable by public relations specialists like themselves.

To many people who are not part of the campaign establishment that benefits from such a development, dealignment is considered a potentially dangerous development. Kevin Phillips, the author of *The Emerging Republican Majority,* expressed the fear that without the mediating influence of the party system, the electorate, especially the middle class, might turn to authoritarian solutions under the influence of the mass media. "American mass culture, epitomized by Hollywood and the movies, was turning to a kindred emphasis on force, will, power, irrationality and mythology in a series of sword-and-sorcery movies", he warned.[37] To the voter getting most information from a television screen, modern elections already may have become as distant from and as contrived and fictional as the movies starring Sylvester Stallone, Arnold Schwartzenegger, Clint Eastwood, and Chuck Norris.

Politicians are tempted to project the same image as these actors. Political leaders are becoming habituated to think, or to act as if they think, that there are no real problems, only public relations problems: "Expressing compassion through photo opportunities at disaster sites or slums takes the place of political action."³⁸ Image sells, not substance, so that George Bush, the "education president," initiates no programs for the schools and declares a "thousand points of light" as the solution to poverty, homelessness, and Third World conditions in the cities. Political leadership has become an exercise in image making rather than the ability to find new solutions to intractable problems, to mediate political differences, and to articulate a political vision. Leadership defined by hype and advertising copy produces political figures bereft of past accomplishment or substance and vision, such as Dan Quayle.

Notes

1. Wilfred E. Binkley, *American Political Parties: Their National History* (New York: Alfred A. Knopf, 1943), pp. 380-381.
2. David Caute, *The Great Fear* (New York: Simon & Schuster, 1978), pp. 267-293.
3. Institute for Labor Education and Research, *What's Wrong With the U.S. Economy* (Boston: South End Press, 1982), p. 316, an excellent popular analysis of the country's economic problems. A good article-length summary of the causes of economic decline in the U.S. is Robert Brenner, "The Deep Roots of U.S. Economic Decline," *Against the Current* 1 (March-April 1986): 19-28.
4. ILER, *What's Wrong With the U.S. Economy,* p. 342.
5. Brenner, "How America Lost the Edge," p. 20.
6. Ibid.
7. ILER, *What's Wrong With the U.S. Economy,* pp. 128-129.
8. Opinion Research Corporation poll reported in the *National Journal,* June 7, 1986, p. 1398.
9. Numan V. Bartley and Hugh D. Graham, *Southern Politics and the New Reconstruction* (Baltimore: Johns Hopkins University Press, 1975), p. 107.
10. Alexander P. Lamis, *The Two Party South* (London: Oxford University Press, 1984).
11. Gerald Pomper, "The Presidential Election," in *The Election of 1984: Reports and Interpretations,* ed. Gerald Pomper (Chatham, N.J.: Chatham House, 1985), pp. 68-69.
12. Kevin Phillips, *The Emerging Republican Majority* (Arlington, Va.: Arlington House, 1969).
13. This idea was promoted by Richard Wirthlin after the 1980 election. For debate about the 1980 election and the idea of a rolling realignment, see the various analyses and data in the post-election edition of *Public Opinion* (January 1981). See also Richard Wirthlin, "The Republican Strategy and its Electoral Consequences" in *Party Coalitions in the 1980s,* ed. Seymour Martin Lipset (San Francisco: Institute for Contemporary Studies, 1981). Phillip's retreat from the realignment thesis can be found in *Post-Conservative America* (New York: Random House, 1982).
14. Richard Wirthlin, "The Republican Strategy and Its Electoral Consequences," in *Party Coalitions in the 1980s,* ed. Seymour Martin Lipset (San Francisco: Institute for Contemporary Studies, 1981), pp. 240-247.
15. Everett Carll Ladd, "Alignment and Realignment: Where Are All the Voters Going?" *The Ladd Report* 3 (1986): 2.
16. Ibid., p. 11.
17. Vic Fingerhut, "Misunderstanding the 1984 Presidential Election," *Campaigns and Elections* (Winter 1985), p. 22.
18. Cited in Lewis Lipsitz, *American Democracy* (New York: St. Martin's Press, 1986), p. 184.
19. See "Portrait of the Electorate," *New York Times,* November 10, 1988, p. 18.

20. Various polls cited in the *National Journal* confirm the extent to which the public was at odds with conservative positions, particularly Ronald Reagan's. For example, see the following issues: August 8, 1984, p. 1494, on taxation and spending cuts; September 15, 1984, p. 1742 on U.S.-Soviet negotiations, especially on underground testing of nuclear weapons; December 15, 1984 on the Equal Rights Amendment, increased spending on education and medicare, relaxing pollution controls, cost-of-living benefits on social security; January 19, 1985, p. 186, on military spending; February 2, 1985, on military spending and arms control; February 9, 1985, on social welfare cuts and ending farm subsidies; May 17, 1986, p. 1224.

21. Fingerhut, "Misunderstanding the 1984 Presidential Election," p. 22.

22. Cited in *National Journal,* March 15, 1986, p. 666.

23. *St. Louis Post-Dispatch,* July 23, 1986, p. B3.

24. Davis, "The Lesser Evil", p. 20.

25. Manning Marable, "Jackson and the Rise of the Rainbow Coalition," *New Left Review* (January-February 1985): 26.

26. Gallup Poll data cited by Thomas Cavanaugh, "The Impact of the Black Electorate," *Election '84,* report 1 (Washington, D.C.: Joint Center for Political Studies, 1984).

27. "The Portrait of the Electorate," p. 18.

28. Marable, "Jackson and the Rise of the Rainbow Coalition," p. 12.

29. Ibid.

30. Ibid.

31. "Declaration of Independence from the War in Vietnam," in *Vietnam and America*, ed. Marvin E. Gettleman, Jane Franklin, Marilyn Young, and H. Bruce Franklin, (New York: Grove Press, 1985), p. 313.

32. Salim Muwakkil, "What Does Jesse want? Now Rainbow's Asking," *In These Times,* December 7–13, 1988, p. 3.

33. Ibid.

34. Maxwell Glen, "Focus on Fundraising," *National Journal,* January 19, 1985, p. 1673.

35. Ibid.

36. Dick Kirschten, "Testing the Waters," *National Journal,* July 20, 1985, p. 1674.

37. Phillips, *Post-Conservative America,* p. 204.

38. Michael Sragow, "Gross Projections," *Mother Jones,* January 1990, p. 25.

Part Three

Protecting Government from Democracy

Chapter 9

The Hidden Governments*

Insulating Government from Electoral Decisions

The writers of the Constitution designed a government that would be insulated from what James Madison called the "sudden impulses and passions" of the people. The original design has worked remarkably well in preserving elites' control over the national government and democratic processes. But Madison's checks and balances scheme was potentially a problem as well as a resource for elites. The fragmentation of national institutions made it almost impossible for government to act in behalf of "popular impulses and passions"; but, in equal measure, institutional fragmentation could also have made it hard for elites to move the national government in any specific direction at all, even when they wanted expeditious enactment of policies that benefited them. Throughout America's national history, elites have had to devise solutions to the fragmentation and potential paralysis of policy making that results from the checks-and-balances policy process.

In the nineteenth century and in the first decades of the twentieth century, political parties and courts were the institutions used by elites to control government policies. Elites were able to build party organizations strong enough to coordinate the actions of presidents, congressional leaders, and state and local officials. The courts provided an ultimate bulwark for protecting the independence of capitalist elites from populist electoral pressures. Judges who owed their long careers to a dominant presidential party (the Republicans for all but sixteen years between 1860 and 1933) nullified congressional and state legislative acts that bore the imprint of movements that aspired to restrict the autonomy of business. The federal courts often struck down states' attempts to regulate corporations, end child labor, provide protection for labor unions, and limit business autonomy. In these ways capitalist elites, especially after the Civil War, overcame a fragmented national government to achieve consistent policy results.

Corruption also served as a mechanism for unifying government. By bribing individual legislators, governors, and judges, capitalist elites ensured that these politicians would put aside their institutional jealousies long enough to enact specific

---

* Authored by David Brian Robertson.

policies that they desired. Because such corruption is an effective and focused instrument for temporarily uniting a fragmented government, elites have turned to it repeatedly in American history. Political corruption is curbed from time to time mainly by the fact that when it is discovered, public officials, threatened by a crisis of legitimacy, repent and enact modest reforms.

In this century elites have had to find new ways to align America's institutions so that they could be put in the service of two goals; enacting specific public policies favoring particular elite interests, and organizing a stronger national government capable of managing the economy. These twin needs have nurtured a fundamental reorganization of policy making. First, specialized and largely invisible subgovernments—alliances among congressional committees and staffs, bureaucratic agencies, and lobby organizations usually representing specific industries—make the consequential decisions involving a large number of important policies. Second, presidents have experimented with new strategies for consolidating their control over money, personnel, and information. Often large corporations with global interests have urged active government domestic and foreign intervention and thus have encouraged this expansion of presidential power. These presidential strategies rely heavily on centralizing political power, manipulating the media, and expanding the definition of "national security" to encompass a constantly enlarging range of government activities.

The effect of the growth of hidden subgovernments has been to move congressional as well as presidential policy making into hidden policy arenas. And thus the national government's policy-making process is more insulated from popular influence than even the Founders might have thought possible.

Checks and Balances for Whom?

The Founders designed government to control the "mischiefs of faction." For the Constitution's authors, the most worrisome examples of such factions in the 1780s were the popular political movements organized by indebted farmers in the rural hinterlands of Rhode Island, Massachusetts, and other states. Thus, the authors of *The Federalist Papers* worried about conflicts between property owners and the propertyless because "the most common and durable source of factions has been the verious [sic] and unequal distribution of property."[1] The Constitution's authors fragmented government in part to prevent propertyless masses from seizing control of the governmental process, thereby preventing a situation in which commercial and propertied interests might be threatened.

The Constitution established an ingenious system for protecting the elite minority's ability to veto government actions. If a majority in the only popularly elected branch of Congress, the House of Representatives, enacted objectionable legislation, it would then have to run a gauntlet of other institutions reliably controlled by elites. Even if the Senate, whose members were selected by state legislatures, agreed with the House and enacted the bill, the president—chosen by the Electoral College—could veto it. Moreover, representatives, presidents, and senators served two-, four-, and six-year terms, respectively, a feature calculated to compound the difficulty of aligning these institutions in the same policy direction.[2] And after the Supreme Court first struck down a federal law as unconstitutional in the case of *Marbury* v. *Madison* (1803), the court inserted itself as an additional veto point in the national political process.

Even mild disagreement could paralyze the complicated policy process at the national level. As a leader in the House of Representatives, James Madison discovered, for instance, that propertied interests were deeply divided over the issue of whether to tax imports. Northern manufacturers wanted to enact a high tariff to reduce foreign competition, but southern planters favored a low tariff because they bought many of their finished goods from Europe and they opposed a punitive tax on these goods. Producers who needed foreign raw materials, such as American rum distillers, also wanted a low tariff on the raw materials they needed for production.[3]

Alexander Hamilton had anticipated such elite rivalries but suggested that their mutual dependence would likely lead to accommodation. He predicted that "there would be no temptation to violate the Constitution in favor of the landed class, because that class would, in the natural course of things, enjoy as great a preponderancy as itself could desire."[4] Hamilton was right. The tariff of 1789, one of the first laws enacted by the new government, constituted a compromise among the various interests that set a low tariff on most goods but taxed steel, cloth, and certain other goods at a high rate in order to protect some manufacturers. This tariff may be seen as a model of how most legislation survived America's complicated policy process: It distributed at least some benefits to most of the elite factions that contended for favorable policy.

By the early 1800s, two institutions had developed that regularly smoothed these conflicts and produced authoritative policy decisions. One of the new institutions, political parties, linked various local elites to the national government and to one another. Members of the House, Senate, and executive branch who belonged to the same party tended to cooperate, and their coalitional agreements helped to overcome the sharp institutional divisions created by the Constitution. Because of the spoils system, each president routinely filled post office, customshouse, and other federal government jobs with members of his party. These partisan bonds provided an informal way to facilitate cooperation and coordination among the executive employees and to link them to members of Congress and to state and local government officials whose careers depended on party fortunes. Thus political parties made it easier to establish "working relationships within and among the branches and levels of the constitutional structure."[5]

Meanwhile, the most difficult policy decisions often were delegated to the least democratic branch of government, the courts. Courts drew the boundaries between the federal government's powers, states' rights, and private interests. For example, the courts had to interpret and reinterpret the rights and responsibilities of corporations because these organizations operated under vague state corporate charter statutes. Over the course of the nineteenth century, the courts struck down a large number of state laws that regulated corporate behavior that gave the public access to corporate decision making. In this way "the judiciary became the chief source of economic surveillance in the nineteenth century."[6]

After the Civil War the courts helped protect laissez faire capitalism from the regulatory measures demanded by the "Prairie Populists" and by the various factions making up the Democratic party. The Republican party successfully fought off the populist challenge in other ways as well—it vastly expanded its fundraising ability, and captains of industry were able to utilize the federal government to harass and intimidate labor leaders and radicals. But this was not enough. Business also wanted government to be able to enact policies that positively promoted its interests. This need contributed to a rapid expansion in the size and number of bureaucratic agencies at the federal level.

The Growth of Bureaucracy

The proliferation of federal administrative and regulatory agencies began in the late nineteenth century and accelerated during the Progressive Era. The creation of the Interstate Commerce Commission in 1887, followed by railroad regulation, the regulation of food and drugs (and the creation of the Food and Drug Administration in 1906), and especially the creation of the Federal Reserve System in 1916, illustrated the new form of collaboration between business and the federal government.

Government activities and responsibilities mushroomed in the 1930s and 1940s. During the Great Depression a multitude of new agencies were created to regulate banks, the stock market, commodity exchanges, and other enterprises, and for the first time the national government took on significant social welfare responsibilities. The growth in the number of federal government employees from 1908 to 1988 is shown in figure 9-1. Clearly, the Great Depression and the Second World War constituted the watersheds in the growth of the federal government's size.

National government administrators have acquired enormous power in contemporary government. That fact by itself poses a challenge to popular control of government in every nation. Scholars studying Western Europe have pointed out that legislative influence erodes as bureaucracies are given increasingly broad delegations of power. Political scientist Alfred Grosser has observed:

> Everywhere legislative initiative has passed into the hands of the administrations. The legislatures sometimes amend, rarely reject, usually ratify. The members continue, indeed, to call themselves collectively "the legislative power" on the law books, but in most cases they merely participate in a procedure of registration.[7]

Civil servants are not elected, and in all governments civil servants now vastly outnumber elected officials. The sheer size and complexity of bureaucracies make it difficult for elected officials to monitor their activities. Because they are experts whose special knowledge gives them power to define policy alternatives, administrative officials frequently dominate the policy process, forcing elected officials to

Figure 9-1 **Growth of Federal Civilian Employment 1910–1988**

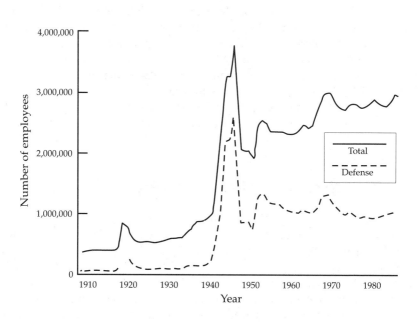

respond to their agenda. Heads of public agencies often have the capacity to defend their budgets and prerogatives against the intrusion of elected legislatures and executives. For ordinary citizens, bureaucratic agencies are even more powerful; frequently they are the only contacts that citizens have with their government.

The courts have confirmed Congress's right to surrender extensive powers to the federal bureaucracy.[8] According to political scientist Stephen Skowronek, in the twentieth century

> American state building progressed by replacing courts and parties with a
> national bureaucracy, and this dynamic yielded a hapless confusion of institu-
> tional purposes, authoritative controls, and governmental boundaries.[9]

Bureaucratic growth profoundly altered the nation's policy-making processes. The growth of bureaucracy shifted the initiative for defining and implementing public policy away from Congress and to the executive branch.

Congress: The Reelection Machine

As it relinquished policy control, Congress began to bureaucratize itself. When it delegated authority to the White House and to civil servants, Congress expanded its staff to increase its ability to scrutinize executive branch activities.[10] Thus, when Congress authorized the president to establish a Bureau of the Budget in 1921, it created a General Accounting Office so that a congressional agency could audit federal spending. When it created the Council of Economic Advisors to help the president manage the economy in 1946, Congress also created a Joint Economic Committee and required top economic policy makers in the executive branch to provide it with economic information and to justify their actions. After President Nixon abused his power by impounding appropriations in the early 1970s, Congress reformed its budget procedures, established House and Senate budget committees, and created a Congressional Budget Office to develop information about federal spending and economic policy independent of the president's Office of Management and Budget.

The increasingly complex job of individual legislators also contributed to the bureaucratization of Congress. Nineteenth-century Congresses largely consisted of individuals who temporarily suspended private careers to attend a few brief legislative sessions. Today members consider service in Congress to be a career in its own right.[11] The average member of Congress has served for a decade. Whereas each member represented less than 50,000 people in the 1830s, each will represent nearly 600,000 in the 1990s. Constituency demands and workloads have increased exponentially. By 1987, the House and Senate received over 100 million pieces of mail annually. The number of public bills enacted has increased fourfold since the 1850s; the 99th Congress (1985–86) approved over 7,198 pages of statute law.[12]

Partly in response to the increased workload pressures, Congress has been transformed into a bureaucracy in its own right. In 1987, Congress employed a total of about 32,000 individuals, including employees in agencies such as the Congressional Budget Office, Library of Congress, the Congressional Research Service, and the General Accounting Office. Over 11,000 of these employees served as personal staff to the 535 elected representatives and senators, a figure that had increased tenfold since 1930. For fiscal year 1990, the budget for Congress alone amounted to nearly $2 billion.[13]

The bureaucratization of Congress has gone hand in hand with the specialization and fragmentation of legislative power. Whereas few standing committees existed in the nineteenth century, such committees multiplied and became the focal point of congressional power early in the twentieth century. Between the 1950s and the 1970s, legislative responsibilities became even more decentralized when committee work was delegated further to subcommittees. By 1989, there were 182 committees and subcommittees in the House of Representatives, and 137 in the Senate. These committees and subcommittees employ about 3,000 staff experts.[14]

These developments usually were justified as necessary for keeping Congress abreast of expanding executive agency activities. The bureaucratization of Congress, however, yielded an unintended dividend for individual legislators: Members of Congress are able to use the formidable resources at their command to help them win reelection campaigns. Incumbent members of Congress, especially representatives, have been able to protect themselves more and more successfully from electoral defeat. Since 1950, more than 90 percent of incumbent U.S. representatives who sought reelection have won. In 1986 and 1988, 98 percent who sought reelection won. Even more striking, members are insulated from defeat even when national electoral trends run against their party. In 1988, for example, voters split their tickets in 148 (of 435) congressional districts, giving a majority to a presidential candidate of one party while electing (that is, nearly always reelecting) a representative from the other party.[15]

Incumbents and their staff have a variety of tools that allow members to publicize their names and maintain favorable images. Members can mail letters, surveys, and other publicity to constituents without paying for postage. Many of these mailings are posted just before an election. In the two months before the November 1988 congressional elections, for example, members sent 60 million newsletters to constituents. Computers in each member's office store extensive specialized lists of constituents who can be sent special mailings tailored to their interests. "Robot" pens personalize a legislator's letters by reproducing "authentic" signatures by the thousands. Congressional recording studios permit members to send live or taped audiovisual messages to their constituents via local television and radio stations.[16]

These resources make it possible for individual representatives to claim credit and take personal responsibility for government actions desired by constituents. Congressional staffers do "casework," that is, intercede with federal agencies on constituents' behalf. Their job is to cut through the bureaucratic maze that regularly frustrates citizens. When a congressional staffer secures a government check for a constituent or cuts through regulatory red tape, the constituent feels grateful. More than one-third of congressional staff are based in members' home districts, where they can most easily respond to constituents' inquiries. On a larger scale, government agencies routinely allow individual members of Congress to announce and therefore claim some of the credit for the construction of major projects, such as locks and dams, interstate highways, and major defense contracts.

Political scientist R. Douglas Arnold argues that working through the bureaucracy makes more sense for individual members' careers than would the direct congressional delivery of benefits.

> Congressmen can claim some of the credit for whatever benefits flow into their districts, but at the same time they have insulated themselves from their constituents' anger when certain benefits cannot be secured. If Congress itself allocated benefits, constituents might well blame their congressmen for failing to acquire benefits, but as long as bureaucrats have the final say, congressmen are partially protected from their wrath.[17]

For congressional members successfully to engage in the machine-style politics that keep individual constituents happy, they must stay on good terms with executive branch agencies. As a consequence, they are not simply advocates for their constituents with these agencies. Rather, they generally try to work out arrangements where everyone in power looks good.

The Hidden Policy Subgovernments

Through committee and subcommittee appointments, individual members try to exercise some influence over a subset of federal activities, such as crop subsidies, military contracts, river and harbor improvements, or labor policy.[18] The dispersal of power among subcommittees gives "many more of [the members] an opportunity to develop close ties to key interest groups and key bureaucratic agencies, thereby increasing their claims for financial support from interest groups and favorable bureaucratic decisions from the agencies."[19] By 1989, about half of all the Democratic representatives in the Democratically controlled House chaired standing committees or subcommittees. The percentage in the Senate was an astonishing 84 percent (a number that was actually lower than in the late 1970s and early 1980s, when all but one or two of the majority party members chaired a committee).[20] The lawmakers who serve on these committees ally themselves with certain bureaus and with interest groups. Congressional committees and subcommittees approve the budget and legislative requests of executive agencies. These agencies implement policy to benefit particular interest groups, and legislators are keen to claim credit for new policies. The interest groups mobilize political support for the agencies, and they are the best source of campaign contributions for members of Congress. Thus, the legislators, public agencies, and interest groups become allies. These allies gather information and share it with one another. "Subgovernments" constructed in this way now dominate most federal policy-making activities.[21]

Dozens of such subgovernments influence federal policies and constitute a "Washington establishment." According to political scientist Morris Fiorina, "These establishments are not malevolent, centrally directed conspiracies against the American people. Rather, they are unconsciously evolved networks of congressmen, bureaucrats, and organized subgroups all seeking to achieve their own goals."[22] The relationships forged in these Washington establishments are genuinely symbiotic: If everyone works together, all the participants can benefit. Though Congress is the center of these constellations of mutual self-interest, Congress undoubtedly relies on the other players:

> The Congress created the establishment, sustains it, and most likely will continue to sustain and even expand it...a lesser proportion of congressional effort is now going into programmatic activities and a greater proportion into pork-barrel and casework activities...[as bureaucracy grows, more and more citizens are interested in specific benefits, or relief from regulations, or the correction of specific mistakes]....Whatever the problem, the citizen's congressman is a source of great succor... In sum, everyday decisions by a large and growing federal bureaucracy bestow significant tangible benefits and impose significant tangible costs. Congressmen can affect these decisions. Ergo, the more decisions the bureaucracy has the opportunity to make, the more opportunities there are for the congressman to build up credits.[23]

One frequently cited example of such a subgovernment consists of the relationship among the U.S. Army Corps of Engineers, the House and Senate public works committees, and such interest groups as the National Rivers and Harbors Congress and local and regional water development groups (often dominated by large agribusiness corporations). The Corps of Engineers is always engaged in dozens of projects for building dams and canals and providing water and navigation. Members of Congress on the House and Senate public works committees typically bundle enough such projects in a package so that a large number of congressional members have a stake in approving the bill. Local elites who benefit from such legislation return the favor in the form of support for the Corps and campaign contributions for the legislators.[24]

Another subgovernment revolves around the tobacco industry. The federal government subsidizes tobacco farming through the Department of Agriculture. Tobacco growers and cigarette companies (led by the industry association, the Tobacco Institute) persistently lobby for these subsidies, and tobacco subcommittees in both the House and Senate help in the effort. Predictably, members of these subcommittees disproportionately represent such tobacco-growing states as North Carolina and Kentucky. Many observers have noted the irony that whereas the U.S. Department of Health and Human Services spends money and energy on efforts to discourage smoking, the U.S. Department of Agriculture and its congressional and interest group allies cancel out these efforts by protecting the federal subsidies that underwrite tobacco production—and thus smoking.[25]

The experience of the Federal Trade Commission illustrates how economic interests can mobilize Congress when an attempt is made to upset the status quo that ties Congress to executive agencies and the lobby groups. When consumer advocate Michael Pertschuk became head of the Federal Trade Commission in 1977, he advocated stricter regulation of the optometry, television, funeral home, used car, and cereal industries. But the affected interests mobilized in response, and Congress intervened. The funeral directors, for example, demonstrated unexpected political strength in congressional districts nationwide. A legislative affairs staffer for the FTC discovered:

> There are funeral directors in every congressional district, and they are very important to elected representatives....The funeral director in a district can make you or break you politically. One congressman told me he goes to thirty or forty funerals a year, and it is a very important means by which he meets constituents....If the funeral director looks kindly upon you and seats you next to the widow, you are in a very good position vis-a-vis the people at the funeral. He is the man who will take you around and put you in contact with a lot of people; he will actually invite you to the funerals.[26]

Congress struck back at the FTC with the Federal Trade Commission Improvements Act of 1980, which restricted the FTC's regulatory powers. After the 1980 election, in which the affected interests contributed heavily to potential supporters, the Reagan administration's FTC appointees significantly reduced the agency's proposed regulations and enforcement, and all the members of the subgovernment were again on good terms.[27]

Subgovernments are not impregnable fortresses of political strength. The groups in a subgovernment may and often do clash with the members of other subgovernments over limited resources or conflicting interests. In a fight with the barge industry, for example, the railroad industry secretly funded environmentalists opposed to a lock and dam project during the late 1970s.[28] Subgovernments may also disintegrate. The alliance supporting sugar subsidies did so in the late 1970s. Once broken apart, a subgovernment may reconstitute itself, as did the sugar lobby in the first year of the Reagan administration.[29] All subgovernments function best under conditions of expanding resources; Reagan's budget director David Stockman's determination to cut the federal budget led him to try to break up sub-governments that he thought protected government programs he disliked.[30]

Even as domestic policy subgovernments came under attack and in some cases were temporarily weakened in the early 1980s, defense contract subgovernments thrived. Most military procurement decisions in the 1980s were made by small, tightly knit groups of policy experts supported by and allied with weapons makers, the Department of Defense, and members of Congress serving on such key committees as the House and Senate Appropriations Committees and the Armed Services Committees. These decisions were poorly monitored and little scrutinized until long after payments were made because the procurement systems were almost completely closed. One study of weapons purchases published in 1982 concluded that

> decisions on defense policy and weapons procurement rest almost entirely in the hands of insiders and policy experts, walled off from outsiders and alternative perspectives. The policy-makers, whose expertise is real and necessary, are also people and organizations with interests to protect and promote: (1) defense contractors whose success is measured by weapon sales, (2) the defense department, with positions and a future to protect and, (3), members of Congress who share in making military policy and are prime targets of industry-Government relations.[31]

A former head of the General Accounting Office described federal government procurements in the 1980s as a "garage sale" with no one in charge.[32]

While the Reagan administration sought cuts in many domestic programs, it presided over an enormous military buildup that fueled the defense subgovernments. Between 1980 and 1985, the Defense Department spent $718.8 billion on salaries, weapons, operations, and maintenance. Another $542.5 billion went to contracts with private industry. As money gravitated from domestic to military programs, members of Congress began to evince more personal interest in military purchases. Rep. Thomas Downey (D. N.Y.) explained the shift by observing, "There's one last really big barrel of pork out there, and it's all federal money." The Defense Department obviously appreciated the changing political calculus. For example, the Navy located the home ports for its expanding fleet to ensure that a maximum number of states and congressional districts would enjoy the economic benefits from military spending. Senator Barry Goldwater (R. Ariz.) frankly described this practice as "pure, unadulterated politics."[33]

The growth of defense spending strengthened the ties between defense firms and individuals in Congress. Defense companies became extremely profitable in the 1980s. In 1984, the ten largest defense contractors averaged a 25 percent return on equity, a figure that indicated that these companies were twice as profitable as the average U.S. manufacturing corporation (where profits averaged a 12.8 percent return on equity). The defense industry invested some of these profits in Congress. Total contributions from the PACs of the twenty largest defense contractors doubled from $1.8 million in 1980 to $3.6 million in 1984. As the Rockwell Corporation's defense contracts increased from $1 billion to $8.4 billion in those four years, its PAC contributions to congressional members soared from $59,635 in 1980 to $328,440 in 1984. Most of the defense industry's contributions were targeted to members of Congress who sat on key committees and supported President Reagan's defense buildup.[34]

The ties between industry and government bureaus can also be extremely close. In 1981, a document was leaked that laid out a detailed chronology of the joint lobbying effort by Lockheed and Defense Department officials to secure appropriations for Lockheed's C-5B airplane. Pentagon officials claimed that such cooperation was neither illegal nor unusual, and an Air Force general explained, "All you're seeing is democracy in action."[35]

Sometimes the line separating an interest group and government official is almost invisible. Frequently, when members of Congress or top federal administrators leave government, they obtain jobs in the private sector in industries that benefited from the government contracts and subsidies they approved while in office. Once in the private sector, such individuals have special access to officials still in government and can peddle their influence on behalf of the industry they recently regulated. The problem of influence peddling and "in-and-outers" is pervasive and open to abuse. There have been several attempts to forbid the practice. In May 1989, a restriction that would have banned federal employees from working on a defense procurement for two years if they had awarded the contract was scheduled to take effect in May. It is revealing that the impending deadline set by the law "sent federal workers and contractors into a panic" and caused at least three dozen top-level federal employees to resign or retire from federal service to avoid the deadline. In response, President Bush delayed the effective deadline by several months.[36]

How Subgovernments Affect Democracy

The fact that hidden subgovernments have developed in the fissures of the American constitutional system creates at least three problems for democracy. First, it protects elected officials from accountability. Interest groups help secure the reelection and therefore the careers of individual members of Congress through political action committees and through "grass-roots" support. Members of Congress return these favors in the form of beneficial legislation and special access. But this system works best in favor of narrow, focused interests that seek a specific benefit: an antitrust exemption for beer wholesalers, delayed enforcement of an environmental regulation that would crimp a company's profits, or a tax break for the real estate industry. This system poorly represents broader, more generalized interests, such as consumer or environmental protection.

Second, corruption is endemic to this system. It is tempting for a legislator tacitly to exchange a campaign contribution for special access and benefits. In 1987, five U.S. senators interceded to delay federal action against Lincoln Savings and Loan of Irvine, California, whose chairman, Charles Keating, sought to hold off a federal closure of his institution. Although Keating was a conservative, he and his associates donated over $1 million to the five senators, four of whom were moderate to liberal Democrats. Confronted with the accusation that their influence on Keating's behalf had been bought by his campaign contributions, the senators defended their action as a legitimate exercise of "constituent service." One of the five, Senator Alan Cranston (D.-Calif.), said, "Obviously if you didn't have to get campaign contributions nobody would be making anything out of it."[37]

Third, because this system is made up of a complex web of tradeoffs and implicit bargains, it is nearly impossible for Congress to come to grips with truly important but divisive issues that threaten to unravel existing arrangements. In 1977, President Jimmy Carter proposed an intricate plan for coping with the energy crisis, but individual members exerted their influence to gut the program of provisions that would hurt their interest group partners. As a result, despite a widespread consensus that the energy crisis required positive government action, little remained of Carter's ambitious proposal a year later.[38] In the 1980s, similar resistance contributed to the annual impasse over the federal budget.

The most simple-minded but far-reaching recent attempt at a solution to such congressional gridlock is the Gramm-Rudman-Hollings law. While Congress and President Reagan failed to agree on budget plans in the mid-1980s, the federal budget deficit grew precipitously. Embarrassed by the spectacle of its inability to agree on a package of tax increases or budget cuts to reduce the federal deficit, Congress approved a deficit-reduction plan proposed by Senator Phil Gramm (R. Tx.) and others in 1985. The Gramm-Rudman-Hollings bill set targets for reducing the federal deficit and provided that, if Congress and the president could not agree on a plan for reducing the deficit before the start of the budget year, federal programs would be automatically cut across the board to achieve the goal.[39] Many critics believe that in permitting the federal budget to be potentially determined by an utterly mindless and simplistic process, Congress abandoned one of the major responsibilities of a legislature in a representative democracy—namely, the job of establishing government spending priorities.

The Covert Presidency

The growth of a complicated bureaucratic maze and the frequent spectacle of congressional deadlock have led inevitably to the concentration of more authority in the executive branch. But presidents find that the size, complexity, personnel protections, and political support of the bureaucracy limit their ability to exercise policy control. Admiration for a strong presidency has increased each time a president demonstrated that he could align the fragmented national government to bring about far-reaching policy changes, as did Theodore Roosevelt, Woodrow Wilson, Franklin

Roosevelt, Lyndon Johnson, and Ronald Reagan. Advocates of an even stronger presidency believe that the office elevates the incumbent and encourages him to exert leadership toward positive goals such as international security, economic planning, and social justice.[40] Motivated by similar aspirations, presidents have searched for new ways to exert more political power. Almost invisibly, each recent presidential administration has added new tools for exerting presidential influence. There now exists a recognizable pattern of hidden powers, a *covert presidency*, that rests on centralizing presidential direction of personnel, budgets, and information; on the manipulation of the media; and on the expanding use of "national security" to control the political agenda.

The Control of Personnel

Before the Second World War, only a handful of personal aides assisted the president. But, like the Congress, the presidency has developed a small counter-bureaucracy in response to the growth of the federal bureaucracy. By 1970, the White House staff had grown to about 500 employees. Though each of them initially pruned the White House staff, Presidents Carter and Reagan permitted the staff to grow back to their original size by the end of their terms. The White House staff is a part of the larger Executive Office of the President, which in 1988 employed more than 1,700 people and had a budget of $140 million.

Compared to the independence and power of established bureaucracies such as the State, Defense, and Treasury Departments, the presidential staff is relatively controllable. Presidential staffers are also uninhibited by strict personnel regulations. Once they are confirmed by the Senate, these presidential appointees comprise a shadow bureaucracy that owes its loyalty solely to the incumbent president. This staff has the will, and increasingly the ability, to exercise control over the federal establishment. Over time, the staff has inventively developed more sophisticated techniques for controlling the behavior of civil servants.

Within three years after the start of both the Nixon and Carter presidential terms, the White House staff had wrested policymaking control from the cabinet. Both Nixon and Carter originally appointed several independent-minded cabinet secretaries to manage federal departments; in both presidencies, the cabinet officials were permitted to select their own subcabinet officers (such as assistant secretaries). It was precisely these independent-minded cabinet officials, often pressed on by career officials in key subcabinet positions, who were the most willing to challenge presidential decisions.

Within a year and a half of Richard Nixon's inauguration, his chief of staff, H. R. Haldeman, and his domestic policy advisor, John Ehrlichman, controlled access to the president. Their influence in setting the president's agenda earned them the title "Palace Guard." Cabinet officials who dissented with the president found their role downgraded, and one especially outspoken cabinet official, Secretary of the Interior Walter Hickel, was fired outright. After 1972, these staffers partially implemented a sophisticated plan to centralize political control further over the day-to-day operations of departments by using personal loyalty to Nixon as the criterion for appointment to cabinet and especially to subcabinet positions.[41]

Like Nixon, Jimmy Carter also started with independent-minded cabinet officers who were allowed to name their own subcabinet officials. In the wake of the Watergate scandal, which was attributed in part to the "Palace Guard," Carter promised not to appoint a chief of staff. By 1979, however, the Carter administration had changed course. Several independent-minded cabinet officials who had dissented openly with the president were pressured to resign. Retreating from his promise, Carter revived the position of White House chief of staff and named his long-time associate Hamilton Jordan to the position.

These experiences taught Ronald Reagan's advisors the importance of appointing officials who are politically loyal to the president. President-elect Reagan's transition staff appointed devoted Reagan conservatives to key cabinet and subcabinet positions. White House control of civil servants also became political and centralized. One of the most direct efforts to control the civil service bureaucracy followed the appointment of Donald Devine as the Director of the Office of Personnel Management (OPM), the agency responsible for managing the civil service system. Devine believed that "there must be response to what the elected officials of the government want" and that the president should exert partisan control over the bureaucracy. Under Devine, the OPM used "reductions in force" to cut the number of career civil servants and to downgrade hundreds of positions. More federal personnel were hired without the protection of civil service. Some of these new officials were hired as political appointees under rules that had been instituted by the Eisenhower administration in the 1950s in order to restore some presidential appointment power in the middle levels of the bureaucracy. The number of such employees increased from 911 in 1976 to 1,665 in 1986, with more than two-thirds serving as mid-level managers who make crucial decisions about implementing politically controversial policies. The number of temporary employees proliferated when Devine granted agencies "broad new authority" to hire temporaries, who already numbered more than 111,000.[42]

The success of the Reagan administration in politicizing the bureaucracy cast doubt on one of the cherished principles of political science—that the bureaucracy is a "permanent government" insulated from radical changes in politics and beyond the capacity of the president to control. Realigning forces in American politics, however, were already exerting an impact before Reagan took office. In 1978, during the Carter administration, Congress passed the Civil Service Reform Act, which was designed to give the president and his appointees more leverage over employees by removing Civil Service protection from large numbers of executives in agencies throughout the government. As the first president to have the law available from the start, the Reagan administration moved aggressively to fill positions with conservative loyalists. Particularly targeted were agencies charged with implementing the programs of the New Deal and the Great Society. The ratio of political to career appointees grew from 7 percent to 18 percent in the Consumer Product Safety Commission, from 35 percent to 40 percent in the Department of Education, from 33 percent to 50 percent in the Federal Home Loan Bank Board, and from 5 percent to 23 percent in the Federal Trade Commission.[43]

The nature of the Reagan transition in 1980 reveals the meticulous planning that went into the assault on the bureaucracy. Immediately after the November 1979 election, nearly one-hundred citizen task forces composed of conservatives were sent into federal agencies throughout the government. The teams were composed not of policy experts but of ideological campaign workers, many of them seeking jobs. Under the direction of Edwin Meese III and William Timmons, they were charged with finding ways of linking various agencies together into a common effort to achieve the conservative agenda. They had full access to agency files (except personnel files) and employees. They gave the Reagan administration briefing books stuffed with recommendations for cutbacks, elimination of programs, and plans for privatization and deregulation.[44]

In 1981, Vice President George Bush was put in charge of a Task Force on Regulatory Relief. The Grace Commission, named after its chairman, J. Peter Grace of the billion-dollar conglomerate W. R. Grace and Co., was asked to find ways of reducing the deficit. The day after Reagan's reelection in 1984, W. R. Grace and Co. began running a series of national television ads, at a cost of $2.1 million, to promote spending cuts. The public and private campaigns alleging inefficiency and overregulation as the principal causes of the federal deficit put the federal bureaucracy under pressure. Pay levels were reduced for many lower-level jobs, at the same time that top political appointees received substantial raises. Uncooperative executives without civil service protection were threatened with geographical transfers in some agencies, such as in the Department of the Interior. A hiring freeze was put into effect for much of 1981.

The politicization of the bureaucracy was most evident at the top. Presidents have been reluctant to place in key positions political appointees who have their own bases of power. But they usually have had to reward various constituencies and interest groups with appointments, even when the appointees did not fully share the president's agenda, and some agencies, over time, came to be regarded as the special preserves of certain groups. Thus, for instance, even under Republicans the Secretary of Labor and key departmental appointments were expected to be representative of the labor movement. Bankers, farmers, small businesses, consumers, environmentalists, and other defined interest groups formed constituencies around government agencies, and they had come to expect some stability in their relationships. When the community of interests was threatened by administration initiatives, it was not hard to persuade a senator or congressperson that a congressional committee or subcommittee should intervene.

The Reagan administration did not put an end to this system, but it did manage to change the composition of some subgovernments and weaken others. Individuals hostile to the interests of constituent groups opposed by conservatives were appointed to key positions. Interior Secretary James Watt, who steered the Interior Department away from its institutionalized role as defender of conservation, was only the most visible and controversial of such appointments. Albert Angrisani, until 1983 the Assistant Secretary of Labor for Employment and Training, described his agency's largest program, the Comprehensive Employment and Training Program, as "just another big welfare program." Rather than acting as a voice to defend the program within the administration, he cooperated in cutting the budget for the program by 20 percent and assisted the White House in replacing it with grants to local private industry councils.[45]

The former corporate executive appointed to head the National Forest Service had a previous career with the timber products industry and not surprisingly advocated getting "more of our wood from the national forests." Rather than seeking any changes in the laws restricting harvests, he increased the budget for timber sales and reduced the amount budgeted for research and conservation. At the National Highway Traffic and Safety Administration, Reagan appointed an administrator who had no previous experience in highway transportation but who had a reputation for opposing strip-mining regulations. Predictably, the new appointee espoused regulatory relief for the automobile companies. Reagan's appointment to head the Federal Communications Bureau had a background in communications, but only as a lawyer representing small-town radio stations; his career was built on defending such stations from challenges to license renewals from groups contending that they were not always serving the public interest. This appointee subsequently succeeded in eliminating the fairness and equal-time doctrines under which broadcasters were required to provide opportunities for response to political advertising and editorials under some circumstances.[46] Reagan's philosophy led to the appointment of Ford B. Ford to be Assistant Secretary of Labor for the Mine and Health and Safety Administration. Ford reduced the authority of mine inspectors and curtailed the number of inspections, citations, and penalties collected. A series of mine disasters slowed the effort, but with support from the mining industry the reduction of oversight in one of the world's most dangerous industries was completed. For his efforts, Ford was promoted to Undersecretary of Labor in 1983.[47]

Ronald Brownstein and Nina Easton, in their book *Reagan's Ruling Class,* reveal that an overwhelming proportion of Reagan appointees have biographies and orientations much like the cases just mentioned.[48] Examples included an Assistant Secretary for Occupational Safety and Health (OSHA) from a construction firm that had been frequently fined by the agency; arms reduction negotiators who believed that the United States needed to increase its military capability; and a head of the Small Business Administration who thought that the agency should be disbanded. There was sometimes a falling out among the conservative zealots, as when budget director David Stockman felt frustrated by Treasury Secretary Donald Regan's resistance to a second round of draconian cuts in social welfare spending. But the overall shape of the federal bureaucracy was profoundly affected by the capture of the Republican party by what Thomas Edsall called "an alliance of conservative ideological leaders, corporate chief executive officers, sunbelt entrepreneurs, independent oilmen, and key representatives of Washington's business lobbying community," joined by conservative intellectuals, some of whom were Democrats.[49]

The Reagan administration could not have exerted such influence over the bureaucracy nor imposed such far-reaching changes without the acquiescence of Congress. Bureaucrats would have simply ignored the task forces, commissioners, and budget cutters. Many of the new policies, however—such as deregulation, budget cuts, and weakening of the civil service protection—were already underway before

Reagan was elected. The new directions are no doubt related to the general shift of the Democratic party away from its New Deal positions and constituencies that we described in chapters 7 and 8.

The Control of Information

Despite the evolution of techniques for improving presidential influence over the bureaucracy, the civil service and the Congress constitute formidable obstacles to direct presidential control. But by manipulating information and public opinion, presidents can undermine the will of these institutions to obstruct presidential goals. Each recent presidency has contributed to the steadily growing elegance with which presidents manage the public's positive perception of themselves and a negative perception about their opponents.

Presidents grasped the potential of direct communication with the electorate in the early years of this century. Theodore Roosevelt began the custom of presidential press conferences, and his cousin Franklin met with the press nearly seven times a month. But the press conference has slowly disappeared because reporters occasionally ask embarrassing questions and presidents sometimes give mistaken answers, and in either case a president's image can be damaged. Eisenhower, Kennedy, and Johnson held about two press conferences a month, Ford and Carter less than one and a half a month, and Nixon and Reagan averaged a press conference only every other month.[50] President Bush began his term by reversing the trend and holding press conferences more frequently; it remains to be seen if this practice will survive when his approval ratings drop, as they do at some time for any president.

In the place of press conferences, presidents have focused more intensely on managing their public image. Television provided unprecedented opportunities to manipulate the public's view of the president, and presidents learned to present themselves and control their message more effectively. Richard Nixon learned that deliberate "packaging" could enhance both presidential electibility and power. A pollster and a media expert exercised unprecedented influence in the day-to-day operations of the Carter White House. During the Reagan administration, media manipulation became an important daily presidential activity. Advisors such as Michael Deaver meticulously manipulated the presentation of the president to deflect criticism and to maximize his popularity, influence and, in 1984, his electoral votes:

> [Deaver's] image-game tactics leaned heavily on polling, used the way soap and cosmetic companies work mass marketing....[Richard] Wirthlin's firm, Decision Making Information, Inc., would "pretest" public attitudes before Reagan went barnstorming on issues....Wirthlin's firm...can do national polls on hot issues within twenty-four hours. Frequently this speed put the Reagan operation far ahead of Congress, the television networks, of Democratic rivals in figuring out the best political line with the public.[51]

This information permitted the White House to use the "line of the day" technique, in which the White House managed information to ensure that network news shows would present the president's views on major issues.

The President and "National Security"

It is obvious that presidents are tempted to define issues as "national security" problems, because in the area of national security the public, Congress, and the courts give the president wide latitude. The Reagan administration was determined to go farther than its predecessors to restrict access to all kinds of information. In 1982, the president issued an executive order that vastly increased the number of government documents classified as secret and made access to these documents more difficult. Federal employees with access to information defined as sensitive were asked to agree in writing that, for the rest of their lives, they would submit for government approval all writings and speeches that might touch on intelligence matters. Over 250,000 federal employees signed the agreements. The administration even attempted to stop university professors from lecturing or writing about advanced technology. Admiral Bobby Inman, deputy director of the CIA, warned that if academics and scientists did not voluntarily limit their dissemination of scientific research on such topics, public opinion "could well cause the federal government to overreact" against the scientists, possibly with criminal sanctions.[52]

The potential for the abuse of presidential power is greater in foreign policy matters than in any other policy arena because presidential discretion goes almost unchecked. Deception in military and foreign policy making is a constant across administrations. The "Pentagon papers," first published by newspapers in 1971, revealed that the Eisenhower, Kennedy, and Johnson administrations had misinformed the press and the public about the nature of the war in Vietnam and the purposes of American intervention. Without congressional approval, President Nixon ordered the secret bombing of Cambodia on Christmas Day, 1970. Although the War Powers Act of 1973 aimed to prevent such unilateral actions in the future, the CIA secretly mined harbors in Nicaragua in 1984.

The National Security Council (NSC) has become partisan and more central to policy making in each succeeding presidential administration. Presidents Kennedy and Johnson elevated the NSC role by relying heavily on the advice of such national security advisors as McGeorge Bundy and Walt Rostow. Henry Kissinger, the most influential foreign policy expert in the Nixon administration, built the largest staff in NSC history and used it to wrest policy control from the State and Defense departments. Although Jimmy Carter expressed an intention to return foreign policy to cabinet responsibility, he came to rely increasingly on his national security advisor, Zbigniew Brzezinski. Secretary of State Alexander Haig attempted to reinvigorate cabinet influence in the early years of the Reagan administration, but Haig was soon eased out of his post and such NSC advisors as William Clark, Robert McFarlane, and John Poindexter became more prominent in many foreign decisions than Haig's successor, George Schultz.[53]

The Iran-*contra* scandal demonstrated that the temptation to abuse national security is endemic to the modern presidency. The White House national security staff established a secret foreign policy network dubbed "the Enterprise" that bargained with numerous foreign governments, sold arms to Iran, and channeled profits to the Nicaraguan *contras* despite a congressional ban on U.S. government assistance to them. A full accounting of this shadowy organization's budget is impossible, but between June 1984 and 1986 the Enterprise apparently received $10 million from private contributors and $34 million from other countries, including $3.8 million from the sale of arms to Iran. With this money the Enterprise purchased airplanes, built an airstrip, bought weapons in Europe, and delivered them to the *contras*. Deceiving outsiders, including the Congress, was considered critical to the success of this operation. As Oliver North told *contra* leader Adolfo Calero, "We need to make sure that this new financing does not become known. The Congress must believe that there continues to be an urgent need for funding."[54]

Such operations as the Enterprise are predictable responses to circumstances in which all presidents find themselves. Although Congress and the courts might act to prevent a recurrence of the specific abuses involved in a given scandal, the circumstances that prompt these abuses have not changed, nor has the inventiveness of presidential staff. Opportunities to enhance their autonomy and power lead presidents to invent national security reasons for bypassing other government institutions in carrying out their policies.

The consequences of military and foreign policy decisions increasingly spill over into domestic politics as the American economy becomes more integrated into international markets. The United States has a long tradition of defining its domestic problems in relation to foreign threats. In the 1950s, federal aid to education (the National Defense Education Act) and interstate highways (the National Defense Transportation Act) were promoted as necessary for the "national defense." In 1988, both parties' presidential candidates endorsed the definition of drugs as a national security problem, and accordingly they favored using the military to combat drugs. A federal antidrug law enacted in 1988 established an Office of National Drug Control Policy in the White House whose director—later referred to as a "czar"—was explicitly authorized to attend National Security Council meetings. As more domestic as well as foreign policy problems become linked to national security justifications, both presidential power and the abuse of that power will continue to blossom.

The Accountability of Hidden Governments

Hidden subgovernments and the hidden presidency pose serious problems for American democracy. Subgovernments thrive when incumbent senators and representatives can successfully maintain subgovernment relationships throughout their careers. In turn, the participants in these closed policy arenas help to ensure that challengers can rarely defeat the incumbents. Hidden subgovernments make the traditional mechanisms of citizen participation, including elections, into little more than symbolic exercises. Important public policies are decided in a complex web of negotiations, tradeoffs and side agreements among the participants in specialized and closed policy systems. Corruption is built into this process. It is becoming increasingly difficult to distinguish between legitimate campaign contributions and quid pro quo payoffs for services rendered by elected officials to powerful private interests.

The presidency relies on a set of hidden governments of its own. In the domestic policy arena, executive agencies owing allegiance strictly to the president have rapidly expanded. In the foreign policy arena—as we demonstrate in the next two chapters—policy making has become shrouded in a cloud of deceit and secrecy.

Notes

1. James Madison, number 10, in *The Federalist Papers* (New York: Mentor, 1961), p. 79.

2. James Madison, number 39, and Alexander Hamilton, number 68, *The Federalist Papers,* pp. 242, 412.

3. John C. Miller, *The Federalist Era, 1789–1801* (New York: Harper and Brothers, 1960), p. 15.

4. Alexander Hamilton, number 60, *The Federalist Papers,* p. 370.

5. Stephen Skowronek, *Building a New American State: The Expansion of National Administrative Capacities, 1877–1920* (New York: Cambridge University Press, 1982), p. 25.

6. Skowronek, *Building a New American State,* p. 27.

7. Quoted in Mattei Dogan, "The Political Power of Western Mandarins: Introduction," in *The Mandarins of Western Europe: The Political Role of Top Civil Servants* ed. Mattei Dogan (New York: Halsted Press, 1975); see also Joel D. Aberbach, Robert D. Putnam, and Bert A. Rockman, *Bureaucrats and Politicians in Western Democracies* (Cambridge, Mass.: Harvard University Press, 1981).

8. Skowronek, *Building a New American State,* pp. 287-288.

9. Ibid.

10. James L. Sundquist, *The Decline and Resurgence of Congress* (Washington: Congressional Quarterly, 1985), p. 37.

11. Roger H. Davidson and Walter J. Oleszak, *Congress and Its Members* (Washington, D.C.: Congressional Quarterly, 1985), p. 37.

12. Davidson and Oleszak, *Congress and Its Members,* pp. 27-36; Norman J. Ornstein, Thomas E. Mann, and Michael J. Malbin, *Vital Statistics on Congress, 1989-1990* (Washington, D.C.: Congressional Quarterly, 1989), pp. 160, 165.

13. Ornstein, Mann, and Malbin, *Vital Statistics on Congress,* pp. 130-135; Janet Hook, "Senators Settle for Moderate Curbs on Mass Mailings," *Congressional Quarterly Weekly Report* 47, No. 5 (November 11, 1989): 3028. Some of the personal staff is assigned to several nonvoting representatives from American possessions and the District of Columbia.

14. Harold W. Stanley and Richard G. Niemi, *Vital Statistics on American Politics,* 2nd ed. (Washington, D.C.: CQ Press, 1989), pp. 200-201; Ornstein, Mann, and Malbin, *Vital Statistics on Congress,* p. 136.

15. Ornstein, Mann, and Malbin, *Vital Statistics on Congress,* p. 56; Rhodes Cook, "Key to Survival for Democrats Lies in Split-Ticket Voting," *Congressional Quarterly* 47, no. 27 (July 8, 1989): 1710-1716.

16. Robert Koenig, "Lawmakers Beat Mail Deadline," *St. Louis Post-Dispatch*, October 15, 1988, p. B1; Steve Blakely, "Congress and Computers," in David C. Kozak and John D. Macartney, *Congress and Public Policy* (Chicago: Dorsey, 1987); Hedrick Smith, *The Power Game: How Washington Really Works* (New York: Random House, 1988), pp. 124-125.

17. R. Douglas Arnold, *Congress and the Bureaucracy: A Theory of Influence* (New Haven: Yale University Press, 1979), p. 209.

18. There were other reasons for the multiplication of subcommittees in the 1960s and 1970s. Liberal Democrats sought the expansion of subcommittees to increase their leverage (given that more conservative Southern Democrats chaired many full committees by virtue of seniority). Lawrence C. Dodd and Richard L. Schott, *Congress and the Administrative State* (New York: John Wiley, 1979), p. 125.

19. Dodd and Schott, *Congress and the Administrative State*, p. 125.

20. Stanley and Niemi, *Vital Statistics on American Politics*, pp. 200-201.

21. There is much disagreement over the issue of whether "subgovernments" have dominated or continue to dominate American national policy. Morris Fiorina discusses this issue in *Congress: Keystone of the Washington Establishment*, 2nd ed. (New Haven: Yale University Press, 1989), and indicates that subgovernment politics still largely describes the national American policy process (p. 121). Jeffrey M. Berry takes the position that these subgovernments have been permanently undermined in "Subgovernments, Issue Networks, and Political Conflicts," in *Remaking American Politics* ed. Richard A. Harris and Sidney M. Milkis (Boulder: Westview, 1989), pp. 239-260; Daniel McCool argues that budgetary constraints have weakened some subgovernments, but that the 1980s have in other ways multiplied and strengthened subgovernments in "Subgovernments and the Impact of Policy Fragmentation and Accommodation," *Policy Studies Review* 8, no. 4 (Winter 1989): 264-287.

22. Fiorina, *Congress: Keystone of the Washington Establishment*, p. 4.

23. Ibid., pp. 4, 44-46.

24. Randall A. Ripley and Grace A. Franklin, *Congress, the Bureaucracy, and Public Policy*, 4th ed. (Chicago: Dorsey, 1987).

25. Ibid., p. 109; Joseph A. Califano, Jr., *Governing America* (New York: Touchstone, 1981).

26. Susan J. Tolchin and Martin Tolchin, *Dismantling America: The Rush to Deregulate* (Boston: Houghton Mifflin, 1983), p. 166.

27. Kenneth J. Meier, *Regulation: Politics, Bureaucracy, and Economics* (New York: St. Martin's Press, 1985), pp. 108-111.

28. T. R. Reid, *Congressional Odyssey: The Saga of a Senate Bill* (San Francisco: W. H. Freeman, 1980).

29. Ripley and Franklin, *Congress, the Bureaucracy, and Public Policy*, pp. 121-123.

30. David A. Stockman, *The Triumph of Politics: The Inside Story of the Reagan Revolution* (New York: Avon, 1987), pp. 36-37.

31. G. Adams, *The Politics of Defense Contracting: The Iron Triangle* (New Brunswick: Transaction, 1982), quoted in Ripley and Franklin, *Congress, the Bureaucracy, and Public Policy*, p. 181.

32. Ripley and Franklin, *Congress, the Bureaucracy, and Public Policy*, pp. 182-183.

33. Jerry Hagstrom and Robert Guskind, "Lobbying the Pentagon," *National Journal* 18 (May 31, 1986): 1316-1321.

34. Jeff Gerth, "U.S. Weapons Makers Ring Up Healthy Profits," *New York Times*, April 9, 1985, p. 40; Steven V. Roberts, "Behind Military Budget Rises: Political Aims of Lawmakers," *New York Times*, May 17, 1985, p. 1.

35. Margaret W. Freivogel, "Pentagon Puts Congress Over a Pork Barrel," *St. Louis Post-Dispatch*, December 21, 1985, p. A1.

36. Macon Morehouse, "Hill Repairing Revolving Door, While Top Employees Exit," *Congressional Quarterly Weekly Report* 47, no. 20 (May 20, 1989): 1186-1187.

37. Richard L. Berke, "Constituent Service," *New York Times,* November 5, 1989, p. 1.

38. David H. Davis, *Energy Politics,* 3rd Ed. (New York: St. Martin's Press, 1982), passim.

39. Lance T. LeLoup, Barbara L. Graham and Stacey Barwick, "Deficit Politics and Constitutional Government: The Causes and Consequences of Gramm-Rudman-Hollings," *Public Budgeting and Finance* 7 (Spring 1987): 83-103.

40. James MacGregor Burns, *Presidential Government: The Crucible of Leadership* (Boston: Houghton Mifflin, 1966).

41. Richard P. Nathan, *The Administrative Presidency* (New York: John Wiley, 1983), pp. 28-55.

42. Robert Pear, "Temporary Hiring by U.S. Is Pushed Under New Policy," *New York Times,* January 2, 1984, p. 1; National Commission on the Public Service, *Leadership for America: Rebuilding the Public Service* (Lexington, Mass.: Lexington Books, 1989), pp. 222-223.

43. Cited in Burnham, "Future of American Politics," p. 237.

44. Burnham, *Critical Elections and the Mainsprings of American Democracy* (New York: W. W. Norton, 1970), p. 4.

45. Kevin Phillips, *Post-Conservative America* (New York: Random House, 1982), p. 204.

46. "Why Reagan Will Be with Us into the 21st Century," *Washington Post Weekly Edition,* September 30, 1985, pp. 21-23.

47. David Moberg, "Unions Are Having Difficulty," *In These Times,* November 21-28, 1984, p. 7.

48. Vic Fingerhut, "Misunderstanding the 1984 Presidential Election," *Campaigns and Elections* (Winter 1985), pp. 21-28.

49. Cited in "The Seamless Web Extends to Politics," *In These Times,* November 21-28, 1984, p. 25.

50. Smith, *The Power Game,* p. 432.

51. Ibid., p. 417.

52. U. Lynn Jones, "See No Evil, Hear No Evil, Speak No Evil: The Information Control Policy of the Reagan Administration," *Policy Studies Journal* 17, no. 2 (Winter 1988–89), pp. 243–260.

53. Karl F. Inderfurth and Loch K. Johnson, "Transformation—Editor's Introduction," in *Decisions of the Highest Order: Perspectives on the National Security Council* ed. Inderfurth and Johnson (Pacific Grove, Calif.: Brooks/Cole, 1988), pp. 89-103.

54. *Report of the Congressional Committees Investigating the Iran-Contra Affair,* Abridged Edition (New York: Random House, 1988), pp. 11-34, 59.

Chapter 10

Democracy
in the Garrison State

The Limited Reach of Electoral Decisions

To America's economic elites, foreign policy is considered a straightforward expression of their right to control decisions about investment, growth, and profits. For more than a century, American foreign policy has been synonymous with the building of an empire. Business elites have not tolerated interference with this process. For this reason, foreign policy making has been gradually removed from domestic democratic processes. Since the Second World War, foreign policy making has involved a relatively small group that routinely operates behind a screen of secrecy and deception.

These developments were pushed along by both political parties. Since the anticommunism hysteria in the years following the Second World War, a bipartisan consensus has existed on foreign policy, with at least three consequences. First, meaningful political discourse has been almost absent about foreign policy issues. At election time, debates about foreign policy amount to contests to see which of the candidates is "toughest" on communism or "communist"-sponsored insurgencies in various countries. Second, as a result voters have never been presented with alternatives outside the Cold War consensus. And third, so many foreign policy decisions have been placed beyond public scrutiny—only surfacing periodically in public "scandals"—that almost all of what passes as official information about foreign policy is manufactured by government agencies for its propaganda effect.

Expanding the Empire

After the Second World War, there was a fundamental redefinition of "normalcy" in American political culture, away from an historic distrust of a large standing military to acceptance of its necessity. From this time forward, any meaningful debates among political and economic elites over whether to finance a peacetime military presence were quickly resolved. The presence of a constantly expanding, well-coordinated military establishment, together with an industry feeding off military spending, was thought to be essential for maintaining American dominance in the postwar world.

Elites made the decision not to return to prewar levels of spending after the Second World War and the Korean War. In constant dollars, the military budget increased by more than ten times between the peacetime years 1940 and 1956. Much of the post-World War II expenditures went for new armaments—notably, nuclear weapons and delivery systems and technologically sophisticated airplanes and ships. The number of military personnel sharply escalated. In 1940, the Untied States maintained only 485,000 men and women under arms, with an additional 256,000 civilians to support them. In 1950, there were over 1.5 million persons in uniform and over 960,000 Defense Department (DOD) civilian employees. By 1975, about 2.15 million people served in the armed forces and there were an additional 1.1 million civilian employees. After falling slightly in the wake of the Vietnam War, civilian employment rose again by 1985 to a level surpassing that of 1978.[1]

As early as 1939, political and economic elites, in collaboration with the executive branch of government, began planning the permanent expansion of the military in order to make possible systematic U.S. intervention in the Third World. Lawrence Shoup's underappreciated research into the activity of a group of business, intellectual, and political elites reveals how the "responsibilities" of the post-war period were not thrust upon, but were actively sought by a group of economic and political elites who wanted to expand and consolidate an American empire.[2]

In September 1939, more than two years before the Japanese attack on Pearl Harbor, the influential New York-based Council on Foreign Relations (CFR) approached the State Department about collaborating on a secret, long-range study of the implications of the European war and how it would affect the role of the United States in world affairs after its conclusion. Financed by the Rockefeller Foundation and with the support of the State Department, various committees began their work, which became known as the "War Peace Studies."

The foreign policy planners first tried to determine whether continued control of the Western Hemisphere would be sufficient to maintain U.S. prosperity and self-sufficiency if Germany were able to control Europe. They concluded that only if the United States expanded its sphere to embrace possessions of the British Commonwealth and the Far East could sufficient access to markets and raw materials be guaranteed. In strict secrecy, the CFR committees and their State Department allies, a group of elites who would have tremendous influence on foreign policy for the next thirty years, defined the U.S. national interest as the economic dominance of two-thirds of the world.

In October 1940, one CFR study group bluntly declared its purpose "to set forth the political, military, territorial and economic requirements of the United States in its potential leadership of the non-German world area including the United Kingdom itself as well as the Western Hemisphere and Far East." The same memorandum indicated that from the start the policy planners considered a permanent military establishment *not as an instrument to deter aggression, but as an instrument of empire building*. It declared that the "foremost requirement of the United States in a world in which it proposes to hold unquestioned power is the rapid fulfillment of a program of complete rearmament." In 1939, elites thought that German hegemony over Europe might be tolerable, but Japanese competition in the Far East was not. On this basis, the CFR recommended that the government aid China and embargo Japan, two policies subsequently adopted by President Roosevelt.[3]

The elites planning postwar foreign policy conceived a world in which American interests might be compatible with a continental Europe controlled by the Nazis; after all, many U.S. leaders regarded Hitler as a useful check on the Soviet Union, and some admired him. But as Japan brought more of Asia under its control and as Germany threatened to militarily defeat Britain and, perhaps, seize control of Britain's vast empire, the CFR committees concluded, eight months before the Japanese attack on Pearl Harbor, that the defeat of the Axis was both inevitable and necessary.

But in preparing for a war with Japan, the Economic and Financial Study group of the CFR suggested to American political leaders that their actual aims—to build an empire—should be covered over with the idea that America was seeking only to protect its immediate interests:

> If war aims are stated which seem to be concerned solely with Anglo-American imperialism, they will offer little to people in the rest of the world. The interests of other peoples should be stressed, not only those of Europe, but also of Asia, Africa and Latin America. This would have a better propaganda effect.

The actual aims proposed by the group were manifestly clear. As one member of the project put it in 1940, it would be necessary to "cultivate a mental view toward world settlement after this war which will enable us to impose our own terms, amounting perhaps to a pax-Americana."[4]

After the formal entry of the United States into the war in December 1941, the CFR and the State Department continued to refine their plans for the postwar period. The work was carried out in secret because both the Council and the State Department recognized that public knowledge of U.S. plans to dominate the Third World (as it was later to be called) could harm America's relationships with other nations that were helping in the fight against the Axis. Equally important, the foreign policy elites knew that it would be damaging to morale at home if the American public learned that its leaders had much more than the defeat of fascism in mind.

An elite consensus was forged that unified the goals of military officers, government officials, and corporations involved in military production. From the very start, the articulation of a public ideology of idealism was considered to be an essential feature of foreign policy planning. Henceforth, America's foreign policies would be rhetorically dedicated to stopping the "international communist conspiracy" and also rhetorically designed (as the opposite side of the coin) to foster democracy and freedom.

George Kennan, a significant intellectual shaper of the postwar order, recognized that a public commitment to high ideals could boomerang later. In a top-secret memorandum drafted in 1946, Kennan laid out the rationale for caution:

> We have about 50% of the world's wealth but only 6.3% of its population....We cannot fail to be the object of envy and resentment. Our real task in

the coming period is to devise a pattern of relationships which will permit us to maintain this position of disparity without positive detriment to our national security. To do so, we will have to dispense with all sentimentality and day-dreaming; and our attention will have to be concentrated everywhere on our im-mediate national objectives. We need not deceive ourselves that we can afford today the luxury of altruism and world benefaction.[5]

In a similar vein, forty years later Lt. Col. John Bacevich, a West Point graduate and International Affairs Fellow with the Council on Foreign Relations, described the motives of U.S. foreign policy in 1986:

We can see today that the Army's primary task down to the present has con-tinued to be precisely what it was in Korea: the application of force to maintain the global status quo that emerged from World War II. While the United States does not claim a formal empire...the Army since 1945 has played the historical role of an imperial defense force, called on repeatedly to protect far-flung American interests threatened by global brush fires by the winds of political change.[6]

Bacevich said that the Army should plan to act as an interventionist force instead of maintaining the fiction that it existed to provide national security. But this would have to be presented to the public "inoffensively, using terms suited to American political discourse" because "an American Army proclaiming itself to be an imperial police force would have difficulty garnering public or congressional support. That statement holds as true today as it would have for the 1950s."[7]

For decades, principles of human rights, democracy, and international law have endured as the guiding rhetorical ideals of America's foreign policy. But the yawning chasm separating these proclaimed ideals from the actual goals underlying foreign policy have been difficult to hide. Because of this discrepancy, soon after the Second World War elites took steps to remove foreign policy from domestic political processes. The most important devices employed—destined to grow more elaborate with every presidential administration—entailed policies of deception and secrecy.

The Foundations of the National Security State

Unlike the post-World War I "return to normalcy," the post-World War II period was marked by the institutionalization of significant "emergency" measures originally adopted to fight the war. Much of this process was accomplished through the National Security Act of 1947. The propaganda apparatus was consolidated in the hands of the U.S. Information Agency; "covert operations" and intelligence gathering were brought together into a Central Intelligence Agency (CIA), though these functions have since spread to all the military branches and into the National Security Council and even the White House; a single Defense Department and a Joint Chiefs of Staff were established to coordinate the independent branches of the military; and the National Security Council (NSC) was created to advise the president on foreign affairs.

A less-noted feature of the act established a National Security Resources Board, which, supplemented by the Armed Forces Procurement Act of 1947 and the National Industrial Reserve Act of 1948, laid the legal foundations for an intimate interaction between military agencies and private industry—the so-called "military-industrial complex." The impact of this legislation was to institutionalize a permanent condition of mobilization for war, breaking with the pre-World War II assumption that the first day of mobilization would be the day that Congress declared war.[8]

This legislation was enacted even though government and military planners believed at that time that the United States would indefinitely maintain an enormous military superiority over the Soviet Union, a nation that had suffered 22,000,000 casualties during the war and which was incapable, even if so inclined, of mounting an effective attack on the United States or Western Europe. The United States alone possessed the atomic bomb. Although the planners erred in believing that their own country would maintain an indefinite monopoly over this technology, not until the late 1960s would the Soviet Union reach any kind of parity with the United States in nuclear weapons.

The institutionalization of militarism under the guise of national security was a logical expression of the aspirations articulated by the Council of Foreign Relations before and during the Second World War. This development was recognized by the historian Charles Beard, who charged in 1948 that Franklin Roosevelt had deliberately led the nation to war and knowingly violated the Constitution to do so.[9] Beard warned at that time that Madisonian principles of checks and balances were in jeopardy and that the executive branch would gain control of foreign policy and war making in the postwar period through the expansion of state secrets.

It is tempting to interpret military growth and foreign policy adventures after the war as the inevitable components of a grand conspiracy among elites to build and consolidate the American empire. But a conspiracy theory must be cautiously applied, even though there is overwhelming evidence that postwar policies were determined in a conscious and coordinated fashion, for it must take into account the genuine divisions that existed among elites about how to handle the Soviet Union. Roosevelt himself seemed to adopt the position that the Soviet Union was entitled to a sphere of influence of its own after the war, and he proceeded to emphasize policies, such as strongly supporting the United Nations, that would have consolidated a grand area for the United States excluding Eastern Europe.[10]

To the ideological right of Roosevelt were influential policy makers like Averill Harriman and George Kennan, who saw the Soviet Union as an expansionist power that needed to be contained without the constraints that might be imposed by a United Nations. Their containment strategy envisioned a military buildup complemented by aggressive diplomatic and economic initiatives. More thoroughly conservative advisers like Dean Acheson favored provocative military measures. Even further to the right stood fanatical anticommunists and opportunists like Joseph McCarthy and Richard Nixon, who argued that the Soviets had penetrated the halls of government within the United States and who advocated "rolling back" the Soviet area of domination rather than merely "containing" it. (Nixon, however, became more pragmatic as his career progressed.)[11]

Even if Roosevelt had not died and been succeeded by the hawkish Harry Truman, developments at home and abroad would probably have accelerated militarization and propelled U.S. foreign policy rightward. The desire by both liberals and conservatives to purge the labor unions and the Democratic party of leftist influence undermined elites who favored a pragmatic orientation towards the Soviets. Stalin's pathological behavior toward his real and imagined political opponents strengthened those who sought to recast the Soviets in place of Nazi Germany as the incarnation of an evil empire that could be deterred only by an aggressive foreign policy backed by a worldwide military presence.

The theory of "totalitarianism" helped legitimate the new national security state by providing the theoretical underpinning for casting the Soviets in the role of aggressor. Proponents of the theory argued that Stalin's Russia and Hitler's Germany were alike because both regimes were characterized by a single party dominated by a charismatic dictator driven by an imperialistic ideology, who used terror and imposed state control over the economy and communications system.[12] It did not seem to matter to promoters of the "Communist conspiracy" theory that there were fundamental differences between the histories and regimes of Germany and the Soviet Union (or that many right-wing policy makers in the United States continued to feel sympathy for the Nazis). The theory was useful in creating an image of an aggressor who would this time be deterred, not appeased—a new enemy that was particularly dangerous because it sought to spread an anticapitalist ideology.

Within the United States, those who sympathized with socialism, Marxism, or communism, or even with civil rights groups, were defined as threats to the security of the nation. Legislation like the Smith Act of 1940, a wartime act aimed at Nazi sympathizers, was now turned not only on Communists but on anyone suspected of holding leftist ideals. In 1950, the Internal Security Act was passed, requiring communist or "sympathetic" organizations to register with the Attorney General, who possessed the authority (under the Smith Act) to declare certain organizations a threat to national security for allegedly advocating the violent overthrow of the United States government. This provision was routinely applied to organizations that had never advocated such a position. Together with the National Security Act of 1947, these pieces of legislation remain as the cornerstone of the government's authority to suppress internal dissent under the guise of national security.

In 1948, bombers capable of striking the Soviet Union with atomic weapons were placed in Britain, and General Lucius Clay, who headed American occupation forces in Germany, tried to convince President Truman to provoke a war with the Soviets. But the Soviet explosion of an atomic bomb in 1949 raised doubts about whether the United States could confront the Soviets without fear of unleashing atomic warfare. The planners were forced to return to the drawing boards.

The result was NSC-68, a document that became the Magna Carta of postwar national security doctrine. It laid a blueprint for moving beyond the concept of defense to the idea of aggressively challenging Soviet interests by any means short of declaring war. In the document, secretly approved by the National Security Council in 1950, foreign policy planners argued against negotiating differences with the Soviets until a new, more terrifying weapon, the hydrogen bomb, could restore unquestioned U.S. military supremacy. In the meantime, it advocated an alliance system dominated by the United States and a buildup of conventional military strength so that U.S. objectives could be met short of resorting to nuclear arms.

Military planners and political leaders realized that implementing this grand design would require mobilizing the American people into a permanent state of quasi war. Accordingly, an emotional substitute for an official state of war would have to be devised. In 1944, Charles E. Wilson, president of General Electric and later Director of Defense Mobilization under President Truman and Secretary of Defense under President Eisenhower, warned in an internal memo that "the revulsion against war not too long hence will be an almost insuperable obstacle for us to overcome. For that reason, I am convinced that we must begin now to set the machinery in motion for a permanent war economy."[13] Almost forty years later, Richard Perle, Assistant Secretary of Defense under Ronald Reagan, argued that "democracies will not sacrifice to protect their security in the absence of a sense of danger. And every time we create the impression that we and the Soviets are cooperating and moderating the competition, we diminish that sense of apprehension."[14]

The Elite Consensus on Militarization

For more than forty years there has been a remarkable degree of consensus among U.S. elites that the nation should preserve a high level of readiness to go to war. Presidential candidates of the two major parties have tried to outdo one another in advocating military preparedness. In the 1960 presidential election campaign, John F. Kennedy said there was a "missile gap" favoring the Soviet Union; twenty years later, the Republicans claimed that the Democrats had allowed American defenses to decline. For voters, the choices have been conducted within extraordinarily narrow limits. From 1945 until 1989, when Soviet Premier Mikhail Gorbachev declared his policy of *perestroika* and the Eastern Bloc governments began to fall, no Democratic or Republican presidential candidate questioned the premises of the Cold War—that the national defense must be constantly strengthened to deter the Communists.

The ideas sustaining the "Cold War," wherein the superpowers have deterred each other from actually going to war by maintaining a balance of terror (MAD, or "mutually assured destruction"), developed only gradually. In the 1950s, foreign policy planners urged a military buildup not as much for deterring as for preparing for an attack on the Soviet Union. In 1955, the Air Force adapted the concept of "Force in Being," which meant maintaining a permanent state of readiness and logistics to fight. "Force in Being" included preparations for initiating a nuclear war. This capacity was supported by a new document adopted by the National Security Council, NSC 162/2, which said that the United States would "consider nuclear weapons to be as available for use as other munitions" in the event of war. President Eisenhower went even further. Concerned that an indefinite arms race might increase the prospects for dictatorial government in the United States, the president suggested in a September 1953 memo to the Secretary of State that we might "consider whether or not our duty to future generations did not require us to initiate war at the most propitious moment that we could designate." When the Army, concerned that emphasis on technology was reducing its mission and budget, objected at a National Security Council meeting that nuclear war was not inevitable, Eisenhower responded, "Since we cannot keep the United States an armed camp or a garrison state, we must make plans to use atomic bombs if we become involved in a war."[15] It is in this context that President Eisenhower delivered an oft-quoted speech about the dangers of the military-industrial complex.

Eisenhower did not go far enough to satisfy the growing number of business, academic, and military figures who advocated and profited from an expanding and permanent military establishment. Advocates of an accelerated military buildup felt thwarted by the method of budgeting under which the amount allocated to military spending was determined after domestic needs were satisfied. The Korean War provided the necessary pretext for military expansion in the early 1950s, but with the end of the war in 1954 and the waning of McCarthyism it was becoming more difficult to maintain momentum. In the late 1950s, a political battle developed between the advocates of accelerating the arms race and those moderates, including President Eisenhower, who continued to fear the impact of a permanent military-industrial complex on domestic politics.[16]

Though it remained far above prewar levels, in the aftermath of the Korean War military spending gradually fell. The militarists vainly struggled to convince Eisenhower and his key advisors to reverse the trend. An opportunity presented itself in 1956, when Eisenhower agreed to establish an ad hoc committee of private citizens to study a proposal for the government to spend $40 billion over a number of years to erect shelters to protect the population from nuclear fallout. The committee, composed of businessmen and academic specialists with close ties to military personnel and large defense contractors, was chaired by H. Rowan Gaither, a lawyer who was also chair of both the Ford Foundation and the Air Force's main "think tank," the Rand Corporation in California. Almost all members of the committee were private consultants to the National Security Council.

The committee took upon itself the task of expanding its mission beyond Eisenhower's mandate by investigating other uses for the $40 billion. When finished, the "Gaither Report" used the same arguments originally advanced in NSC 68 to argue for a military buildup and to accuse the Eisenhower administration of "complacency" in the face of the Soviet "threat." It exerted pressure on the administration to maintain not only the capability to initiate a nuclear war, but to undertake covert actions against guerrilla insurgencies and to fight a large-scale conventional war. It advocated a boost in military spending to $48 billion per year, $10 billion more than the amount recommended by the Eisenhower administration. The committee said that military "needs," irrespective of domestic priorities, should henceforth be identified as the standard for determining the Pentagon's budget.

The Gaither committee's recommendations were based on its assessment of how much spending would be needed to offset what it saw as a constantly expanding

Soviet military capacity. The committee, however, vastly overstated the Soviet buildup. It predicted, for example, that the Soviets would develop and deploy enough intercontinental ballistic missiles by 1960 to destroy American retaliatory capability. In fact, however, by 1961 the Soviets had deployed only ten missiles. The United States, under Presidents Kennedy and Johnson, would be the first country to massively deploy such missiles.

The Gaither committee's report remained classified, but militarists discovered that selective disclosure of military secrets could tilt public debate in their favor. Parts of the report were deliberately leaked to the media and sympathetic politicians. Democrats were particularly eager to use the report's findings to discredit the Republican administration. In the 1960 presidential campaign, John Kennedy invented an alleged "missile gap" to embarrass Vice President Nixon. After he was elected, Kennedy brought the militarists into his administration and put their recommendations into effect.

Considering that the Democrats and liberals were as committed to military spending as the Republicans and conservatives, it is hardly surprising that Eisenhower's warnings about the growing power of the military-industrial complex have fallen on deaf ears. Today, over 30,000 companies are engaged in military production. During the Second World War, production was carried out in 1,600 federally owned plants; only fifty-eight currently are owned by the government. Each year, more than 15 million contracts (over 52,000 each day) are signed between government and private companies. In fiscal 1985, the United States spent almost $1,100 per person on the military, in contrast to its European allies, which spent an average of $250 per person. In the mid-1980s, about $146 billion in private military business was generated by the Pentagon each year. During the Reagan administration, spending for military research increased 62 percent above the rate of inflation, while funding for civilian research fell by 10 percent.[17]

Grossly exaggerating the Soviet buildup long has comprised the principal strategy for building political support for military spending. In the 1950s, the public was told that the Soviets would have 600 to 700 long-range bombers by 1960. When 1960 came, the USSR had 190. It was said that the Soviets would have 500 to 1,000 intercontinental ballistic missiles by 1961; the USSR had only ten by that time. In the 1960s, the warning went out that the USSR would soon have 10,000 interceptors in a nationwide antiballistic missile system. But the Soviets actually deployed sixty-four, almost all of them designed to hit bombers rather than missiles. In the 1970s, the official government line was that new "highly accurate" Soviet SS-19 missiles could destroy all U.S. land-based missiles. Actually, the SS-19 proved far less accurate than originally claimed.[18]

Estimating actual Soviet military expenditures likewise has been a politically loaded enterprise. The U.S. Arms Control and Disarmament Agency estimated Soviet spending at $233 billion for 1980 and $248 billion for 1983, but the respected Stockholm International Peace Research Institute estimated Soviet military spending at $154 billion for 1980 and $162 billion for 1983. The source book *World Military and Social Expenditure* utilizes a method that results in somewhat higher estimates than those of the Stockholm Institute, but these comparisons still show that U.S.

military spending far exceeds Soviet spending. For 1982, the sourcebook estimated U.S. expenditures at $196 billion, 6.2 percent of the Gross National Product. Soviet expenditures were estimated to be $170 billion, amounting to 10.9 percent of the USSR's smaller GNP. Total NATO (North Atlantic Treaty Organization) expenditures were estimated at $310 billion, 5 percent of combined GNP, compared to Warsaw Pact total expenditures of $187 billion, 9 percent of GNP.[19] In 1983, the CIA admitted that earlier estimates ran about double its new, revised estimate and that the USSR had not actually increased its military spending during the Carter years (1977–1981) at all.[20]

Even if Mikhail Gorbachev continues to deprive American hawks of a convenient enemy, the militarization of the economy has created a complex system of dependence on military spending that will not easily be broken. Only nine of the 3,041 counties in the United States received less than $1,000 from the Defense Department in 1984. With so many constituents on the military payroll, few congressional representatives can afford to attack waste and fraud vigorously or to challenge the Pentagon's priorities without fear of retribution. In 1983, Defense Secretary Caspar Weinberger accused Congress of tacking nearly $3 billion worth of unnecessary items onto the Pentagon budget. Roughly 3,275,000 jobs in the United States are in defense industries, up from 314,000 in 1940. There are almost 1.5 million military retirees in addition to the 3,295,000 people on the civilian and active military payrolls.[21] The link between corporations and the military is solidified by the retention of retired officers as employees of private contractors. Employed by 157 major military contractors were 1,350 former high-ranking military officers, plus 316 former high-ranking officials of the Defense Department.[22]

The boom in military expenditures and the extraordinary profits to be made have shifted the priorities of many companies not previously associated with military production. Profits for arms suppliers rose from an average of 19.4 percent from 1970 to 1979 to 23.3 percent from 1980 to 1983; for durable goods as a whole, in contrast, profits fell from 14.4 percent in the 1970s to 10.6 percent in 1980 to 1983. Thus, "the profits gap between commercial and military businesses widened enormously."[23] In response, such companies as Singer, IBM, Goodyear Tire, AT&T, and Westinghouse turned to military production. In 1975, Singer, famous for sewing machines, earned only 15 percent of its revenues from aerospace electronics; by 1985, it earned 80 percent from that source. Morton, once famous for salt, has become Morton-Thiokol, builder of rocket engines.

The considerable influence of the military-industrial complex with Congress has been reinforced by the system of campaign financing. Political action committees representing the largest twenty defense contractors increased their contributions 225 percent during the first six years of the Reagan administration. Military agencies are prevented by law from forming their own lobbies, but they have found functional substitutes in "legislative liaisons," maintained at taxpayer expense.[24] The influence of the military lobby is further enhanced by the fragmentation of congressional oversight and the presence of hidden subgovernments that bring lawmakers, contractors, and military agencies into mutually beneficial alliances. Public scandals about contractors defrauding the government have led to proposals to consolidate congressional oversight, but this is unlikely to be successful because of the desire of senators and representatives to chair key committees and win elections.

Even the most seamy, costly, and threatening political scandals since the Second World War have so far failed to slow the transformation of American society into a garrison state. This was demonstrated in the political aftermath of the Vietnam War.

The "Vietnam Syndrome"

By 1945, Indochina had been a part of the French empire for almost three-fourths of a century. After the war, the French colonialists faced a determined effort by Vietnamese patriots, led by the Communist party and Ho Chi Minh, to resist a reimposition of colonial rule. The fact that the Communist party dominated the anticolonial forces made the rebels entirely unacceptable to U.S. political and military leaders. The United States committed itself to supporting France, and after France's military defeat in 1954 the United States initiated a gradual process of intervention.

Against all logic and evidence, some military planners and foreign policy specialists in the Reagan administration asserted that an inadequate military effort had brought about the American defeat in Vietnam. More than 3 million U.S. soldiers served in Vietnam, including 524,000 at the peak of the war in 1969 (plus 86,000 additional air force and naval personnel based offshore and in Thailand). From 1965 to 1975, the U.S. spent between $159.4 billion (DOD's estimate) and $239.6 billion (U.S. Senate estimate) on the war. The 14,392,302 tons of explosives (more than used against Japan in the Second World War) left more than 25 million craters in a country smaller than the state of California and reduced all North Vietnamese cities south of Hanoi to rubble. More than 400,000 tons of napalm and 19 million gallons of herbicides (including 11 million gallons of Agent Orange) were used to destroy the croplands and half the forests in the country. Some 58,655 U.S. troops were killed.[25] More than 2,000,000 Vietnamese—one-ninth of the population—were killed.[26]

The Vietnam War differed from the Korean War in a crucial respect: Conscription and the high cost in lives generated discontent at home, but an antiwar movement also emerged. Ordinary citizens, at first led by college students and youth, became dissenters. They were followed by large numbers in the intellectual community, then journalists, and finally by liberal politicians. The FBI, the CIA, and other units of the national security apparatus selectively persecuted protesters. Unlike the McCarthy cruades of the 1950s, however, open and systematic repression backfired. The antiwar protests threatened to mushroom into a broader movement for social change that might have knit together civil rights activists, feminists, the youth movement, and liberal elements in the labor unions and the Democratic party. This was too high a price to pay for continuing the war. Even Richard Nixon, who built his early career on the political hysteria of McCarthyism, eventually accepted the necessity of a strategic retreat.

The political fallout from the war troubled elites. A rising cynicism and distrust of basic institutions threatened political stability. Especially undermined was the linchpin institution of the national security state, the presidency. To justify the war, Presidents Johnson and Nixon had resorted to "secrecy, control and manipulation of information, deceit, and spying on and interference with the legitimate exercise of the political rights of American citizens." This was a judgment offered not by critics of U.S. policy but by the authors of a study conducted by the National Defense University.[27] These actions constituted logical extensions of past governmental strategies to keep foreign policy secret and beyond citizen influence. This time, however, the pattern of deceit became boldly illuminated by media publicity. Under normal circumstances this would not have happened (see chapter 3), but the exposure of government secrets and spying became one component of the Watergate scandal.

In 1971, secret documents were leaked to the *New York Times* revealing that President Johnson and other people in the government had repeatedly lied about Vietnam. Congress reacted to the "Pentagon Papers" scandal by imposing new legal constraints on the president's war-making authority, most notably in the War Powers Act of 1973, which required the president to report to Congress when U.S. forces were committed to activities in which combat was a strong possibility. The act also required congressional approval to maintain troops in such a combat position for more than ninety days and authorized Congress to demand their immediate withdrawal by means of a resolution.

Other legislation placed new restrictions on the activities of the FBI and the CIA. Congressional oversight of the CIA was strengthened after Senate investigations revealed extensive domestic spying, involvement in the overthrow of the democratically elected government of Chile, a CIA-directed "secret war" in Laos, use of assassination in covert operations, and CIA activities to undermine elections in Chile and in several other countries.

These new restrictions on the executive branch's ability to conduct foreign policy making in secret endangered the carefully constructed post-World War II elite consensus about the need for a big military budget, unrestricted executive authority, and the legitimacy of intervening in the affairs of other countries. Elites were convinced that foreign policy simply could not be opened up to public debate. If this happened, their freedom to pursue interventionist strategies would surely be compromised.

The defeat in Vietnam was a learning experience for the American people that left them with little enthusiasm for more wars. In 1974, only 48 percent of those responding to a national poll were willing to defend Japan with military force in case of Soviet attack and only 37 percent was willing to defend other major allies. By 1980, the figures would rise to 74 percent and 68 percent, respectively, but even as late as 1982 enthusiasm for intervention in the Third World was notably lacking—for example, only 20 percent of the public favored the use of military force to prevent a guerrilla victory in El Salvador.[28]

President Carter attempted to adjust to this new atmosphere by recognizing the limits of what could be accomplished by military force. Carter found himself under attack from conservatives for having negotiated the eventual return of the Panama Canal to Panama and for concluding a new arms control agreement (SALT 2) with the Soviets. A combination of his own confused ideology, major revolutions in Iran and Nicaragua, economic recession at home, and the Soviet invasion of Afghanistan hastened Carter's conversion to militarism. In the last two years of his term, Carter cut domestic spending and increased military expenditures, planned new missile deployments in Western Europe, announced a new doctrine committing the United States to war in the Middle East in case revolutions threatened any Western allies, and began training a "rapid deployment force" for use against Third World revolutions.

Carter's presidency was still on the skids when an Iranian mob, angered by years of U.S. support for the Shah's violent dictatorship in their country and encouraged by an opportunistic, fundamentalist religious elite, seized the American embassy in Iran and held its inhabitants hostage for more than a year. The media kept the hostage story before the public night after night (this was the origin of ABC's program *Nightline*). A botched rescue attempt during the 1980 campaign contributed to Carter's difficulties. There can be little doubt that the episode contributed to his defeat.

The hostages were released literally as Ronald Reagan took the oath of office. (There is some evidence that Reagan struck a deal with the Ayatollah during the 1980 campaign not to release the hostages until after the election in exchange for a promise of future arms shipments. This may have been the first step in what emerged later as the Iran-*contra* scandal.)[29] The new president and his handlers recognized that the affair was an excellent catalyst for rallying public opinion behind an aggressive policy agenda that involved reversing the tendency toward congressional influence in foreign affairs, drastically increasing military spending, and waging counterinsurgency warfare through surrogates or mercenary armies in Africa, Southeast Asia, Afghanistan, and (most forcefully) Central America.

The Reagan administration came into office determined to reassert the executive branch's ability to conduct foreign policy as it saw fit. A threefold strategy was devised. First, new strategies of intervention were utilized to ensure that foreign policy could be conducted as far from public view as possible. Second, the public was subjected to a carefully orchestrated propaganda campaign. And third, the administration undertook to revitalize the military as an instrument of foreign policy.

Government Secrecy and the Reeducation of the Public

Since 1981, an avalanche of literature on so-called "low-intensity conflict" has emanated from military planners and conservative theorists. "Low-intensity conflict"— or "peaceful engagement"—the new phrase favored by the Bush administration—are euphemisms for wars conducted in Third World countries out of sight of the American public which rely on hired mercenaries clandestinely working at the direction of the CIA (this way American soldiers do not die, which upsets the public). Much of the literature advocating this new method of making war takes the view that our constitutional traditions must be bent or redefined in the struggle for American supremacy. Sam Sarkesian, an academic specialist who chairs the Interuniversity Seminar on Armed Forces and Society, asserts that revolution is inherently undemocratic and that counterrevolution must therefore "develop [its] own morality and ethics that justify any means to achieve success. Survival is the ultimate morality." This means that the United States must sometimes support sides in conflicts in which "all of the ingredients for a 'dirty', ungentlemanly, terror-oriented conflict are there; and it is likely to be protracted and increasingly costly." As a consequence, "American policy may support nondemocratic regimes in the name of democracy." To do this, Sarkesian argues that the United States needs a stronger, independent intelligence and covert operations capability. Americans must be "educated" to understand that we must employ or support measures overseas "inconsistent" with our constitutional traditions at home.[30] People like Sarkesian believe that, in the absence of a successful effort to "reeducate" Americans about the nation's best self-interests, the government must act in secrecy.

Based on this logic, the Reagan administration organized a secret government within the executive branch to conduct foreign policy. The people within this group gained complete autonomy from Congress, operated without the knowledge of the public, and even worked outside the established foreign policy and intelligence agencies.[31] In 1986, the administration proposed legislation to repeal the War Powers Act. Congress already had been induced to increase funds to build up the Special Operations Forces (SOF), which are authorized to carry out covert operations not subject to congressional oversight. For both SOF units and the CIA, more emphasis was placed on training in sabotage and "psychological operations."[32]

In 1982, CIA operatives were caught mining Nicaraguan harbors and newspapers published the contents of a CIA manual used to train the *contras* to carry out sabotage and assassination against civilian targets. Congress reacted by enacting restrictions on CIA involvement in Nicaragua. The administration found a way around the law in the Special Forces, which were coordinated from the National Security Council. The Special Forces employ and train terrorists to carry out acts of violence for political purposes. The victims are not armed opponents but civilians.[33] To prevent these victims from appearing as statistics in State Department human rights reports, civilian victims of the Salvadoran military and Nicaraguan *contras* were categorized as legitimate military targets in flagrant violation of international human rights treaties to which the United States is a signatory.[34]

The new theorists understood that terrorist attacks against civilians in Nicaragua constituted an explicit strategy that they had helped devise. Neil Livingstone, a self-styled "terrorism expert" with close ties to the Reagan administration, recommended that in order to fight covert wars military units must be trained "to hunt down and kill terrorists" accused of acting against Americans and that "debate be reopened on murder as an instrument of national policy."[35] For Vernon Walters, a top Reagan policy maker and former deputy director of the CIA, the reluctance of the American public to endorse such tactics "could have been" due to "effective covert action...carried out by the Soviet Union against the United States." Walters wrote a scenario in which he imagined a Soviet long-term planning group in 1948 discussing, "with great sophistication and profound understanding of the American national character and of the 'American dream,'" a plan to weaken American resolve to resist their plans for "world domination." He advocated that we use the same tactics as he imagined the USSR has used, especially including psychological warfare and propaganda, and develop in addition the "ability to recognize when covert action is being used against us and the means to thwart it."[36] What did Walters have in mind as the means to "thwart" such ingenious Soviet "propaganda"? One of the documents he authored for the administration urged that psychological operations of the same type used by the United States in other nations "may be necessary" to win the hearts and minds of Americans.[37]

But Walters's recommendations had already been implemented by the Reagan administration. The Pentagon had at its disposal a 1,000-member, $100 million-a-year worldwide public relations operation with which it generated its own propaganda, as it did in the case of the invasion of Grenada when it alleged a much larger Cuban presence and much greater threat to American lives than actually existed.[38] Besides the Pentagon, taxpayer-funded institutions like the National Endowment for Democracy and its Central American branch helped finance "demonstration elections" and friendly human rights agencies in other nations so that favorable "information" could be generated for the human rights reports produced by the State Department.[39]

Public relations has been a principal tool used to rehabilitate the image of the military services. Livingstone, who regularly rang the terrorism alarm bells in the mainstream media, was an executive with Gray and Co., a Washington public relations firm, when he played a key part in the Reagan election campaigns. During the first term, Reagan administration propaganda was coordinated by Michael Deaver. After Deaver's departure, White House chief of staff Donald Regan established a new team, headed by W. Dennis Thomas, which met every day to chart ways to influence public opinion. Thomas summarized the group's philosophy:

> The notion absolutely is that you establish themes through repetition. You've got to establish unanimous agreement on the part of those who have to put it forth; then you have to say it, resay it and figure out different ways to say it.[40]

Such a public relations operation actually amounted to a kind of domestic covert operation similar to the operation implemented by the United States elsewhere to influence the internal politics of other nations.

Rebuilding the Military

It is not much of an exaggeration to say that the U.S. military had nearly collapsed as an effective institution during the Vietnam War. Over 1,000 commissioned and noncommissioned officers were "fragged"—that is, assassinated—by their troops. There were more mutinies and refusals to engage in combat than in any previous American war. According to official Army figures, 28 percent of troops in Vietnam used hard drugs such as heroin and cocaine. The quality of the officer corps declined.

At all levels, fraudulent medals were awarded. The number of awards for bravery actually increased as the level of combat declined.[41]

Without a knowledge of history other than what they were told in high school and through the media, few soldiers understood the war. The enemy used guerrilla hit-and-run tactics and was virtually indistinguishable from the non-combatant population. This fact led to vicious racism and contempt for the Vietnamese people. Black soldiers were less susceptible because of their experience with racism in the United States. Some taped to their helmets the slogan, "No gook ever called me nigger"; a few retreated into their own Saigon enclaves where military police were afraid to follow. For whites and blacks alike, drugs constituted a logical refuge from the horror, and the enemy did not have to supply them. To protect political allies in Thailand and elsewhere, the CIA guarded poppy fields and transported heroin on one of its "company" airlines, Air America.[42]

Some military planners and politicians believed that the problem of discipline lay in the social base of the army, which was disproportionately made up of the poor and minorities. After the war, with the abolition of the draft and implementation of the all-volunteer army, the problem threatened to grow worse, since there was little incentive for middle-class citizens to enroll. Blacks were recruited at a rate three times higher than their proportion in the population. Rates of hard drug use were estimated to have been 35 percent higher than Vietnam levels, and 38 percent of the Army's troops were being released from service after less than three years for "mental, moral or physical reasons."[43]

By the late 1970s, however, substantial progress was made to rebuild the military. An all-voluntary army replaced the draft, and the services' recruitment budgets shot up. The Reagan administration fine-tuned these efforts. In fiscal year 1986, the four branches of the military spent over $1.8 billion on recruitment, an average of nearly $5,400 for each of 333,600 recruits, $1,400 more than the average for the previous year. Advertising alone totaled $216 million, including $60,000 for a rock video featuring break dancing. There were about 15,000 military recruiters, one for every 185 high school seniors in the country. In 1986, there were 227,448 high school students enrolled in Junior Reserve Officer Training Corps, compared to a total of 287 twenty years earlier. The Pentagon spent $52.1 million on texts, arms, and uniforms for these students.[44]

Job training and tuition credits accumulated in the military make military service before entering college or the job market the only viable option for many high school seniors, a point hammered home in Pentagon advertising featuring teenage actors discussing career options in the soda shop. Such benefits probably account for a significant proportion of reenlistments, which went up 65 percent from 1985 to 1986. In reality, there is little more to this approach than the traditional method of promising impressionable young people advantages that the services cannot deliver. For all of the emphasis on opportunities for training for high-tech careers, only 17 percent of Army jobs require such skills.[45]

On college campuses, students must now prove that they have registered with the Selective Service to receive financial aid. With tuition rising and nonmilitary aid falling, the Reserve Officer Training Corps (ROTC) becomes an increasingly attractive option. In 1986, there were 530 active ROTC detachments with 110,872 students, up 50 percent since 1975. At the graduate level, 4,000 students were funded by the Pentagon.[46]

By the mid-1980s, the military was no longer recruiting from the "lower depths" of American society. Of first-time recruits, 93 percent of the 1985 group and 92 percent of the 1986 group had graduated from high school.[47] Although recruitment promises may be inflated, the military is effectively competing with higher education as a major institution providing opportunities for job training. Although the children of elites continue to eschew military service, the lower- to middle-class ranks of society are becoming heavily populated by people who have made the rite of passage through military service.

The propaganda benefits from this rite of passage are not lost upon military planners. In 1977, when the prestige of the military was at a postwar low and disenchantment with the defeat in Vietnam still restrained military adventures abroad, Thomas Carr, Director of Defense Education under President Carter, asserted that military service was becoming an increasingly important means for socializing young people:

> By 1984, given the involvement of such a large proportion of our young people
> with military service, the military will have become a major instrument for
> youth socialization—assuming a large portion of the role once dominated by
> the family, church, the school, and the civilian work setting.[48]

Young people not exposed to such socialization through military service are subjected to a propaganda barrage that has much the same objective. Television advertising, especially concentrated in spot ads shown during sports events, portrays a positive image of military life and of the military image.

The Internal Politics of the Garrison State

On July 4, 1987, as Independence Day celebrations focused on the two hundredth anniversary of the Constitution, chances are that most Americans over-looked news reports that Lt. Col. Oliver North and other members of a secret Reagan administration task force had formulated a plan to suspend the Constitution and declare martial law in the event of either urban riots or widespread domestic opposition to a military intervention. In such a case, national government control was to be transferred to the Federal Emergency Management Agency and military commanders would have been appointed to run state and local governments.[49]

William French Smith, then attorney general, hushed up the plan, and government officials subsequently brushed aside reports about it, claiming that this kind of contingency planning is an ordinary function of government and a necessary preparation for emergencies, such as nuclear war. But in fact, North and his National Security Council aides had been planning an operation designed to involve the United States in exactly the kind of foreign intervention that might have provoked internal opposition. And the NSC was not merely running amok; Elliot Abrams, Assistant Secretary of State for Inter-American Affairs (after 1985) and chief public advocate of the Administration's policy toward Central America, was a staunch advocate of an invasion of Nicaragua, as he admitted early in 1989.[50]

The *contras,* then virtually under North's direction, were to swarm into an area of Nicaragua and declare it "liberated." North knew that this action would inevitably provoke a counterattack by Sandinista forces and that the United States would be under pressure to commit ground combat troops to rescue its mercenaries (the plan was very similar to the Bay of Pigs operation in Cuba in 1961). North, who had begun his career in Vietnam, understood that successful prosecution of a land war in Central America would almost surely require suppression of dissent at home. Part of his plan for accomplishing the necessary repression would have involved the establishment of internment camps, similar to those used during the Second World War to incarcerate American citizens of Japanese ancestry. North could have some confidence in overcoming the legal obstacles to such a plan. After all, the present Chief Justice of the Supreme Court, William Rehnquist, helped Nixon's attorney general John Mitchell draft a similar strategy to use against people protesting the Vietnam War.

North had already heavily influenced the shape of the Central America debate. For example, pro-*contra* legislators, including Senator John Danforth, were fond of quoting from a 1981 speech by Nicaraguan Interior Minister Tomás Borge in which he proclaimed the Sandinista revolution as one that "goes beyond our borders." Danforth's quote came from information provided by a white paper, "Revolution Beyond Our Borders," prepared by the Office of Public Diplomacy of the State Department. It failed to quote the rest of Borge's remarks, including the explanation, "This does not mean we export our revolution. It is sufficient—and we cannot avoid this—that they take our example." The oversight is understandable. The unofficial coordinator of the Office of Public Diplomacy was Oliver North.

The Office of Public Diplomacy was actually a small operation compared to the entire public relations campaign being used to sell the Reagan administration's policy. A tax-exempt organization called the National Endowment for the Preservation of Liberty, working with the support of Lt. Col. North and President Reagan, solicited millions of dollars from citizens to coordinate "private" support for the *contras.* A public relations firm, International Business Communications (IBC), helped in the effort,[51] which was headed by two former government employees.

The American public was the chief target of the IBC and the Office of Public Diplomacy. By relying on "private" donations, the IBC was able to lobby members of Congress, using methods that would have been considered suspect if utilized by public agencies. For example, the IBC organized letter writing and phone campaigns wherein "citizens" would express their opinions to congressmen.

On March 13, 1985, a staff member of the Office of Public Diplomacy sent a memorandum to White House director of communications Pat Buchanan to describe the "White 'Propaganda' Operation" being organized by IBC. He gave five examples of the campaign. One included an op-ed editorial in the *Wall Street Journal,* written by a history professor who had received funds and assistance provided by "our staff." Two other op-ed pieces appearing in the *New York Times* and *Washington Post* were written entirely by the Office of Public Diplomacy, though they were signed by *contra* leaders. All this was done despite the fact that the 1985 Appropriations Act specifically prohibited using public funds "for publicity or propaganda purposes not authorized by Congress."[52]

While Congress and the media focused the public's attention on the question of whether or not Reagan knew about the diversion of profits from the sale of arms to Iran to the *contras,* the larger issue was the existence of a permanent "secret government" that ran not only the *contra* war but a variety of other covert actions. Many of these actions were actually carried out by secret organizations and networks that supplied their own funding to supplement what they received from the CIA through drug trafficking and arms merchandising.[53] When Congress outlawed military aid to the *contras,* this network went into action to save the *contras.* It was a largely private network that operated in coordination with, but not under the control of, American intelligence agencies.

In the face of an increasingly complex, well-coordinated, and insulated national security apparatus, the information available for public debate about foreign affairs becomes subject to an overwhelming degree of manipulation. Decisions are carried out in secret and the volume of state secrets has mushroomed with every presidential administration. After decisions are made behind closed doors, strategies are devised about how to manipulate mass opinion in favor of decisions or actions already undertaken. Domestic electoral decisions do not lead to governmental policies. Instead, public opinion campaigns are orchestrated to build support for decisions already reached.

Notes

1. Employment data taken from Francis A. Beer, *Peace Against War* (San Francisco: W. H. Freeman, 1981), p. 199; Center for Defense Information, "Militarism in America," *The Defense Monitor* 15, no. 3 (1986): 4.

2. See Shoup, "Shaping the Postwar World: The Council of [sic] Foreign Relations and the United States War Aims During World War II," *The Insurgent Sociologist* 5, no. 3 (Spring 1975): 9-52; Shoup and William Minter, *Imperial Brain Trust: The Council on Foreign Relations and United States Foreign Policy* (New York: Monthly Review Press, 1977).

3. Shoup, Ibid., pp. 18-20.

4. Shoup, Ibid., p. 34.

5. Kennan, "Review of Current Trends, U.S. Foreign Policy," report by the Policy Planning Staff, U.S. State Department, PPS/23, in *Papers Relating to the Foreign Policy of the United States,* vol. 1, 1948, p. 524.

6. A. J. Bacevich, *The Pentomic Era: The U.S. Army Between Korea and Vietnam* (Washington, D.C.: National Defense University, 1986), pp. 151-153.

7. Ibid.

8. Patrick L. Vawter, *Industrial Mobilization: The Relevant History* (Washington, D.C.: National Defense University, 1983), pp. 9-10.

9. Charles Beard, *President Roosevelt and the Coming of the War, 1941: A Study in Appearances and Realities* (New Haven: Yale University, 1948).

10. See Stephen Ambrose, *Rise to Globalism: American Foreign Policy Since 1938,* 4th ed. (New York: Penguin Books, 1985), pp. 1-115.

11. Ibid. and Walter LaFeber, *America, Russia, and the Cold War, 1945–1984*, 5th ed. (New York: Alfred Knopf, 1985).

12. See Carl J. Friedrich and Zbigniew K. Brzezinski, *Totalitarian Dictatorship and Democracy* (Cambridge, Mass.: Harvard University, 1956).

13. Quoted in *In These Times*, December 17-23, 1986, p. 4.

14. Cited in "Militarism in America," *The Defense Monitor* 15, no. 3 (Washington, D.C.: Center for Defense Information, 1986), p. 3.

15. Quotations found in A. J. Bacevich, *The Pentomic Era*, pp. 12-38.

16. This account of the Gaither Report and its consequences relies on John C. Donovan, *The Cold Warriors, A Policy-Making Elite* (Lexington, Mass.: D.C. Heath, 1974), pp. 130-149.

17. "Militarism in America," p. 3.

18. Ruth Leger Sivard, *World Military and Social Expenditures, 1985* (Washington, D.C.: World Priorities Press, 1985), p. 17.

19. "Soviet Military Power: Questions and Answers," *The Defense Monitor* 9, no. 1 (Center for Defense Information), 1986 spending.

20. Sivard, *World Military and Social Expenditures*, p. 23.

21. "Militarism in America," p. 3.

22. Ibid. Number of retired officers in industries calculated from data in Francis A. Beer, *Peace Against War* (San Francisco: W. H. Freeman, 1981), pp. 206-209.

23. Bennett Harrison and Barry Bluestone, *The Great U-Turn: Corporate Restructuring and the Polarizing of America* (New York: Basic Books, 1988), p. 148.

24. "Militarism in America," p. 3.

25. Will Reissner, "How the NLF Won," *Intercontinental Press*, April 29, 1985, p. 253.

26. Sivard, *World Military and Social Expenditures*, p. 11.

27. James K. Oliver and James A. Nathan, "The American Environment for Security Planning," in *Planning U.S. Security*, ed. Philip S. Kronenberg (Washington, D.C.: National Defense University, 1981), p. 37.

28. Polls cited in John E. Reilly, *American Opinion and U.S. Foreign Policy 1983* (Chicago: Council on Foreign Relations, 1983), p. 31, and in Alvin Richman, "Public Attitudes on Military Power, 1981," *Public Opinion* 4 (December-January 1982), pp. 44-46.

29. Barbara Trent, Gary Meyer, and David Kaper, producers, *Coverup*, a film (Empowerment Project, Santa Monica, California, 1988).

30. Sam C. Sarkesian, "Low-Intensity Conflict: Concepts, Principles and Policy Guidelines," in *Low Intensity Conflict and Modern Technology*, ed. Lt. Col. David A. Dean (Washington, D.C.: National Defense University, 1986).

31. See Jonathan Marshall, Peter Dale Scott, and Jane Hunter, *The Iran-Contra Connection* (Boston: South End Press, 1987). The idea of a "secret government" has been popularized by the Washington-based religious center for public interest law, the Christic Institute. See also "Coverup; Beyond the Iran-Contra Affair," a film produced by Barbara Trend, Gary Meyer and David Kasper (Santa Monica, CA: The Empowerment Project, 1988). On Congress' failure to exercise oversight, see Jane Hunter, "Overseeing the Overseers," *NACLA Report on the Americas* 22 (September-October 1988): 22-27.

32. Frank Greve, Steve Stachlow, and Tim Golden, "U.S. Official Guided Secret American Flights to Contras, Crew Says," *St. Louis Post Dispatch*, January 18, 1987, p. 1. Frank Greve and Mark Fazlollah, "White House Linked to Combat Squads," *St. Louis Post Dispatch*, July 26, 1987, pp. 1, 8, taken from the Knight Ridder news wire. The Knight Ridder news service provided a number of revealing investigative reports, but few reports appeared in mainstream papers like the *New York Times* and *Washington Post*. On overall buildup of Special Operations

Forces, see "America's Secret Soldiers: The Buildup of U.S. Special Operations Forces," *Defense Monitor,* 14, no. 2 (1985).

33. See Friends Committee on National Legislation, "Terrorism—Bringing the War Home," *Washington Newsletter* (American Friends Service Committee, May 1986).

34. *Critique: Review of the Department of State's Country Reports on Human Rights Practices for 1985* (New York: The Watch Committees, 1986).

35. Neil C. Livingstone, "Fighting Terrorism and 'Dirty Little Wars,'" in *Defense Planning for the 1990s,* ed. A. Buckingham, Jr. (Washington, D.C., National Defense University, 1984).

36. Vernon Walters, "The Uses of Political and Propaganda Covert Action in the 1980's," in *Intelligence Requirements for the 1980's,* ed. Roy Goodson (Washington, D.C.: National Strategy Information Center, 1981).

37. Robert Kupperman Associates, "Low Intensity Conflict," study prepared for U.S. Army Training and Doctrine Command (1983), p. 39, cited in Sara Miles, "The Real War: Low Intensity Conflict in Central America," *NACLA Report,* 20 (April-May 1986), pp. 17-48.

38. See Jeff Blyskal and Marie Blyskal, *PR, How the Public Relations Industry Writes the News* (New York: William Morrow, 1985), pp. 9-32.

39. Tom Barry and Deb Preusch, *The Central America Fact Book* (New York: Grove Press, 1986), pp. 74-75.

40. "A New Team of Stage Managers Maximizes Reagan's Star Quality," *National Journal,* January 18, 1986, pp. 162-163.

41. Richard A. Gabriel, "Modernism vs. Pre-Modernism: The Need to Rethink the Basis of Military Organizational Forms," in *Military Ethics and Professionalism,* ed. James Brown and Michael J. Collins (Washington, D.C.: National Defense University, 1981).

42. Cincinnatus (pseudonym for a U.S. military officer), *Self-Destruction: The Disintegration and Decay of the United States Army During the Vietnam Era* (New York: W. W. Norton, 1981), pp. 67-98. David E. Engdahl, "Foundations for Military Intervention in the United States," in *Military Intervention in Democratic Societies,* ed. Peter J. Rowe and Christopher J. Whelan (London: Croom Helm, 1985), pp. 1-50.

43. Gabriel, "Modernism vs. Pre-Modernism," p. 43.

44. See Richard Halloran, "High School Graduates Revive Volunteer Force," *New York Times* (October 11, 1987), p. 42. Figures on 1986 recruitment are from "Military Manpower Strength Assessment" (Washington, D.C.: Department of Defense, 1986). See also, "Militarism in America," pp. 5-6.

45. "Military Manpower Strength Assessment," passim.

46. "Militarism in America," pp. 5-6.

47. "Military Manpower Strength Assessment," passim.

48. Quoted in "Militarism in America," p. 5.

49. See "North Worked on Martial Law Plan," *St. Louis Post Dispatch,* July 5, 1987, p. 1, another Knight Ridder story. Greve and Fazlollah, "White House Linked to Combat Squads," pp. 1, 8.

50. "North Worked on Martial Law Plan," ibid.

51. Peter Kornbluh, "The Contra Lobby," *The Village Voice* (October 1987). Also see Theodore Draper, "An Autopsy," *The New York Review of Books* XXXIV/20 (December 17, 1987), pp. 68-69.

52. Ibid.

53. Barbara Trent, Gary Meyer, and David Kaper, producers, *Coverup* (Empowerment Project, Santa Monica, California, 1988).

Chapter 11

Exporting the Facade*

A Mirror

As Noam Chomsky has pointed out, the policies of an imperial power toward the nations within its sphere of influence reveal the character of its own politics and culture:

> We naturally look to the Central America-Caribbean region...if we want to learn something about ourselves, just as we look to Eastern Europe or the "internal empire" if [we] want to learn about the Soviet Union.[1]

In the Caribbean and in Central and South America, the United States has acted as an imperial power for more than a century, and during that time U.S. political and business elites have exerted a guiding influence in the establishment of political systems. The portrait that comes into focus through the lens of empire reveals that the elites who manage U.S. foreign policy have no attachment to democracy *except as a device to legitimate* their political and economic domination. For this purpose the symbols of democracy are useful indeed, and this explains why elections in the nations south of the U.S. border have been sponsored by the United States both as instruments for managing client states and as a means to influence American public opinion. Such elections are carefully staged media events designed to "demonstrate" the worthiness of U.S.-supported regimes.[2]

The overriding concern of U.S. elites has been the construction and maintenance of a system of governments that will protect inequality and class privilege at least as effectively as in the United States. When President Reagan said in 1982, "What I want to see above all else is that this country remains a country where someone can always get rich and stay rich—that's the thing we have that must be preserved,"[3] he was expressing in unusually candid terms a sacred tenant of America's political tradition. The nations within the orbit of the empire have been subjected to devastating doses of violence coordinated by U.S. corporations and government officials when they have failed to demonstrate allegiance to the same principle.

---

* Coauthored with Lynne Silverman.

The Guiding Motives

In the late nineteenth century, rapid industrialization motivated America's capitalists to seek new markets for their products and to search for a continuing supply of raw materials for use in their factories. During the period of aggressive overseas expansion that began in 1898, the United States annexed Puerto Rico, Guam, and the Philippines; made Cuba a U.S. protectorate in 1903; established control over the Panama Canal in 1904; and launched a series of occupations of Cuba, Haiti, the Dominican Republic, Honduras, and Nicaragua. On the eve of the Spanish-American War of 1898, Senator Albert Bevridge presciently predicted aggressive expansion and intervention abroad:

> [American factories] are making more than the American people can use...fate has written our policy...the trade of the world must and can be ours....We will cover the ocean with our merchant marine. We will build a navy to the measure of our greatness. Great colonies, governing themselves, flying our flag, and trading with us, will grow about our ports of trade. Our institutions will follow....And American law, American order, American civilization and the American flag will plant themselves on shores hitherto bloody and benighted by those agents of God henceforth made beautiful and bright.[4]

The United States emerged from the Spanish-American War with the status of an imperial power capable of securing the political and economic domination of Latin America. A doctrine to justify an imperialist policy soon followed. In 1905, President Roosevelt added the Roosevelt Corollary to the Monroe Doctrine, asserting the moral right of the United States, as a superior civilization, to act as "policeman" in the hemisphere. He stated: "All that this country desires is that other republics on this continent shall be happy and prosperous; and they cannot be happy and prosperous unless they maintain order within their boundaries and behave with a just regard for their obligations toward outsiders."[5] The "outsider" that Roosevelt had in mind was, of course, the United States.

In the years between 1900 and 1930, government and big business cooperated closely in the twenty-eight military interventions (almost one per year, on average) that accompanied the North American expansion throughout the Caribbean Basin.[6] During this era of "Gunboat and Dollar" diplomacy, the economic penetration of Latin America mushroomed, from $21 million in investment in 1897, to $93 million by 1914,[7] to $206 million by 1929.[8] The bulk of direct investment went into mining and banana and sugar plantations in Costa Rica, Guatemala, Honduras, Cuba, the Dominican Republic, and Nicaragua. While the Guggenheim family bought up copper and silver mines in Mexico and South America, the Boston-based United Fruit Company acquired huge tracts of land and, "like a veritable octopus spreading its tentacles over the whole of the region,"[9] created a network of railroads and port facilities for the shipment of fruit across Central America. U.S. bankers supplied the capital to build an infrastructure suitable to the needs of business, such as roads, electric plants, and communications systems. The U.S. government repeatedly rushed in the military to prevent revolutions that seemed to threaten corporate power. In

1935, Major General Smedley D. Butler reminisced about his career in the Marine Corps during this period. He spoke of the intimate relationship between military intervention and corporate investment:

> I spent 33 years and 4 months in active service as a member of our country's most agile military force—the Marine Corps....I spent most of my time being a high-muscle man for Big Business, for Wall Street and for the bankers. In short, I was a racketeer for capitalism...

> Thus I helped make Mexico...safe for American oil interests in 1914. I helped make Haiti and Cuba a decent place for the National City Bank boys to collect revenues in....I helped purify Nicaragua for the International banking house of Brown Brothers in 1909–12. I brought light to the Dominican Republic for American sugar interests in 1916. I helped make Honduras "right" for American fruit companies in 1903.[10]

By the early 1930s, most government leaders had learned to avoid frank assessments of U.S. policies such as Butler's. Rising dissent against U.S. foreign policy forced a shift in rhetoric; an enemy had to be found to justify intervention. The idea that Soviet bolshevism was threatening the region "with the help of the Mexican labor movement"[11] was put forward in 1938 when President Lázaro Cardenas of Mexico nationalized foreign oil companies in response to their refusal to pay workers the amount mandated by the Mexican Supreme Court. Anticommunism provided the new justification for U.S. involvement in Latin American affairs. Now it was the "global responsibility" of the United States to oppose "communist" or "Marxist" movements that "threatened" the hemisphere. The spectre of communism, in tandem with the idea that U.S. interventions were motivated by a selfless desire to spread democracy and freedom, became the newly revised justifications for U.S. intervention in Latin America.

New Styles of Intervention

As the rhetoric used to justify American domination over Latin America shifted from the building of empire to the Red Menace, the style of intervention changed accordingly. Frequent invasions and prolonged military occupations gave way to efforts to install governments that would act as surrogates protecting U.S. economic and political interests. From one country to another, these governments acted in remarkably consistent ways: They freely used terror and repression against their own citizens.

In the Dominican Republic, the dictator Rafael Trujillo provided a model for the sort of government favored by U.S. elites. Trujillo had risen through the ranks of Dominican society and military during the U.S. Marine occupation of 1912 to 1924. Described by U.S. military officers as "one of the best in service," he was promoted to the rank of general and put in charge of the country's police force, which became the National Army in 1927. By 1930, having eliminated all of his rivals by means of bullets or exile, Trujillo became president through an election in which he was the only remaining candidate. Until 1962, Trujillo controlled Dominican society through his military, which he "welded into a machine of terror which he refined over the years":[12]

> Thousands of his political enemies, automatically called "Communists," died in secret police dungeons, many of them after suffering hideous tortures perpetrated with electrical devices, nail extractors, decapitation collars, and leather-thonged whips. Young ladies who spurned his advances were found dead in "accidents." Even those who fled abroad lived in constant dread of kidnapping and death at the hands of Trujillo agents who, after performing their murderous tasks were themselves marked for extinction. In 1937 he supervised the massacre of from 15,000 to 35,000 Haitian squatters in two days.[13]

Using such means he was able to provide the Aluminum Corporation of America (ALCOA) and United Fruit, among other American corporations, the stable environment and docile work force they desired. Government and business leaders in the United States hailed Trujillo as the "man responsible for the great work of Dominican progress, the man who brought trade between the Republic and the other American nations to a peak."[14] American public relations firms worked diligently for Trujillo, placing full-page newspaper advertisements designed to sell the dictator to the American public as "their friend and best ally in the fight against communism."[15]

With a combination of direct and tacit approval from the United States, similar dictators proliferated throughout Latin America: Jorge Ubico in Guatemala, Tiburcio Carias Andino in Honduras, Maximiliano Hernández in El Salvador, and Anastasio Somoza García in Nicaragua. Loyal only to the United States and supported by a small privileged elite within their own countries, the dictators became firmly entrenched by sharing with the multinational corporations the benefits of maintaining a receptive environment for U.S. investment. Washington supplied arms and financed and trained military officers and police forces in counterinsurgency strategies and methods of torture to be used against civilian populations. In most cases, the United States built modern military and police organizations from the ground up because in most Latin American countries they were badly organized and armed, and thus not sufficiently adept at maintaining oligarchic control.

Post-War Capital Penetration

Citizens of the United States are bombarded with an official government propaganda that promotes the notion that America is the leader of a free world dedicated to spreading democracy, protecting freedom where it exists, and advancing freedom where it is denied. Hand in hand with this rhetoric is a language of capitalism that extols the value of free trade and free enterprise as the only means of bringing economic well-being to the people living in the world's underdeveloped countries. Guided by such an ideology, investments abroad have served as a vital source of capital accumulation for U.S. corporations. These investments have returned huge profits, with a consistently higher return for dollars committed than investments made domestically. This unusually high rate of return has been ensured by a history of military intervention to protect the property and autonomy of U.S. investors and corporations, and by policies that have always placed "good business climate" above all other goals.

Beginning in the late 1940s, a new wave of investment washed over Latin America. Investment in banking, manufacturing, tourism, and service industries added to the already well-established markets in agriculture (mostly bananas and sugar), mining, and lumber, thus expanding the total volume of direct corporate investment in Latin America from $3 billion in 1946 to $8 billion by 1961.[16] The formation of the Central American Common Market (CACM) in 1961 spurred yet another frenzy of multinational investment. The United Nations Economic Commission originally conceived the idea of the CACM as a way to promote development throughout Central America. Formulated to benefit the less developed economies of Honduras, Nicaragua, and Costa Rica, the CACM established a gradual process to eliminate trade barriers between these countries, thus expanding the markets for their local goods to the whole of Central America.

The notion of a planned market system linking these countries was abhorrent to U.S. elites, because it might compete with or even sometimes exclude U.S. trade and investment. By offering a $100 million grant to establish the CACM, the United States replaced the United Nations as the sponsor and ignored its mechanisms for regional planning.[17] The remodeled CACM and the Agency for International Development (AID) provided the technical and financial assistance to multinational corporations to speed the flow of U.S. capital into Central America. Although the large U.S. corporations of Castle and Cooke, R. J. Reynolds, Gulf+Western, United Brands, and Hershey continued in agricultural production, most companies diversified their holdings into other areas such as food processing plants, plastic plants, cement plants, breweries, gambling casinos, and tourist hotels. Banks and financial institutions such as Citicorp, Bankamerica, and Chase Manhattan sprinkled branches through the region to make both private and public loans. By 1981, finance-related investment amounted to about 40 percent of all U.S. direct investment.[18]

The rapid expansion of the fast food industry in the United States during the 1960s and 1970s opened a huge market for cheap Central American beef. Investments in livestock mushroomed when the Latin American Agribusiness Development Corporation—which included as members Goodyear Tire and Rubber Company, Borden Inc., Caterpillar Tractor Company, and Chase Manhattan Overseas Banking Corporation, among others—poured $75 million into livestock investment and deforestation in Guatemala, Costa Rica, Honduras, and Nicaragua.[19] Seventy-five million dollars in loans from the World Bank, AID, and the Inter-American Development Bank underwrote beef production projects in Costa Rica alone. Beef exports from Central America increased from 13.7 thousand tons in 1960 to over 114 thousand tons in 1970. At the same time, beef consumption fell by 41 percent in Costa Rica, by 38 percent in El Salvador, and by 13 percent in Guatemala and Nicaragua, because the cattle being raised were reserved for export. A study published in 1981 concluded that one-third of the forest land in Costa Rica and 250 square miles of forest land each year in Nicaragua (until the Sandinistas took power in 1979) had been converted to pasture for cattle grazing for markets controlled by multinational corporations.[20]

By the late 1980s, investment in Latin America accounted for 80 percent of all U.S. direct investment in Third World countries, with $5.3 billion of it in Central America.[21] In the Caribbean Basin, where Rockefeller family corporations dominate investment in resorts, oil, and banking, $16.9 billion was invested in banking and finance. Sixty-seven of the top 100 U.S. corporations and one-third of the top 500 corporations did business in Central America, and over 500 firms provided services needed by Central American businesses.[22]

The U.S. Development Model

Between 1950 and 1965, corporations invested $3.8 billion in Latin America and earned $11.3 billion in profits. This compares to a $8.1 billion investment in Europe that returned $5.5 billion in profits during the same period.[23] The Department of Treasury has estimated that two dollars is returned to the United States for every one dollar that the United States puts into the World Bank.[24] Ronald Reagan's 1981 Caribbean Basin Initiative made the business climate even better by eliminating tariff barriers, allowing U.S. manufacturers to treat the area as an extension of the American economic system while still paying Central American workers one-eighth of the average wage rates paid in the United States for the same work.

Numerous studies show that capital investment in Third World countries has led to income concentration favoring a few and a deterioration in the quality of life for the vast majority of citizens. Economists Irma Adelman and Cynthia Morris report a decline in per capita personal income of up to 60 percent in Third World countries experiencing rapid economic growth as a result of outside investment. Their findings suggest "no automatic or even likely trickling down of the benefits of economic growth to the poorest segments of society."[25] A 1982 United Nations study reached the same conclusion: Although multinational corporate investment sometimes contributes to high rates of growth in "host" countries, the benefits flow "to domestic elites associated with foreign interests" and "basic needs of the population such as food, health, education, and housing" are ignored.[26]

While corporations reap huge profits from their investments in the Caribbean and Latin America, the social and economic well-being of the masses can best be described as desperate. The annual income of 90 percent of Haitians is less than $120, and the poorest 20 percent of the people in El Salvador earn $46 annually.[27] Malnutrition, which affects over half the Central American population, causes mental retardation in 80 percent of children born in rural Honduras.[28] Dysentery, tuberculosis, and parasites thrive in the crowded conditions of slums and squatter settlements of Latin American cities.

Throughout Latin America, growth has occurred but development has not. For example, in Brazil, whose growth rate in the 1960s and 1970s was labeled an "economic miracle," 52 percent of the population was considered malnourished in 1970. Infant mortality grew by 45 percent between 1960 and 1973.[29] In Mexico, 1 percent of workers earn 66 percent of the nation's total income; the majority of workers are unable to earn enough to meet their most basic needs. In the 1980s, declining per capita income has contributed to the further deterioration of an already desperate situation.[30] Two development economists have advised that the "only hope of significantly improving the income distribution in these countries lies in a transformation of the institutional setting."[31] This is precisely what U.S. foreign policy is designed to prevent.

The intimate connection between politics and the climate for U.S. corporate investment was noted in 1972 by David Rockefeller, when he observed during his Latin American tour that "often the more democratic the country, the more hostile it is to foreign investment."[32] In the same year, Frank Zingaro of Caltex called attention to the opposite side of the same coin when he noted that in the Philippines, the imposition of "Martial law has significantly improved the business climate."[33]

The important features of a "good" business climate are: a tractable, low-paid labor force; an absence of worker-controlled unions; weak or nonexistent environmental protection laws; lax health and safety regulations in the workplace; tax concessions and government subsidies for business; the use of public money to provide the infrastructure necessary for the functioning of business; and laws permitting tax-free repatriation of corporate profits back to the United States. Because political revolutions commonly arise in reaction to such a system of exploitation, the control of the political system is inseparable from a "good" business climate. One of America's largest corporations, Gulf+Western, once boasted that it was a "model for American companies in Latin America." A company spokesman told the Committee on Foreign Affairs in 1982 that "our experience has shown that free enterprise can work for the benefit of the developing world."[34] Indeed, Gulf+Western's experience was extensive and it had been able to fine-tune its model for development, especially in the Dominican Republic.

Gulf+Western came to the Dominican Republic in 1966, two years after an invasion by U.S. Marines. Aided by major tax concessions granted by President Balaguer to foreign investors, economic penetration of the country quickly followed U.S. military and political intervention. With loans from Chase Manhattan Bank, Gulf +Western gained a foothold in the island's economy with its purchase of the South Puerto Rico Sugar Company. By 1976, its investment had grown to $300 million in sugar, meat, citrus, tourism, and tobacco. Other transnational corporations also operated in the Dominican Republic, but Gulf+Western dominated the economy as the country's largest landowner, employer, and exporter. Because the yearly revenues of Gulf+Western were greater than the Dominican Republic's Gross National Product, it could accurately be called "a state within a state."[35]

Immediately on entering the country, Gulf+Western broke the sugarcane workers' union, Sindicato Unido. Denouncing the union as communist controlled, the corporation fired the entire union leadership, annulled its contracts, and sent in police to occupy the plant while the American Institute for Free Labor Development (an agency financed in part by the CIA) formed a new union that obtained immediate acceptance from the Dominican president. The possibility of free unions on Gulf's sugar plantations disappeared (along with dozens of labor leaders), with the result that of the country's 20,000 cane cutters, only one out of ten is Dominican. Most of the cane workers are Haitian immigrants paid $1.50 to $3.00 a day to do what Dominicans call "slave work."[36]

Gulf+Western set up the first of the industrial free zones that thrive in the Dominican Republic. Often called "runaway shops" (because businesses relocate there from U.S. communities) or "export platforms," such zones offer a low-wage labor force, government subsidies, and freedom from taxes and environmental regulations. Unions are not permitted in these zones, and thus in the mid-1980s 22,000 workers earned an average of 65 cents per hour working in factories surrounded by barbed wire and security guards. Dominican Law 299 grants corporations a 100 percent exemption from Dominican taxes and also provides them a 70 percent government subsidy of plant construction costs to set up business in the zones.[37] Bestform, Esmark, Milton Bradley, Ideal Toys, Fisher Price, and North American Phillips are among the U.S. corporations that take advantage of the free zones to assemble and manufacture their products for export back to the United States.

Because investment benefits a tiny upper class in the Dominican Republic, the living conditions of Dominicans are grim. In 1985, 90 percent of Dominicans suffered from malnutrition and 20 percent lived in "absolute poverty." Illiteracy stood at 54 percent, with 1 million school-age children not attending school. The Dominican Bishops' Conference issued a report stating that 63 percent of Dominicans received an income of less than $58 a month and that within the country 400,000 Haitians worked under a system of "virtual slavery."[38]

Advertisements in U.S. newspapers have long extolled the benefits of investing in a beautiful Caribbean Basin atmosphere free of any government regulation. A nineteen-page supplement designed to lure investors to the Dominican Republic appeared in the *New York Times* on January 28, 1973. A photograph showed President Joaquin Balaguer and Teobaldo Rosell, General Director of Gulf+Western, locked in an embrace above the caption "cooperation between government and industry."[39] The supplement promoted the La Roomona Free Zone as a haven for investors. Tax breaks were featured under a headline that read, "Tourist Law Offers Incentives":

> Foreigners enjoy the full protection of the law (and indeed the Dominican Republic has never in all its history confiscated any foreign owned property). The law extends even to apartments, hotels, condominiums, discotheques.... Benefits include 100 percent freedom from income taxes for 10 years with provisions for a possible additional five years...exemptions on construction formation of the corporation, licenses, municipal taxes, tariff duties, and import duties on equipment, furnishings and anything else necessary for the creation of business...even duty-free liquor—an unusual measure.[40]

Another headline urged, "Industrialists Dream of Chances Like These":

> ...both government and labor organizations traditionally combine to cooperate with capital in attracting and keeping industry profitable....The federal minimum in most categories of skilled and semi-skilled labor is 25 cents per hour.[41]

With the help of repressive governments, corporations in countries within the orbit of the Monroe Doctrine operate using the Gulf+Western model (though Gulf

+Western sold its Dominican holdings in 1984, when sugar prices fell). In El Salvador, women at the Maidenform assembly plant earn $4 a day stitching bra cups to straps. Bras are among El Salvador's ten leading nonagricultural exports to the United States.[42] In Haiti, with its "tradition of respect for private property and foreign ownership," women working for Rawlings Sporting Goods for $2.70 a day sew all of the baseballs used by the two major leagues in the United States. With over $60 million in annual sales from Haiti, Rawlings is the third largest corporation operating in that country.[43]

When Democracy Is Unacceptable

Democratically elected governments founded on principles of social justice, land reform, and national independence have sometimes emerged in the countries encompassed by the Monroe Doctrine. When that has happened, the U.S. elites have consistently decided that democracy is inimical to their own interests. The Dominican Republic, Guatemala, and Chile provide three examples of how U.S. elites regard popular democracy.

In 1962, with 59 percent of the popular vote, Juan Bosch won the Dominican Republic's first free election ever held. Only seven months later, he was overthrown by military officers and forced into exile. In 1965, however, with support from the poor, the urban working classes, and the professional middle classes, Bosch was again elected, and he announced plans to restore the 1963 constitution. The United States intervened by sending 23,000 Marines to topple his government. An estimated 2,500 civilians were killed in the weeks following the invasion.[44] The Marines remained in the Dominican Republic through June 1, 1966, "pacifying" the population while the U.S. government organized elections to legitimate a government that would meet with its approval.

President Lyndon Johnson initially justified the invasion to the American public as a rescue operation. Unless the United States intervened, he claimed, "American blood will run in the streets."[45] Other justifications soon crept into the president's speeches. On April 30, 1965, he stated that the invasion was undertaken "to preserve law and order."[46] By May 1, he was explaining, "Our goal in the Dominican Republic...is that the people of that country must be permitted freely to choose the path of political democracy, social justice, and economic progress."[47] On the following day, he argued, "Communist leaders, many of them trained in Cuba, seeing a chance to increase disorder, to gain a foothold, joined the revolution. They took increasing control. And what began as a popular democratic revolution...very shortly moved and was taken over and really seized and placed into the hands of Communist conspirators."[48]

From the day he was elected, U.S. foreign policy elites regarded Bosch as anathema. Like other parties on the democratic left struggling to exist in Latin America, Bosch's Dominican Revolutionary Party sought to gain both economic and political independence from the United States. Bosch was opposed by the estimated 7 percent of the population that made up the privileged classes of Dominican society.

His support came mainly from the 93 percent of Dominicans who, collectively, were 70 percent illiterate and 30 percent unemployed, and who received an average annual income of less than $150.[49] Bosch promised at his 1962 inauguration: "We are changing our image—the moral, political and economic image of the country....We are changing it into a revolutionary democracy."[50]

Though the seven months of his presidency was too brief to realize extensive social reforms, Bosch made significant moves toward establishing economic independence from the United States and restructuring Dominican society. Although he did not nationalize corporate holdings, Bosch placed some restrictions on property owned by foreigners, forced foreign investors to share profits with local firms and workers, and imposed a tax on sugar profits. To break the stranglehold that the United States had imposed on the Dominican economy, Bosch traveled to Europe to secure a $150 million loan from a bank in Zurich. Under the land reform program guaranteed by the 1963 constitution, 1,400 families were given state-owned lands. Schools were established to educate the peasants in the organization and management of farm cooperatives. To finance his social reforms, Bosch cut the salaries of the military and the bureaucracy in half, including his own, which he reduced from $2,400 a month to $1,500 a month.

With the reestablishment of a right-wing military government after the 1965 coups, foreign investment, which had slowed to a trickle, once again flowed. During the military junta's first few months, $175 million in new foreign investment flooded in, two contracts for U.S. oil refineries were signed, six private U.S. banks made loans totaling $30 million, and the World Bank granted a $1.7 million loan for a hydroelectric study.[51]

Joaquin Balaguer was elected president in U.S.-sponsored elections held in 1966. From the moment President Johnson reacted to the CIA's recommendation that Balaguer be elected president by urging, "Get this guy in office down there!" the outcome of the Dominican election was assured.[52] It is hardly surprising that the U.S.-backed candidate won in a country occupied by U.S. troops, where an estimated 300 members of the opposition party were assassinated during the election campaign.[53] While the U.S. media applauded the triumph of Dominican democracy, a fresh reign of terror was unleashed on the Dominican people. With financial backing from the United States, death squads targeted political dissidents for torture and murder. By 1971, over 1,000 people had been killed.[54]

All Latin American governments face the reality that the U.S. government stands ready to unleash a reign of terror if governments are installed that seek independence from international corporations and U.S. imperial ambitions. This lesson was brought home to Guatemala in unmistakable terms in 1954, and to Chile in 1973.

In 1951, Jácobo Arbenz Guzman became president of Guatemala through free elections. Arbenz desired to implement reforms that would ameliorate desperate social conditions in his country. Following United Nations recommendations, he expropriated lands that were held by the United Fruit Company, offering to pay what United Fruit had claimed the lands were worth when it filed its taxes. Though Arbenz sought to enact reforms within a capitalist framework, he aimed to break the economic domination that the United States had asserted over his country since the early twentieth century.

U.S. foreign policy elites went into a frenzy, labeling Guatemala as a "beach-head of international communism," "a threat to the oil wells of Texas," and a "danger to the Panama Canal."[55] In 1954, the Arbenz government was overthrown by a mercenary army trained by the CIA on a United Fruit plantation in Honduras. U.S. pilots bombed Guatemala City as the mercenaries quickly seized power. A new president chosen by U.S. foreign policy personnel was flown to Guatemala in an embassy plane. He became the first of a line of dictators that crushed Guatemalan resistance to U.S. domination. Between 1954 and 1982, 90,000 persons were killed in Guatemala.[56]

As part of the platform that he was elected on in 1971, Salvador Allende Gossens nationalized Chile's major industries in an attempt to use the nation's resources for internal development. Allende's program worked—unemployment dropped and salaries rose for the masses.[57] For U.S. corporations, that was unacceptable. In October of 1971, executives of ITT, Anaconda, Ford, and other U.S. corporations were personally assured by Secretary of State William Rogers that "the Nixon Administration is a business administration. Its mission is to protect business."[58] A three-pronged strategy was developed to destabilize the Allende government, which involved strangling the Chilean economy by eliminating loans and trade agreements, strengthening the Chilean military, and exacerbating social tensions by means of CIA covert activities. In 1973, Allende was killed in a coup d'etat coordinated by U.S. military and CIA personnel. In the year following the coup, more than 30,000 people were assassinated by Chile's government. This heavy dose of terrorism was an omen of things to come. For more than sixteen years, Chile was ruled by one of Latin America's most repressive military regimes, presided over by General Augusto Pinochet. He finally was replaced by a civilian president in an election held on December 14, 1989, though Chile's constitution continues to guarantee the independence of the armed forces from civilian rule. Before relinquishing the presidency, Pinochet indicated that any attempt to investigate the years of human rights violations would trigger a military coup.

Models of Democracy: A Tale of Two Nations

In September 1973, former Representative and later New York City Mayor Edward Koch expressed concern that the Chilean coup might convince the American public that elites were interested in democracy only as a facade:

> If democracy is perceived as a mere facade to protect the power and privileges of the oligarches, to be swept away when the results do not please the elite, then the only other response that can be taken by people who seek social justice is violent revolution....It would be the greatest tragedy of the coup if its final legacy was that democracy itself was to be characterized as a fraud.[59]

Motivated by a similar concern, foreign policy elites go to great lengths to try to demonstrate their sincere support for democracy. Thus, U.S. opposition to mass-based democratic governments is one side of a coin. On the other side, the United States sponsors elections regularly in contexts where electoral participation can have nothing but symbolic meaning. The election in the Dominican Republic in 1966 constituted the first of a series of elections that Edward Herman and Frank Brodhead have described as "staged" by the United States. The staged election has become an international media event complete with international observers and journalists. It serves the purpose of pacifying a restive home population, reassuring it that ongoing interventionary processes are legitimate and appreciated by their foreign objects.[60]

The Reagan administration described Nicaragua's election held in 1984 as a phony, "Soviet-style" exercise, and it went to considerable lengths to try to sabotage it. Meanwhile it praised El Salvador's U.S.-sponsored elections held in March 1982. The way that the United States responded to these two elections should give pause to anyone who thinks that U.S. elites are dedicated to democracy except as a symbolic device to protect elite interests.[61]

As early as the 1850s, Nicaragua was regarded as a strategically important route for moving goods between the Caribbean and Pacific, and in the pre–Panama Canal days it was considered a potential site for a canal to connect the two oceans. Accordingly, U.S. military forces intervened in Nicaragua in 1850, 1854, and 1857. Through the remainder of the century, competition with Europeans and with nationalistic Central Americans involved the United States in several more efforts alternately to overthrow or prop up Nicaraguan governments. When a pro-American regime was threatened by a peasant revolt in 1912, the U.S. Marines invaded and occupied the country. They left briefly in 1925, but returned again in 1927 to try to suppress a revolt led by Augusto Cesar Sandino, a nationalist who rallied thousands of poor peasants to his cause. In 1927, Undersecretary of State Robert Olds explained that his country was intervening because any kind of independence from the United States established an unacceptable precedent:

> Until now Central America has always understood that governments which we recognize and support stay in power, while those which we do not recognize and support fall. Nicaragua has become a test case. It is difficult to see how we can afford to be defeated.[62]

To prevent Sandino from triumphing, the Marines occupied Nicaragua until 1933. They left after they had trained and equipped a Nicaraguan army, the National Guard, to take their place. In 1934, supporters of the U.S.-chosen commander of the Guard, Anastasio Somoza, assassinated Sandino while he was in Managua at Somoza's invitation to negotiate a truce. Somoza then consolidated his power.

Somoza established a family dictatorship through control of the Guard and he amassed a tremendous fortune as well as a reputation for exceptional greed and violence. For forty-five years the Somoza family received political and military support from the United States. In 1961, a small group of students founded a movement, the Sandinista Front for National Liberation, to renew Sandino's fight against U.S. domination. The Front grew in strength as women, workers, peasants, students, middle-class professionals, and thousands of others joined mass organizations in support of its struggle. By 1979, it had become a disciplined army. In the final year of the rebellion the Somoza dictatorship lost much of the support of the Nicaraguan business community and middle classes, which had come to resent its extreme corruption and brutality. The murder of ABC news producer Bill Stewart in 1979 by the Guard, shown on television across the United States, precluded any effective public relations job to prop up public support for Somoza. On July 19, 1979, the Sandinistas entered Managua after a war that had cost more than 50,000 Nicaraguans their lives.

The Reagan administration came to power in January 1981 committed to overthrowing the Sandinista government by sabotaging the economy, characterizing the revolution as a product of an international communist conspiracy, and training and arming a mercenary army to invade from a neighboring country. Several groups were given financial aid, but the most cooperative proved to be forces organized by former officers of Somoza's National Guard. With U.S. support, they launched an invasion from Honduras in 1981 during which they killed, tortured, and kidnapped health and literacy workers, land reform workers, religious supporters of the Sandinistas, and even landowners who had chosen to try to work with the new government.[63] By 1987, the "contras" had failed to take control of any populated area inside Nicaragua and had been condemned by independent human rights agencies. Congress offered some resistance to the policy, but consistent with the usual level of political "debate" in the United States, the Republicans and Democrats differed more about the most effective means of undermining the Sandinista government than about its character.

Even before coming to power, the Sandinistas had promised to hold free and fair elections. They were under pressure to make good on this promise by European and other Latin American countries, which conditioned support for the new government on its respect for human rights and democracy. The Sandinistas surprised everyone by scheduling elections for November 1984, two years earlier than they had originally promised. A president, vice president, and representatives to an Assembly were to be chosen, with the Assembly charged to write a new constitution and determine rules for subsequent elections. Sweden provided financial aid to help pay for the election. The United States refused any such support and instead spent money to bribe opponents of the Sandinistas to boycott the elections. Never having had a free election, the Nicaraguans sent delegations to various Western democracies to study how elections were organized. The United States refused to grant a visa to the delegation so that it could study the U.S. electoral system.

Six parties, three to their left and three to their right, put up candidates against the Sandinistas. Those on the right divided into factions over the issue of whether or not to participate at all. Though the right-wing factions never publicly proclaimed an alliance with the *contras,* they were supported financially by the United States and together put forward a viable candidate, Arturo Cruz, to represent their position. They formed an opposition, the Coordinadora, which received U.S. financial support through the CIA. Although the CIA subsequently persuaded Cruz not to file as an official candidate, the Nicaraguan government nevertheless allowed him to run an informal campaign.

To assess the openness and fairness of the elections in Nicaragua, the Latin American Studies Association (LASA) in the United States sent a delegation to observe the election process.[64] The LASA team sought to investigate not only whether the procedures were fair but also whether overall conditions permitted a fairly contested election. The team randomly selected a number of complaints by opposition parties and investigated them to determine whether they were valid. In this way they were able to evaluate the claim frequently reiterated by the U.S. government that the Sandinistas had rigged the elections in advance.

The official U.S. observers sent to monitor El Salvador's U.S.-financed elections held in March 1982 were not so thorough as the LASA. As in Nicaragua, the government had promised elections and was under international pressure to make good on its word. The Salvadoran regime and the United States hoped to use elections to legitimate the government's rule at the same time that U.S. advisors trained and equipped the Salvadoran army to fight a revolutionary movement demanding land reform, freedom of speech and association, and democracy. The United States tried to dictate the outcome by financing the campaign of the largest political party, the Christian Democrats (PDC), headed by José Napoleón Duarte.

U.S. involvement in El Salvador dates back to the nineteenth century, when North American and European investors forced the Salvadoran government to allow the United States to take over its collection of customs taxes. One of the purposes was to protect Salvadoran coffee growers and U.S. corporate landowners from taxation. In 1932, peasants revolted in protest against forced labor on coffee plantations. In response, the military slaughtered more than 30,000 peasants, the vast majority lined up and executed gangland style after the revolt had already been quelled. This single massacre killed 2 percent of the nation's population, and it completely destroyed the Indian culture of the country. Though the United States did not participate, U.S. air units in nearby Nicaragua were put on alert and two destroyers and a unit of Marines were stationed off the Pacific coast. Their job was to step in if the Salvadoran military could not efficiently carry out its job.

After the Second World War, foreign investment in El Salvador's economy expanded and diversified, and as a result conditions deteriorated for rural peasants and the urban poor. Eleven percent of the rural population was landless in 1961, but this proportion shot up to 40 percent by 1975 and to 60 percent by the early 1980s. Less than 1 percent of landowners owned 78 percent of the land. One U.S. government study found in 1977 that 73 percent of El Salvador's children suffered from malnutrition. Not surprisingly, when the Sandinistas came to power in Nicaragua, where economic and social conditions were somewhat similar, the U.S. and Salvadoran elites worried that a similar revolution might succeed in El Salvador.[65] El Salvador's guerrillas, the Faribundo Martí Front for National Liberation (FMLN), attracted growing popular support. Mass organizations representing workers, peasants, and the poor in the cities and countryside were prospering.

In October 1979, young military officers led a coup against a brutal military government that had lost the support of the Carter administration. The officers were joined by political reformers from various political parties who believed that the country was facing its last chance to avoid civil war. But with the CIA's assistance, the Salvadoran oligarchy and its military allies pushed the young military reformers out and launched a campaign of assassination and terror against the civilian population. In April 1980, Archbishop Oscar Romero, an outspoken critic of oligarchy, was assassinated while leading mass in San Salvador. In response, the largest parties, unions, and mass organizations formed a political coalition named the Democratic Revolutionary Front (FDR). The Front formally allied itself with the FMLN, but it was not itself made up of guerrilla fighters. In November, the Front's seven most important leaders were surrounded by uniformed military and police at a high school in San Salvador and taken away by men in civilian dress. Their mutilated corpses were found shortly afterwards.

In December 1980, four American Catholic churchwomen who were doing work with the poor were raped and murdered by Salvadoran troops, which led the Carter administration to suspend aid temporarily. The crisis in the government led the United States to install José Napoleón Duarte as president. Duarte's Christian Democratic Party had been decimated by military terror and many of its leaders had defected to the FDR. Already, the military had prevented Duarte from assuming the presidency after winning elections in 1972, but he evidently saw the U.S. invitation to take power as a second chance.

In January 1981, the guerrillas launched a major offensive that they hoped would lead to the overthrow of the government. Despite pleas to President Carter from Archbishop Romero's successor, the Carter administration quickly restored military assistance, and since then the United States has escalated its involvement in El Salvador, which receives more U.S. aid than any other Latin American country—$1.4 million a day in 1989, about half the country's total budget.

As accounts of human rights abuses filled the front pages in U.S. papers, it became more difficult for the Reagan administration to convince Congress and the public that the Duarte government was worthy of aid. Hence the administration prevailed on the real power in El Salvador, the military, to permit elections in March 1982 for the purpose of choosing a Constituent Assembly. The Assembly would choose an interim president and establish rules for subsequent elections. Duarte called on the FMLN to lay down its arms and for FDR leaders to participate in the elections. The FMLN-FDR responded that conditions in the country did not permit free elections to take place.[66]

Two Elections

The integrity of the Sandinista-sponsored elections in 1984 and the U.S.-sponsored election in El Salvador in 1982 can be judged by reference to six "contextual" criteria: freedom of speech; access to the media; the ability of social organizations to form without intimidation; freedom for party organizations to field candidates and freely campaign; the absence or presence of state-sponsored terror; and the degree of coercion and fear imposed on the general population.[67]

Freedom of speech. The 1982 campaign in El Salvador was staged in the midst of a declared state of siege, during which constitutional guarantees were suspended. Although the state of siege was officially lifted during March, the month when the election was held, Salvadoran citizens were not informed of this fact until after the elections. According to church-sponsored human rights groups, security forces were responsible for killing about 30,000 people since the October 1979 coup and over 1,500 unarmed civilians in the three months leading up to the elections. Even if legal guarantees had been kept in place, it is unlikely that anyone would have felt safe to criticize and debate in El Salvador.[68]

In Nicaragua no general state of siege existed despite the intensity of stepped-up *contra* attacks. A limited state of emergency that circumscribed some rights had been in place but was lifted for the three-and-a-half month campaign. The Coordinadora, though connected to the *contras* and funded by the CIA, was presented with only one restriction in its latitude to criticize the government: It could not legally urge people not to register and vote. Even in this case the Sandinistas were tolerant. Thinly veiled statements by Coordinadora leaders that could easily be construed as advocating abstention were frequently published in *La Prensa,* a newspaper partially financed by the CIA. But all other criticisms were allowed, and Arturo Cruz freely entered and toured the country making speeches critical of the Sandinistas. On at least one occasion, Sandinista police and political leaders protected Cruz from angry Nicaraguans who tried to prevent him from speaking.

The delegation representing the Latin American Studies Association (LASA) was able to identify a few instances in which opposition candidates were harassed by Sandinista supporters but found no evidence that these incidents were orchestrated or condoned by Sandinista military and civilian leaders. One of the incidents amplified by U.S. media turned out to have been provoked by the Coordinadora itself, not by the government. The LASA delegation found that the electoral commission, composed of representatives from the Sandinistas and six parties that ran against them, investigated complaints seriously and even initiated investigations of its own.

Overall, the LASA delegation concluded that freedom of speech was widely exercised during the campaign:

> Even the casual observer could not fail to be impressed by the profusion of prominently displayed opposition-party billboards, posters, wall paintings, and graffiti which in some cities seemed to occupy every available square inch of space. The opposition could, and did, get its message out.[69]

In contrast, Salvadoran critics risked death-squad assassination for speaking out. Unlike Cruz, FDR leader Guillermo Ungo could not openly enter El Salvador and expect to exit alive.

Access to the media. In El Salvador the press, radio, and television, if not owned by the government, operated under strict government censorship. There were three major newspapers in El Salvador in the 1970s. One, the official paper of the Roman Catholic church, was bombed in 1977 and repeatedly shut down by the government after that. Another was closed in 1980 after its editor and two employees were kidnapped, killed, and their bodies mutilated. The third was invaded and destroyed by the army in 1981. The only independent radio station, which was run by the church, was bombed five times after the 1979 coup. At least twenty-six domestic and foreign journalists were murdered. During the campaign, a death list of thirty-five journalists was circulated by security forces, just before the murder of four Dutch journalists.[70]

There was little press censorship in Nicaragua until March 1982, when limited censorship was instituted as part of a state of emergency issued in response to *contra* attacks. Censorship was lifted in August 1984, with the exception of news about military and economic matters related to the war. The LASA delegation reported some political censorship of the main opposition newspaper, *La Prensa,* which received financial support from the CIA. Nearly all of the articles censored spread rumors, often false, about imminent food shortages, or carried information about the military. There was no censorship of Nicaragua's thirty-nine radio stations, including the several controlled by private groups and the Catholic bishops. The two television stations, both taken over by the government from Somoza interests, carried uncensored debates involving all seven parties, as did those radio stations owned by the government. All political parties were given uncensored access to 15 minutes per day of free, uninterrupted television time and 30 minutes per day of free radio time on all state-run stations.[71] Thus in contrast to El Salvador, the Nicaraguan electoral campaign was conducted in a climate of media criticism and open debate.

Organization freedom for intermediate groups. Groups and associations stand as a buffer between the individual and the state. They are especially important for poor people because they are the only means of giving a collective voice to those who lack money and social standing. In El Salvador, unionists, religious leaders, teachers, and students have been special targets of military death squads because of their organizing activities. In July 1982, the Salvadoran teachers union reported that 292 teachers had been murdered, sixteen disappeared, and fifty-two arrested. In 1980, the university was invaded and shut down by the military. Its officials, including eight deans, were later arrested. All strikes were declared illegal. By March 1982, approximately 150 union and peasant leaders and nearly 1,100 students had been murdered. No military or police official has ever been arrested or prosecuted. A delegation of U.S. labor union leaders concluded in 1983: "Union leaders and members who participate in normal trade union activities routinely risk imprisonment or murder. Peasants active in land reform are still massacred. This climate of violence against the opposition severely circumscribes the rights of thought, expression and political assembly."[72] The judiciary, which is controlled by the right wing, guarantees that these crimes go unpunished.

The same labor union delegation investigated political conditions in Nicaragua. Although concerned about limitations on the right to strike, the delegation concluded that

> although opposition unions in Nicaragua have been harassed, they have been allowed to exist and press their demands....These unions have been free to main-

tain offices, meet with their members, distribute their publications, conduct workshops, and solicit funds. Most significantly, these unions have been allowed to voice their opposition to the Sandinista Government without fear of extinction.[73]

Sandinista organizers have raised the percentage of workers organized into unions from 6 percent before the revolution to 40 percent afterwards.

Freedom of party organizations to campaign. As noted, the FDR in El Salvador was subjected to a wholesale slaughter of its leaders prior to the election, a period during which about 150 civilians were being murdered each week. Even Duarte's Christian Democratic Party (PDC) was subjected to terror. By April 1981, forty of its activists had been killed. No party to the left of what remained of Duarte's party dared contest the election, and even Duarte's supporters found that the United States could not protect them from right-wing terrorism.

The opposition to the Sandinistas included parties on the left (including the party officially recognized by the Soviet Union as the official communist party in the country) that favored closer ties to the Soviet Union and criticized the Sandinistas for allowing 60 percent of the economy to remain capitalist. On the right, three opposition parties charged in the campaign that the Sandinistas had aligned Nicaragua too closely to the Soviet Union and that it was moving too fast to institute social and economic reforms. The LASA report concluded that "the Nicaraguan voter had a wide range of options on major issues—considerably wider, for example, than in recent elections in El Salvador and Guatemala."

In El Salvador, the FDR-FMLN offered to negotiate with the government for the establishment of conditions that could lead to free elections in which they would agree to participate. But Duarte, under pressure from the United States, insisted that the rebels would have to lay down their arms and participate under the existing conditions. The Sandinistas insisted that the *contras* could not participate as long as they continued to try to overthrow the government forcibly. Despite the close ties between the Coordinadora and the *contras,* however, the Sandinistas agreed to negotiate with Coordinadora leaders in an attempt to get them to contest the elections. When it became clear that the Sandinistas were willing to meet the demands of the Coordinadora, the CIA pressured Arturo Cruz to break off the talks. According to the president of Venezuela, who was close to the negotiations, the United States "just didn't want someone of the prestige of Cruz to enter the elections, because it would validate them. They wanted to demonstrate that there was no freedom of elections in Nicaragua." Their strategy was "simply to take away legitimacy."[74] In this effort, U.S. diplomats inside the country also made frequent attempts to persuade opposition candidates to drop out of the race, resorting in at least one case to bribery of lower-level party officials.[75]

Absence or presence of state-sponsored terror. Besides the official security apparatus, paramilitary groups operated freely in El Salvador. Church and other independent human rights groups documented that the vast majority of the 30,000 killed in El Salvador were civilian victims of rightist violence. If the number of political murders carried out by such forces were extrapolated to proportions reflecting a population the size of the United States, there would have been 1,170 politicians, 6,000 peasant and labor union leaders, 1,125 clergy and religious workers, 49,050 students, 10,080 teachers, 1,170 journalists, and probably more than 1,000,000 farmers and workers murdered—all in only twenty-nine months![76]

In Nicaragua, the LASA delegation found that the United States was the principal source of an attempt to create a "climate of fear and intimidation" during the Nicaraguan elections. In the week of October 21, forty-three civilians were killed as a result of *contra* attacks. Besides the fear caused by these attacks, U.S. warplanes flew daily flights across Nicaraguan skies, emitting sonic booms that caused "a sense of near panic among the population."[77] Nevertheless, during the campaign, LASA observers had little difficulty finding opponents who were stridently critical of the Sandinistas. The observer noted that "not one person lost his life as a result of campaign violence—a remarkable record in a country experiencing its first open electoral campaign in any Nicaraguan's lifetime, at a time of armed conflict and high emotions."[78]

Degree of coercion and fear. Voting in El Salvador was required by law. The week before the election, El Salvador's top military commander told the nation over the radio that the failure to vote would be considered an act of treason. This constituted, in effect, a death threat for those found after the election without a stamped ID card and an ink mark on their thumb. Local authorities were required to check and report nonvoters within ten days of the election. Government-backed organizations pressured their members to vote for the Duarte and other Christian Democratic candidates, the U.S.'s preferred alternative, as U.S. advisers to these groups admitted in congressional testimony.[79] Allegedly in an effort to minimize the high degree of fraud that had characterized earlier elections, transparent ballot boxes were used. This could hardly have been reassuring to Salvadoran voters, who had to drop their ballots in these boxes while armed soldiers stood guard. Finally, ballots were marked with the identification number of the voter, making it possible to trace ballots to the individual voters.

In Nicaragua, registration, but not voting, was required. Polling booths were curtained. As requested by opposition parties, registration cards submitted by voters to prove their eligibility were kept by election judges so that government officials could not afterwards seek out abstainers or check to see who voted for the opposition. Only civilian employees and election judges were allowed in the polling areas. Voters had their thumbs put in ink to prevent them from voting more than once, but the LASA observers reported no evidence that this was used to identify and punish abstainers later.

Procedures and results. In El Salvador the United States had hoped for a big turnout. There can be no doubt that both the apparent and actual turnouts were manipulated for the benefit of the U.S. media. In all of San Salvador there were only thirteen places to vote. In some areas, there were an estimated 50,000 potential voters per polling precinct, inevitably causing long lines that looked visually pleasing on

North American television news programs. In contrast, the average size of a precinct in Nicaragua was 400 voters.

A study by the Jesuit-run Catholic University in San Salvador showed that the government's claim that 1,555,687 voters went to the polls was fraudulent. Under the most optimistic conditions, only about 750,000 could possibly have voted. In fact, before the election, government officials were claiming that there were 1.3 million registered voters. Remarkably, with an estimated 750,000 Salvadorans living in refuge outside the country, with tens of thousands prevented from voting because of fighting between the FMLN and government forces in eastern provinces, and with perhaps one-quarter of the population living in areas controlled by the FMLN guerrillas, 250,000 more ballots were cast than there were registered voters.[80] In Nicaragua, an estimated 70 percent of the adult population voted. The Sandinistas won the presidency and vice presidency by a 67 percent majority. But because they had deliberately structured the allocation of votes for the Constituent Assembly to maximize the representation of smaller parties, the Sandinistas took only sixty-one of ninety-six seats (63.5 percent).[81]

The outcome in El Salvador was embarrassing for the United States. The combined vote for the three main right-wing parties gave them a majority over the U.S.-favored PDC, Duarte's party. Many observers felt that many Salvadorans voted for right-wing candidates because they were intimidated in areas where death squad forces were present. Other Salvadorans may have voted for right-wing candidates to protest the obvious U.S. support for Duarte. Despite the glass ballot boxes, 14 percent of the population cast blank ballots, a form of protest employed throughout Latin America. Fewer than 1 percent did so in Nicaragua, even though the privacy of the ballot was protected.

If the electoral results had been respected, former Major Robert D'Aubuisson, personally involved in death squads and the murder of Archbishop Romero, and labeled a "pathological killer" by Jimmy Carter's ambassador to El Salvador, would have been chosen as provisional president of the Constituent Assembly. This outcome would have precipitated a major public relations embarrassment for the United States. After secret behind-the-scenes negotiations with U.S. advisers, who threatened a cutoff of military aid, D'Aubuisson was forced to settle for majority leader of the Assembly. The oligarchy was thereby assured that all reforms would come to a halt because right-wing parties controlled the Assembly. But the "demonstration" effect for U.S. public opinion was kept intact.

In 1984, Duarte won a runoff election to gain the presidency in a contest conducted much like the election of 1982. As in 1982, the results of the Salvadoran elections were widely reported and enthusiastically praised in the U.S. media. A congressional delegation and other observers representing the U.S. ventured out of the luxurious Sheraton Hotel where they were staying just long enough to see the long lines of voters and pronounce the elections as fair and honest. In the same year the Reagan administration declared that the Nicaraguan elections were fraudulent. Asked how the United States could condemn the Nicaraguan elections while endorsing the elections in El Salvador, where all political groups to the left of the Christian

Democrats were unrepresented, a senior U.S. official defended the use of an infinitely variable standard:

> The United States is not obliged to apply the same standard of judgement to a country whose government is avowedly hostile to the U.S. as for a country, like El Salvador, where it is not....That allows us to change our yardstick.[82]

The standard for evaluating democracy employed by U.S. elites seems to be infinitely variable, depending on whether the regime in question is controlled by the United States. But this does not mean that the United States has no standard at all for judging democracies that have been established in Latin America. The United States is reliably comfortable with "democracies" where few of the conditions for democracy exist. Freedom of speech, access to the media, freedom to organize groups, the freedom to field candidates, the absence of state-sponsored terror, absence of coercion and fear—when these conditions exist, U.S. elites are nervous because the results are unpredictable. Above all else, what U.S. elites demand of "democracy" in Latin America is that the regimes that emerge victorious from election processes be loyal to U.S. interests. Since this is the priority, the United States pronounces elections as democratic in those circumstances when they are meaningless exercises in legitimating U.S.-backed regimes; conversely, elections are judged as fraudulent precisely when the conditions best favor genuinely democratic politics.

The Nicaraguan elections of February 1990 presented the United States with an unusual case. With the *contras* defeated as an effective military (but not terrorist) force, the Bush administration decided to give their political counterparts the green light to participate in the electoral process. The pro-*contra* parties joined with other internal opponents to form the United Opposition Front, UNO, which chose Violeta Chamorro, widow of a respected newspaper publisher murdered by Somoza, as its presidential candidate. The National Endowment for Democracy, run as a private foundation but almost completely funded by the U.S. government, funneled between $12 million and $18 million into the Chamorro campaign, and there was doubtlessly covert support from the CIA as well. Although there were restrictions, the Sandinista government established legal channels for such support, in contrast to the United States, where campaign contributions from foreign governments are prohibited. As incumbents, the Sandinistas had acquired certain advantages themselves, but these were little more than what incumbents normally enjoy in electoral democracies. Even more than in 1984, the elections and the campaign itself were to be closely monitored by international observers, including delegations from the United Nations, the Organization of American States, and the Carter Center (linked to former President Jimmy Carter).[83]

Despite all these efforts, independent polls by respected agencies indicated that the UNO campaign was headed for a landslide defeat. Therefore, U.S. policy was put on two tracks. On the one hand, the U.S.-favored opponents would campaign and try to win as much support as possible so that an internal opposition could be established. If they lost, as seemed likely, the U.S. would have condemned the elections as unfair and held in a climate of violence but at the same time would have urged the opposition to accept whatever legislative seats it won. For this purpose, a second track of attempting to discredit the elections through disinformation was put into operation, and the administration positioned itself to continue a policy of hostility toward Nicaragua after the elections by continuing to claim, with no conclusive evidence, that the Sandinistas were sending arms to the FMLN in El Salvador.

In an open bid to buy votes, President Bush announced during a visit by Chamorro to Washington that if she won the election the U.S. economic blockade would be lifted and a massive new aid program would be initiated. The president's message to the Nicaraguan people was clear: reelect the Sandinistas and you will have additional years of economic privation and *contra* terrorism. Elect our preferred candidate, and not only will we lift the siege, we will shower you with money.

Chamorro pulled off a major upset and won the election. The administration and the corporate media predictably called the result a victory for democracy. Where most of the world credited the diplomatic initiatives of the Central American presidents for having made UNO participation in the elections possible, the Bush administration credited the *contras*. Actually, the *contras* had been busy attacking civilian targets all through the campaign, during which twenty-three Sandinista party workers were killed.[84]

A Disturbing Image

By the 1980s, there were signs of a diminishing effectiveness in campaigns to engineer consent in support of foreign policy goals. The Vietnam Syndrome lingers in expressed public opposition to the use of American troops in any international conflict that might arise in the 1980s. ABC and *Washington Post* polls conducted in 1982 revealed a 79 percent to 18 percent opposition to sending U.S. troops to aid the Salvadoran government.[85] Sixty-five percent of those polled said they perceived the war to be "much like the war in Vietnam," and a 51 percent majority said "they would support young men who refused to go to El Salvador if the United States were drafting soldiers and sending them to fight there."[86]

The American public's current unwillingness to support direct intervention in Third World affairs has not changed the U.S. policy commitment to maintain a system of client states by force and terror. During the Reagan administration alone, at least 150,000 Central Americans died as a result of U.S.-sponsored terrorist forces. In El Salvador over 50,000 people have died since the mid-1950s, and in Guatemala almost 100,000 people have been killed by government forces. In Nicaragua the number of civilians killed by *contra* attacks during the Reagan administration totaled 30,000.[87]

By the end of 1988, it appeared that the *contra* war had failed in its objective of overthrowing the Sandinistas. U.S. officials expressed fear that "its failure is going to have long-term costs for us."[88] In El Salvador, Haiti, Honduras, Guatemala, Chile, and countries outside the hemisphere, U.S.-sponsored repression feeds revolutionary fires. Perhaps U.S. elites fear that mass-based democracies in these countries might set a bad example for American citizens. For elites, it is essential that democracy invests them with legitimacy; and it is equally critical that democracy not be captured by populist movements. *Elites "sponsor" elections within the U.S. in a manner similar to the way they "sponsor" them abroad:* to legitimate rule by the rich and well born and to preserve a system of class privilege. If elections are used for any other purpose, they are labeled as fraudulent and heavy doses of terrorism are frequently applied to nullify their results. Elites have not employed these tactics within the United States—that is, they have not overturned democratic institutions and processes, as they have so often done elsewhere. They have not found it necessary to do so because elections within their own country have never escaped their control.

Notes

1. Noam Chomsky, *Turning the Tide: The U.S. and Latin America.* 2nd rev. ed. (Montreal, N.Y.: Black Rose Books, 1987), pp. 4-5.

2. Edward S. Herman and Frank Brodhead, *Demonstration Elections, U.S.-Staged Elections in the Dominican Republic, Vietnam, and El Salvador* (Boston: South End Press, 1984).

3. Jeff McMahan, *Reagan and the World Imperial Power in the New Cold War* (London: Pluto Press, 1984), p. 16.

4. Quoted in Jenny Pearce, *Under the Eagle: U.S. Intervention in Central America and the Caribbean* (Boston: South End Press, 1982), p. 9.

5. Quoted in Walter La Feber, *Inevitable Revolutions: The United States in Central America* (New York: W. W. Norton, 1983), p. 37.

6. Ibid.

7. Ibid., p. 35.

8. Tom Barry and Deb Preusch, *The Central America Fact Book* (New York: Grove Press, 1986), p. 4.

9. Gordon Connell-Smith, *The United States and Latin America: An Historical Analysis of Inter-American Relations* (London: Heinemann Educational Books, 1974), p. 123.

10. Quoted in *Guatemala in Rebellion: Unfinished History,* ed. Jonathan L. Fried, Marvin E. Gettleman, Deborah T. Levenson, and Nancy Peckenham (New York: Grove Press, 1983), p. 87.

11. La Feber, *Inevitable Revolutions,* p. 65.

12. Piero Gleijeses, *The Dominican Crisis: The 1965 Constitutionalist Revolt and American Intervention* (Baltimore: The Johns Hopkins University Press, 1978), p. 21.

13. Dan Gurgman, quoted in Edward S. Herman, Frank Brodhead, *Demonstration Elections: U.S. Staged Elections in the Domican Republic, Vietnam and El Salvador* (Boston: South End Press, 1984), p. 20.

14. Gleijeses, *The Dominican Crisis,* p. 22.

15. Ibid., p. 23.

16. Pearce, *Under the Eagle,* p. 26.

17. Ibid., p. 47.

18. Roger Burbach and Marc Herold, "The U.S. Economic Stake in Central America and the Caribbean," in *The Politics of Intervention: The United States in Central America,* ed. Roger Burbach and Patricia Flynn (New York: Monthly Review Press, 1984), pp. 193-199.

19. Norma Stoltz Chincella and Nora Hamilton, "Prelude to Revolution," in Burbach and Flynn, *Politics of Intervention,* pp. 193-199.

20. Ibid., pp. 227-228.

21. Barry and Preusch, *Central America Fact Book,* p. 13.

22. Ibid, p. 22.

23. Howard Zinn, *A People's History of the United States* (New York: Harper & Row, 1980), p. 557.

24. Barry and Preusch, *Central America Fact Book,* p. 22.

25. Irma Adelman and Cynthia Taft Morris, *Economic Growth and Social Equity in Developing Countries* (Stanford: Stanford University Press, 1973), p. 189.

26. Quoted in Michael Parenti, *The Sword and Dollar: Imperialism, Revolution, and the Arms Race.* (New York: St. Martin's Press, 1989), pp. 21-22.

27. Barry and Preusch, *Central America Fact Book,* p. 129.

28. Ibid.

29. Noam Chomsky, *Turning the Tide,* p. 159.

30. E. Bradford Burns, *Latin America: A Concise Interpretative History* (New Jersey: Prentice-Hall, 1986), p. 350.

31. Adelman and Taft, *Economic Growth and Social Equity in Developing Countries,* p. 190.

32. Richard J. Barnet and Ronald J. Muller, *The Power of the Multinational Corporations* (N.Y.: Simon and Schuster, 1974), p. 86.

33. Ibid., p. 94.

34. Barry and Preusch, *Central America Fact Book,* p. 16.

35. Pearce, *Under the Eagle,* p. 65.

36. Barry, *Other Side of Paradise,* p. 293.

37. Ibid., p. 298.

38. Chomsky, *Turning the Tide,* pp. 152-153.

39. The *New York Times,* January 28, 1973, advertising supplement.

40. Ibid.

41. Ibid.

42. Barry and Preusch, *Central America Fact Book,* p. 137.

43. Barry, *Other Side of Paradise,* p. 336.

44. Pearce, *Under the Eagle,* p. 63.

45. McMahan, *Reagan and the World Imperial Power,* p. 149.

46. U.S. Department of State, *American Foreign Policy, Current Documents (1965)* (Washington, D.C.: U.S. Government Printing Office, 1968), p. 1956.

47. Ibid., p. 960.

48. Ibid., p. 962.

49. Jose A. Moreno, *Sociological Aspects of the Dominican Revolution* (Latin American Studies Program Dissertation Series, Cornell University), p. 140.

50. Richard J. Barnet, *Intervention and Revolution: The United States in the Third World* (New York: The World Publishing Company), p. 164.

51. Ibid., p. 168.

52. Ibid., p. 46.

53. Ibid., p. 38.

54. Ibid., p. 51.

55. Fried et al., *Guatemala in Rebellion,* quoted in introduction by Guillermo Toriello Garrido, p. 15.

56. Ibid.

57. Burns, *Latin America,* p. 312.

58. Barnet and Muller, *The Power of the Multinational Corporations,* p. 83.

59. Burns, *Latin America,* p. 313.

60. Herman and Brodhead, *Demonstration Elections.*

61. A good summary of the professed U.S. position on electoral democracy in South America can be found in "Democracy in Latin America and the Caribbean," *Current Policy,* no. 605 (Washington, D.C., U.S. Department of State, Bureau of Public Affairs).

62. Quoted in Barry and Preusch, *Central America Fact Book,* p. 4.

63. Robert Matthews, "Sowing Dragon's Teeth," *NACLA Report on the Americas* 20 (July-August, 1986).

64. LASA, "Report of the Delegation on Nicaraguan Elections," *LASA Forum* 15 (Winter 1985): 9-43.

65. Herman and Brodhead summarize the situation and cite the relevant studies in *Demonstration Elections,* pp. 94-119.

66. Ibid.

67. The following schema relies on Herman and Brodhead, ibid., pp. 11-16.

68. The conditions are described in detail by Herman and Brodhead, ibid., basing their findings on internationally respected human rights organizations. See, for example, the Americas Watch Committee (New York), *Report on Human Rights in El Salvador,* January, 1982, and supplements of July 20, 1982 and July 19, 1983.

69. LASA, "Report of the Delegation."

70. Herman and Brodhead, *Demonstration Elections.*

71. In January 1986, the principal radio station of the Catholic bishops was shut down after failing to broadcast the Nicaraguan president's New Year's message, as required by law, and for refusing to comply with the government's request for an explanation. In June, *La Prensa,* the main opposition newspaper, was closed indefinitely after disclosures in the U.S. media that it had received funds from a CIA-connected organization and immediately after the U.S. Congress authored $100 million for the *contras.* The right-wing opposition in Nicaragua claimed that both shutdowns were unjustified and that this was evidence of the "totalitarian" inclinations of the Sandinistas. It is important to note that both shutdowns occurred well after the 1984 campaign when both media outlets were operating and vigorously criticizing the Sandinistas.

72. *The Search for Peace in Central America, A Special Report by the National Labor Committee in Support of Democracy and Human Rights in El Salvador* (New York, 1985), p. 24. The AFL-CIOs continue to support U.S. policy in Central America. The dynamic of conservative union officials joining conservatives in the name of anticommunism can be traced back to the purging of the left from the unions after the Second World War, as described in chapter 8.

73. Ibid., p. 25.

74. Barry and Preusch, *Central America Fact Book,* p. 293.

75. Testimony by a U.S. labor official cited in Brodhead and Herman, *Demonstration Elections,* pp. 127-128.

76. Ibid., p. 123.

77. LASA, "Report of the Delegation," p. 36.

78. Ibid, p. 34.

79. Herman and Brodhead , *Demonstration Elections,* pp. 127-128.

80. Ibid., pp. 130-133.

81. LASA, "Report of the Delegation," pp. 19-23.

82. Ibid., pp. 42-43.

83. Central America Resource Network, *Executive News Summary,* February 21, 1990.

84. Notimex (Official Mexican News Agency), February 21, 1990.

85. Kenneth A. Oye, Robert J. Tieber, Donald Rothchild, eds., *Eagle Defiant* (Boston: Little, Brown, 1983), p. 57.
86. Ibid.
87. Noam Chomsky, *The Culture of Terror* (Boston: South End Press, 1988), pp. 28-29.
88. Ibid., p. 90.

Chapter 12

Must Democracy in America Be a Facade?

Three Sources of Crisis for American Democracy

Electoral processes and institutions in America have always been put in the service of maintaining the political authority and class privilege of elites. Even so, elections have been arenas for important and sometimes crucial political struggles. Though they were never useful in energizing populist movements for long, competing elite factions sometimes used elections as opportunities for mobilizing mass publics behind political agendas; on these occasions political discourse and electoral competition was enlivened, though these political openings occured within strict ideological limits. By the 1980s, however, elections had become little more than opportunities for elites to manipulate mass opinion; elites use them as occasions for passion-play entertainment and symbolic proof of their right to govern. Though campaigns offer a mirage of competition and political debate, it is an illusion artfully maintained by the professionals who run them as a lucrative new service industry of the postindustrial age. Educational institutions recognize the growing economic importance of campaigns, and as a consequence programs are springing up to train people for careers in the politics industry. The Graduate School of Political Management in New York City, for example, offers "advanced certificate programs consistent with its stated objectives of providing students with the knowledge and skill base for professional work in political management."[1]

Recently it has become popular to quote Alexis de Tocqueville, who argued in the mid-nineteenth century that there was a danger of mass tyranny in American politics.[2] Benjamin Ginsberg, echoing this view in a recent popular book, argues that mass opinion promotes state power; indeed, he illuminates how during the present century modern communications technology has put public "opinion," a phenomenon constantly measured and reported, at the service of power.[3] But public opinion does not exist as some objective phenomenon, waiting to be measured and amplified by the media. The media, the education system, the campaign industry, and government leaders constantly shape it. And when it does not conform to their massaging, elites have a significant capacity to ignore it, in proportion to the electorate's diminishing ability to hold government accountable.

It should be understood that the campaign "industry," like other industries, is dominated by corporations, it runs on money, and the participants expect to make a profit. Money and politics always have been intimately entwined in American politics. In the age of electronic mass media, the relationship between money brokers and politicians is tighter, possibly, than at any previous period in our national history. High-tech campaigns are extraordinarily expensive, so that the ability to raise money substantially decides who realistically can win public office. At both ends—the politicians' purchase of campaign talent and media advertising, and at the other "end," fundraising and contributions—corporate elites wield decisive influence. The nature of this system has become so obvious that even some incumbents worry that the legitimacy of the political system may become broadly questioned. In this spirit the Senate minority leader, Robert Dole, called for campaign reform in 1989 to reduce the 7-to-1 advantage in PAC contributions that incumbents enjoy. Claiming to be troubled by the 99 percent success rate of congressional incumbents in the 1988 elections, he said, "Republicans are determined to bring grass-roots politics back to the campaign scene."[4] The reforms he proposes would reduce the upper limit on individual and PAC contributions. Such reforms would certainly not restore "grass-roots politics," but the entrepreneurs who bundle small contributions together would have more to do, presumably. In any case, does anyone believe that reform is a priority for the beneficiaries of the present system? Dole's proposal will make some good "sound bites" for the television ads in his next reelection campaign, and that is no doubt its actual intention. Promises of reform, like most statements politicians make in the electronic age, are offered up for their public relations impact.

The first crisis of American democracy, the privatization of electoral politics, has led to the second crisis: the privatization of the national government's policy making processes. The policy subgovernments we described in chapter 9 are remarkably closed systems. The Defense Department and military contractors constitute perhaps the most well-known and thoroughly insulated policy subgovernment. But these subgovernments are numerous: The National Forest Service and the lumber industry are engaged in a constant, complicated dance, together with key senators and representatives who receive appropriate campaign contributions. The oil industry does its dance in a subgovernment composed of oil-state politicians, their committees, and the Energy, Interior, and Commerce Departments. And so forth. What passes for political "debate" in the United States skirts around the margins of these systems, does not impact them significantly, and therefore does not affect policy to any substantial degree. Such a tight relationship between politicians and business in the making of policy has probably not existed in the United States since the time of the "robber barons" in the late nineteenth century. Most policies that matter to Americans are now for the most part put up for sale. Like campaigns and elections, the everyday policy processes of American government have been privatized.

The third crisis of American democracy is the growth of an enormously powerful, autonomous, and secret national security apparatus. The insulation of foreign policy-making from domestic electoral processes came about because civilian and military foreign policy and corporate elites sought shelter from any accountability in the building of an American empire. They needed to conduct their business in secrecy and at a far remove from domestic political processes in direct proportion to the barbarity of their strategies to control the people and governments of other nations. More than any other reason, this is why foreign policies have been papered over so thoroughly by deceit and secrecy. Perhaps because America's elites find bloodthirsty policies so efficient, they are not willing to put these policies up for debate in the political arena. The public is able to exert influence in this realm mainly through protest activities such as mass demonstrations and civil disobedience.

It is an exercise in mythology to suppose that "foreign" and "domestic" policy making can be neatly demarcated. As Richard Barnet has observed, "Exempting foreign policy from the operation of democracy while preserving popular government in domestic affairs is becoming impossible now that the fragile membrane separating 'foreign' and 'domestic' issues is fast disappearing."[5] Domestic politics have always been heavily influenced by the foreign policy agenda. During and after the First World War, the government's carefully orchestrated repression of labor leaders and social-ists was justified on national security grounds. The code words "national security" again guided domestic repression of the 1940s and 1950s. Subsequent events also illuminate the intimate connection between foreign and domestic politics, as repre-sented by an executive power that has moved beyond the Constitution. The Watergate scandal should be understood in this light. At least in that case, the principal perpetrator was driven from office and his party punished at the polls. Several key players were prosecuted for their crimes. Nixon's vice president, Gerald Ford, who had no direct role in the scandal, was defeated in part for pardoning the former president.

But this episode stands in stark contrast to the latest scandal. In the Iran-*contra* scandal, the Reagan administration was able to prevent full judicial prosecution of Lt. Col. Oliver North and his coconspirators simply by withholding documents from the courts in the name of national security. Congress acquiesced in limiting full disclosure of the conspiracy, fearing that the public reaction might endanger all covert activities, which are essential to the U.S. capacity to intervene freely in the affairs of other nations. During Congress's televised hearings, when any representative or senator attempted to delve into issues such as the involvement of officials in drug running or the contingency plan to declare martial law and intern political opponents of the administration's Central American policies, the questions were ruled out of order by the committee chair, a Democrat. Before the television audience, North was able to project himself as the hero and the congressional investigators as the villains. His congressional inquisitors made this outcome more or less inevitable when they so frequently said they agreed with his aims but not with his methods, and when they dutifully added that state secrets were necessary and good. It is hard to imagine what other type of person they would want for the job. They seemed to be harping on extremely minor points—mainly, whether he had kept *them* informed (in secret sessions, of course). With this as their main concern, the lawmakers could not help but seem petty and self-serving.

The Iran-*contra* affair revealed the astonishing size and independence of the national security state. What it failed to show was that the presidency as an institution has grown enormously and that it is able to exert its will in domestic politics as surely as in foreign policy making. The "two presidencies," domestic and foreign, are closely interdependent. Before the Second World War, the White House managed the cabinet departments through the help of a few key aides, most of whom were personal acquaintances of the president. By 1970, the White House staff had mushroomed to more than 500 people. In 1988, the Executive Office of the President had a budget of $140 million, and employed more than 1,700 people.[6] The White House employees are on call to do many duties, and these jobs are not necessarily separated into separate "foreign" and "domestic" spheres.

During the 1988 presidential campaign, the circle joining domestic politics and the national security agenda was closed. George Bush visited a flag factory and questioned Michael Dukakis's patriotism. His handlers adroitly exploited racism and fear of crime through the prison furlough ads. To complete the trilogy, Bush called Dukakis a "card-carrying" member of the American Civil Liberties Union. The third "issue" linked the other two: "card-carrying" works as a codeword for "communist" or at least "leftist" in traditional American discourse, and the ACLU often has championed the rights and civil liberties of accused criminals. The themes of the 1988 campaign perfectly illustrated the way in which the national security state has influenced domestic politics.

The Culture of Violence

Voltaire wrote, "Those who can make you believe absurdities can make you commit atrocities." There are those who excuse the complicity of U.S. foreign policy in the slaughter of Third World people as an unfortunate by-product of our competition with the Soviets. But the endorsement and practice of human rights abuses and dictatorship overseas and the cynical manipulation of the democratic ideal has profound consequences for American democracy and for American culture. No American in the 1990s can avoid the consequences of living in a culture permeated by ideas and images of violence, war, and conquest.

Consider, as an example, the extraordinary prevalence of militaristic themes in movies. Such movies always have been popular, but they became a leading genre of the 1980s. Their motivating energy was a belligerent nationalism and racism. In 1984 Cannon Films released *Uncommon Valor,* followed by *Missing in Action* and *Missing in Action II,* all of which depicted privately organized covert operations in Vietnam to rescue American prisoners of war. Movies like *Red Dawn* and *Invasion USA* portrayed fanciful and glorified wars against Third World and Soviet invaders, led by teenagers. ABC television weighed in with a communist takeover of *Amerika* in early 1987. *Delta Force,* a product of the Cannon-Norris team, featured U.S. soldiers changing the history of the 1985 Lebanese high-jacking of a U.S. plane. Hundreds of Arabs are killed in the film while only one U.S. soldier dies—and his death is compared to Christ dying on the cross.

Of course the all-time champion in this class is Sylvester Stallone's *Rambo, First Blood II,* in which racist images of brutal, duplicitous Vietnamese are interwoven with the idea that liberal bureaucrats and politicians are weak on communism. As in other films of this type, the action is staged in the Third World, where the American defeat in Vietnam can be rerun with a "happier" ending—we win. This is achieved, notes critic Susan Jeffords, through a "reaffirmation of the American male and the values of the masculine war experience." She quotes lines from a key scene in *Uncommon Valor* that could just well been spoken by Rambo:

> There's a bond between you men as strong as the bond between my son and me. 'Cause there's no bond as strong as that shared by men who've faced death in battle. You men seem to have a strong sense of loyalty because you're thought of as criminals. Because of Vietnam. You know why? Because you lost. And in this country, that's like going bankrupt.[7]

Pentagon officials understand the value of such films and provide logistical support for their production. U.S. allies such as South Africa and Israel have made major investments in television and film production to influence world opinion. For example, the Chuck Norris films are produced by Israel G.G. Studios, founded by Israelis Menahem Golan and Yoram Globus, who received a $13.2 million grant from the Israeli government, signed by Ariel Sharon, defense minister at the time of the Israeli invasion of Lebanon. Immediately after constructing new studios just outside of Jerusalem, the team began filming *Delta Force.* In addition to war films, Golan and Globus produce slasher movies (e.g., *Texas Chainsaw Massacre II*). Ironically, they also received the right to construct a $50,000,000 theme park called "Bible Land" next to their studios.[8]

The chief competition to the "low-intensity warfare" and "peaceful engagement" movies are provided by a multitude of police, detective, and crime flicks. Without doubt, the most usual story line in these films has a sadistic rapist/mass murderer on the loose, and all because the criminal laws let him out on a technicality or loophole. Clint Eastwood's *Dirty Harry* series best epitomized this plot, but there were countless imitators. For the summer 1989 movie season, *Criminal Law* added a new twist by tying in a contentious social issue. The crazed killer, who is acquitted through the wiles of a crafty criminal lawyer, stalks women who have had an abortion. He is driven mad by the thought that they have murdered their babies.

Television series that debuted in 1987 and 1988 took the logical next step of depicting "unsolved mysteries," profiling actual criminals on the loose or reconstructing heinous crimes while inviting viewers to phone hot lines with tips for solving the crimes in question. In a society of gaping inequities and a permanent underclass, a high level of crime can scarcely be avoided. But in a political culture addicted to military solutions, crime becomes, like communism was, a frightening enemy that requires a paramilitary readiness to combat.

Themes of militarism and violence permeate the culture of childhood in America. By 1985, ten war-theme cartoons were being beamed at children each week, with another eight added in 1986. Among these were *Rambo* and *Karate Kommando,* the latter based on a Chuck Norris character. Most such cartoons were sponsored by the toy industry, which, thanks to such efforts, increased its sales of war toys by 600 percent between 1982 and 1985. By 1985, war toys accounted for seven of the leading ten toys. Broadcasters made huge profits off cartoons promoting the toys because they spent nothing for the programs, which were provided free by the war toy industry (most children's shows depicted characters that were also sold in stores and advertised during the programs). One innovative show *(Thundercat)* even provided broadcasters with a 5 percent cut on the profits from the sales of toys. Both the Federal Trade Commission and Federal Communications Commission made requests to protect the nation's children from this barrage. Congress demonstrated its concern about the problem in 1985 when it passed legislation to protect the toy industry. The new law provided that any retail store selling a counterfeit Rambo doll (for example) could be fined up to $1,000,000 for the first offense, and $5,000,000 and fifteen years in prison for the second. In 1988, Congress finally legislated restrictions on advertisements aimed at children, but these were vetoed by President Reagan.

By the age of sixteen, the average American child will have watched some 20,000 hours of TV containing 200,000 acts of violence and 50,000 murders or attempted murders involving 33,000 guns.[9] Popular Reagan-era shows were *The A-Team* and *Miami Vice,* both featuring military assault weapons in their plots. Popular cartoon programs featured "death ray" weapons much like artists' drawings of the proposed Star Wars program. The culture's images accurately reflect its love affair with arms. The United States is the largest producer of firearms in the world, accounting for 70 percent of the world's arms sales, and it also has the weakest gun control laws of any Western democracy. In the mid-1980s, American citizens owned about 40 million registered handguns and over 100,000 registered machine guns, and an estimated 500,000 unregistered military-style assault weapons. The Pentagon did its part to build this arsenal by sponsoring a program that distributes surplus M-14s to people who pass a certified marksman program.

"To survive a war, you've got to become a war," says Stallone as Rambo in *First Blood II.* In 1985, one of every 131 white male deaths and an astonishing one of every twenty-one black male deaths (almost 5 percent) were homicides. In 1979, the United States spent $13.8 billion on police protection and $21.7 billion on property protection.[10] According to the FBI, in the early 1980s sixteen survivalist camps taught paramilitary tactics. Graduates of these schools freelance as anticommunist mercenaries in the Third World; one graduate was arrested in an assassination attempt on the life of Indian Prime Minister Rajiv Gandhi. Graduates and other paramilitary specialists keep in touch with one another through magazines like *Soldier of Fortune, SWAT, International Combat Arms,* and *Firepower.*[11]

The proliferation of arms, together with training by right-wing organizations, suggests that "covert" violence easily could be turned against American citizens. The problem is likely to become more widespread as propaganda portrays the threat to national security as internal and emanating from groups working for peace and justice or from such organizations as the ACLU. The death squads who operated with such devastation in El Salvador; the terrorists that attacked clinics and schools in Nicaragua and shot down civilian airlines in Afghanistan; the military officers and the police officials who tortured and "disappeared" citizens in Guatemala were all armed and trained by the United States. It is painfully obvious that such government-supported terrorism could logically be directed to individuals and groups inside America's own borders.

Are world events now likely to reverse these trends? The Soviet Union has, in effect, withdrawn itself as the main adversary of the United States. Pentagon spending seems about to level off for the first time in more than a decade. The Warsaw Pact states have, one by one, gone through remarkable political changes. Pieces of the Berlin Wall were on sale in department stores in time for the Christmas holidays in 1989.

One should not, however, underestimate the ability of America's elites to invent new enemies. Struggles for self-determination and national independence will continue to be regarded as revolutions that must be snuffed out. In its search for enemies, the United States will find all it wants in revolutions throughout Latin America and the Third World. As long as America's elites regard aspirations for social and economic justice elsewhere as a threat to U.S. security and affluence, they will, without fail, find endless enemies.

Of course, the "enemies" can be found within as well as elsewhere. The drug war is a convenient means for expanding the national security state, and here no distinctions are possible between foreign and domestic policy. The architects of the drug war imagine that military and paramilitary action in Colombia and other nations as well as at home will somehow solve the drug problem, despite a consensus among police and drug enforcement authorities that interdiction of drugs has not had and cannot have anything but a marginal effect on supplies. At home, the drug "czar," William Bennett, said that he would not object to the idea of public executions and the beheading of drug sellers. National and local news stories obsessively chronicle daily drug busts and shootouts. The killing of "drug lords" is openly celebrated. This is the best kind of war for America's elites and for political conservatives because it is in no danger of being won with the methods employed, and can be used to justify an indefinite expansion of state power.[12] In the face of this endless enemy, who needs the Soviet Union? The militarization of American society can proceed even if the superpowers achieve rapprochement.

But even in the contemporary political culture of the United States, militarism is not irresistible. American public opinion continues to register disapproval for the deployment of American ground troops in any protracted wars in the Third World. Several films such as *Salvador, Platoon, Missing,* and *Born on the Fourth of July* have portrayed realistic views of war and U.S.-backed terror abroad. Military recruitment is still based as much on a materialist as on a patriotic appeal, and there is little to suggest that army morale could sustain engagement in any prolonged war. Public reaction to revelations about illegal arms deals and slush funds for the *contras* showed that most Americans can still be outraged by abuses of executive power. Millions of people have been mobilized into disarmament and antiwar groups, like the Nuclear Weapons Freeze Campaign and the Committee in Support of the People of El Salvador (CISPES). Public opinion continues to favor arms control agreements and to oppose military intervention in Central America.

The Democratic Prospect

Those who would work for something besides a democratic facade had best anticipate the opportunities and dangers that a crisis of legitimacy would present in America. Perhaps the best first step in a struggle for mass-based, broadly representative democracy is for people to understand how the present system is self-managing in the way that it induces passive acceptance of elite rule. A challenge to current policies will have to place a premium on popular organization and mobilization, which are difficult to achieve, but such challenges to elite power have been recurring events in America's historical tradition.

Political scientists have long argued that elite rule is not monolithic, that because of competition among elites and because individual citizens come together to promote common interests, organized groups participate in the political process all the time, not just during election campaigns. The *Dictionary of American Government and Politics* says

> traditional democratic theory, with its emphasis on individual responsibility and control, is transformed into a model that emphasizes the role of competitive groups in society. Pluralism assumes that power will shift from group to group as elements in the mass public transfer their allegiance in response to their perceptions of their individual interests.[13]

But pluralists have underestimated the obstacles that ordinary citizens face in recognizing and then acting on their interests, which is most dramatically demonstrated in the biases toward corporate wealth built into the campaign finance system and in the control of mass media by corporate capital.

Though the ability to communicate ideas on a mass scale is dominated by the corporate media, there are opportunities to challenge the prevailing consensus as it is articulated by elites. There remains in the United States a space for the expansion of alternate politics and communication. As a first step to protecting and expanding this space, individual citizens must avail themselves of a full range of information. The views and agendas of corporations and of the ideological right are amply represented in numerous mass-circulation publications such as *Time, Newsweek, U.S. News & World Report,* and the *New York Times.* A different point of view, often labeled "left," can be found in small-circulation publications such as *The Guardian, In These Times, The Nation, Z Magazine, The Progressive,* and *Mother Jones.* Most regions of the country are served by community radio stations that carry National Public Radio or the Radio Pacifica News Network. For television news, World Monitor offers an alternative to the official sources, sound-bites-between-commercials type of entertainment news shown by the networks. For the most part, however, the electronic and print media remain a vast wasteland that reflects the poverty of political discourse in American life.

There is a positive political tradition in America, consisting of skepticism about concentrated power, defense of rights enumerated in the Constitution, and a belief in the right to equal opportunity. These aspects of the American experience need to be defended against those who would abrogate civil rights and liberties in the name of national security or a war against drugs. Even if the Constitution were left unmolested by elites, however, it is not democratic enough. Reforms are long overdue to make it easier for citizens to register to vote. Perhaps in no other area of substantive reform are the prospects so favorable because Democratic party officials are pressured to move on this issue on one side by the Republican financial advantage and on the other by the Rainbow Coalition. Another crucial reform would mandate the counting of blank and spoiled ballots cast in protest—or even the option of a binding "none-of-the-above" vote. Voters desperately need an alternative to the lesser-of-two-evils choice that invariably is presented to them.

It is likely that in the next few years there will be changes in the campaign finance system simply because the corruption endemic to American politics has become so blatant. But it is not sufficient merely to add regulations and rein in the PACs. It is much more important to strengthen the enforcement ability and the representativeness of the Federal Election Commission, provide access to mass media for any party or candidate who qualifies through a petition process (instead of a fund-raising process) to get on the ballot, and replace private financing of electoral campaigns with public financing. Finally, the number of terms that senators and representatives can serve should be strictly limited[14] so that incumbents do not so easily become members of entrenched, hidden subgovernments.

Among other structural reforms, the most important may be changes in the way that parties get access to the ballot and in the way that representation is allocated to parties. Access to the ballot should be uniform throughout the country and require a fixed percentage of signatures of registered voters, with many fewer further qualifications requiring geographic dispersion of signatures across congressional districts. Within each state, a system of proportional representation should be implemented for elections to the House of Representatives as a first step in encouraging the development of a multi-party system.

Even if reforms were to open up the electoral system, it is possible that militarism in America has proceeded to the point that elites might be willing to use force, if they deem it necessary, to prevent significant social and political change. It should occasion no surprise that the government has become a significant threat to the people it is supposed to represent. The American national government has lasted for 200 years mainly because the elites who have controlled it have had a significant capacity to protect themselves from effective challenge. The degree to which they are able to use the government to protect their interests has never been greater. While nations in Eastern Europe and elsewhere are embarking on historic experiments in democracy, the U.S. political system—ironically—becomes less democratic every day.

Aristotle understood that "The real ground of the difference between oligarchy and democracy is poverty and riches. It is inevitable that any constitution should be an oligarchy if the rulers under it are rulers by virtue of riches."[15] America has a government run by elites who use the political system to protect wealth and privilege; thus, it is accurate to say that America's oligarchy is also a plutocracy—a government run by the wealthy.

Since the 1980 election, when plutocratic government in the U.S. became fully institutionalized by the new system of campaign finance and refined technologies of campaigning, a significant redistribution of wealth toward the top has been successfully initiated. In one decade the incomes of the wealthiest 20 percent rose by 29 percent, which was eight times faster than for the population as a whole.[16] The incomes of the top 1 percent of wage earners increased by 74 percent, or by $233,332 each—an amount that is five times the income level of the average family in the U.S.[17] All this occurred during a decade when workers' wages fell, the first time since the Second World War this has happened during an economic recovery.

Specific public policies facilitated this rapid redistribution of wealth. Tax "reform" lowered taxes for the rich, but raised them for most other people. High real interest rates benefited investors who were already made wealthier by relaxed regulation of antitrust laws and of financial institutions. The evidence of the redistribution of wealth and incomes is obvious every day, in the newspaper articles on the savings and loan scandal, which made fortunes for some, like George Bush's son Neal, to reports on the rising number of homeless, and the growing underclass, and the new crime wave in the cities.

How would elites respond if there were a serious political challenge to their new gains? Imagine the following scenario: Sometime in the 1990s a candidate proposes during a presidential campaign to drastically reduce the military budget and to stop all Star Wars research; meaningfully increase taxes on the rich to fund housing, health, and education programs; and reorient U.S. policy to support national self-determination by Third World countries. Against all odds he or she wins the presidency. Would the institutions of the national security state accept the electorate's verdict, or would they turn their well-honed skills of political manipulation and terror used so frequently against the people of Latin America against a "national security" threat at home? To survive in America, must democracy be a facade?

Notes

1. Quoted from the letter that accompanies the brochures describing the Graduate School of Political Management, New York City (1989).

2. See Alexis de Tocqueville, *Democracy in America* ed. and abridged by Andrew Hacker (New York: Washington Square Press, 1964), especially pages 90-107 and 299-327. Unfortunately, less attention is being paid to de Tocqueville's warning about the growing danger of a business aristocracy; see pages 217-220.

3. Benjamin Ginsberg, *The Captive Public: How Mass Opinion Promotes State Power* (New York: Basic Books, 1986).

4. Bob Dole, "Republicans Want Real Campaign Reform," *St. Louis Post-Dispatch,* April 28, 1989, op ed, p. 2B.

5. Richard J. Barnet, "The Costs of Intervention," in *Low Intensity Warfare: Counterinsurgency, Proinsurgency, and Antiterrorism in the Eighties,* ed. Michael T. Klare and Peter Kornbluth (New York: Pantheon Press, 1988), p. 220.

6. David Brian Robertson, "The Covert Presidency," in John C. Shea, *The Argument Book* (Pacific Grove, Calif.: Brooks/Cole, 1989).

7. Susan Jeffords, "The New Vietnam Films: Is the Movie Over?," *Journal of Popular Film and Television* 13 (Winter 1986): 186, 190.

8. National Coalition on Television Violence, *NCTV News* 7 (January-March 1986).

9. Ibid.
10. Ibid.; also "Militarism in America," pp. 6-7.
11. "Militarism in America," pp. 6-7.
12. See John Dillin, "White House Seeks New Powers in Fight Against Drug Abuse," *Christian Science Monitor,* May 18, 1990, pp. 1-2.
13. Jay M. Shafritz, *The Dorsey Dictionary of American Government and Politics* (Chicago: The Dorsey Press, 1988), p. 407.
14. See Michael H. Klein, "Limiting Congressional Terms: A Historical Perspective" and "The Twenty-Second Amendment: Term Limitations in the Executive Branch" (Washington, D.C.: Americans to Limit Congressional Terms, September 25, 1989).
15. *The Politics of Aristotle,* trans. Ernest Barker. (London: Oxford University Pres, 1958), p. 116.
16. Larry D. Hatfield, "Prosperity slipping, study says," *San Francisco Examiner* (September 3, 1990) pp. A1, A14, reporting on a study by the Economic Policy Institute, Washington, D.C., released September 2, 1990.
17. Ibid.

Index

Index

Guatemala, 50, 222, 224, 225, 229, 230, 231, 242, 253
Gulf+Western, 225, 227, 228, 229
Gun control, 62, 121
Gunboat diplomacy, 222

Haig, Alexander, 195, 196
Haiti, 222, 226, 228, 229
Hamilton, Alexander, 180
Harris Poll, 75, 78, 162, 166
Hart, Gary, 134, 146, 167, 169
Hegemony, 9, 14, 35, 154, 202
Helms, Jesse, 40, 44, 104, 134, 137
Heritage Foundation, 33
Hidden governments, 13, 196–197, 209
Hidden primary, 12, 144–147, 167
Hispanics, 29, 100, 103, 169, 170
Hitler, Adolf, 202, 205
Homelessness, 174
Honduras, 53, 222, 224, 225, 226, 231
Hoover, Herbert, 69, 169
Horton, Willie, 76, 77, 102, 121
House Committee on Un-American Activities, 155
House of Representatives, 11, 134, 137, 147, 179, 180, 183, 185, 186, 210, 255
House Ways and Means Committee, 148
Housing programs, 155, 156
Human rights, 35, 163, 168, 203, 213, 233, 235, 238, 250
Humphrey, Hubert, 66, 68, 119, 123, 131, 155, 160

Ideology, 47, 104, 113, 120, 121, 122, 137, 140, 154, 156, 166–167, 168, 202, 205, 211
Illiteracy, 91, 94
Immigrants, 12, 22, 24, 25, 26, 92, 93, 94, 158, 228
Imperialism policy, 221, 222
Income distribution, 226, 227
Incumbents, 13, 65, 71, 134, 137, 140, 141, 149, 150, 183, 184, 190, 196, 241, 248
Independents, 162
Individualism, 64, 72, 156
Industrial Workers of the World (IWW), 7, 92
Intelligence community, 50, 54
Interest groups, 98, 185, 186, 188, 192
Interior, Department of, 192, 248
Internal Security Act, 155, 156, 205
Intervention, 32, 56, 166, 168, 170, 195, 201, 203, 210, 212, 216, 222, 223, 225, 232, 253
Iran-*contra* scandal, 118, 162, 196, 212, 249
Israel, 163, 170, 251
Issue voting, 112, 113, 114, 115

Jackson, Jesse, 75, 97, 98, 101, 120, 121, 147, 163, 167–170
Jacksonian democracy, 2, 11, 90
Japan, 34, 56, 104, 105, 158, 168, 201, 202, 211
Japanese-American detention camps, 8, 217
Jefferson, Thomas, 1, 21
Jews, 24, 156, 163
Johnson, Lyndon (President), 56, 67, 68, 116, 119, 190, 194, 195, 208, 211, 229, 230
Journalists, 43, 45
Judiciary, 178, 181
Justice, Department of, 48, 54, 155

Kennedy, John F. (President), 67, 68, 123, 166, 194, 195, 206, 208
Khomeini, Ayatollah, 49, 71, 212
King, Jr., Martin Luther, 28, 123

Korean War, 48, 51, 67, 116, 201, 203, 207, 210

La Prensa, 55, 236, 237
Labor, 92, 135, 140, 148, 154, 156–160, 227
  laws, reform of, 168
  leaders, 136, 157, 158, 159, 160, 181, 223, 249
  movement, 156–160, 192
  unions, 48, 136, 140, 144, 178, 205, 210
Latin America, 14, 27, 34, 54, 56, 85, 222, 223, 224, 225, 226, 227, 229, 235, 240, 253, 256
Latin American Studies Association (LASA), 234, 236, 237, 238, 239
League of Women Voters, 84, 95
Leftist, 76, 155, 156, 159, 171, 205, 250
Legitimacy, 8, 15, 87, 88, 106, 107, 179, 238, 243, 248, 254
Legitimation, 5, 10, 62, 89
Liberal, 63, 120, 121, 140, 149, 154, 160, 161, 205, 210, 251
  alternative, 56, 153–156
  bias, 43, 47
Democrats, 130, 189
Liberals, 47, 103, 105, 123, 149, 154–156, 161, 166, 167, 169, 170, 171, 205, 208
Literacy testing, 91, 93, 97, 100
Livingstone, 213, 214
Lockheed, 149, 188

Machine politics, 92, 93, 94, 103, 129, 184
Madison, James, 11, 89, 178, 180
Madison Avenue, 63, 70, 71, 72
Mandate, 87, 111, 115
Marbury v. *Madison, 180*
Marines, 227, 229, 232, 234
Marshall Plan, 155
Martial law, 216, 249
Marxism, 205, 223
McCarthy, Eugene, 120, 135
McCarthy, Joseph, 67, 155, 156, 204, 207, 210
McGovern, George, 111, 120, 131
Media, 10, 12, 43, 52, 67, 74, 75, 125, 129, 144, 153, 167, 171, 172, 173, 179, 190, 208, 211, 212, 214, 218, 221, 230, 232, 236, 239, 240, 242, 247, 248, 254, 255
  advertising, 248
  "alternative," 57
  bias, 43, 47, 65, 70
  consultants, 65, 68, 70, 76, 78, 153, 161, 172, 194
  ownership of, 40
  spots, 68, 172
  underground, 56
Meese III, Edwin, 102, 192
Middle East, 27, 212
Middle-class, 95, 147, 150, 161, 162, 163, 173
Militarism, 72, 168, 204, 205, 206–210, 212, 251, 253, 255
Military, 51, 53, 54, 64, 187, 195, 196, 200, 201, 202, 203–210, 212, 223, 234, 235, 248
  buildup, 73, 187, 188, 204, 214–216
  recruitment, 215, 216, 253
  spending, 158, 166, 168, 201, 207, 208, 209, 211, 212, 256
Military-industrial complex, 204, 207, 208, 209
Minorities, 98, 148, 158, 215
Missile gap, 206, 208
Mondale, Walter, 62, 64, 72–74, 97, 101, 121, 124, 125, 134, 155, 160, 161, 167–169, 170

Index